PSYCHOLOGY LIBRARY EDITIONS:
CHILD DEVELOPMENT

Volume 7

THE BIOLOGISING OF CHILDHOOD

THE BIOLOGISING OF CHILDHOOD

Developmental Psychology and the Darwinian Myth

JOHN R. MORSS

FOREWORD BY ROM HARRÉ

Routledge
Taylor & Francis Group
LONDON AND NEW YORK

First published in 1990 by Lawrence Erlbaum Associates Ltd.

This edition first published in 2018
by Routledge
2 Park Square, Milton Park, Abingdon, Oxon OX14 4RN

and by Routledge
711 Third Avenue, New York, NY 10017

Routledge is an imprint of the Taylor & Francis Group, an informa business

British Library Cataloguing in Publication Data
A catalogue record for this book is available from the British Library

ISBN: 978-1-138-74142-3 (Set)
ISBN: 978-1-351-27384-8 (Set) (ebk)
ISBN: 978-1-138-03773-1 (Volume 7) (hbk)
ISBN: 978-1-138-03783-0 (Volume 7) (pbk)
ISBN: 978-1-315-17768-7 (Volume 7) (ebk)

The Biologising of Childhood: Developmental Psychology and the Darwinian Myth

John R. Morss

Lecturer in Education
University of Otago,
Dunedin, New Zealand.

Foreword by
Rom Harré
Linacre College
Oxford

LAWRENCE ERLBAUM ASSOCIATES, PUBLISHERS
Hove and London (UK) Hillsdale (USA)

Lawrence Erlbaum Associates Ltd., Publishers
27 Palmeira Mansions
Church Road
Hove
East Sussex, BN3 2FA
U.K.

British Library cataloguing in Publication Data

Morss, John R.
The biologising of childhood: developmental psychology and the Darwinian myth.
1. Children. Development. Biological factors
I. Title
155.4

ISBN 0-86377-129-7

Typeset by Acorn Bookwork, Salisbury, Wilts
Printed and bound by BPCC Wheatons, Exeter.

Reproduced by courtesy of the Trustees of the British Museum

At length for hatching ripe
he breaks the shell

William Blake

Contents

Foreword xi

Preface xiii

Acknowledgements xvii

1. **Introduction** **1**
   Introduction 1
   Notes to Chapter One 9

2. **Charles Darwin and the Origins of Developmental Psychology** **11**
   The "Natural History of Babies": Darwin on Child Development 11
   Evolution and Recapitulation 16
   Darwin's Immediate Impact 19
   The Influence of Evolutionism 23
   Notes to Chapter Two 26

3. **Biology and the Developmentalists: Hall, Baldwin, and Freud** **31**
   Introduction 31
   Granville Stanley Hall: Zealot of Evolution 32
   James Mark Baldwin and the "Embryology of Society" 37
   Sigmund Freud and the Ancestral Imperative 43
   Notes to Chapter Three 48

4. Biology and the Developmentalists: Vygotsky, Piaget, and Werner 51
Introduction 51
Minor Developmentalists in Europe and America 51
Lev Vygotsky and the Ontogeny of Culture 57
Jean Piaget and the Biology of Knowledge 59
Heinz Werner and the Morphology of Thought 67
Notes to Chapter Four 70

5. "The Prisoner of the Senses": Sensationism in Developmental Thinking 73
"Prisoner of the Senses" 73
Notes to Chapter Five 81

6. Infancy 83
Introduction 83
The Newborn 84
Knowledge of the World 91
Knowledge of People and Knowledge of the Self 101
The Psychoanalytic Tradition 107
Notes to Chapter Six 112

7. Childhood 115
Introduction 115
From Autism to Egocentrism 116
The Origins and Functions of Language 119
Reasoning and Logic 124
Drawing and Spatial Representation 132
Children, Peers, and the Adult World 140
Notes to Chapter Seven 147

8. Adolescence 151
Introduction 151
Adolescence and the Acme of Intellect 152
Adolescence and Turmoil 159
The Adolescent in Culture 164
Notes to Chapter Eight 170

9. Models and Processes 173
Introduction 173
Progress and Directionality 175
Processes of Change and Processes of Stability 181

Differentiation and Integration 186
Notes to Chapter Nine 193

10. Biology and Alternatives to Biology in Contemporary Developmental Psychology 197
Introduction 197
Biological Theories: Ethology and Psychobiology 199
Alternatives: Lifespan Theories 204
Alternatives: Formal Theories 207
Alternatives: Theories of Social Context 211
Alternatives: Theories of Social Construction 214
Notes to Chapter Ten 219

11. Conclusions 227
Introduction 227
The Foundations of Developmental Psychology 228
The Darwinian Myth in Developmental Psychology 230
The Future 232
Notes to Chapter Eleven 234

References 237

Reference Notes 251

Author Index 253

Subject Index 259

Foreword

Dissatisfaction with the orthodox accounts of how human beings mature has been growing for more than a decade. Serious objections to the idea that there is a uniform and inevitable schedule of developmental stages first showed up in the field of moral development. Kohlberg's mapping of Piaget's stages of cognitive development onto human moral sensibility turned out to be the celebration of a peculiarly American preconception of moral maturity. Cultural conventions ordered different kinds of moral reasoning into a hierarchy, but real children drew on whatever form seemed strategically appropriate at the time. Piaget's dominance of the field of developmental psychology was never complete but his influence was pervasive. Doubts arose piecemeal as investigators like Margaret Donaldson and Peter Bryant demonstrated the plain falsity of many of his claims. Yet the very idea of a schedule of development has never seriously been challenged. John Morss's study is the first to go right to the heart of the matter. Something very fundamental must be awry.

Having been involved myself in a long running attempt to get social psychology on to something like the right lines, I know how far academic psychology is from the natural sciences in the way its practitioners respond to empirical discoveries which run counter to their hypotheses and to conceptual developments that displace or marginalise popular theories. The job of putting developmental psychology "back on track" involves much more than pointing out factual errors and conceptual confusions. It is as if there were still chemists who favoured the ideas of Paracelsus, others who were followers of Stahl and sought the negative specific gravity of phlogiston. The great merit of Morss's study is that it goes deeper than any critical work so far to a reflection on the very idea of development. As Morss shows, a peculiarly pre-Darwinian biological assumption of hierarchical progression underlies the various attempts to create a psychology of human maturation: that is, such maturation is almost universally construed as *development.*

Alone amongst the great psychologists Lev Vygotsky realised that the biological metaphors were misplaced. His way of understanding how human beings acquire adult status is rooted in the idea of social appropriation. We become whatever we can take from the circumambient environment of social practices. There is no internal schedule of maturation that parallels the internally driven schedule of physical development, preformed in the genetic material. With the acquisition of language (free from Chomskian constraints of preformation) a person at whatever age can take whatever society offers and whatever is legitimate for such a one to acquire. But Morss has another insight that complements his celebration of the genius of Vygotsky. It is the realisation that sensationalism in the psychology of perception is a pervasive and distorting viewpoint rooted in the very same general biologising psychology that has influenced developmentalists. In this field too there has been an innovator of the same stature as Vygotsky, namely J. J. Gibson, whose ecological optics demonstrates the way that an infant human being, fully equipped with a perceptual system, explores the ambient flux of energy for the invariants that are the very presence of the things and events of the material world. We simply do not perceive by integrating sensations.

It is a very great pleasure to introduce this book because it has the kind of cutting edge that may perhaps finally shift the community of students of human maturation from their current assumptions. But we cannot be too sanguine. The history of recent attempts to carry forward other psychological specialities is not encouraging. Yet progress is made. The old errors are eventually transcended. And this book will surely play an important part in bringing a new era into existence for "developmental" psychology.

Rom Harré
Linacre College
Oxford

Preface

It is widely accepted that developmental psychology has been strongly influenced by biology. But evaluations of this influence differ: Its nature, its extent, and its desirability are all still matters for intense debate. Some contemporary thinkers would wish to re-establish developmental psychology on non-biological foundations: But this may be an impossible dream. This book uses an analysis of the history of developmental psychology in order to examine the role of certain key biologistic assumptions in its classic formulations. My claim is that developmental psychology has been profoundly influenced by notions which have long been abandoned in their original disciplinary context: notions which I group together as "non-Darwinian." The formulations even of contemporary developmental psychology, I argue, retain the indelible stamp of those source notions. What modern developmentalists measure, investigate, even perceive in their subject-matter is, therefore, still defined by these outdated biological concepts. What developmentalists discover in their empirical work may be determined in advance: by non-Darwinian (and this really means *pre*-Darwinian) biology.

These are strong claims, and a much larger book would be required to provide definitive support for them. The strategy followed here is to investigate the influence of the identified source notions on the "founding fathers" of the discipline (and the discipline has indeed been a male-dominated one); and to indicate in rather less detail the persistence of the early formulations, and hence the perpetuation of the initial influences, down to the present day. It is therefore to *continuities* in theoretical formulations that most attention is given: To the carrying-over of basic presuppositions from one theorist to another. Most general accounts of classical theories in developmental psychology offer a separate chapter on each figure chosen, with little account of cross-fertilisation. Such a procedure severely overestimates the originality even of a Freud or a Piaget. This book takes what I hope is a more "historical" perspective; it is in this respect a *developmental* analysis of developmental psychology.

The structure of the book is broadly chronological, although deviations occur at a number of points as specific issues are addressed. Following the Introduction, the second chapter sets the scene with a discussion of Darwinian and non-Darwinian biologies in their historical context, with especial emphasis on developmental issues. The third and fourth chapters introduce six major figures (and some minor ones) by means of an investigation of the biological presuppositions adopted by each. All of these major figures—Hall, Baldwin, Freud, Vygotsky, Piaget, Werner—are met with again (but some more than others) in subsequent chapters; some repetition and some recapitulation is therefore unavoidable. It is hoped that this increases clarity. The short fifth chapter is concerned with issues of a more philosophical nature, but which are intimately bound up with the biological ones.

Issues raised in these early chapters are brought to bear on more substantive topics in Chapters Six to Eight, which divide up the developmental course into three segments; and in Chapter Nine which discusses formulations on models and processes of development. This chapter also serves to bring earlier material together to some extent. Chronologically, the focus has moved from the late 19th century to the mid-20th, with the discussion of standpoints which could broadly be referred to as classical and foundational ones in the discipline. The tenth chapter surveys the recent and contemporary scene in developmental psychology against the background of the historical analysis. Following this, Chapter Eleven attempts to draw some conclusions concerning the overall influence of the factors under investigation.

Notes accompany each of the eleven chapters indicating further reading as well as specific sources. They appear at the chapter end. In this context I would like to give a special acknowledgement to two crucial sources: Gould's *Ontogeny and phylogeny* and Sulloway's *Freud: Biologist of the mind.* Neither of these authors is a developmental psychologist, yet Gould —palaeontologist and historian of biology—and Sulloway—Darwin scholar and historian of science—were the first to indicate the real extent of the discipline's non-Darwinian foundations. In my view the implications of Gould's and Sulloway's work have not yet been adequately assimilated by developmental psychology: This book is an attempt to begin this process.

John R. Morss
Irish Hill, Ballyclare, Ireland
and Mt. Mera, Dunedin, N.Z.
July 1988

Acknowledgements

I would like to express my thanks to George Butterworth, for very substantial help and encouragement throughout this project; Alan Costall, for his help and erudition; Peter Bowler, whom I was most fortunate to have as a nearby colleague; and John Broughton for continual support. I am indebted to Frank Sulloway and to Stephen Jay Gould for inspiration and encouragement. I owe a very great deal to my contact with Tom Bower, arguably the most gifted developmental theorist of his generation; here, specifically, in connection with the role of sensationism and associationism in developmental thinking.

I have received help and encouragement from many colleagues, friends, and members of my family. In particular I would like to thank the following: Rachel Baskerville; Lise Bird; Ben Bradley; John Freeman-Moir; Sheila Greene; John Groeger; Rom Harré; Peter Hobson; Greta Jones; Paul Light; Andy Lock; Wolfe Mays; Brendan McGonigle; Bruce McMillan; James Moore; Michael Morgan; Mark Olssen; Mel Pipe; Malcolm Reed; Martin Richards; Robert Richards; James Russell; John Shotter; Anne Smith; Bob Young. A number of anonymous reviewers have contributed very substantially to this final version.

Early versions of some material was presented at research seminars in various centres; at meetings of the "Darwiniana" group based at Queen's University, Belfast; and at Conferences of the British Psychological Society (especially, of the Northern Ireland Branch and of the Developmental Psychology Section.) These forums have been stimulating and challenging as well as convivial. Three Heads of Department—Max Taylor, Julian Leslie, and Ted Glynn—have been supportive and facilitative. I would also like to express special thanks to Tony Chapman, Tony Gale, and Brian Stratford. I am grateful to the University of Ulster for study funds. Finally, I would like to acknowledge the help of library staff at the Universities of Ulster and of Otago, and at the British Library, London.

1 Introduction

INTRODUCTION

The influence of Charles Darwin on developmental psychology is a major focus of this book. This influence has been widely recognised, and indeed widely advertised within the discipline. But the nature of Darwin's influence has not been as straightforwardly benevolent as some histories of developmental psychology would imply. Some such histories give the impression that early developmentalists recognised fairly readily what is now identified as the Darwinian message; the discipline was therefore able to shake off any pre-Darwinian ideas and set off on the upward path toward its present state. Such influence as the older, misguided biologies may have exerted were thus inherently transitory; and certainly of no more than antiquarian interest now. Developmental psychology's "official" history, if I could call it that, records the discipline's progressive assimilation of the Darwinian enlightenment.[1] That the discipline is now truly Darwinian is rarely questioned.

I exaggerate, of course. But accounts of the history of developmental psychology have certainly been "triumphalist" in tone, and the appeal to Darwinism is as much rhetorical as substantial.[2] Moreover, the claims which are specific to developmental psychology rest on more general, traditional assumptions concerning the Darwinian influence, and these assumptions are themselves coming to be seen by historians of biology as quite misleading.[3] The triumphalist account perpetuates some serious errors concerning the nature of Darwin's so-called "revolution." Darwin scholars have, over the past few decades, re-evaluated this formulation which greatly distorts the relationships between Darwin's work, that of his predecessors, and his scientific community. The ideas and claims which are now termed Darwinism stand out much more clearly with hindsight than they did in their time. Darwin's own writings reflected changes in emphasis as his ideas developed; Darwin himself consistently endorsed "non-Darwinian" principles, as later identified; Darwin himself exaggerated the distance between his own claims and those of such earlier writers as Lamarck. Again, the reception of Darwin's ideas was multi-faceted, differing from one country to another. For example, resistance was total and long-lasting in France. Even where the environment was more receptive, Darwinism cannot be seen as having swept all alternatives before it. The substance of these alternatives has also been represented as being chiefly of a religious nature: but some religious thinkers of the time were very positive toward the "natural theology" they saw in Darwin. Much more serious was the opposition from other kinds of biology, especially versions emphasising an overall order to the scheme of evolution. These alternatives seemed indeed to have triumphed over Darwinism by the closing years of the 19th century.[4]

The most basic, but erroneous, assumption of the triumphalist account is that a Darwinian revolution swept aside all opposition. As a consequence of this key assumption, the influence of non-Darwinian ideas on early developmentalists is treated as necessarily superficial. Darwinism, after all, was right and the alternatives were wrong (and Lamarck, of course, was wrong *and* silly). Such a simplistic framework must distort more detailed considerations. There is a tendency also to include under Darwinism various notions which are considered to have been desirable influences, even though they may be common to other frameworks: Thus Darwinism is used rather loosely as a category for positively-toned attributions of biological influence. All in all, it would seem fair to describe developmental psychology's appeal to Darwin as a *myth*: A myth of origin and a myth of legitimacy.[5]

Clearly, the definitions of "Darwinism" and of "non-Darwinism" are quite crucial here. By Darwinism I shall refer to the set of claims centred on the primacy of *natural selection* as the mechanism for evolutionary change: Essentially, that variations occur basically by chance, and that selection for better adaptiveness takes place on such chance variations. This standpoint is usually referred to by historians of biology as *neo*-Darwinism, a term which recognises that Darwin himself did not hold such a radical position and that its formulation was a later development. Readers should therefore be prepared to discover that Darwin himself was not always, or not strictly, a Darwinian in this sense. This situation, even if confusing, is not meant to be pejorative: It has been argued quite persuasively that Darwin's own, more eclectic position is one which still has much to recommend it.[6] On this point of the evaluative tone of the terms used, I should admit that "non-Darwinism" is employed more than once in an accusatory way in the chapters which follow; that is, an adherence to non-Darwinian biologies is treated somewhat as a guilty secret to be unearthed. This practice is stylistic and is intended to be more than a little ironic in tone.

Alternatives to Darwinism have been referred to and categorised in several ways in the relevant literature. The major non-Darwinian "name" is Jean-Baptiste de Lamarck, but the term "Lamarckist" requires just as much qualification as Darwinist; and, again, Lamarck himself was no Lamarckist. Non-Darwinians of the latter 19th century brought to centre stage a mechanism which, for Lamarck, had been of quite minor significance: The assimilation into genetic material of habits acquired during an animal's lifetime. This "use-inheritance" or the inheritance of acquired character—a mechanism consistently endorsed by Darwin himself—is what is here referred to as Lamarckism (again more accurately, "neo-Lamarckism"). Lamarck himself shared with the later non-Darwinians a more general and more profound conviction: That the animal kingdom manifests design and order in its progressive transformations. That is, evolutionary change has direction, an overall plan. For Darwinism, in contrast, evolution is determined "from the bottom up," by low-level, proximate mechanisms.[7]

Non-Darwinian biology focused on high-level laws governing evolutionary change, and hence on directionality and progress in evolution. The Lamarckist mechanism was invoked as a means by which direction could be given to variations: variations originate as direct adaptations or accommodations to the environment (certainly not, however, as mere efforts of will). Evolution is thus directed by *habit*, and natural selection is allowed the minor role of weeding out inappropriate variations (those which arise in nonadaptive ways). Many alternative formulations for mechanism were proposed, giving different weight to use-inheritance, to natural selection, and to other factors; but the adherence to high-level "laws" of evolution was paramount. This insistence on general laws gave legitimacy and significance to perhaps the most general of the *developmental* claims of the non-Darwinians: The claim encapsulated in the notion of *recapitulation*.

The term recapitulation has been defined and employed in different ways by different writers.[8] Since the strongest version of the claim has lost credibility, many authors have been at pains to establish that their own approach (or that which they wish to endorse in another) is most definitely *not* recapitulation. I shall use the term to refer to any proposal, however loosely formulated, by which some aspects of a *sequence* of developmental change are held to be parallel across contexts (where "contexts" refers to individual development; the course of evolution; the history of civilisation;

the history of science). What this amounts to in general is that the same "laws" are held to be operating in individual development (ontogeny) and in evolution (phylogeny). The above qualification regarding *sequence* is important, since the proposal that such different contexts are similarly subject to laws of mechanics, or of physiology, is not considered to be recapitulation. To repeat: My most general use of the term "recapitulation" refers to the identification of unitary underlying laws *of development*. In such cases, authors seem to be seeing such phenomena as the growth of the individual or the course of evolution as examples or manifestations of "Development" (with a big "D").

The most fundamental claim of this general kind of recapitulation is that different "series" represent manifestations of the same ordered sequence of states, that is the same *hierarchy*. Relationships of superiority-inferiority are essential to this picture. If it is such relationships on which a particular proposal lays stress then the term *hierarchical recapitulation* will be used. Other versions place more emphasis on the kinds of change observed to characterise the ascent of the scale (increasing "differentiation" or "integration", for example). In all such cases the connection between the different contexts is essentially a "transcendental" one: It operates at a level above (or alternatively, below) the actual cases themselves. Phylogeny does not cause ontogeny, and neither does ontogeny cause phylogeny. Both in a sense are "caused" by a more general force or process: the process of Development. The different series might be described as "parallel" or "corresponding" or perhaps "correlated." All of these terms convey the point that the two series stand on an essentially equal footing. The term "homologous" could also perhaps have been used, since it refers to similarities which arise from common descent (as in the similarities between a human arm and a bird's wing); but "descent" has Darwinian overtones which would be quite misleading in this context.

Any time the term recapitulation is used in the chapters which follow, then, the more general sense at least is being identified. The more specific and stronger versions involve additional claims. As well as the kind of mystical connection by which two series partake of Development in general, various claims on causative relationships may also be made. The clearest example is the "biogenetic law" of Ernst Haeckel, according to which phylogeny (evolutionary ancestry) *causes* the sequence of stages in ontogeny. This account is referred to as *ancestral recapitulation*. Other writers have proposed that some causal effects can work the other way round: That aspects of individual development can guide the direction of evolution. Some have even attempted to show that causal effects operate in both directions, such that the relationship between development and evolution is a "dialectical" one.

An interest in causal relationships between individual life-courses and the course of evolution has often involved some reference to the Lamarckist principle of use-inheritance. The doctrine has been applied in the context of an animal's habits or behaviour, such that *learning* may in some cases be seen as giving rise to evolutionary change. Learning, in turn, has often been identified as being based on the organism's reception and interpretation of *sensations*. This doctrine of "sensationism" has been of very considerable influence on developmental thinking, as discussed in Chapter Five and elsewhere; in particular, it has led to some long-standing and very tenacious assumptions concerning the nature of early development. What I term sensationism is very closely related to the epistemological tradition of "sensationalism," a doctrine based on the empiricist claim that all cognition ultimately derives from sensory experience.[9] This assumption stems from such 17th-century thinkers as Locke and Gassendi and has always had close links with biological thinking, since it tends to de-emphasise uniquely human features of the acquisition of knowledge. Sensationalism stressed "the continuity of animal and human reason, the associationist view of intelligence, materialistic psychology, and habit as the key to mental progress". The importance of this philosophical stance includes its "significant influence" on the subsequent development of evolutionary theories; a demonstration of this is its employment by Darwin and its role in the definition of the concepts of instinct and of intelligence.

Excepting for some glances further back, especially in Chapter Five, the book takes the middle to late 19th century as its point of departure. Some comments should therefore be made on those intellectual traditions which, like the sensationalism noted earlier, prepared for and provided the background to the emergence of evolutionist thinking and of empirical developmental psychology. A starting-point for such a discussion is somewhat arbitrary, but mention should certainly be made of the notion of *progress* in human affairs as explored in the French Enlightenment of the 18th century. Focusing in particular on the modern history of Europe, such writers as Condorcet were able to argue that (despite irregularities and variations) the present should be seen as essentially better than the past, and that the course of human progress should be expected to continue into the future. The tradition against which Condorcet was arguing was the "Classical" position which viewed modern civilisation as secondary and essentially inferior to that of ancient Greece and Rome. Condorcet was writing in the period just prior to the French Revolution, an upheaval in which considerable appeal was made to this notion of progress. And although Condorcet's own concerns were principally with human society, others such as his younger colleague Pierre-Jean Cabanis were discussing the issue of the perfectibility of *animals*: That is, a universal tendency toward developmental progress. Such a tendency depended on the acceptance of continuity among animal types *and* between animals and mankind:

A notion central to the construction of theories of evolution during the next century. Cabanis' claims were of direct influence on Lamarck, and, indirectly, on Darwin. More generally, the notion of progress in human affairs came to dominate 19th-century thought.[10]

One approximate contemporary of Condorcet was Jean-Jacques Rousseau, whose writings were an important source for the Romanticism of the early 19th century. Associated with this movement were such idealist philosophical traditions as those of Schopenhauer, Hegel, and Fichte. In German-speaking Europe, in particular, there emerged an attitude to man and nature known as "Nature-philosophy" which sought for general laws and general processes underlying change in either organic or inorganic matter. *Developmental* change—change which seemed to be progressive and systematic—was a central concern of Nature-philosophy, as it was for the wider Romantic movement. Development was seen as a general process in Nature, becoming manifest not only in the growth of the individual but also in the relationships among different animal species. Thus, ontogenesis—the development of the individual—was seen to correspond in some way to observed patterns of genesis within the animal kingdom.

The Nature-philosophers, and those scientists influenced by them, were not working with a Darwinian model of evolution with species descending one from another by modification. Neither indeed was Lamarck, who was writing at the turn of the century but who adhered to older intellectual traditions than Nature-philosophy as such. However, the Nature-philosophers *did* see animal species very much as ranked in a scale, from "lower" to "higher." In the accounts of such early 19th-century biologists as Meckel and Serres, this animal series was seen to correspond to steps in the development of the individual human. Thus ontogenesis appeared to reflect or recapitulate the animal series; "lower" animals had simply "run out of steam" before making it to the human state. Stages of development in the human correspond to the *adult* forms of "lower" animals: The correspondence perceived here being essentially of a mystical or transcendental nature.[11]

In mid-century the prevailing mood of romantic idealism was challenged by a vigorous revival of materialism: A movement appealing to progress in the physical sciences rather than to the humanities. In the social sciences and philosophy, positivist formulations such as those of Comte emerged. Developments in associationist philosophy—such as the work of James Mill in England, and Herbart in Germany—gave rise to systematic formulations of the ways in which mental contents are derived from sensations. Such developments represented the continuation of the sensationalist traditions of the previous century. This associationism coverged with experimental physiology to give rise to an empirical kind of psychology.

Psychology prospered in this empiricist and materialist environment, and was able to assimilate such methods as the "psychophysics" of Fechner, itself related much more closely to the older Nature-philosophy. Indeed, what became known as the "new psychology" towards the end of the 19th century—the psychology of Wilhelm Wundt—had roots also within idealist traditions.[12] Certain features of the earlier Romantic Idealism were quite successfully revived at the end of the 19th century, especially in philosophical debate; and in the new century, such writers as Henri Bergson exemplified a reaction against the earlier positivism. Even so, the psychology of the 20th century adhered quite rigidly to the positivism, the empiricism, and the associationism of that of the 19th.

Meanwhile, the middle part of the 19th century had seen the first publication of Charles Darwin's (1859) *The origin of species*, and various responses to it. Most significant for the history of developmental psychology was the response of Ernst Haeckel. It was Haeckel who formulated and promoted the notion of *ancestral* recapitulation as being implied by Darwin's claims. He thus discerned a precise recapitulation of evolutionary ancestry in the growing organism: Phylogeny (the supposed course of evolutionary ancestry) is thus the direct cause of the changes observed in the growing individual. Ontogeny recapitulates phylogeny. The complex issue of whether this argument of Haeckel's was or was not true to Darwin is discussed in some detail in the second chapter. It is important to note that—as for the Nature-philosophers—it is still the *adult* forms of infra-human animals to which stages of human ontogenesis are held to correspond. With evolution, it is argued, the various ordered animal states get compressed back earlier and earlier in the life cycle of the individual. Some may even get deleted, but the overall sequence is retained.

As already noted, psychology as an empirical discipline emerged from a background of positivism and associationism. What of *developmental* psychology as such? Here it must be stressed that developmental psychology has never stood in a straightforwardly subordinate relationship to psychology in general. It has not emerged "out of" a general or higher-level psychology; some aspects of its origins (in Nature-philosophy for example) are quite distinct. The psychology of ontogenesis may perhaps be seen as having differentiated out of a more general "comparative" or "genetic" psychology. In any event, it is important to see developmental psychology by and large as progressing *alongside* experimental psychology, the science of adult human behaviour. Thus the "new" psychology of Wilhelm Wundt—emerging at the end of the last century—saw issues of development as outside the scope of an experimental science. The experimental and the developmental disciplines can probably be said to have influenced each other to about the same extent; and some influences such as Darwinism have impacted on the two fields in different ways. Developmental psychology, then, may properly be regarded as a science in its own right.

The evolutionist thought of the late 19th century has exerted the most profound influence on the 20th. "Social Darwinism" in its various guises (and whether or not accurately named[13]) has been a major force in the social sciences and humanities. References to evolutionist thinking in anthropology are made throughout this book; sociology still retains its imprint (evolutionism being a major target for such innovators as Giddens[14]). The term "biologism" as I employ it is intended to be in some respects of wider reference than "evolutionism," although there is a great deal of overlap; the former including Lamarckism for example, and the nonevolutionary assumptions of Nature-philosophy.

To speak as this book's title does of "the biologising of childhood" might seem to imply that childhood was at some earlier time constructed in nonbiological terms. I have not attempted to explore this issue. However, it might be that childhood had previously been defined in moral terms, or in terms of rights; and some contemporary thinkers would like to proceed in this way now. More generally, this book concentrates on what I see as the baleful influence of biology rather than on possible alternatives. My claims concerning the history and present state of the discipline of developmental psychology are not meant to depend on the validity of any particular alternative. Having said this, however, it will be clear that I do in fact favour certain nonbiological approaches: namely, those that emphasise the social construction or social production of individual development. A defence of this kind of alternative is presented in the final chapters, but is meant to be no more than an indicative treatment of these issues. More detail on my own favoured approach or approaches would, I feel, unbalance the book.

A related point should be made concerning "alternative" features of some of the classic figures whose work is discussed. Lev Vygotsky, in particular, can be interpreted as having anticipated much contemporary thinking in terms of alternatives to biology. The same can be said, although to a lesser extent, of the writings of James Mark Baldwin. My discussions of both these figures are intended to give some indication of their nonbiological contributions. George Herbert Mead would have received similar treatment, in that his work is giving inspiration to contemporary debate on these issues, but his slight influence on developmental psychology up till the present makes this inappropriate. In general, the alternatives to biology offered by these earlier writers constitute something of an undercurrent in the mainstream, or a counterpoint to the main theme of biological hegemony. The supremacy of biological thinking which is the topic of this book might be seen as having given rise to the suppression or occlusion of alternative forms of description. If so, a critique of that supremacy should be a liberating exercise, not a destructive one. My motto is taken from William Blake, who saw human development as the transcending of organic constraints. Perhaps the time has come for developmental psychology, at last, to break the shell.

NOTES TO CHAPTER ONE

[1]Recent histories of developmental psychology include the accounts of Cairns (1983), Dixon and Lerner (1984; 1985), and Reinert (1979). See also however, the recent re-evaluation of Darwin's influence in Costall (1985) and in the Charlesworth symposium (Charlesworth, 1986a; 1986b; Costall, 1986; Ghiselin, 1986). This issue is discussed further in Chapter Eleven. More general historical and philosophical issues are explored by various contributors to Lerner (1983). Comparative summaries of classical formulations in developmental psychology may be found in Crain (1980), Lerner (1986), and P. Miller (1983).

[2]Leahey (1986) has identified a number of ways in which psychology's history of itself tends to be distorted and self-serving. It follows the tradition of 'Whiggish" or "presentist" histories of science, which: "view[] the past as a series of progressive steps leading to the supposed wisdom of the present." Leahey identifies the following "sins": internalism, the exclusive concern with technical problems as defined by the science itself; the "Great Man" orientation according to which "giants" singlehandedly create or remake a field of enquiry; and historical ignorance and shallowness. It is not easy to avoid such sins entirely but the effort is made, in this book, at least to keep them under control.

[3]See especially Bowler (1983; Note 1; 1988) and the collection by Kohn (1985).

[4]See Bowler's *The eclipse of Darwinism* (1983).

[5]Barthélemy-Madaule (1979/1982) has discussed the *mythical* quality of the role of Lamarck (and see Chapter Two), and Sulloway (1979) has discussed "the myth of the hero" in connection with Freud.

[6]See Gould (1985), Gould and Vrba (1982).

[7]On Lamarck, see Chapter Two (footnote 7); also Bowler (1984).

[8]My account of recapitulation theory is based on Gould (1977). Many similar issues are also discussed by Sulloway (1979). Also see De Beer (1958), Mayr (1982).

[9]"Sensationalism" and its profound influence on evolution theories—including the issue of perfectibility of animals (text)—is discussed by Richards (1979; 1982; 1987), from whom my quotations are taken.

[10]Manicas (1987, pp. 53, 72) writes: "It is hardly an exaggeration to say that, without noticeable exception, 19th-century thought was preoccupied with the idea of progress . . . No one in the 19th century could quite free themselves from the idea of progress [defined as unilinear growth]. Nor has our century."

[11]Gould (1977).

[12]For a wide-ranging account of psychology's history, see Buxton (1985). The re-evaluation of Wundt is due to Blumenthal (1980; 1985) and Danziger (1980). Its importance is stressed by Leahey (footnote 2); describing Wundt (Leahey, 1986, p. 649) as "an empiricist of the British mould" is an error that has been corrected by "the new historians of psychology," as has the "myth of a lineage of British Empiricism." Such revisions—and the history of psychology in general—are set in a broader context of the history of the social sciences by Manicas (1987).

[13]It has been common to defend Darwin from complicity in "Social Darwinism" but this may be too apologist a stance (Moore, 1986; Young, 1985a).

[14]Giddens (1984, pp. 228–243) notes the centrality of the concept of *adaptation* to evolutionist explanation in the social sciences, but finds its definition to be diffuse and vacuous. Giddens' analysis parallels that of Gould (Gould & Lewontin, 1979; Gould & Vrba, 1982) in which "adaptationism" is found to be equally impoverished as an explanatory concept in the *natural* sciences.

2 Charles Darwin and the Origins of Developmental Psychology

The work of Charles Darwin has been seen by many developmentalists as the single most influential source of ideas in the theory of child development.[1] In this chapter, Darwin's own views on developmental issues are investigated. These views are then set in the broader context of evolutionary thinking towards the end of the 19th century, a context in which Darwin's theory of natural selection was only one of several competing doctrines. This context, rather than Darwin's theory as such, was the intellectual background from which early developmental psychology emerged. The chapter includes a discussion of the impact of Darwin on his contemporary developmentalists, especially Wilhelm Preyer, George Romanes, and James Sully.

THE "NATURAL HISTORY OF BABIES": DARWIN ON CHILD DEVELOPMENT

Charles Darwin (1809–1882) is widely regarded as the greatest biologist of the 19th century.[2] Many of his ideas were developed on his round-the-world voyage on H.M.S. *Beagle* which took place between 1831 and 1836. Within two years of his return he had opened the first of a series of notebooks on issues relating to human, as well as to animal, evolution. At the end of Notebook M, which was completed in 1838, Darwin wrote the following:

> Natural History of Babies
> Do babies start (i.e., useless sudden movement of muscles) very early in life
> Do they wink, when anything placed before their eyes, very young, before

> experience can have taught them to avoid danger Do they know frown when they first see it?[3]

The notebooks covered numerous topics, including much material on emotional expression in man and animals. Darwin's notebook material on human babies was based on secondhand evidence, but a year later his first child, William, was born. Darwin made careful observations on William's early development, including the issues he had identified in 1838. This material remained unpublished by him until 1877, when some extracts appeared as "A biographical sketch of an infant."[4]

The relationship of man to the animal kingdom was perhaps Darwin's greatest and most longstanding concern. His major claim was for the existence of *continuity* between man and the animals, and his interest in the behaviour of babies was closely related to this issue of continuity. In *The descent of man*, published in 1871, Darwin argued that the "mental and moral faculties" of man have been gradually evolved from animal ancestry, and: "That such evolution is at least possible, ought not to be denied, for we daily see these faculties developing in every infant."[5] From the time of the early notebooks onwards, Darwin was searching for evidence of continuity. Anatomical structure was a major source of evidence, but behaviour was seen as being of equal importance. Behaviour was critical because those scientists who wished to deny continuity—who wished, that is, to treat mankind as distinct and special—focused on human behaviour as being unique. Such characteristics as the use of language, moral sensitivity, and sociability were held to be found only in humans. These kinds of behaviour were therefore of vital importance to Darwin's case.

For Darwin, the evidence for continuity was particularly strong in the case of the expression of emotion. Therefore, in addition to material on emotionality in animals and adult humans of all kinds, evidence from human babies was crucial. For if emotional responses such as startle and fear could be demonstrated in the young infant, the individual acquisition of these responses would seem to be ruled out. It would have to be concluded that the responses were an inheritance from animal ancestry. Evolutionary descent, and the continuity between man and the animal kingdom, would hence be demonstrated.

The early notebooks contain numerous remarks about the early appearance of emotional expressions in children. Some of this material was later used by Darwin in *The expression of the emotions in man and animals*. This book brought together various evidence for continuity in the means of expression (especially facial expression) and attempted to provide an explanation for the origins of specific expressions. Such explanations focused primarily on use-inheritance: On the assimilation into germ-material of movements originally habitual and adaptive.[6] For example, facial expressions relating to disgust were traced by Darwin to mouth movements involved in vomiting. Man's ancestors, for Darwin, possessed much greater voluntary control than ourselves over the muscles involved in vomiting: Vomiting for them was a *habit*. In modern man, all that remains is an attenuated version of the same muscular movement, now hereditary and universal. In general, reactions which arose as adaptive and functional responses have come to be inborn. As presented in the "Biographical sketch" of 1877, the evidence includes the newborn's starting and blinking to a sudden sound as a manifestation of fear.

Nothing has yet been said on the issue of *natural selection* as a mechanism for evolutionary change. Darwin's theory of natural selection was announced in 1859 in *The origin of species*. By analogy with "artificial" selection—the breeding of domesticated animals, and plants, by humans—Darwin proposed that evolution could work by those animals happening to possess favourable characteristics living longer and producing more offspring. If it was granted that the favourable characteristics were heritable, then animals with such characteristics would come to predominate. Those without such inborn advantages would perish. Critically, for the theory of natural selection, the advantages were seen as inborn from the start. That is, some individual happened to be born with a new, potentially advantageous, characteristic. Natural selection was a process that was able to seize on such a characteristic and breed it into a population, in much the same way—but without intention—as a farmer might breed long wool into his sheep. No animal could be forced, or encouraged, to elongate its wool; but if a long-woolled animal did arise, it could be used as breeding stock.

Throughout his work, Darwin saw natural selection only as one of several processes involved in evolutionary change. The major additional process involved the inheritance and transmission of characteristics actually acquired in the lifetime of an animal. This process has usually been associated with the name of Lamarck, the French zoologist whose work was carried out at the very beginning of the 19th century.[7] Darwin endorsed the inheritance of acquired characters throughout his writing, from the time of the early notebooks to *The descent of man* (1871) and through to the later editions of *The origin of species*. To the extent that the childhood material relates to one or other mechanism, it is the inheritance of acquired characters which receives more support. The theory on the origins of emotional expression is an example of this. Indeed, the theory of the inheritance of acquired characters makes developmental claims quite directly. Evidence in its favour consists of the observation in young offspring of characteristics known to have been acquired (rather than inherited) by the parent or more remote ancestor. Such examples, as quoted by Darwin, include the observation that the children of blacksmiths have strong arms and the suggestion that the human foetus has thick skin on its soles because of the pressure exerted on generations of adults in walking.[8]

Darwin was thus quite happy with the view that behavioural characteristics of man might have been inherited from the acquisitions, as well as from the inborn qualities, of ancestors. In general, such inherited features, such as the means of emotional expression, would remain through individual development: The animal ancestry would form a permanent component of the adult human. For Darwin, of course, this was strong evidence for continuity and hence for the theory of descent. In some cases, however, characteristics of children were seen by Darwin as being outgrown by the adult. The child demonstrated vestiges of animal ancestry which the adult in some sense left behind. In the early notebooks, examples include the "violent passions" of young children and the fact that children, but not adults, pout like apes. Further[9]: "Children have an uncommon pleasure in hiding themselves & skulking about in shrubbery, when other people are about: this is analogous to young pigs hiding themselves; a hereditary remains of savages state."

Thus, certain aspects of *child* behaviour demonstrate evolutionary ancestry more ancient than that shown by the adult. Further examples are given in the "Biographical sketch". For example, the intonation of early language in his child offers support, for Darwin, to his claim that: "before man used articulate language, he uttered notes in a true musical scale as does the anthropoid ape Hylobates [gibbon]." Further, his child's fear of large animals at the Zoo prompts Darwin[10] to the following remark:

> May we not suspect that the vague but very real fears of children, which are quite independent of experience, are inherited effects of real dangers and abject superstitions during ancient savage times? It is quite conformable with what we know of the transmission of formerly well-developed characters, that they should appear at an early period of life, and afterwards disappear.

These examples of Darwin's thinking might suggest that he endorsed a straightforward recapitulation theory of child development, with the course of evolution being repeated by the individual. However, Darwin's thinking was rather more complex than this. He argued that the *embryos* of modern species might well resemble the *embryos* of their ancestors, simply because evolutionary change would have affected adult states, leaving the embryo largely unchanged. For the same reason, modern species having common ancestry would show resemblance between their embryonic states: Both species, in descending from the common ancestor, having maintained their embryonic patterns. For Darwin, evolution is a conservative process: Features will remain unchanged unless and until strong forces for modification arise. In general, the embryo and the young animal are sheltered from such forces.

Darwin emphasised that the characteristics of adults would re-emerge, through the operation of heredity, at the appropriate age in the descendants. Adult modifications were not pushed back into earlier stages of development, but largely replaced by new adaptations. Recapitulation theory demands that adult features come to be located in the young and embryo of descendants. Thus, the embryo *changes* with evolution. For Darwin, as we have seen, the embryo remains unchanged. This conservatism was for Darwin good evidence of continuity in descent: As he argued in the sixth edition of the *Origin*, alternative interpretations could hardly explain such invariance. Thus, at least in the context of embryology, Darwin rejected the recapitulation of ancient adult states. His view was influenced by the writings of the Russian embryologist von Baer (more accurately, Baer[11]) who had emphasised that it is the *embryos* of related species which resemble each other. The trend is from a general plan to a specific form; such a trend having no connotations of evolutionary transformation as far as Von Baer himself was concerned.

Darwin agreed with the earlier writer that, in general, evolutionary change involves increasing *differentiation* of adult from embryo. That is, modern animals differ more from their embryos than earlier animals did from theirs. As a result, but in a rather incidental and indirect fashion, modern embryos might in fact resemble ancient adults: The ancient adults were little different to the ancient embryos, which were little different from *modern* embryos. For Darwin, however, this possibility was simply speculative. It was an interesting hypothesis which would require considerable empirical evidence (on the fossil record) to enable a judgement on its merits to be made. It was not an established result or law which could be used for predictive purposes.

Following this necessary digression into Darwin's general theory, what can be said about his views on early childhood? In general, Darwin considered early development as an hereditary endowment, a baseline from which variation might emerge in the *adult* state. Many aspects of child behaviour, such as emotional expression, would remain fixed through the lifespan: They were of interest only as a source of evidence for continuity and descent. Some aspects certainly arose from the inheritance of characters formerly acquired in the lifetime of ancestors, for whom they had been of adaptive value. Adaptation to current function was not of great significance during early development: If anything, adaptation was for future (adult) activity. Thus the important aspects of child behaviour were those which were to remain as permanent characteristics. As we have seen, however, Darwin also noted examples of child characteristics which were outgrown by the adult human but were exhibited by adults of "lower" species. It would appear that, for Darwin, the human child resembles the adult animal only because, and insofar as, the adult animal resembles the young animal: As discussed earlier, from the combination of conservatism and differentiation in evolutionary progress. Darwin might thus be said to have rejected recapitulation as an explanatory mechanism, but arrived at conclusions which remained highly consistent with it. Darwin's approach is not completely clear, and may not have been entirely consistent. Ernst Mayr has concluded that Darwin's formulations effectively gave "silent blessings" to recapitulation theory.[12] In any event, an adherence to the doctrine of the inheritance of acquired character itself gives rise to a rather ad hoc form of recapitulation, as in the example of the thick-skinned sole of the foetus. Darwin's contemporaries and successors appear to have paid little attention to the finer points of the argument. Rightly or wrongly, Darwin was generally seen to have both endorsed and authorised the recapitulation account of early human development.

EVOLUTION AND RECAPITULATION

Developmental psychology has its roots in the latter part of the 19th century, a period dominated in many ways by ideas relating to evolution. The term evolution must, however, be taken very broadly, and it was certainly not the case that Darwin's theory of natural selection swept away all alternatives. The concept of a "Darwinian revolution" may well be misleading in a number of ways.[13] In fact, one of the effects of Darwin's own proposals was to stimulate the opposition into clarifying and systematising its alternative position. Such non-Darwinian views on evolution can be seen to have exerted much wider influence than Darwin's natural selection. Where natural selection proposed a nonteleological mechanism, leading to a branching system of adaptations to different habitats, the nonDarwinian approach proposed that evolutionary change must have some direction and overall design. Lamarck's own system was based on this assumption: Different animal series being seen as climbing up through a fixed hierarchical sequence. The inheritance of acquired character, for which he is now best known, played rather a minor part in Lamarck's system. Much more central, for Lamarck and for the later neo-Lamarckians, was the assumption of direction and design in evolutionary change (although of a natural, not a theological kind). This assumption gave rise to a linear picture of development: A single track of developmental progress, up which all organisms and civilisations have to climb.

As we have seen, Darwin himself endorsed certain aspects of Lamarckism and he also made frequent use of the single-track model. Indeed, his central claim for the continuity of man and the animals was closely tied to such an account. An appeal to ontogeny as evidence for continuity and descent requires that the sequence of developmental change is, in certain respects, a unitary one. The same evolutionary course is to be traversed by the infant as by the species. The notion of a single track of development is an ancient one, often referred to as the "Scala Naturae" or the Great Chain of Being: The conceptualisation of animals, man, and (occasionally) angels as ranged on a single, continuous scale.[14] Non-Darwinian forms of evolution theory were, essentially, *pre*-Darwinian: they represented the continuation of a tradition into which Darwin had intruded, but which he failed to overthrow. As Stephen Toulmin[15] notes: "The idea of a Sovereign Order of Nature is not dead. It has roots elsewhere than in the field of biology, and has survived (though transformed) the revolutions produced in biology by Cuvier, Darwin and their successors."

Another feature on which the non-Darwinians differed from Darwin was the origin of variations. As proposed by Lamarck, animals might themselves sometimes play an active part in directing evolutionary change; the classic example being the giraffe stretching for higher branches and hence, through the greater exercise of appropriate muscles (*not* as a direct result of will), slightly lengthening its neck. Darwin accepted that such modifications, once acquired, might become hereditary, and he laid great stress on the fact that the animal could not in any meaningful sense direct the change (erroneously asserting that this had been Lamarck's claim[16]). Certainly, Darwin's early thinking gave a major role to habit, and hence departed less from Lamarck than he appears to have wished. For the nonDarwinians the organism's own behaviour was of crucial importance in guiding evolutionary change. This was one important way in which the uncontrolled, opportunistic nature of Darwin's natural selection could be circumvented. For those of the non-Darwinians who accepted that evolutionary change has no overall plan, an emphasis on the active contribution of the organism represented an attractive alternative: A compromise between outright teleology and radical mechanism.

In many ways, Darwin himself failed to propose a clear-cut, radical alternative to the more traditional accounts of evolution. The most important step in this direction was taken by August Weismann who, in 1885 (three years after Darwin's death), outlined an argument for the impossibility of the Lamarckian mode of inheritance. Weismann argued that the "germ plasm"—the inheritable material in an organism—was isolated from any effects occurring during the organism's lifetime, and therefore that the only heritable features were those themselves inherited. Natural selection was thus the only means by which evolutionary change took place.[17] Weismann's was a radical Darwinism. Its impact was considerable in biology, splitting evolutionists into two opposing camps, the neo-Darwinists led by Weismann and the neo-Lamarckians. On developmental psychology, then beginning to emerge, its impact was almost negligible. Almost without exception, developmentalists refused to accept that acquired characters could not be transmitted directly.

The contribution of one younger contemporary of Darwin should be discussed in more detail, since its influence on developmental psychology was perhaps as great. Ernst Haeckel (1834–1919) of Jena saw himself as a follower of both Darwin and Lamarck, and his account of evolutionary change had an immense appeal to both scientific and popular audiences in the final decades of the 19th century.[18] Much of his technical work was in embryology, and he presented evidence that the human embryo passes through stages of development at which it *corresponds* to the adult forms of various species of animal. For Haeckel, the human embryo is literally recapitulating its evolutionary ancestry. The adult forms of "lower" animals are expressed and transcended as the human climbs up its own ancestral tree. This was Haeckel's "biogenetic law": That ontogeny is the short and rapid recapitulation of phylogeny. In fact, for Haeckel, the ancestry drives the individual development: Phylogeny is the *cause* of ontogeny. This picture was seen as a derivative of Darwinism[19]:

> Of all the branches of anthropology, not one is so affected and altered by the theory of descent as psychology . . . In order to understand correctly the highly differentiated, delicate mental life of civilized man, we must, therefore, observe not only its gradual awakening in the child, but also its step-by-step development in lower, primitive peoples and in invertebrates.

For Haeckel, and for those who followed him, the process of recapitulation was so precise that embryological evidence could be used to reconstruct the evolutionary sequence itself. Very early stages of the embryo yielded information on the earliest and most primitive ancestors of man, no longer represented by any living organism. Such procedures seemed to Haeckel, with some justification, as compatible with Darwinism and indeed as an application of Darwinism. For Haeckel, evolutionary advance involves additions of various kinds to the behavioural repertoire of adult animals. Such additions come to be transmitted by the Lamarckian mechanism. Changes are thus made at the *end* of the developmental sequence and, unless the lifespan were to expand without limit, earlier (older) acquisitions thus have to be packed down into a shorter period of time. Therefore any acquisition moves back earlier and earlier in the lifespan, eventually into the embryo, as advance in the species takes place. These acquisitions, representing earlier adult forms, become compressed into early development to make room for new acquisitions. Past ancestral states are not really transcended, but are merely added to the obstacle-course of life which faces each new individual.

Finally, something should be said concerning one of Darwin's most influential contemporaries, Herbert Spencer (1820–1903). Spencer's approach to evolution was but one aspect of a grand theory of the universe and of human society. The central proposal of the theory was that the general trend in all developmental processes was one of differentiation, from homogeneity to heterogeneity. In this view he was strongly influenced by the work of the embryologist von Baer, for whom (unlike for Haeckel) the human embryo exhibits a *generalised* vertebrate and then mammalian form before its final specification as human. As Spencer expressed it himself:[20] "the series of changes gone through during development . . . constitute an advance from homogeneity of structure to heterogeneity of structure . . . [this] is the law of all progress." This differentiation theory is inconsistent with the strong version of recapitulation, according to which the embryo is seen as passing through the *adult* forms of ancestral species. The inconsistency was recognised by von Baer himself when he subsequently rejected the Haeckelian interpretation (as he also rejected the Darwinian theory of descent with modification[21]).

Spencer found a general form of the recapitulation theory to be compatible with his differentiation theory of development, although he did not explore its ontogenetic implications in a systematic manner. This approach was consistent with Spencer's adherence to the Lamarckian doctrine of the inheritance of acquired character. Spencer, who coined the phrase "survival of the fittest," exerted immense influence on the scientific and popular community at the end of the 19th century, not least in the United States; the impact of his ideas, if not of his name, may be traced through to contemporary formulations.

DARWIN'S IMMEDIATE IMPACT

This section discusses Darwin's influence on three younger contemporaries, all of whom had special interests in developmental topics. These three—Preyer, Romanes, and Sully—represent the next generation after Darwin, all three having been born around the time Darwin was observing the early development of his own children. In Germany, William Preyer—more usually referred to as Wilhelm—published the first full-length baby biography in 1882. In England, George Romanes applied Darwin's ideas directly to developmental issues; and James Sully discussed child development against the background of contemporary evolution theory. All three were personally acquainted with Darwin.

George Romanes (1848–1894) was Darwin's direct heir, his protégé, to whom Darwin left manuscript material concerning the evolution of mental faculties and instinct. Although Darwin's junior by some 40 years, Romanes lived only 12 years longer. His central commitment was to the continuity between animal and man, especially in the area of mental abilities. As Romanes[22] himself put it: "the human mind itself, is but the topmost inflorescence of one mighty growth, whose roots and stem and many branches are sunk in the abyss of interplanetary time." As this quotation might suggest, Romanes was also influenced by Herbert Spencer[23]. "Mind," said Romanes, "is everywhere continuous." Thus, all differences in mental attainment represent differences of degree, not of kind: In Romanes' words, not differences of "*origin*, but differences of *development*." Development as a continuous process was of central interest for Romanes. Going beyond Darwin, he attempted to formulate a systematic account of the progressive stages of mental functioning in the animal kingdom and in man. He constructed a comprehensive diagram of mental evolution, divided into 50 successive degrees of "elaboration." For each degree, both a stage in human ontogenesis and a group of animals were given. Thus level 24, which was characterised by the communication of ideas (and hence sympathy), corresponded to the 5-month-old human infant *and* to the bees and wasps. The whole scheme, for Romanes, portrayed "the probable development of Mind from its beginnings in protoplasmic life up to its culmination in the brain of civilised man".

The details of Romanes' recapitulation theory are of little interest in themselves, although his scheme was more concerned with infancy and early childhood than was Haeckel's, which focused on the embryo.[24] Unlike Haeckel, also, Romanes carried out empirical observations to seek evidence for the theory. In particular, he studied the development of communication in his own children. In doing so he was directly following Darwin's lead; examples of gestural communication in the one-year-old were included in the "Biographical sketch." Romanes' research was more detailed, and it led him to question the significance of the traditional boundary between infancy and childhood—the emergence of spoken language. For Romanes, communicative functions are continuous across this boundary; and this continuity itself comprises strong evidence for a developmental account of evolution. Romanes described a sequence of steps by which the child first parallels and then outstrips the achievements of other animals. The lowest or "perceptual" level of thought is common to many species; the next, "receptual" level is shared by the 18-month child, the parrot, and higher mammals. At this level the child can point to a tumbler (for a drink), just as the dog can "beg" for water. Both can comprehend speech to a certain extent, and both can respond with appropriate gestures or movements. Similarly, the very young child can tug at an adult's clothing in order to get a door opened. It is only the human child, however, who is able to proceed beyond this level.

Wilhelm Preyer (1841–1897) was born in England but achieved eminence in Jena, Germany, where Ernst Haeckel was professor of zoology and comparative anatomy. Preyer himself was principally a physiologist and embryologist; he considered himself to be a close follower and interpreter of Darwin (of whom he wrote a biography in 1896). Preyer's approach to child development was based on an adherence to the ancestral version of recapitulation and to Lamarckian principles of evolution[25]:

> The mind of the new-born child, then, does not resemble a *tabula rasa* . . . the tablet is already written on before birth, with many illegible, nay unrecognizable and invisible, marks, the traces of the imprint of countless sensuous impressions of long-gone generations . . . each [man] must . . . fill out and animate anew his inherited endowments, the remains of the *experiences and activities of his ancestors.*

Thirty years later, just before his death, Preyer stated[26]:

> Individual development . . . is an abbreviated repetition of phylogenesis . . . the mental development of all mankind can be found in the child in an abbreviated form.

The origins of developmental characteristics were to be sought in heredity, not acquisition by the individual. Thus, for Preyer (writing in *The mind of the child*, 1882), preverbal concepts such as the concept of food could *not*, in the growing individual, be "formed otherwise than it was formed by our ancestors." The original acquisition had taken place in such ancestors, so that current effects represent (again) the "traces of the imprint of countless sensuous impressions of long-gone generations."

In Preyer's application, a highly orthodox one for his time, the sensory experience was projected back into the evolutionary past so that the modern child was still seen as replaying its ancestry. Recapitulation was thus seen as a kind of *memory* of ancient events and experiences, the idea being that the original experience had imparted vibrations to certain particles in the germ material. These "vibrations" continued to resonate in the descendants. Preyer's work, especially *The mind of the child*, was immensely detailed on certain aspects of early development, but its overall theoretical framework was non-Darwinian biology. Indeed, Preyer's developmental work (together with that of Romanes) received considerable praise from Haeckel himself, writing at the end of the 19th century.[27]

James Sully, who occupied the Grote chair in mind and logic in the University of London, exerted his influence mainly by writing textbooks. In terms of his interests, he might be said to have been more primarily a psychologist than either Romanes or Preyer. An early paper on "Babies and science" (1881), which was characterised by recapitulationary argument[28], was followed by *The teacher's handbook of psychology* in 1886. Here Sully noted that children's fear of strangers, or of certain animals, and their love of human companionship: "appear to point to the effects of ancestral experience. Numberless experiences of the pleasure of human companionship, and of the dangers connected with strangers and wild animals during the past history of the race, have left their organic trace in the shape of an inherited association."

More generally, but consistent with this neo-Lamarckism, Sully's account of child development at this point is an associationist one: There is a "uniform order of development of the faculties," namely Sensation, followed by Perception, followed by Representative Imagination, followed by General or Abstract Knowing. Essentially this is Herbert Spencer's account, and Sully agrees with Spencer that developmental change is characterised by progress "from vague to distinct knowledge" ("differentiation"); from simple to complex ("integration"); from external sense to internal thought (from the "presentative" to the "representative"); and from the knowledge of individuals ("concrete things") to that of classes ("abstract qualities"). It should be stressed that all these claims were entirely orthodox and commonplace, being set within the nonDarwinian biology and the associationist psychology then dominating scientific thought.

In his subsequent book *Studies of childhood* (1895), Sully employed recapitulationary logic in a systematic manner. This allowed him to make comparisons between children and modern-day adult "savages" for[29]: "As we all know, the lowest races of mankind stand in close proximity to the animal world. The same is true of the infants of civilised races." The "savage" was held not to have advanced beyond the state of prehistoric man, and the civilised child had to pass through an equivalent state on his way to civilised adulthood. Various similarities were described by Sully, including the attribution of life to inanimate objects (a phenomenon usually described as "animism"); the belief that dreams were real and had locations in space; and bizarre notions of causality, such as the movement of a tree being thought to make the wind blow. Similarly, a belief in the control over distant events by one's own actions was observed by Sully in both the child and the "savage." Sully tells us in his autobiography[30] that:

> A point of peculiar interest to me in connection with these researches was the tracing of an affinity between the ideas and impulses of the child and those of backward races. In working out the analogies between them, I found it necessary to look more closely into ethnological records of savage peoples, and also to seek information from anthropologists like Professor E.B. Tylor.

It was Tylor who, in his *Primitive culture* of 1871, had explored the "animism" of the thinking of "savage peoples."

The child's art is, for Sully, also similar to that of the "savage": Several views of an object being displayed at once, hidden features being shown as if visible, and vertical displacement being used to indicate depth. This last feature was also described as parallel to a stage in Egyptian art. In general, for Sully, primitive perception exhibits a "natural realism": The child, said Sully, is "a Berkeleyan, in so far at least that for him the reality of things is reality for his own sense-perceptions." It should be noted that Sully's analyses included empirical observations as well as recapitulationary argument, and some of Sully's observations have proved extremely well founded. But the framework for explanation was recapitulation and the Lamarckian mechanism of heredity. Moreover, neurological speculation was included. For Sully, "lower" (more primitive) neural centres come to be overlaid, with development, by higher inhibitory centres. This model was an application of the influential proposals of J. Hughlings Jackson in 1884 concerning a hierarchy of levels in the brain; and Jackson was greatly influenced by the global evolutionism of Herbert Spencer. [31] Neurology and evolution theory thus combined to yield a coherent and systematic picture of developmental change in human childhood.

THE INFLUENCE OF EVOLUTIONISM

Sully's employment of recapitulationary logic, and especially the systematic comparison of the child with the "savage," was typical of the scientific thought of the late 19th century.[32] Different formulations had different purposes, depending upon the direction of argument—whether from the (presumed known) "savage" to the child, or vice versa. Most included a mixture of direct ancestral comparisons (such as child with prehistoric man, or "savage" with animal) as well as indirect or parallel comparisons ("savage" with child). For all such comparisons to be worthwhile, the course of development has to be seen in terms of a single track or sequence. Both individual development (ontogeny) and evolutionary progress (phylogeny) are thus seen in terms of a linear series of states or stages. Darwin's natural selection predicted a radiation or branching, but still, in general, Darwinism was taken to offer support to the recapitulation theory. Indeed, Darwin's work was taken as a vindication of the Scale of Nature, rising up through the various classes of animals and various races of men and reaching its apex with the white European male.

Comparisons between the child, higher animals and "savages" were commonplace in the literature of the late 19th century and beyond. Some went further: Havelock Ellis, British sexologist, found that posture and locomotion in country people, the "plebeian," and in women all compared closely to that in children. Women, for Ellis, were "nearer to the infantile condition than men."[33] Emotional expression was described almost universally in terms of recapitulation. For one turn-of-the-century writer, the expression of pain in the infant resembled that of "a monkey or Negro," while that of the three-year-old presented "the picture of a savage." Racism and recapitulation theory are deeply interwoven. In this connection, some aspects of the *practical* application of evolutionist thinking should be noted. For example, John Langdon Down explored the idea that certain forms of mental retardation might represent throwbacks to earlier (more primitive) states. Such primitive states were also seen as represented by modern nonEuropean races; hence "Mongolian idiocy." The condition is now named Down's Syndrome.[34] In fact, idiocy (as in the microcephalic) had been used by Darwin himself in the context of the demonstration of continuity. A second example is the influential work of the Italian criminologist Lombroso, for whom certain kinds of criminal represented throwbacks or "atavisms." More general parallels between criminals and young children were a commonplace in scientific writing.

The closing years of the 19th century were the heyday of what might be called "global parallelism" as applied to the conceptualisation of childhood. Evidence from a vast range of sources—primates, "primitives," prehistory—was amalgamated into an encyclopaedic account of the thought processes of the child, unified by the principles of evolutionism. A typical compendium of such material was published in the year 1900 by Alexander Chamberlain, an anthropologist brought to Clark University by the developmentalist Stanley Hall. Parallels were described in connection with counting games and primitive rituals; make-believe names and the concealment of names; indiscriminate eating; the love of adornment; and belief in the reality of dreams. According to Chamberlain[35]: "The child and the savage meet on this ground, some young boys and girls being as firmly impressed with the reality of their dreams as are the Brazilian indians."

The issue of dreams was of importance in other ways also. Many of the parallels to which appeals were made involved aliens, such as prehistoric man, primitive tribes, or the criminal. One major parallel, however, came closer to home: The comparison of the mental life of the child with the dream state in the civilised adult. The most systematic and influential contributor to this line of argument was Sigmund Freud. Freud stated in *The interpretation of dreams* (1900)[36]: "Dreaming is a piece of infantile mental life that has been superseded." In fact, comparisons between child thought, the thought of the mad, and the dream state had been made before. The comparison of the later two (madness and dreaming) was noted by Freud himself in such earlier writers as the philosophers Kant and Schopenhauer as well as in Freud's contemporary, the psychologist Wilhelm Wundt. In the late 19th century, the comparisons were unified by Hughlings Jackson's hierarchical model of the central nervous system by which "lower" levels were seen as becoming overlaid, and inhibited, by "higher" levels. Progress up the hierarchy was taken to characterise evolutionary change *and* development in the individual; and the stratified structure allowed *regression* to lower levels even when higher states had been achieved.

One of those who adopted the hierarchical model was one of Freud's teachers in Vienna, Theodore Meynert. A brain anatomist and psychiatrist, Meynert considered hypnotism to be dangerous *because* it tampered with the higher, inhibitory centres, thereby loosening their control over the lower levels (a major concern of these primitive levels being sex).For Meynert, as for others, development from infancy involves the progressive emergence of inhibitory centres: Thus acute hallucinatory psychosis and dreaming were both compared to the "primary-ego" state of infancy.[37] Indeed, it was becoming commonplace to treat dreaming as a regression to ancient (ancestral) states, a procedure highly compatible with the hierarchical model. Both James Sully and Havelock Ellis, for example, described dreams as a regression to ancient or archaic impulses and feelings, to 'the old ways of looking at things and of feeling about them." The comparison with the mental life of childhood was at least implicit here. Moreover, the hierarchical model of mental functioning, read in an evolutionary way, was highly compatible with the theory of recapitulation. The experience of ancestors was taken as forming the basic substrate of the early mental life of the child, a mental life, moreover, which was unconscious. Adult dreams regressed to this child-like level, and hence to ancient ways of thinking. The role of Lamarckism was central here: It was the experience and feelings of ancestors, not their inborn adaptations, which were replayed in childhood and in dreams.

A catalogue of the use of recapitulationary logic at the end of the 19th century would be of little value.[38] If for no other reason, the formulations selected here were equalled if not excelled by those of the major developmentalists themselves. Recapitulationary logic, with its associated assumptions on parallels between the child and the "savage," was widespread and wholly orthodox at the time when such figures as Stanley Hall, James Mark Baldwin, and Sigmund Freud were developing their own lines of interest in ontogenesis. Many scientists concerned with child development considered themselves to be Darwinians. Frequently, however, it was the Lamarckian and recapitulationary aspects of Darwin which they were taking up. Haeckel's "biogenetic law" was put forward, and broadly accepted, as consistent with Darwinism. The arguments of Weismann for the impossibility of the Lamarckian mechanism had little impact, especially on developmental thinkers. James Sully, for example, referred disparagingly to to "the fashionable Weismannism of the hour." The overall effect of Darwin's biological writings on developmental thinking was, paradoxically, to strengthen assumptions about the child which were in fact pre-

Darwinian ones. That which was original to Darwin was largely ignored. But, due at least in part to the *impact* of Darwin—if influenced rather little by his precise claims—a new science had emerged by the end of the 19th century: The science of developmental psychology.

NOTES TO CHAPTER TWO

[1]The general impact of Darwin on psychology is discussed by Boakes (1984); by Gottlieb and others in Hearst (1979); and in Woodward and Ash (1982).

[2]On Darwin see the series of books by Bowler 1983; 1984; 1987; 1988), and the recent authoritative collection by Kohn (1985). For a broader history of biology, see Mayr (1982).

[3]Gruber (1974, p.297); punctuation as in original. Beer (1985, p.558) has noted that: "in 1838 [Darwin's] preoccupation with psychological development was at a height and accompanied his struggle with the idea of species development and transmutation. Ontogeny thus authenticates in a very general way . . . the inquiry into phylogeny."

[4]The background to the "Biographical sketch" (Gruber, 1974) is described in more detail by Keegan and Gruber (1985).

[5]Darwin (1871, p.123).

[6]Richards (1977, p.15) comments that, in *The expression of the emotions in man and animals*, Darwin: "relied almost entirely on the principle that individually acquired habits could in time become instinctive in a species and heritable by its progeny." Also see Browne (1985).

[7]The inheritance of acquired characters played a minor role in Lamarck's theory (Bowler, 1984; Lamarck, 1809/1914; Mayr, 1982). Lamarck himself emphasises that this mechanism has the effect of distorting the basic trend in the animal series, which is that of increasing organisation and "perfection." It represents the influence of environmental variation on relatively *non*essential organs. The heritability of the effects of use gives rise only to "lateral ramifications" from the basic series. Thus (Lamarck, 1809/1914, p.70): "Progress in complexity of organisation exhibits anomalies here and there in the general series of animals, due to the influence of environment and of acquired habits." Lamarck stresses that the occurrence of these anomalies must not be allowed to distract attention from the underlying sequence. Lamarck's project was the application of a notion of organisational complexity to the animal kingdom, and it was carried through with great rigour. A system of classification ordered according to these principles would: "represent[ ] as nearly as possible the actual order followed by nature in the production of animals." The tendency to increase in complexity and hence perfection—that is, toward human organisation—was seen as a tendency inherent in organic material: Animal life is continuously generated but at the lowest level, and drives itself upward through the predetermined sequence. Adaptation to specific environments merely distorts this process. As emphasised by Barthélemy-Madaule (1979/1982, pp. 73, 81), the heritability of parental experience was simply taken for granted by Lamarck as it had been since the writer of the book of Genesis (Genesis 30, pp. 37–42). Again, observations on pregnancy contained in the Notebooks of Leonardo (Richter, 1952, p.164) include the comment that: "one soul governs two bodies, as when one sees that the mother desires a certain food and the child bears the mark of it."

[8]Darwin (1871, p.32). Darwin also reports (p.31) that U.S. sailors had been found to have shorter arms and longer legs than soldiers, the first difference being explained by sailors' extra practice at pulling. 'Whether the[se] . . . modifications would become hereditary, if the same habits of life were followed during many generations, is not known, but it is probable." For Darwin's commitment to use-inheritance, see Grinnell (1985); Richards (1981). The primacy of *habit* in Darwin's accounts at this time is also noted by Burkhardt (1985).

[9]Gruber (1974, p.343); punctuation as in original.

[10]Ibid., p.469 ("A biographical sketch of an infant," 1877).

[11]Von Baer's real (Russian) name was K.M. Baer (Scudo & Acanfora, 1985, p.737). There is some confusion over his nationality (Ridley, 1982, has him as a German), and more over his theoretical stance. Toulmin (1981) has von Baer as a recapitulationist, a mistake also made by James Mark Baldwin (1930, p.11), by Jean Piaget (1967/1971, p.83) and by Dixon and Lerner (1985, p.263). Also see Gould (1977).

[12]Mayr (1982, p.474). In his autobiography (Barlow, 1958, p.125), Darwin observes that his account of embryological development in the *Origin* had been largely ignored at the time, credit for the account having subsequently been given to Haeckel among others. On Haeckel see text.

[13]See, especially, Bowler (1983; Note 1; 1988).

[14]The "Great Chain of Being" was investigated by Lovejoy earlier this century (Glass, Temkin, & Strauss, 1968). See the Glass collection also for other pre-Darwinian formulations. Lovejoy's work has recently been re-evaluated in a collection of papers in the *Journal for the History of Ideas* (1987, Vol.XLVIII/2). The "phylogenetic scale" in relation to psychology is discussed in Hodos and Campbell (1969). See also Wertheimer (1985).

[15]Toulmin (1982, p.56).

[16]Darwin erroneously described Lamarck as having proposed that will-power drives evolutionary change (Richards, 1981, p.195). Darwin's misrepresentation may have arisen from the highly influential "eulogy" of Georges Cuvier (Barthélemy-Madaule, 1979/1982, pp. 77, 108; Jordanova, 1984, p.102) which attempted to ridicule Lamarck's proposal that life-forms can change one to another. Also see Richards (1982, p.268) where the persistence of Darwin's error is noted in such contemporary scholars as Howard Gruber and Michael Ruse; and see Grinnell (1985).

[17]Weismann himself later retreated from this radical stance (Mayr, 1985; Ridley, 1982). However his contribution had already had its effect. Essentially, Weismann's claims gave rise to redefinitions both of Lamarck and of Darwin (Barthélemy-Madaule, 1979/1982, p.82): The inheritance of acquired character was now perceived as central to Lamarck, and the significance of Darwin was now perceived as due to his formulation of an alternative. It is important to note that Lamarck's work was revived and redefined in France just as elsewhere; that is, French neo-Lamarckism was part of a general trend of the times, not the continuation of an unbroken tradition. In the mid-19th century Lamarck appears to have been forgotten in France as elsewhere (but see Barthélemy-Madaule, 1979/1982).

[18]For Haeckel and his influence see De Beer (1958), Gould (1977). Haeckel saw himself, and was seen by his contemporaries, as a champion of Darwinism in Germany (cf. the biography by Bölsche, 1900/1906). Haeckel visited Darwin twice (p.241).

[19]Haeckel (1866); cited in Jaeger (1982, p.308).

[20]Spencer (1864, p.324). Especially see Smith (1982a); also see Jones (1980); Manicas (1987); Ridley (1982). For Spencer (Richards, 1985, p.307): "the chief mechanism of evolution was the internalizing of external relations most frequently encountered . . . this mechanism progressively drove anatomical forms and conjoint mental structures from more generalized adaptive states to more definite correspondences with the environment, from simpler, more homogeneous patterns to more complex and heterogeneous configurations."

[21]Scudo and Acanfora (1985).

[22]Romanes (1889); cited in White (1983, p.59).

[23]Romanes is discussed by Boakes (1984); by Richards (1977); by Ridley (1982—including the Spencer influence); and by Sulloway (1979).

[24]Romanes' *Darwin, and after Darwin* (1892/1897) contains detailed descriptions of recapitulationary phenomena in the newborn human, such as inflection of feet so as to facilitate the grasping of branches and the strong grasp—as demonstrated by Robinson in 1891 (op. cit., p.80)—"in order to hold on to the hair of the mother when she is using her arms for the

purposes of locomotion." Similarities with the chimpanzee and the gorilla are detailed. The correspondence between ancestral and individual forms is exact (op. cit., p.101): "Every individual of every species . . . exhibit[s] in its own person a history of developmental change, every term of which corresponds with the structural peculiarities of its now extinct predecessors—and this in the exact historical order of their succession in geological time." The theoretical importance of embryological evidence is stressed by Romanes: he concludes the Embryology chapter by noting: "we cannot wonder that evolutionists should now regard the science of comparative embryology as the principal witness to their theory."

[25]Preyer (1869); cited in Tobach (1985, p.215) (emphasis added). The work of Preyer is discussed in such histories of developmental psychology as Cairns (1983); but now most comprehensively in Eckardt et al. (1985). Most contributors to the latter are committed to the description of Preyer as a true Darwinian.

[26]Preyer (1897); cited in Eckardt (1985, p.183).

[27]Haeckel (1899/1906, pp.37–38). Haeckel writes here (p.37) of: "the long scale of psychic development which runs unbroken from the lowest, unicellular forms of life up to the mammals, and to man at their head." The metaphorical use of the term "head" should be noted. Further, "The psychic difference between the crudest savage of the lowest grade and the most perfect specimen of the highest civilisation is colossal." Compare Darwin (1871, p.64): "Differences . . . between the highest men of the highest races and the lowest savages, are connected by the finest gradations. Therefore it is possible that they might pass and be developed into each other."

[28]Cavanaugh (1985). In 1885 Sully wrote an introduction to a translation of Perez's *The first three years of childhood* (1878). Here Sully noted (pp. vi–vii) that: "We are learning to connect the individual life with that of the race . . . In the light of the new doctrine of evolution, the early period of individual development, which is pre-eminently the domain of instinct, . . . is seen to be the region which bears the clearest testimony to this preparatory work of the race." Perez himself is cautious about the recapitulation hypothesis, describing Darwin's claims concerning the child's fear of large animals as "exaggerated." He also expresses grave reservations over a recapitulationary theory of colour vision which he ascribes to "Gladstone and Magnus." According to this theory, mankind in general, and the individual child, move forward from a total lack of colour vision (as "before Homer"!) through the acquisition of the primary colours, the last being blue (a process held by its proponents to be "not yet far advanced" in some portions of humanity). Sully also comments here (p.xvii) on the respective roles of mother and father in infant observation: "The father cannot . . . hope to accomplish the task alone. His restricted leisure compels him to call in the mother as collaborateur . . . The mother's enthusiasm and patient brooding watchfulness are needed quite as much as the father's keen analytic vision. The mother should note under the guidance of the father, he taking due care to test and verify."

[29]Sully (1895, p.5).

[30]Sully (1918, p.239). Tylor is cited by R. Spencer (1957, p.214) as follows: "The savage state in some measure represents an early condition of mankind, one out of which the higher culture has gradually developed or evolved . . . the result showing that, on the whole, progress has far prevailed over relapse." R. Spencer continues: "Tylor and his contemporaries . . . were [directed] to a conceptual ordering of mankind in terms of a psychic unity that leads to a *unilinear* growth and development of human institutions" (my emphasis).

[31]Hughlings Jackson's work and its influence are discussed by Smith (1982b) and by Sulloway (1979).

[32]General accounts of the recapitulationary parallels popular at the end of the 19th century may be found in Gould (1977); Stocking (1968); Strickland (Note 3); and Sulloway (1979). Kessen (cited in Wertheimer, 1985, p.22) has referred to: "a riot of parallel-drawing between animal and child, between primitive man and child, between early human history and child."

[33]Ellis (1894); cited in Gould (1977, p.118).

[34]See Gould (1984, p.134) (also for Lombroso). More recently, persons with Down's Syndrome have been described in the scientific literature as being characterised by "slow development." This notion is in many ways an evolutionist one. Indeed, as cited by Rynders in Pueschel, Tingey, Rynders, Crocker, and Crutcher (1987), Down's Syndrome had been considered by Crookshank (*The mongol in our midst*, 1924) as a reversion to the orang-utan. The concept of "slow development" in Down's Syndrome is subjected to an empirical critique in Morss (1985a). "Slow development" is combined with other evolutionist arguments in recent writings by Lynn (1987) on the origins of racial differences in I.Q. (but note: The term "mongoloid" is used in this context as a racial grouping; on this issue of ethnic categories see Gould, 1977, p.127).

[35]Chamberlain (1900); cited in Gould (1977, p.118).

[36]Freud (1900: S.E. V, p.567).

[37]On Meynert, see Sulloway (1979).

[38]One indication of the general popularity of these claims is their frequent reference in the Sherlock Holmes stories, written in the 1890s (Conan Doyle, 1981). Holmes discusses Darwin on the prehistoric origins of music in *A study in scarlet* (p.37), commenting that "there are vague memories in our souls of those misty centuries when the world was in its childhood"; (to this Watson responds "That's rather a broad idea"). Again, in *The empty house* (p.494) Holmes discusses the career of Moriarty's henchman Col. Moran as having taken a bad turn after a brilliant start: "I have a theory that the individual represents in his development the whole procession of his ancestors, and that such a sudden turn to good or evil stands for some strong influence which came into the line of his pedigree. The person becomes, as it were, the epitome of the history of his own family." Watson comments "It is surely rather fanciful." Atavistic throwbacks play a part in several of the stories, including *The hound of the Baskervilles*. Here, also, the Who's Who entry for Dr. Mortimer (p.671) is of interest: Mortimer's articles include *Is disease a reversion*, *Some freaks of atavism*, and *Do we progress*? (Mortimer is covetous of Holmes' skull for its interesting shape; elsewhere, Holmes uses size of hat as a measure of intellect.) Holmes also uses the character of progeny as a guide to the true personality of the parent. On these and other aspects of Sherlock Holmes as psychologist, see Radford (1988). Popular science fiction remains of interest in this way: *Star Trek*, for example, making frequent use of recapitulation, as did Kubrick's *2001: A Space Odyssey*.

3 Biology and the Developmentalists: Hall, Baldwin, and Freud

INTRODUCTION

This chapter and the next discuss the general influence of biological ideas on the developmental psychology of six major figures in the history of the discipline. These "major" figures are: Stanley Hall, James Mark Baldwin, Sigmund Freud (Chapter Three); Lev Vygotsky, Jean Piaget, and Heinz Werner (Chapter Four). These chapters are designed to introduce the theoretical assumptions of these major developmentalists: More is said on each in subsequent chapters. In addition, consideration is given in Chapter Four to the work of certain "minor" figures. In this context, some comments are also made on certain schools or traditions within psychology at large, including the "Gestalt" school. These two chapters are concerned with a more recent period than the previous one. Indeed, they bring some aspects of the story up to date in that many of the claims made by these "major" theorists remain central to modern developmental thinking. At the same time, the material is a direct continuation of that in Chapter Two, since several of these modern figures had already begun their work by the end of the 19th century.

As will be seen, recapitulationism in its several versions forms a central theme of these chapters. Another closely related topic is that loosely termed Lamarckism—the doctrine of the inheritance of characters acquired in an ancestor's lifetime. Partly because of its emphasis on the (originally) adaptive nature of behaviour or "habits"—and hence on processes of learning—this Lamarckism has exerted a constant fascination for psychologists. The doctrine has close connections with recapitulation theory, for it supplies the mechanism by which an incremental process of evolution may take place. Thus the young animal may be seen as recapitulating first its remote ancestry and later its parentage, adding new adaptive habits to its adult repertoire. Innovatory adaptive responses, novel to the animal in its own lifetime, might possibly, in turn, become assimilated into the germ material for the benefit of later generations. The central assumption here is of evolutionary progress as a single track: A formulation *more* central to Lamarck himself than the hereditary mechanism per se, and a formulation necessary to the doctrine of recapitulation. A further issue is that of *periodicity* in development: The concept of cycles or phases. Periodicity is related to the notion of repetition (the periodic return to a certain state) and thus, again, to recapitulation. As will be seen, the concept of periodicity was of central importance for several major developmentalists.[1] One expression of this is the model of developmental progress as taking place by a series of waves or thrusts. And the concept of a developmental stage—one of the most central ideas in the discipline—is intimately related to this model.

Chapter Two has outlined the biological background to the material in these two chapters. Darwinism was one among many views competing for domination at the end of the 19th century, and the available versions of Darwinism were many and varied. Darwin himself had endorsed the Lamarckian mechanism, and the version of evolution theory popularised by Haeckel owed as much to Lamarck as it did to Darwin. Ancestral recapitulation—the doctrine of ontogenesis as a replay of evolution—was seen as being consistent with Darwinism. In the broader context, long-standing prejudices concerning non-European races seemed to find support in popular Darwinism. Non-Europeans had been described as "children" since the beginning of the 19th century, and a Darwinist recapitulation theory appeared to put this interpretation onto a scientific footing. Racist thinking has always aspired to scientific respectability and Darwin, certainly unintentionally, provided what was sought. This issue is of relevance here because the supposed equivalence of the "savage" and the civilised child gave rise to much that became central to the conceptualisation of child thought. The effect in the other direction—the more systematic application of "childishness" to other races—is not within the scope of this book.[2]

GRANVILLE STANLEY HALL: ZEALOT OF EVOLUTION

G. Stanley Hall was the first American developmentalist and although his stock is now low his influence has been considerable. At the beginning of the present century he commanded international respect as an authority on individual development[3]. The esteem was perhaps greatest among such professional groups as teachers; many of Hall's peers, William James in particular, admiring his determination more than his intellect. From the standpoint of the 1980s Hall is seen as having contributed little that was original, and as having championed mistaken and even bizarre theoretical claims. As Hall put it himself, towards the end of his career, "How hard I rode my hobbies!" To a large extent, Hall's influence arose from his enthusiastic advocacy of certain current ideas which he found congenial. The biggest of these ideas championed by Hall was ancestral recapitulation. Hall saw his "genetic" (i.e. developmental) psychology as a new method for psychology as a whole, and in formulating it he attempted to incorporate what he considered to be the best in contemporary science. Much of this was, in a broad sense, biological.

Stanley Hall (1844–1924) was, by chronology, of the generation of Romanes, Sully, and Preyer, but did not reach the peak of his influence until the turn of the present century. He spent two important periods of his higher education in Germany. First, around 1870, he studied philosophy and became interested in the developmental approach expressed by "Nature-philosophy." Hall put the central message of this world-view as follows[4]: "Mind was matter awakened, and vegetable and animal life and mind showed the stages of this awakening." Despite his subsequent rejection of philosophy as such, much of this approach remained with Hall. When he later embraced evolution theory it was very much as a grand, global Idea with which to unify natural and human science. Hall studied experimental science in his second German period around 1880, during which time he briefly attended Wundt's laboratory of experimental psychology in Leipzig as well as studying with physiologists. For Hall, the development of consciousness could be traced back to the activity of muscle tissue in primitive (ancient) organisms. With recapitulationary logic, he argued that the emergence of "attention" in the individual should be seen as paralleling its evolutionary history: The "successive waking of the different elements of psychical life." Hall was not yet centrally concerned with the development of the individual, but much of the direction of his later thinking was already determined.

Following his second German period, Hall became deeply involved with educational theory and practice in the U.S.A. His approach to education was a recapitulationary one[5]: "The pupil should, and in fact naturally does, repeat the course of the development of the race, and education is simply the expediting and shortening of this course." This picture was not original to Hall: It was a doctrine influential in Germany and elsewhere in Europe. A version of it had been suggested by Jean-Jacques Rousseau in the 18th century. This educational theory of "cultural epochs" argued that the child should be brought through a sequence of cultural systems corresponding to stages in the social evolution of civilised man. The school curriculum should therefore be a "developmental" one, determined at each point by the needs of the child.[6] It is important to remember that the child's needs were defined by reference to a recapitulationary model. In the context of the late 19th century, this gave rise to a convergence of interest between education and child study. The common goal was the delineation of the correct or natural course of child development. By the 1880s this research programme was well under way in Europe, detailed accounts of the first three years or so of life having been published in 1878 by Perez and in 1882 by Preyer. Others were using questionnaires to explore "the contents of children's minds." Hall adopted the questionnaire method and played a major role in the establishment of a "Child Study" movement in the U.S.A.[7]

Hall attained the post of President of Clark University in 1889 and began to develop a systematic theory of the development of the child. By this time, the work of Romanes had appeared, indicating what purported to be the Darwinian approach to child development. Hall's own perception was that his own psychology had become Darwinian. The mature form of his "Genetic Psychology" now took shape. It was doubly influenced by the theory of recapitualtion: Through his earlier "child study" work, based on a recapitulationary theory of education; and through his ideas on biology, from nature-philosophical to popular Darwinian. Attention will be focused here on Hall's most influential work, *Adolescence* (1904). Although most centrally concerned with adolescence and young adulthood, this book also expresses most clearly Hall's overall picture of individual development. Hall's objective was an ambitious one: The demonstration that his "genetic" psychology was the one true method for psychology in general. Earlier approaches to psychology, argued Hall, had mistakenly based themselves on static views of knowledge and "the soul." Here he made savage attacks on philosophy in general and on epistemology (the theory of knowledge) in particular. Mankind and Mind must, for Hall, be described in terms of progressive change, not of fixed characteristics. This plea for "process" has been echoed many times since, and by many for whom Stanley Hall would be a strange bedfellow indeed.

One mistake identified by Hall was the assumption that the present state of Man is a final state, the pinnacle of evolution. Instead, Hall urged, Man is still actively evolving towards a higher state: An "ascendant super-race." Critically, for Hall, it is adolescence and not adulthood which must provide the jumping-off point for evolutionary advance. Adolescence is plastic in a way that adulthood is not. Individual development through childhood was seen by Hall as rigidly controlled by the process of recapitulation. The state of adolescence itself is the highest point of development, with adulthood representing a falling away, a decline into a state of rigidity. Future evolutionary change will lead to present-day adulthood being pushed back into the years of childhood, eventually, perhaps to "shrivel to a rudiment." This simple picture of evolutionary change, with a single track of development becoming increasingly condensed and contracted, relies (as we have noted) on the mechanisms of Lamarckian inheritance as well as on recapitulation. Hall's grand vision of the course of evolution gave coherence to his interpretation of individual development. Moreover, it imparted a zealous and evangelical flavour to his writings on adolescence itself.

Although never as systematic as Romanes, Stanley Hall agreed with the earlier writer in discerning stages of individual development corresponding to protozoa, amoebae, fish, amphibians, mammals, and anthropoid apes. His major interest in direct parallels concerned the more recent evolutionary past (as reconstructed). The recapitulation of animal species is complete by early childhood, but the prehistoric ascent of man has still to be repeated. Thus, for Hall, the modern 8 to 12-year-old represents the adult of a prehistoric ancestor. This putative ancestor thus reached adulthood at 8 to 12 years of age. *His* sexual maturity must therefore have been reached several years earlier, at around 6 years. Traces of this ancestral puberty can, for Hall, still be discerned in modern 6-year-olds. The indications are general instabilities of health (in itself an uncontentious proposal: The close relationships of sexuality and health being taken for granted by Hall's contemporaries). Such indications in present-day children were described by Hall in a memorable phrase as "the ripple-marks of an ancient pubic beach."

Such speculations were not merely fanciful. They enabled Hall to argue that the modern child is essentially similar to the posited ancestor. The ancestor had been small and the inhabitant of a warm climate. Like his pygmoid ancestor, the modern 8 to 12-year-old is happy and well adjusted to his physical environment. Such activities as hunting, fishing, and roving were appropriate and to be encouraged (in the boy, at least). As a contemporary of Hall put it: "The boy in the woods building his fire . . . is living over again the wild outdoor savage life of his ancestors."[8] This account of pre-puberty also contributed to the explanation of adolescence. The evolutionary stage of the happy pygmoid was left behind on the way to modern man, his tranquility disrupted by an evolutionary surge. "Old moorings were broken and a new level attained." The new form was larger, an increase in size represented in the modern adolescent by a growth spurt. More significantly, the trauma associated with the evolutionary wrench had to be relived by every modern adolescent. For Hall, the doctrine of recapitulation thus explained the instability which had long been considered characteristic of the adolescent (by Rousseau, among others). The assumption was now given evolutionary authority. In passing into adolescence, the young person was reliving one of the most abrupt transitions of his evolutionary history. Partly as a result of Hall's advocacy, the notion of "storm and stress" as an inherent and definitive characteristic of adolescence has become one of developmental psychology's most tenacious dogmas.

Hall's employment of recapitulationary logic was global. Fear of water, for example, was explained in terms of reptilian and amphibian stages of evolutionary ancestry. The reptilian state was considered more recent than the amphibian. Therefore, the land-based "reptile" stage manifests an aversion to the watery environment which its former, amphibian state had enjoyed. Hence the child, at the appropriate (reptilian) age, develops a fear of water. As well as children's fears, another central concern of Hall was play. The reconstruction of evolution from present-day childhood should, for Hall, eliminate as far as possible the effects of culture, and the spontaneous nature of play seemed to qualify it for this purpose. Play for Hall is archaic, the "motor habits . . . of the past of the race." Like the tail of the tadpole it is essential to subsequent development even though it is as rapidly lost. An alternative theory of play was proposed by Karl Groos in 1899, according to which play represents practice for essential adult habits. For Hall, however, the theory of Groos was "superficial and perverse." Hall held play in an almost mystical reverence, partly for its virtue of revealing ancestral processes. He was certainly not the last to do so, and to discount more functional explanations.

Another basic characteristic postulated by Hall for ancient man was periodicity in behaviour. Ancient behaviour was held to have been more directly under the control of the seasons and the tides than is that of modern man. Such periodicity is, in fact, for Hall, still retained to some extent in modern youth and celebrates "its highest triumphs" in women. Periodicity is "perhaps the deepest law of the cosmos." It is more clearly manifested in vagrants and criminals than in the law-abiding population, and thus the instilling of an artificial daily routine into the criminal is particularly difficult. The issue of periodicity had been of considerable interest to Darwin himself, for whom the phenomenon provided evidence of continuity between species. And Hall's younger contemporary Sigmund Freud was giving careful consideration also to the implications of human periodicity. Hall became greatly interested in Freud's work in general and was responsible for Freud's successful visit to the U.S.A. in 1909.

Many general uses of recapitulationary logic were made by Hall. The "developmental" perspective was, for Hall, essential for an understanding of animals, children, "savages," "defectives," cases of "psychic devolution," and even of sexual perversion.[9] The rigid repetition of evolutionary ancestry did, however, give rise for Hall to something more flexible. The ancestral experience formed a kind of resource on which the adult could draw: A profoundly Lamarckian notion, and one also developed by Freud's younger colleague Carl Jung. Genius, for Hall, represents the most flexible and creative use of this inherited resource. Most adults are denied, or deny themselves, the freedom to access this store. The resource is fundamentally instinctive and is the location of "much that makes the human soul really great and good." Instinct is the "wisdom beneath us": That is to say, the wisdom of our ancestral past.

An explicit appeal to recapitulation was therefore central to Hall's thinking. Ironically, Hall himself contributed to the eventual downfall of the theory, for he was responsible in 1889 for appointing the anthropologist Franz Boas to a post at Clark. Boas found the evolutionary approach, at least with regard to culture, quite unacceptable. For him, different cultures had to be seen in their own terms, not as early stages in a linear progression culminating in the civilisation of Europe. Boas' views had little direct effect on the thinking of developmentalists but did, later, inspire the highly influential work of Margaret Mead (discussed in Chapter Eight). In many ways, Hall himself distrusted consciousness and rationality. At the same time, he liked to see himself as a hard-nosed scientist, scornful of philosophical speculation. Idealist or speculative forms of philosophy were adolescent excesses to be outgrown, and hence were once compared by Hall to masturbation. It is thus perhaps ironic that Hall's current status is evaluated in terms of his theoretical claims rather than his empirical contributions. These theoretical claims were derived directly from biology; and the biology which influenced Hall—which, rather, swept him off his feet—was a speculative, Nature-philosophical biology in Darwinian dress.

JAMES MARK BALDWIN AND THE "EMBRYOLOGY OF SOCIETY"

During the period when Stanley Hall was the dominant force in developmental psychology in the U.S.A. the major alternative voice was that of James Mark Baldwin. Baldwin (1861–1934) opposed Hall over a number of issues, both academic and professional. Where Hall despised philosophy, Baldwin considered it indispensible for an understanding of individual development. At the same time, Baldwin's understanding of biology and of the Darwinian contribution was far deeper than that of the older man. In spite of this, much of Baldwin's writing expresses versions of recapitulationary thinking, even if of a more sophisticated kind than that of Hall. Unfortunately, perhaps, as Baldwin moved away from the biology of recapitulation theory he also moved away from empirical observation, becoming increasingly concerned with epistemological issues albeit in the developmental context. Partly for this reason, Baldwin's influence on developmental psychology was and has remained less than it deserves to be.[10] Another reason for this lack of influence is Baldwin's premature withdrawal from the U.S. academic scene in 1908, his subsequent career being based in France. After a long period of neglect, interest has recently revived in Baldwin's contribution.[11]

For Baldwin, empirical research and observation always played a secondary role to theory. His major aims were philosophical ones. Like Hall, he saw the developmental approach to psychology as a general method and his own "genetic epistemology" as a unification of the major philosophical trends of the 19th century. One of these trends was "evolutionism," a movement which for Baldwin included not only the contribution of Darwin but also that of the more speculative Herbert Spencer, as well as the Idealism of Hegel. Hegel had dominated German philosophical thinking in the early part of the 19th century and, posthumously, exerted great influence in the U.S.A. in the last decades of the century. Hegel's philosophy concerned the progressive evolution of human consciousness as expressed in culture and nationhood. It was a form of Idealism because it held the spirit or essence of a nation or state to be something real and objective. For Hegel, individual human subjects were not the centre of existence: Groups or nations were in a sense "more" real. Hegelian thinking was centrally concerned with process and change, with history as a kind of development. This approach had nothing to do with the work of Charles Darwin. Rather, it reached back to the Nature-philosophy of early 19th-century Germany, with its interest in unified processes of change in the natural world. Such an orientation is highly compatible with the more general forms of recapitulationary thinking.

Baldwin's philosophical concerns thus included the processual, dynamic nature of knowledge. At the same time, however, Baldwin held to a picture of *correspondence* between the mind and the world: A relationship which, for earlier thinkers, had been taken as rather a static one. Baldwin hoped to synthesise the dynamic and the static in his theory of knowledge and his work in the area of developmental psychology should be seen as part of this project. Baldwin's earliest views on psychology centered on the issue of correspondence. At this time, in the 1880s, psychology was emerging as an experimental science whose major concern was the investigation of the relationships between stimuli and sensations. This was "psychophysics," the demonstration (in Baldwin's words) of "a necessary connection between mind and body." Indeed the underlying philosophy of psychophysics (as espoused by one of its founders, Gustav Fechner) was a form of "monism" in which mind and body were treated as twin aspects of one reality. Although Baldwin paid less and less attention to experimental psychology as his ideas developed, the concept of a psychophysics remained basic. For example, *Development and evolution* (1902) explicitly set out to explore the *evolutionary* significance of this epistemological stance.

Like Hall, Baldwin was influenced by the work of Romanes. In addition, he had two infant subjects to hand: His daughters, on whom nearly all of his empirical observations were carried out. Baldwin published a number of articles in the 1890s (a number of which were later included in the text of *Development and evolution*) and also two major books: *Mental development in the child and the race* (1895) and *Social and ethical interpretations in mental development* (1897). Recapitulationary arguments play a part in each of these books, Baldwin's acceptance of at least the general principle of recapitulation being total. The basic processes underlying evolution and individual development were seen as identical. The infant, for Baldwin, is "plainly recapitulating the items in the social history of the race" and thus "the embryology of society is open to study in the nursery." Both the growing infant and the scale of phylogeny manifest "more and more developed stages of conscious function." As stated in the preface to *Mental development*, a "doctrine of race [i.e. species] development of consciousness" is "essential" for an understanding of mental development in the individual: Individual and race development are "identical."

Social and ethical interpretations is concerned with the social nature and the social development of man. The book is radical in many respects, and especially in its insistence on the constitutive role of social intercourse ("A man is a social outcome rather than a social unit"). Here Baldwin's arguments are directed against an individualist tradition in philosophy which he traces back to the writing of Thomas Hobbes in the 17th century. Baldwin's account of social development in the individual is a complex and sophisticated one, giving detailed consideration to such processes as social transmission and imitation in its various forms. However, the principle of recapitulation is given whole-hearted endorsement within this context. Baldwin is concerned with the origins of such social behaviours as "bashfulness" and modesty (following Darwin, and anticipating Freud, in this concern): And "origins" means location within the history of the race. Quite straightforwardly, Baldwin proposes that the human race has developed through an "animal" or biological epoch, followed by a social-cultural epoch leading up to the present. Two forms of recapitulation correspond to these two epochs: The first is biological and the second anthropological. These processes are seen by Baldwin as distinct and as having sometimes complemented each other and sometimes been in conflict. The development of the child manifests the combined influence of both, and it is the task of the scientist to tease the two apart.

As well as endorsing the "biological" or ancestral form of recapitulation, then, Baldwin also clearly endorses the cultural version. In fact, Baldwin's account in *Social and ethical interpretations* is probably the most systematic *combination* of these two to be found in any developmentalist. The biological form introduces material from distant, animal ancestry, while the cultural form introduces more recent acquisitions derived from human prehistory. Detailed comparison is made between specific stages in individual development and the supposed history of early social evolution. Like ontogenesis, "the progress of race culture shows . . . transitions from the savage to the gregarious and nomadic, and then to the reflective forms of co-operation." Baldwin sums up his position in this way[12]: "The race had to reconcile the instinctive tendencies which came down from the animals with the co-operative tendencies which social life prescribed; and *it was done by the race in the same way that it is done by the child: the race became reflective, intelligent, and so started on a career of social development . . .*" In common with many contemporaries, then, Baldwin sought to reconstruct man's prehistory from observations of the child. Certainly, his version of recapitulation is not the crude and rigid version of Hall. Ontogeny for Baldwin is not simply secondary to phylogeny: Causal relationships operate in both directions in a *dialectical* fashion. Individual development is not simply a mechanical replay of ancestry. As Baldwin's thinking progressed he moved away from an appeal to recapitulationary doctrine as an explanatory device, the related phenomena becoming, rather, issues to be explained. Thus *Development and evolution* attempts to explain *why* (on the basis of his own evolutionary theory) it should be the case that development should recapitulate evolution. The reasons Baldwin adduces include the claim that "the process which shows itself as recapitulation" is "the only one by which nature could make individuals *like their parents*; the way, that is, of bringing them up through serial processes of genetic development, each stage being necessary to the next." (Another reason is the wisdom of Nature in preserving the achievements of past generations, to constitute "so much capital or stock in trade" for the progeny.)

Recapitulationism became increasingly embedded in Baldwin's larger theory of evolution ("orthoplasy") but always remained central to it. It also played a crucial role in his later and more technically philosophical studies of individual development (*Thought and things*, 1906–1911). Baldwin came to approach psychic development as corresponding, in certain respects, to the history of Western philosophy: Both, he claimed, presenting a sequence of epistemological world views (such as dualism). Another version of this formulation can be found in Baldwin's *History of psychology* (1913)—an avowedly "recapitulationist" study, as Baldwin's Introduction makes clear. Here the history of psychology (of formulations on what psychology *is*) is treated as parallel to the development of the child, since "in social evolution [of the race] we see a re-statement of the greatest stages of individual development . . . The individual's development in consciousness of self recapitulates . . . the evolution of self-conscious reflection in the human race."

One biological issue on which Baldwin stood alone as a developmental psychologist was that stimulated by the claims of Weismann. Propounded in 1885, ten years before the publication of *Mental development*, the doctrine of the isolation of germ-cells threatened to overturn the Lamarckian principle at a stroke. If, as Weismann claimed, germ-cells remain uninfluenced by the body then individual experience cannot possibly affect them and such experience could never be transmitted. Baldwin accepted this claim and might thus be seen as having attempted a truly Darwinian developmental psychology. However, while accepting that Lamarck's mechanism as such could not work, Baldwin still considered the process of natural selection inadequate to explain evolutionary progress. In parallel with several contemporaries he searched for a viable alternative to the Lamarckian mechanism. The outcome was the doctrine of "organic selection," now sometimes known as the "Baldwin effect."

Organic selection relies on the principle of "coincident variation," by which appropriate new (congenital) variations are held to emerge under the protection of actual adaptation by individuals. This adaptation (or in Baldwin's terms, "accommodation") principally consists of changes of *habit*. Such accommodation might be opportunist (the enlargement of habit repertoire) or it might be a response to environmental change. These individual acquisitions could not be transmitted directly by heredity (although they might well be transmitted socially from one generation to another). However, the accommodations "keep a species afloat" until the "right" *genetic* variation comes along. Behaviour thus points the way forward for evolutionary progress. Throughout Baldwin's writings, natural selection is seen as a negative "weeding-out" process; evolution, for Baldwin, requires positive processes as well and organic selection is one of several he proposes. Indeed, the function of organic selection is to hold natural selection at bay while new accommodations get a foothold.[13] If *neo*-Darwinism is the doctrine of the supremacy of natural selection (a doctrine given strong support by Weismann), then Baldwin was certainly no neo-Darwinian. Baldwin took Weismann seriously, but did not accept the full implications; one of his contemporaries noted that Baldwin "both admits and denies Weismannism."

Baldwin's account of adaptation in the individual—presented at greatest length in *Mental development*—represents an application of his more general evolutionary stance. Fundamentally, for Baldwin, adaptation involves the *selection* of behaviour. His formulations on selection in the individual centre on two processes, habit and accommodation. Variations arise initially by a trial-and-error process and are first tested "internally" before being tried out. This pre-testing is the role of habit, which can eliminate a new variation as soon as it arises if it is too discrepant with existing structures. It should be noted that there is nothing particularly

Darwinian about this "weeding-out" process: Such a form of selection has no contribution to make to enhancing overall adaptation. *Progressive* change, for Baldwin, is the responsibility of "accommodation." Habit, if it does not reject the new variation, keeps it going in a circular, repetitive fashion; it is maintained in the repertoire by rehearsal. New variations are kept as it were on a stationary orbit, awaiting the intervention of accommodatory processes to test them against the external world. The most basic form of accommodation involves slight variation as the behaviour is repeated, and the model of repetition-with-variation became central to Baldwin's account of infant development. This process was at this time termed the "circular reaction." As is made clear in *Development and evolution*, the concept of the "circular reaction" is closely related to the psychological utilitarianism usually associated with the names of Herbert Spencer and Alexander Bain: The claim that movements get to be repeated to the extent that they result in pleasure. For Spencer, and for Baldwin, early movements are *over-produced* and the successful ones selected post hoc (this is Baldwin's "functional selection"). A fundamental tendency for repetition or the reproduction of movements is thus a basic requirement of a learning organism—hence the "circular reaction."

Baldwin's employment of biology was thus considerably more complex than that of Hall, and involved theoretical innovation in a way that Hall's did not. This may have been one reason for its relative lack of success. The biological contribution to Baldwin's picture of child development includes some elements of fairly straightforward recapitulationism. However, Baldwin was able, as most of his contemporaries were not, to give learning a meaningful role in development. Those who were strongly influenced by Haeckel and Romanes, and indeed by Darwin's own developmental writing, took infancy and childhood to be basically repetitive. Adaptation to current needs was seen rather as "noise" in the system, distorting the true ancestral signal. For various and complex reasons, Baldwin felt adaptation and learning in early life to be of crucial importance. He chose not to see this emphasis as contradictory to recapitulation theory, a decision which is perhaps to be regretted. The fact that Baldwin's own recapitulationism was of a general, "soft" variety undoubtedly played a part here. Be that as it may, learning for Baldwin remained bound up with evolutionary presuppositions. Many of those who subsequently studied infant learning without the baggage of recapitulation theory also lacked the breadth and depth of Baldwin's concerns with developmental change.

Baldwin's influence on psychology has always been hard to evaluate. His unplanned departure from the academic scene in the U.S.A. (in 1908) certainly attenuated any direct influence on American developmental psychology. Up to that date he had represented the major alternative to the approach and claims of Hall. However, he continued to work in exile and in Paris became a close colleague of the French psychologist Pierre Janet. Through Janet, as well as through his books, Baldwin exerted a profound influence on the young Jean Piaget who, in a Baldwinian circular reaction, retained and varied the approach of America's most original developmentalist.

SIGMUND FREUD AND THE ANCESTRAL IMPERATIVE

The influence of Sigmund Freud on Western thought has been immense, and the impact of his formulations on individual development has only been one component of that influence. To a considerable extent, however, Freud's contribution to developmental psychology has been one of systematisation and synthesis rather than true originality. Many of Freud's claims were made by other contemporaries, although none forged them into a coherent system as he was able to do. Freud's concerns were broad; he wished to delineate the nature of civilised man, and the study of psychological disturbance was largely a means to that end. His interest in individual development was a subsidiary one, contributing both to the explanation of adult disturbance and more directly to the issue of the process of civilisation. Biological presuppositions were central to these interests, and it is appropriate to focus on biological aspects of his developmental claims. In this area, his sources of influence overlapped with those of contemporaries whose concern for individual development as such was greater than that of Freud himself. Like so many writers of the turn of the century, his biology was derived from Haeckel; it was based on Lamarckism and recapitulation theory.[14]

Sigmund Freud (1856–1939) was turning to developmental questions during the 1890s, at much the same time as Hall and Baldwin in the U.S.A. Freud's scientific career was already well advanced by this time. His first and highly successful interest had been in neuroanatomy, and his first research involvement with children related to neurological damage such as cerebral palsy. This was to remain his only detailed, direct research with children. Freud's medical career, begun in 1886, appears to have represented a rather reluctant and pragmatic alternative to the more attractive career of full-time neuroanatomical research. He soon specialised in neurotic disturbance, then referred to under the blanket term of "hysteria," and with his colleague Josef Breuer published an influential theory of hysteria. This theory was concerned with an "economic" model of mental life, that is, one based on a consideration of energy and its distribution. At this point, in the mid-1890s, Freud's interest in individual development was limited to case histories. His views on the origins of neurosis focused on early experience of a sexual nature, or rather the premature exposure to adult sexuality. Such experience was seen as essentially *passive*: It included, for example, a nurse's stimulation of a baby's genitals in play as well as more extreme interference. It was referred to by Freud (for its effects rather than for its intentions) as "seduction."

For various reasons, however, Freud had abandoned the "seduction" theory of neurosis by 1897. More generally, he had rejected the assumption that neurosis arises simply from specific experiences in an individual's lifetime. Increasingly, individual development was seen against a background of universal sequences of change: Specific outcomes were due to perturbations in the universal sequence, rather than to specific experiences as such. Evolutionary arguments were tentatively explored in Freud's *Project for a scientific psychology* (written in 1895). The "Project," which was never completed, was an attempt to formulate a precise neuropsychology of mental functioning. Evolutionary thinking came to dominate Freud's theoretical approach. A contribution to this trend came from Freud's friendship with Wilhelm Fliess, who formulated a radical and wide-ranging theory of development based on recapitulation and periodicity. Freud's first major book, *The interpretation of dreams* (1900) made extensive use of recapitulationary thinking. Thus dreams themselves reveal prehistoric ancestry: "Dreams . . . have merely preserved for us . . . a sample of the psychical apparatus's primary method of working . . . What once dominated waking life, while the mind was still young and incompetent, seems now to have been banished into the night—just as the primitive weapons, the bows and arrows, that have been abandoned by adult men, turn up once more in the nursery."[15] For Freud, then, dreams in the adult represent a throwback to primitive ways of thinking, just as the war-play of small children represents a throwback to the real warfare of prehistoric man. Freud's younger collaborator Carl Jung was to develop the idea further, in terms of a "collective unconscious" or race memory, again solidly based on Lamarckian principles.

Freud's own view was an orthodox one for the time; his original contribution lay in the attempt to delineate the nature of the primitive thought processes. In Freud's formulation, "primary process" thinking is the form available to the *unconscious*. The latter concept was one of general interest to scientific thought in the final decades of the 19th century. In this connection, especial attention was focused on the phenomena of hypnosis and multiple personality. These phenomena suggested that much of mental life goes on in camera, conscious awareness being directed only at a narrow zone at any one time. Such a hierarchical formulation of consciousness fitted closely with Hughlings Jackson's neurological model of a hierarchy of levels of control and inhibition. Lower levels were considered primitive and ancient, and generally inaccessible to consciousness. It was the function of newer, higher levels to inhibit the older and lower. Where this control was slackened in dreams or eliminated by brain damage, the lower levels could reassert themselves.

The universal course of development in the individual came to be of major theoretical importance to Freud. It brought together issues of specific outcomes (such as neurosis) and issues of evolutionary ancestry. In its turn, sexuality was central to Freud's view of ontogenesis. Sexuality was the major sphere for the operation of periodicity in human behaviour, as investigated by Wilhelm Fliess (and by Hall). Like play in children, sexual behaviour was seen as relatively free of cultural influence (at least in its more physiological aspects). It was the adherence to recapitulation which led Fliess to look for sexuality in children, for if the child was repeating stages of development of prehistoric adults then sexuality should be present. Stanley Hall was moving in rather the same direction, at the same time, but was looking for residual signs rather than active evidence of precocious sexuality. Fliess himself, and other contemporaries, did observe what they considered to be evidence of sexuality in young children, and Freud incorporated these findings into a coherent system. Indeed, it would appear that Freud relied on his friend Fliess for observations on real infants, and that access to his own infants for such purposes was denied to Freud by his wife.[16]

Freud's account of individual development underwent changes throughout his working life, and also varies somewhat from one context to another. Freud's most systematic description of ontogenesis is presented in his writings on sexuality, starting with the first edition of *Three essays on the theory of sexuality* (1905). The development of sexuality was essentially the development of "libido," and the libido theory incorporated all aspects of human behaviour. Libido provides the reservoir of instinctual energy whose means of discharge changes with the development of the individual. Both intellectual and social development were seen by Freud as deriving from the sequential redistribution of libido. For Freud, then, sexuality in a sense explains all human behaviour: But this must be seen as an extension of the meaning of sexuality rather than as a reduction of other phenomena *to* sexuality. For example, Freud held that the thinking of modern neurotics and of man's primitive ancestors could alike be described as especially dominated by sexuality. For Freud, the infantile form of sexuality is either a general, diffused form, distributed across the whole body surface (causing the infant to be "polymorphously perverse"), or is focused on the mouth and the anus. The latter version came to dominate Freud's account, but it should be emphasised that both received support from recapitulationary logic. Both, for Freud, could be held to characterise the sexuality of animals: either general and diffuse or located at one or other end of the digestive tract. The human child was seen by Freud as growing through an animal phase of sexuality on his way to the adult human variety (mainly "his": Freud's account of psychosexual development was essentially male-centred).

A two-phase model was settled on by Freud in 1915, with an initial "oral" stage being followed by an "anal" stage. The existence of these "pre-genital" stages of sexuality—that is, stages prior to the adult's genital centred sexuality—was fundamental to Freud's general claims concerning neurosis and perversion. The proper course of development involves the passing through, and transcending, of these pre-genital phases. Failure to do so leads to pathology. The abandonment of the early erotogenic zones is at the same time an ontogenetic and a phylogenetic turning-point. Both in development and in evolution, for Freud, the pre-genital stages are followed by a period of "latency" in which libidinal reservoirs build up without a means of discharge. The sexual energy is dammed up, to burst forth at a later time. In evolutionary terms, for Freud, this controlled source of energy was responsible for the emergence of civilisation. Culture is a by-product of the diversion of libidinal energy from immediate gratification. For the modern individual, the energy is built up during the late years of childhood until released at adolescence, when sexuality comes to be focused on the genitals.

A later addition to the sequence was the "phallic" stage, described by Freud in 1923 as the culmination of pre-genital sexuality. For both sexes, at the age of four years or so, interest focuses on the phallus but not yet in an adult manner (not truly genital). The sequence of stages finally arrived at by Freud was therefore as follows: oral, anal, phallic, latency, genital. Recapitulationary logic was central to Freud's derivation of these stages. The whole sequence is necessary and predetermined: It is "the course of development laid down for civilised men." And as emphasised in the preface to the third edition of the *Three essays*[17]: "Ontogenesis may be regarded as a recapitulation of phylogenesis, in so far as the latter has not been modified by more recent experience. The phylogenetic disposition can be seen at work behind the ontogenetic process."

Various other aspects of Freud's thinking could be selected to illustrate the role played by recapitulationary logic. Thus *Totem and taboo* (1912–1913), a study of anthropology and prehistory, is premissed on recapitulationary parallels. Its subtitle is "Some points of agreement between the mental life of savages and neurotics." Freud's account was based partly on ethnographic evidence, particularly on the Australian aborigine, and partly on the reconstruction of prehistory. Freud was searching for the origins of civilisation in the individual and in the species. True to his conviction that culture and sexuality are closely linked, the taboo on incest plays a central role in the book. For Freud this taboo, with its guarantee of exogamous marriage, is universal and a biological necessity. Its significance to the individual is built on ancestral experience.

A central characteristic of the primitive mind, for Freud, is a belief in the omnipotence of one's thoughts. This "overvaluation" of psychical acts is most clearly expressed in "animism". This term had been popularised by Edward Tylor in his influential book of 1871, *Primitive culture.*[18] For Freud, animism is natural to prehistoric man who "knew what things were like in the world, namely just as he felt himself to be." Magic is the "technique" of animism: It attempts to impose the laws of thought onto physical reality. Such features were taken by Freud to recur in the young, modern individual by recapitulation. Later, the concept of super-ego was developed by Freud, again in the context of an account of man's prehistory. This concept came to play a central role in Freud's account of moral development and the "Oedipus complex." Even Freud's rather more obscure concept of Thanatos (the "death instinct") is at root a recapitulationary notion. A death instinct is the logical culmination of a tendency to repeat or to return to a former state: The urge for the most basic state of all, the zero state of absolute stability.[19]

The centrality of Lamarckism to Freud's thinking must not be forgotten. Freud wrote in 1917 that Lamarckism "coincide[s] with the final outcome of psychoanalytic thinking." Thus the enormous personal impact of such developmental events as the Oedipus complex may be seen in part as due to the accumulative effect of the experience of countless ancestors. The experience of individuals was seen by Freud as building up a massive heritage of disturbance, accumulating with each generation. In this claim Freud was supported by his one-time collaborator Carl Jung, for whom ancestral experience forms a "collective unconscious" or race memory. For Jung, adult minds "still bear the marks of the evolutionary stages we have traversed, and re-echo the dim bygone in dreams and fantasies". And Jung was quite emphatic that the early stages which are now repeated were *adult* (not childhood) states, that is, characteristics of *adult* ancestors as in the classic formulations of ancestral recapitulation[20]: "Myths . . . are on the contrary the most mature product of that young humanity. Just as those first fishy ancestors of man, with their gill-slits, were not embryos, but fully developed creatures, so the myth-making and myth-inhabiting man was a grown reality and not a four-year-old child." Jung himself did not pursue the ontogenetic implications of this position, being more concerned with adulthood. Like those who did—and especially Freud—his major theoretical assumptions were based on Lamarckian principles. Lamarckism, recapitulationism, periodicity, and the developmental stage were central notions for Freud. His account of individual development is a profoundly biological one. And, as with so many of his contemporaries, the contribution of Darwinism to Freud's biology was overwhelmed by older, perhaps more primitive ideas.[21]

NOTES TO CHAPTER THREE

[1]The importance of the notion of periodicity is discussed by Sulloway (1979), for example in the context of Freud's mathematical formulations on human development.

[2]A discussion of the employment of recapitulationary logic in racist thinking may be found in Gould (1977). The long history of the notion of "the childhood of the race" is discussed in Boas (1966, p. 65). Boas cites Hastings as stating in 1911, in the *Encyclopedia of religion and ethics*, that "The 'childhood of the race,' originally a metaphor, has become an almost technical term, through the establishment of the law of recapitulation." Boas traces the popularity of the notion back to Comte and to Vico. As Boas (op. cit., p. 65) notes: "When one thinks of the child as a duplicate of primitive man, of the youth as a duplicate of mediaeval man, and of the adult as representative of positivistic man, one has taken over the Law of Recapitulation and given it a psychological turn. The social and psychological applications of this law belong on the whole to the twentieth century."

[3]On Hall, see especially Ross (1972); also McCullers (1969).

[4]Hall (1923); cited in Ross (1972, p. 47).

[5]Hall (1882); cited in Ross (1972, p. 120).

[6]The "cultural-epoch" theory of education can be traced back at least as far as Condillac (Compayré, 1887/1909, p. 312) and Rousseau, in the 18th century. Goethe is cited by Drummond (1908, p. 58) as having said: "Although the world in general advances, the youth must always start from the beginning, and as an individual traverse the epochs of the world's culture." The 19th century educationalist Herbartians applied a similar principle, as did Herbert Spencer, in whose hands (Compayré, 1887/1909, p. 338): "this hypothesis [of Condillac] becomes a law." Spencer himself makes the following comment (1860/1896 pp. 110–111): "Thus . . . we are on the highway towards the doctrine long ago enunciated by Pestalozzi, that alike in its order and its methods, education must conform to the natural process of mental evolution—that there is a natural sequence in which the faculties spontaneously develop . . . so in education we are finding that success is to be achieved only by rendering our measures subservient to that spontaneous unfolding which all minds go through in their progress to maturity." Also see Gould (1977); Kern (Note 2); Strickland (Note 3).

[7]Examples of the widespread use of recapitulationary parallels in the Child-study literature may be found in Drummond (1908). Child-study interests the anthropologist, for example, because (op. cit., p. 4): "unable to discover a living specimen of primitive man, [he] turns to the child as his nearest representative." Again (op. cit., p. 16): "when the student has studied the child as an animal, he is in a better position for studying . . . how the characteristic human faculties are grafted upon or grow out of . . . the animal nature of the child." Drummond notes (1908, p. 18) that: "the higher human attributes . . . having appeared late in the history of the race, are yet unstable, and vary greatly in different individuals . . ." Drummond himself urges, however, that the concept of recapitulation be used flexibly and to some extent metaphorically. He also makes the comment (op. cit., p. 251) that: "children, and especially young children, are not so much interested in the appearance of an object, or its colour, or structure, or form, as in what it does or what it affords them the opportunity of doing."

[8]Starr (1895); cited in Gould (1977, p. 136).

[9]Hall (1904, Vol. II, p. 550).

[10]For Danziger (1985, p. 324) it was Baldwin's cast of theorising, especially his interest in dialectical description, which: "sufficed to make it totally incomprehensible to virtually all psychologists in his own country." Danziger continues (p. 326): "The majority of develop-

mental psychologists ignored Baldwin's insights." It has been observed (Ridley, 1982, p. 67) that: "Baldwin's contemporaries found him verbose and obsessively self-important."

[11]See especially Broughton and Freeman-Moir (1982); also Cairns (1980); Danziger (1985); Kessel and Bevan, in Buxton (1985, p. 286); Mueller (1976); J Russell (1978). Baldwin is cited by Mueller as having said in 1906: "The psychology of the future will be social to the core."

[12]Baldwin (1897/1913, p. 228) (emphasis in original).

[13]"Organic selection" is discussed in more detail in Chapter Nine in the context of theories of developmental process. A critical analysis of Baldwin's own formulation was made by Groos (1896/1898, p. 63; 1898/1901, p. 282) against the background of Darwinism and neo-Darwinism. Groos notes here that: "there is a steady and constantly increasing current against [Darwin's] teaching" and refers to a "saying" that "it is high time that biology recovered from its 'Englische Krankheit'." Groos himself was particularly concerned with play, which he argued was so important that it explains the existence of the period of youth. "Animals would certainly make no progress intellectually if they were thus blindly left in the swaddling-clothes of inherited impulse." Groos thus rejected recapitulation as an explanation of play. On children's predilection for climbing trees, he notes (1898/1901, pp. 87–88) that: "we naturally attribute this to the habits of their progenitors, but a simpler explanation of their enjoyment may be that their elders cannot get at them."

[14]On Freud, see especially Sulloway (1979); also Ellenberger (1970); Kern (Note 2); Roazen (1974). Freud's appeal to recapitulation theory is also discussed by Boas (1966, p. 66).

[15]Freud (1900; S.E. V, p.567).

[16]Sulloway (1979, p. 190).

[17]Freud (1915; S.E. VII, p. 131).

[18]Tylor's endorsement of a unilinear trend in human evolution is noted in Chapter Two. R. Spencer has noted the related commitment (of Herbert Spencer and others) to *progress* and "the gradual upward trend of man"—a notion itself related to the assumption of perfectibility, of man as "innately good and improvable". This notion can also be found in popular religious writings well into the 20th century: for example Codd's account of reincarnation (1917). Codd (1917, p. 13) writes that the implication of Darwinian evolution theory is that: "every form of life is in itself both the result of a previous process of gradual development and the promise of still further unfoldment; a stage in a continual ascent from lower and simpler towards higher and more completely organised forms, expressing the varying powers of life with increasing precision and delicacy." Reincarnation is "the doctrine of evolution applied to the soul."

[19]The recapitulationary implications of Thanatos are explored by Sulloway (1979, p. 404). The "death instinct" was initially formulated by Sabina Spielrein, ex-patient of Carl Jung and subsequently training-analyst of Jean Piaget (Carotenuto, 1982; see footnote 5 to Chapter Seven).

[20]Jung (1912/1956, p. 24).

[21]Jung (1973, p. 164) commented on Freud's theoretical (and ethnic) roots in a letter to G. Adler in 1934, discussing Freud's "materialistic, rationalistic view of the world . . . [Freud] is simply a typical exponent of the expiring 19th century, just like Haeckel, Dubois-Reymond. . . ."

4 Biology and the Developmentalists: Vygotsky, Piaget, and Werner

INTRODUCTION

The three figures discussed in the previous chapter were very much products of the 19th century. Hall, Baldwin, and Freud all received their education and training in the latter part of that century, and all had published substantial works by its close. Before discussing some figures whose influence is more recent, we now consider some "minor" developmentalists whose contributions were made during the second and third decades of the present century. The figures discussed include John Watson, Arnold Gesell, Edouard Claparède, Karl Bühler, and William Stern. These psychologists were all born in the decade 1870–1880 and may be taken to represent the next generation after Baldwin and Freud. It should be stressed that the term "minor" is very much a relative one: All of these middle-period developmentalists exerted great influence over a wide range of concerns in psychology, education, and child care. Minor status for Gesell, for example, is justified on the grounds of his theoretical contribution, which was considerably exceeded by his practical influence. For the others, an interest in individual development was only part of a broader project.

MINOR DEVELOPMENTALISTS IN EUROPE AND AMERICA

Turning first to the U.S.A., several trends may be discerned in relation to developmental thinking during the early part of this century. One strong tradition was that derived from studies of animal learning. To a considerable extent this represented the continuation of a tradition deriving from Darwin and Romanes, although substantial deviation from this tradition occurred with the proclamation of "behaviourism" by John Watson in 1913. A major influence on Watson was the psychologist Edward Thorndike, who had investigated the learning capacities of various animals in experimental settings. Thorndike had already established himself as a critic of Stanley Hall (whom he accused of adherence to "a distorted and fallacious form of the doctrine of evolution") and had published a critique of Hall's theory of recapitulation. For Thorndike, the theory was so flexible as to be useless. A single stage of ontogenesis could be made to correspond, on different occasions, to a range of (supposedly ancestral) animal types. Exceptions to the theory vastly outweighed positive instances. To the extent that characteristics or "tendencies" do in fact emerge at regular times or in a regular sequence, such regularity is to be attributed to natural selection. Rather than replaying ancestral progress, the timing of emergence and sometimes disappearance of these tendencies reflects the pressure of survival: Timing, and the point of emergence within ontogenesis, is determined by the selectively optimal location of the tendency. Thorndike's "theory of utility" was a straightforwardly Darwinian alternative to recapitulation (if perhaps a simplistic one). However, Thorndike's direct influence on developmental psychology has been limited.

John Watson (1878–1958) argued that methods of investigation and theory-construction in animal learning—as in the experimental work of Thorndike—should be applied to human psychology. This was the essence of behaviourism. Watson himself had attempted to correlate learning abilities with neurological growth in the rat, but concluded that learning abilities could not be predicted from the maturational state of nerve fibres. He also observed various aspects of the early development of his own children, noting in 1904 "a baby is more fun to the square inch than all the rats and frogs in creation." Watson began systematic experimentation with human infants in 1916. By this time he was professor of psychology at Johns Hopkins University, a post once held by Stanley Hall: His invitation to the post had come from James Mark Baldwin, then head of the department of philosophy.[1]

Watson's interests in children centred on the issue of instinct and on the processes of habit formation. He argued that there were very few true instincts, that is, reactions existing from birth. In his early accounts, Watson described three true instinctive responses—fear (as to a noise), anger (as to restraint), and love. This last was explicitly linked by Watson to Freud's views on infant sexuality, in that gentle stimulation of the baby's whole body surface was taken to elicit sensual pleasure. All other responses, for Watson, should be attributed to learning: To the conditioning of these basic responses as a result of experience. Fear of the dark must arise from the conditioning of the initial fear reaction: The child must have experienced fear in the dark, and the dark must thus have become what was termed an "adequate stimulus" for fear. Following the First World War, Watson set out to study such learning processes experimentally. Most notable was the conditioning of "Little Albert": The experimental inducement in a baby of fear of a rat, by the pairing of exposure to the rat with the loud banging of a metal bar. Throughout his writing on infancy, Watson maintained the position that the newborn's behavioural repertoire is fragmented and that the emergence of organised systems of response must be due to learning (that is, conditioning) processes. This behaviourist tradition of development is itself an extension of the Spencer-Bain utilitarianism noted in connection with Baldwin—the position according to which successful actions become "strengthened" with experience. Such behaviourist approaches to individual development have proved tenacious and powerful and it was these formulations—rather than, for example, Thorndike's Darwinist arguments—that seemed to provide the major alternative to recapitulationary viewpoints in the early decades of the present century.

Alongside the development of behaviourism, others in the U.S.A. were continuing the tradition of G.S. Hall. The central figure was Arnold Gesell (1880–1961), director of a narrowly defined and productive research programme at Yale from the 1920s onwards. Gesell had completed his Ph.D. at Clark University, where Hall was President, before taking medical qualifications and then embarking on his research career. Recalling Hall's teaching, Gesell[2] was later to write:

> G. Stanley Hall was the acknowledged genius of the group at Clark . . . He had . . . an empathetic propensity to revive within himself the thought processes and the feelings of other thinkers. This same projective trait enabled him to penetrate into the mental life of children, of defectives, of primitive peoples, of animals, of extinct stages of evolution.

Gesell enthusiastically accepted Hall's recapitulationism, writing in 1912 that: "recapitulation is one of the most wonderful of scientific generalizations . . . [The child] has a pedigree, both human and biological, and to appreciate him we must think historically." For Gesell, individual development essentially represents the expression of growth in the nervous system. The same overall processes are at work in the course of evolution as in ontogenesis. Gesell noted that the infant "grows and adapts in a manner which is measurably comparable to the evolutionary process." Gesell's developmental psychology was "genetic": That is, one concerned with general processes of growth, as Hall's had been. For Gesell, the "supreme genetic law" was that all present growth hinges on past growth;

and growth itself, for Gesell, was "an historical complex" which incorporates its past. Later he was to note that Hall's adherence to (strict) recapitulation might have been exaggerated; but the general aspects of recapitulation, with its emphasis on unitary processes, certainly retained their influence on Gesell's thinking.

The methodological implications of Gesell's growth approach to development included a reliance on observational techniques and the seeking of norms related to chronological age. The empirical method comprised the systematic observation of "normal" behaviour in relatively naturalistic settings; cine film was used extensively; experimental methods were eschewed as not yielding information on spontaneous, "natural" aspects of development. The course of development was assumed to be stable and could thus be explored piecemeal, like a foreign country: A massive pictorial account of early development published in 1934 was aptly termed an "Atlas." Individual differences in such aspects as handedness or intelligence were assumed to be largely determined by inheritance. A belief in the existence of a correct course of development was central to Gesell's approach: As he noted, "the inevitableness and surety of maturation are the most impressive characteristic of early development." The assumption that the observed pattern of developmental change is *right* is a concomitant of the more general forms of recapitulation. If all developmental change, whether in the species or in the individual, manifests the same unitary process then the outcome of this process must be considered as true and correct. This claim had been expressed clearly by Haeckel and was also central to Freud.

Gesell's assumptions on the nature of individual development were consistent with those of the leaders of the mental testing movement. Mental testing or psychometrics was emerging in the first decades of the 20th century as a major force in psychology. One of the founders of mental testing in the U.S.A., Lewis Terman, carried out his Ph.D. research alongside Gesell at Clark. The thesis, "Genius and stupidity" (presented in 1905) made use of test items similar to those devised earlier by the French psychologist Alfred Binet. Binet himself had aimed at practicality and the coverage of a wide range of abilities relating to school performance. Terman's aim, however, was to arrive at a score on a general measure of intelligence, a characteristic of the individual assumed to be largely constitutional (hereditary). Terman went on to formulate the Stanford-Binet intelligence scale, first published in 1916, which became the standard I.Q. test throughout the English-speaking world. Similarly, Gesell's general "developmental" tests for infants came to dominate the scene for both clinical and research purposes. The developmental assumptions inherent in I.Q. testing itself should not be overlooked.[3] Fundamentally, development is regarded as the regular accretion of age-linked competence. This viewpoint is entirely consistent with Gesell's concept of the "mental manifestation" of growth. The concept of "growth" stands at the centre of both the psychometric and the maturational models of development and in many ways growth models were seen as representing the main contribution of biology to the description of ontogenesis. The history of intelligence testing lies outside the scope of this book, but its influential role in reinforcing the grip of the "growth" orientation to development should not be underestimated.

A short comment should perhaps be made on the institutional aspect of child development research in the U.S.A. in this period. Numerous Child Study Centres were established from the 1920s on, with various sources of funds, and a number of large-scale and long-term research projects were initiated. The work of such centres could perhaps be classified as "normal science" as defined by the historian of science T.S. Kuhn: That is, effort was directed at the exploitation of available ideas and methods rather than the expansion of theoretical perspectives.[4] "Normal science" is, by its nature, conservative. During this period, then, with the traditions of Watson and of Gesell firmly established, theoretical innovation needed to emerge from Europe (and beyond). The major developmental voice in French-speaking Europe at this time was that of Edouard Claparède (1873–1940). In 1912 Claparède founded the *Institut Jean-Jacques Rousseau* in Geneva, where developmental research went on alongside teacher education. Claparède took what was termed a "functional" approach, attempting to describe the child's behaviour and development in terms of the adaptation to current needs. In this approach Claparède believed himself to be following the approach indicated by Rousseau himself. For Claparède, an emphasis on current needs necessarily casts doubt on the role of recapitulation, which is concerned with ancestral needs. His own empirical work included the study of problem-solving in children, where he employed the technique of having the child talk through the process of solution as it went on. For Claparède, past habits, if inappropriate, might themselves form obstacles to success. Here consciousness must intervene: For Claparède, consciousness arises only when automatic functioning meets with failure. This was one aspect of his influential "law of becoming conscious."[5]

Claparède's approach might be considered representative of a new form of biological reasoning as applied to developmental issues. The emphasis was now on the immediate adaptiveness of behviour. Like other post-Darwinian formulations of biological psychology, the "functionalist" approach claimed Darwinian descent. Certainly the notion of adaptation was central to Darwin. But for Darwin, adaptation was in a sense anticipatory (in any specific case): A new variation was generated which happened to be adaptive to the new circumstances it encountered. The notion of deliberate and consciously directed adaptation was much closer to Lamarckian and other non-Darwinian formulations. Since only the adult animal could reproduce then pre-adult features could not be held as of fundamental significance in the classical Darwinian account. Independent of a recapitulationary interpretation of childhood, the Darwinian version certainly played down the role of adaptation (that is, accommodation) to the immediate environment and its demands.

Alongside Claparède's work, the immediate, problem-solving orientation was receiving an important boost from another source. During the second decade of the century the Gestalt school of psychologists emerged, partly in response to trends within the prevailing orthodoxy of Wilhelm Wundt's approach. Working in Leipzig, Wundt had developed what might be called the first "official" psychology: An experimental tradition whose influence was immense. Wundt himself established a productive research laboratory, a journal for the dissemination of results, and perhaps above all trained the next generation of both European and American psychologists.[6] The methodology employed well-established techniques of psychophysics, and attempted to delineate the mental processes of human subjects as they attended to and processed stimuli. Wundt placed emphasis on the voluntary, active features of adult human mentation and hence argued that psychological processes must of necessity be studied in the adult subject, who is capable of introspection and verbal report. The study of childhood, for Wundt, was more akin to *social* psychology, the study of the cultural products of thinking, for which experimental techniques are inappropriate.

The Gestalt school attempted to focus directly on what was, for them, the central feature of cognition: The appreciation of wholes and of patterns. The perception of the real environment, with all its demands, was taken as the basic role of behaviour. Many of the experimental techniques of the Gestalt school were developed in the study of animal intelligence. Most notably, Wolfgang Köhler studied the problem-solving capacity of chimpanzees. These studies, carried out during the First World War, presented the animal with a piece of food which could only be obtained by some novel behaviour, such as putting two sticks together to form a longer stick. The focus was on the animal's immediate needs and on its immediate perception of the problem scenario. The Gestalt approach was therefore very much a functionalist one. Two Viennese psychologists, Charlotte and Karl Bühler, applied Köhler's methods to young children. Karl Bühler himself was an important contributor to mainstream Gestalt psychology.[7] During the 1920s the Bühlers tested infants on tasks such as using a stick to reach a distant object. For Karl Bühler, a "chimpanzee age" could be defined for the human infant: A stage of equivalence with respect to problem-solving capacity. Thus the theory of recapitulation reappeared even in the context of highly functionalist investigation.

A final "minor" figure is William Stern (1871–1938). Stern's *The psychology of early childhood* (1914) was authoritative and highly influential. Stern's method was trained observation: Experimentation on children he considered dangerous. His theoretical interpretations were cautious. He acknowledged Wilhelm Preyer to be the founder of child psychology, but felt that Preyer's theoretical deductions were "too intellectual". With respect to biology, Stern treated the ancestral version of recapitulation as an hypothesis held by those interested in prehistory. Stanley Hall's recapitulationary theory of play was considered only a partial explanation. However, the more general form of recapitulation is given strong endorsement by Stern: The notion that the same processes must underlie all forms of change in the natural world. Stern is worth quoting at some length on this issue[8]:

> [Hall] lays especial stress on the essential agreement between the attitude of mind and action in young children and human beings of early civilisation, but there are also *formal* agreements that have not, necessarily, anything to do with atavism [ancestral throwbacks]. All psychic development, whether in the individual child or in humanity as a whole, follows certain laws of sequence, in accordance with which primitive and more roughly hewn life-forms precede the more complicated and finely differentiated.

Stern's statement expresses with considerable clarity the more general version of recapitulation, in which correspondence is formal rather than causal. Further, Stern's version points the way ahead in the sense of a subsequent return to the more general versions of recapitulation. Stern's influence may, indeed, have contributed to this change. His most noted student, Heinz Werner, adopted this approach with gusto. The most extensive application of general recapitulation was carried out by a protégé of Claparède, Jean Piaget. Piaget was also influenced, although less directly, by the Gestalt movement and by the work of the Bühlers. But the more direct heir to the Bühler approach was the developmentalist to whom we now turn: Lev Vygotsky.

LEV VYGOTSKY AND THE ONTOGENY OF CULTURE

The three remaining "major" figures to be discussed represent, if not a new generation, certainly a younger cohort of developmental psychologists: All born in the 1890s, and hence receiving their education at the beginning of the present century. Lev Vygotsky, Jean Piaget, and Heinz

Werner are parallel figures, each knowing of and commenting on the work of the others (to varying degrees). Of the three, the influence of Piaget has certainly been the greatest to date. However, Werner's ideas have been perpetuated by a series of co-workers and students (in the U.S.A.); and interest in Vygotsky has increased considerably in recent years with the translation of some of his writings into English (*Thought and language* in 1962 and 1986[9]; and *Mind in society* in 1978). During his brief but highly productive research career, Lev Vygotsky developed a synthesis of the psychological traditions of central Europe and the Marxism of the Soviet Union. The psychological sources included, principally, the Bühlers; his views on Stern were generally critical. It was the functional approach to child development which most influenced his thinking—the emphasis on problem-solving and the intelligent use of tools in naturalistic, adaptive contexts. Vygotsky extended this work in important directions, investigating the nature of language and its relation to thought, and the role of social factors in development. Assumptions of a strictly biological kind perhaps play a relatively minor role in his thinking; but they are present, and it is a testament to the tenacity of these ideas that they retained a grip even on someone as original as Vygotsky.

Lev Vygotsky (1896–1934) had broad interests in the humanities and in education, and his psychological work should be seen in that context. His adult life was spent under the Soviet system, and Marxism plays a major role in his thinking. This adherence to Marxism itself carries with it certain assumptions of a biological nature. Marx himself, writing in the 1860s, had emphasised the central and constitutive role of productive (economic) activity in the life of man, and had thus traced a continuity between tool use in animals and human work. Problem-solving and practical intelligence —changing the world through action—were given even greater emphasis by Marx's collaborator and interpreter, Friedrich Engels. Engels himself endorsed Haeckel's doctrine of ancestral recapitulation.[10] Thus the Marxist tradition in early Soviet Russia itself incorporated biological assumptions, one illustration being the optimistic neo-Lamarckian expectations for the rapid improvement of people and of crops within a few post-revolutionary generations.

The Darwinist tradition in Marxism was employed by Vygotsky chiefly for its emphasis on continuity between man and the animals. The demonstration of intelligent action in infants, prior to the emergence of language, was to become one of the major planks in Vygotsky's argument on the development of language and thought. Comparative evidence from higher animals—that is, Köhler's work on problem-solving in chimpanzees—was vital support for this position. But this evidence could only be employed if continuity were accepted. It should however be emphasised that Vygotsky saw no value in Bühler's concept of a "chimpanzee age" in the human infant, although the Bühlers' findings were of great interest to him. It was the demonstration of practical intelligence in the infant which excited Vygotsky, and especially the demonstration that such "technical thinking" precedes the emergence of speech. Vygotsky was committed to the acceptance of significant parallels between primates and human infants and such parallels cannot but be flavoured, at least, with recapitulationary thinking.

Vygotsky's general model of ontogenesis has pronounced recapitulationary overtones. He makes it clear that human infancy is dominated by functions which also operate in animals; "elementary processes" such as tool use and communicative signalling. Following infancy, these biological processes increasingly become interwovern with the sociocultural processes unique to humans[11]: "The internalisation of socially rooted and historically developed activities is the distinguishing feature of human psychology, the basis of the qualitative leap from animal to human psychology." More explicitly, the mastery of tool use is held to be linked, both ontogenetically and phylogenetically, with the mastery of one's own behaviour through the medium of signs. "In phylogenesis we can reconstruct this link through fragmentary but convincing evidence, while in ontogenesis we can trace it experimentally."[12] Essentially this was the claim of Romanes, and the assumption of Hall.

Vygotsky himself denied adherence to what he took to be the doctrine of recapitulation, and certainly there are important distinctions made in his account between the course of evolution and the course of individual development[13]. Most centrally, the emergence of the human species is seen as representing a transition out of the animal kingdom in various respects —a definite move *from* the biological *to* the sociohistorical—whereas the development of the individual involves a close intertwining of the two. This issue cannot be resolved definitively except by close reference to the Marxist tradition on human nature. In general, at least, Vygotsky cannot therefore be said to have freed himself entirely from the grip of recapitulationary thinking. In view of its influence on his intellectual forebears it would have been remarkable if he had done so.

JEAN PIAGET AND THE BIOLOGY OF KNOWLEDGE

Jean Piaget (1896–1980) was born in the same year as Vygotsky but survived him by nearly 50 years. His theoretical system evolved continuously during his long research career and it is difficult to give a definitive summary of its biological characteristics.[14] Indeed, Piaget's account of individual development is biological in a more comprehensive way than that of perhaps any other major figure: It can, however, be argued that the biological character of Piaget's theory became established very early and did not change in any substantial way. The evolution of his system consisted in the assimilation of more and more material with, perhaps, rather little accommodation of the pre-existing structures. Throughout his career, Piaget was explicitly anti-Darwinian, as several commentators have noted;[15] some have suggested that he failed to understand certain of the Darwinian claims.[16] This section discusses Piaget's early writing in some detail, but also gives consideration to late statements such as are contained in *Biology and knowledge* (1967) and *Behaviour and evolution* (1976). Later chapters will return to these issues in particular substantive contexts, and some general points are re-examined in Chapter Nine.

Piaget's initial training was in zoology and his first substantial publications concerned molluscs. Very early, however, he also developed interests in philosophy and in social science. A major early influence of both a philosophical and a biological nature was that of the most prominent French philosopher of the time, Henri Bergson. Bergson was deeply concerned with the nature of life processes and the theory of evolution. Darwinism he found too mechanistic, and Lamarckism, though superior, still too individualistic.[17] For Bergson, the progress of evolution was like a great cavalry charge, driven by a vital force (the "*élan vital*"). Adaptation to specific environments was a secondary matter: It explained only "the sinuosities of movement of evolution, not its general direction still less the movement itself." Bergson's "creative evolution," as described in his 1907 book of the same name, was a "big bang" theory: Evolutionary change resulting from the aftereffects of an "original impetus of life" like a great explosion. The influence of Bergson on Piaget, considerable in many ways, was certainly a profoundly non-Darwinian one. This influence would have been generally consistent with Piaget's scientific training, in that French science (including that of French-speaking Switzerland) remained especially resistant to Darwinism into the early 20th century.[18] One direct influence of Bergson, according to Piaget himself, was his decision (taken in his late teens) to "consecrate [his] life to the biological explanation of knowledge." Piaget's overall aim was a genetic theory of knowledge, that is a "genetic epistemology." Such an objective had also been held by Baldwin, as we have seen, but where Baldwin's version was substantially theoretical, Piaget's involved extensive experimentation, an area in which he was supremely gifted.

In general it appears that Piaget was not greatly influenced by other developmentalists (such as Hall and Baldwin) prior to his own empirical research with children. His formative influences were philosophical and biological, and the latter involved an adherence to Lamarckism. Indeed, Piaget carried out experimental work in this area, seeking for evidence of the hereditary transmission of properties acquired by individuals. He claimed that the shells of aquatic molluscs were directly modified by the extent of water movement (variable with depth of habitat) and that such modifications could be transmitted to offspring. Consistent with the current French viewpoint, Piaget in 1918 could in his own words "decide in favour of Lamarckism without any qualms."[19] The Darwinian mechanism of natural selection was considered secondary, and Weismann's demonstration of the impossiblity of the Lamarckian mechanism was dismissed. Like Baldwin before him, Piaget sought to establish an active role for behaviour in the evolutionary scheme; later, Piaget developed his own formulation of Baldwin's "organic selection."

A related standpoint concerned the concept of the species. Darwinism came to be synthesised with a model of heredity derived from Mendel's gene theory, leading to a position which emphasised the distinction between fluctuating and hereditary variations. A fluctuating variation did not breed true, and could play no role in evolutionary change. Piaget rejected this distinction, seeing the species merely as the fixed version of what had formerly been a fluctuating variation. Again, this standpoint was essentially a Lamarckian one. It should also be noted that a long-term interest of Piaget—the issue of the relation between wholes and parts—arose first in this biological context. It was in terms of species (as wholes) and individuals (as parts) that his first views on this important issue were formulated.

A central polarity in Piaget's theory of individual adaptation is that between *assimilation* and *accommodation*. These twin concepts were initially derived by Piaget from their employment (one under a different name) by the philosophically oriented biologist Felix Le Dantec. Le Dantec, who died in 1917, was the author of several Lamarckian works on biology and was an adherent of recapitulation theory.[20] Le Dantec saw the life process as a state of conflict between two fundamental tendencies, "functional assimilation" and "imitation." The former is a conservative force, represented by the animal's effort to retain its integrity of structure and habits, both from moment to moment (during its lifetime) and by reproduction of its own kind. Thus habits (and functions in general) become assimilated into the individual, and thence assimilated into the species. Lamarck's mechanism is thus a manifestation of functional assimilation. The conservative process is opposed by the deforming effect of the environment, by which an individual is moulded into a representation or reflection of that environment. This antagonistic process was termed "imitation." For Le Dantec, assimilation and imitation stand in simple opposition: An increase in one can only take place at the expense of the other. Piaget's adoption of this model (announced in 1918) included one radical change. The two processes could not be in simple opposition, Piaget argued; rather, they must grow together, in direct proportion to each other. Piaget's was a dynamic reformulation of Le Dantec's essentially static account. Le Dantec's attractively simple version may well have had limited applicability to developmental issues. It is possible that Piaget's transformation may, in attempting to extend the account for such purposes, have sacrificed some of the validity of the original concepts of "assimilation" and "imitation."

Certainly Piaget himself had no qualms on the validity of the assimilation-imitation dichotomy in the developmental context. Introducing a change of terms a few years later, Piaget substituted "accommodation" for "imitation": Thus the model of assimilation and accommodation was obtained. Since the change took place subsequent to Piaget's reading of Baldwin, it may be assumed that he wished in this way to incorporate certain of Baldwin's claims into his own account. This may have been unfortunate, although perhaps typical of Piaget's procedure. The central point to note is the biological origin of the assimilation-accommodation dichotomy. Piaget continually explained these terms by reference to strictly biological functions such as digestion. These examples should not be seen as analogies for intellectual processes: If anything, the intellect should be seen as an analogy for digestion. As Piaget put it in a late account, "cognitive functions are an extension of organic regulations"; or, less formally but with no less seriousness, "A rabbit that eats a cabbage doesn't become a cabbage; it's the cabbage that becomes rabbit—that's assimilation."[21]

Le Dantec's simple formula for assimilation and imitation involved a balance or equilibrium between the two. For Piaget, both grow reciprocally; the animal's increasingly complex set of habits, to which external reality is assimilated, is paralleled by an increasing openness to experience. Piaget, however, also wished to maintain Le Dantec's stress on the importance of equilibrium processes in the organic world. The concept of a dynamic equilibrium became central to Piaget's subsequent thinking. In turn, it was related to the issue of part-whole relationships: Parts and wholes of any structure must, argued Piaget, manifest a relationship of equilibrium in which the integrity of both is preserved. Certain states of awareness—such as the awareness of logical necessity, or of moral obligation—may be taken to indicate the particularly *stable* equilibrium between parts and wholes. In the context of moral behaviour, for example, stable equilibrium would represent a state of harmony between individual and collective rights. Other states were taken to represent the domination of either parts or wholes (examples being drawn from aspects of visual perception). The preoccupations and formulations of these early years—that is, before his experimental work with children—remained firmly embedded in Piaget's thinking. The objectives, the methods, and the interpretive frameworks of his subsequent empirical programme can probably be understood only by reference to this early thinking. As Piaget put it himself, in looking back on the work of that period, at that stage he had no psychological training and therefore "I was bound to limit myself to the construction of a system."[22]

Piaget's early attitude to the theory of recapitulation is unclear. He must certainly have been introduced to it in his zoological and palaeontological studies. His own retrospective accounts of his early thinking suggest that a conviction of the existence of recapitulationary parallels was of long standing. Throughout his career, Piaget explored the implications of the more general formulations of recapitulation (according to which the development of the individual is subject to the same laws as the course of evolution). His standpoint on the stronger formulations is less easy to establish; this issue is considered in the latter part of this section.

A parallel on which Piaget has laid much emphasis is that between individual development and the cultural progress of knowledge. He has described this parallelism as "the fundamental hypothesis of genetic epistemology." The notion is a variant of the "cultural epoch" theory of education, according to which the child must be brought through progressively higher (i.e. more recent) stages of civilisation through appropriately chosen materials. This theory derived in part from the writings of Jean-Jacques Rousseau, a Swiss like Piaget; and the *Institut J.-J. Rousseau*, at which Piaget carried out all his major work, took its nominal connection to Rousseau seriously. It might also be noted that the cultural epoch approach to education had reached its most influential status at around the turn of the century, and Piaget may be assumed to have been at least familiar with the theory as an approach to education.

Brief mention should be made here of a slightly more innovative feature of recapitulation theory which Piaget explored in his research programme. Some 19th-century biologists had suggested that recapitulation might take place *within* the development of the individual, as well as between individual development and evolutionary ancestry. The chief example of this was held to be seen in the segmentation of the animal body, and the anatomical relationship of the skull to the vertebrae of the spine. Thus one segment could be seen as the repetition of another, or in terms of the repeated presentation of the same basic template.[23] A very early version of this "metameric" theory had been propounded by Goethe at the end of the 18th century. Goethe himself, it should be noted, was a founder of the Romantic movement (with a considerable interest in the nature of growth and development) and also of the Nature-philosophy approach in general. Piaget's version of repetition within development is concerned with knowledge structures rather than bone structures. It gives rise to a "spiral-staircase" model in which patterns of growth are repeated with development but at progressively higher levels. More accurately, but less elegantly, each spiral should be seen as connected to the next by an elevator. The most basic example of this repetition within development is the shift from the level of action (as in infancy) to the level of thought. Piaget's term for this kind of shift is *décalage* (vertical *décalage* in this case).

This conceptualisation of the transition from infancy to childhood and the rest of development remained central to Piaget's thinking. But he also applied the notion of *décalage* to finer details of developmental progress.

One example of this is found in Piaget's account of the development of spatial representation, in which a series of states traversed by the infant are seen as reappearing at a higher level, and to be traversed again, during childhood. For present purposes, it is important to re-emphasise the recapitulationary overtones of this concept of internal repetition or *déca-lage*. The concept of developmental stage, and the related concept of periodicity in development, are intimately related to the general theory of recapitulation. The "spiral-staircase" model requires that each circuit is qualitatively different to the next. Repetition of stages with coherent and integral characteristics relies on such qualitative distinctions. The notion of stage in development has philosophical as well as biological origins (although some ancestry is shared in common). Piaget's own stage theory is better examined in more concrete contexts, but the fact that a stage analysis is demanded by recapitulation theory should not be overlooked.

Towards the end of his long career, Piaget collected his thoughts on the relationships between biology and development in *Biology and knowledge* (1967) and in *Behaviour and evolution* (1976). Some relevant statements may also be found in *The principles of genetic epistemology* and in *Psychology and epistemology*, both first published in 1970. Here we shall look first at Piaget's mature position on Lamarck—including his evaluation of Baldwin's "organic selection"—and then at his position on recapitulation. Lamarckism is discussed in *The principles of genetic epistemology*, where it is labelled as essentially an "empiricist" theory of evolution: One stressing the imposition of the environment onto a passive animal. In this interpretation, Lamarck's claim was that habits are created quite directly by environmental pressure (and are thence taken into the germ material). For Piaget, this notion of direct "imitation" (as he would once have called it) is Lamarck's central error. Writing as he is in the latter part of the 20th century, Piaget might find it difficult to maintain his adherence to orthodox Lamarckism (now described by him as "abandoned long ago"). A cynic might suggest that Piaget is using the demise of Lamarckism as a somewhat dubious means of making certain points on empiricism.

Darwinism for Piaget can be seen as the opposite extreme to Lamarckism as an account of the role of behaviour in evolution. Piaget acclaims Lamarck's insight, while rejecting his actual solution, and here he gives an evaluation of Baldwin's "organic selection." Piaget considers Baldwin's formulation to be "helpful and worth retaining" and limited chiefly in that it falls short of his own "phenocopy" theory. The latter account describes accommodations as coming to be replaced by equivalent genetic instructions, whereas (according to Piaget) Baldwin's model tends to emphasise a more open-ended, facilitative role for adaptations. That is to say, Baldwin claims that "organic selection" gives the species a chance to "come up with" appropriate variations, without determining such new variations in any direct sense. This feature of Baldwin's model should be seen as part of his attempt to avoid Lamarckism; it is a generally Darwinist position in that sense. Piaget's position, on the contrary, should probably be seen as a disguised return to a form of Lamarckism—disguised because Piaget has rejected Lamarckism as he has defined it. Piaget's position is Lamarckist in that (against Baldwin) he wishes to argue for a fairly direct linkage between habit and genome (phenotype and genotype). At the same time he wishes to distance himself from Lamarckism qua "empiricism." Baldwin is incorrect because the directive role of habit it too loose; Lamarck because its role is too tight (and for Darwin, habit is said to play no part at all). As on other occasions, Piaget attempts to establish his position by distancing himself *simultaneously* from a number of classic alternatives: Not for the only time, these simultaneous distancings are not entirely consistent.

Piaget's mature statements on recapitulation might be seen as of a similar kind to those on Lamarckism: Rejecting the label while retaining the substance. Certainly, Piaget wishes to disavow what he considers classic recapitulationism to be. Thus[24]: "embryogenetic development is not a mere 'recapitulation' of phylogenesis, which is what de Serres, F. Müller, and von Baer thought it was." The "mere" should be noted well (and Piaget is quite wrong in referring to von Baer in this context). In any event, this quotation is followed immediately by the following parenthetical remark: "(Their idea remains valid in the main, provided allowance is made for the influence of changes in speed and short circuits)." But this qualification was recognised even by Haeckel, who emphasised the importance of such corrective factors. The same kinds of qualification are noted elsewhere in the same work, such as "ontogenesis is not an exact and detailed recapitulation of phylogenesis." The position *rejected* by Piaget is therefore a most extreme and simplistic version of recapitulation: One held by no serious developmental thinker. If Haeckel and Baldwin can legitimately be termed recapitulationists then so must Piaget. To quote Piaget again[25]: "the law of ontophylogenetic 'recapitulation' . . . is valid by and large."

The standpoint expressed in *Psychology and epistemology* is weak in a similar manner. Here Piaget[26] notes: "As for theories of evolution, even if the parallels between ontogeny and phylogeny have been exaggerated (and in detail they are far from exact), there is little doubt that embryology has given new perspectives to evolutionary theory . . ." Piaget's rejection even of the strong, ancestral form of recapitulation is a highly qualified one. More positively, Piaget emphasises that the connection between the two series of ontogeny and phylogeny consists of a lawful sequence of *stages*. Thus "evolution, in its phylogenetic aspects, submit[s] to the laws of embryogenetic development"; and, in comparing the history of ideas in child development and in evolution[27]: "[Ontogenetic development] has always been seen (contrary to the notion of evolution which was discovered late) as implying, first, an ordered series of stages and a causality connection linking each stage to the next." The issue of the history of ideas may seem an intrusion here, but for Piaget it is all part of the same grand scheme by which universal laws of developmental change work themselves out in different contexts.

Finally, some comment should be made on Piaget's notion of "convergent reconstruction" as discussed in *Biology and knowledge*. This process refers to an aspect of developmental progress whereby formations at one level of functioning are "reconstructed" at a higher level (for example, action structures becoming reformulated as cognitive operations). As Piaget makes clear, his previously formulated notion of "vertical *décalage*" is an example of this process; as is "reflective abstraction." In all such cases, Piaget distances himself from the ("empiricist") suggestion that reflection or translation is in any sense direct or determinate. The relationship is held to be more creative than this in a certain sense; at least insofar as new properties emerge from the transition. It appears that Piaget wishes to retain strong and explanatory relationships between the two series but also to insist on qualitative and hierarchical distinctions between them.

Piaget's attitude to the strong, ancestral version of recapitulation theory was perhaps an ambivalent one. It could be suggested that he appealed to it when it seemed appropriate but denied it quite strenuously when it did not. In any event, Piaget's adherence to the more general form of the recapitulation argument could not be denied. For Piaget all manifestations of development, whether individual or phylogenetic, are to be seen as the outcomes of a unitary process. Piaget might therefore be seen as a modern exponent of Nature-philosophy. The assumption of unitary process (and more specifically, of the "single track" in developmental progress) is central to Piaget's thinking. In true recapitulationary style, he has observed that prehistoric man would be the ideal subject for the investigation of the genesis of knowledge. The child is in a sense a poor substitute. At the same time, Piaget sees the modern child as still, in some important respects, more primitive than adult prehistoric man. Piaget's appeal to biology was a very flexible one.

There are many similarities between the biological approaches of Piaget and that of James Mark Baldwin, although Piaget applied such notions as recapitulation much more systematically to the *empirical* investigation of individual development than Baldwin had done. Certainly Piaget read Baldwin's works, and Pierre Janet, under whom Piaget studied in Paris, had weekly lunches with the American émigré. Baldwin was the more sophisticated as a philosophical thinker, and perhaps for this reason focused his interest on the epistemological side of genetic epistemology.

Piaget's major contribution was to the genetic (that is, developmental) component; and here, the major influences and the major presuppositions were derivative of biology. Like Hall and Freud before him, and consistent with his intellectual background, Piaget's biology had little to do with the arguments of Charles Darwin.

HEINZ WERNER AND THE MORPHOLOGY OF THOUGHT

These chapters introduce the major figures in developmental psychology by focusing on the biological influences on their thinking. In doing so, the spotlight has moved from the U.S.A. (with Hall and Baldwin) to Europe (with Vygotsky and Piaget). With a discussion of Heinz Werner (1890–1964), who emigrated from Germany to the U.S.A. in the 1930s, the circle is complete. Werner's European years had included, most notably, study under William Stern at Hamburg. Stern saw his own approach as sharing some of the features of the Gestalt school of psychology, developed in Germany earlier in the century, with its orientation to holistic analysis. Stern did not endorse the Gestalt ideology whole-heartedly, but Werner did, making an attempt to construct a developmental psychology based on Gestalt principles.

Subsequent to his arrival in the U.S., Werner was offered the G. Stanley Hall Professorship in Genetic Psychology at Clark University. Here he pursued both empirical and theoretical researches into a structural, holistic developmental psychology. Werner's own term for his approach was "organic," contrasting it with alternative "mechanistic" approaches.[28] The stated goal of Werner's developmental psychology was the grasping of the structural patterns of different levels of functioning and of the relationships between different levels. With respect to the structured nature of levels or stages, Werner went beyond Piaget's stage-analysis in significant ways. True to the Gestalt tradition, a level was treated as self contained and complete in itself—a whole. It needed to be grasped as a totality, not in terms of components. One necessary consequence of this holistic approach is that difficulties arise in attempting to understand transitions from one stage to another. If one state is complete, how and why can change take place? Piaget had recognised this as a problem inherent in an approach based on Gestalt principles, describing the resulting model as "structure without genesis." He did not, however, see it as inherent in *any* stage theory, including his own. In Werner's account the holistic analysis of stages had further consequences: If levels are complete in themselves, then establishing an order or hierarchy among levels becomes problematic. The usual criteria for the ordering of levels—for claiming, in crude terms, that one level is better than the preceding one—would seem to evaporate. Development no longer occurs at all.

This issue is connected with the biological theme of this chapter. Species are, in a sense, "wholes," complete in themselves, and yet they must be seen as in some sense descending one from another. One of the major sources of influence on Werner's biological views was Jacob von Uexküll. Von Uexküll—a "prominent opponent of Darwinism"[29]—shared some philosophical assumptions with certain of the early Gestalt thinkers, tending to rationalist and idealist views including an emphasis on innate ideas. Von Uexküll had attempted to describe perceptual worlds unique and special to each species. Such a perceptual world (or *Umwelt*) would have to be essentially inborn. These views were adopted and applied in a developmental context by Werner's contemporary, the ethologist Konrad Lorenz.[30]

Werner's approach to the issue of recapitulation was essentially an extension of Stern's. He rejected the ancestral recapitulation of Haeckel and Hall, because it was "mechanistic" and "extreme": This approach "sought to treat as materially identical various developmental sequences when the data warranted only the assertion of similarity or parallelism." For Werner, the *appearance* of recapitulation—of the repetition in ontogeny of evolutionary change—arises from the parallel manifestation of unitary processes of development. Werner's "formal" recapitulation, like that of Stern, was therefore of the general, hierarchical variety. For Werner, developmental change is a general phenomenon, and thus different "series" might well show correspondence. But primitive, ancient states are only approximated by any modern adult: Parallelism relates more to formal characteristics of mental structure. The stated aim of Werner's developmental psychology was the description of levels of mental function, not the reconstruction of a speculative history of mankind (although Werner did occasionally stray into the latter territory).

In this respect, Werner departed from the more orthodox employment of findings on modern-day "primitives." Although greatly interested in formal aspects of such anthropological findings, Werner did not take contemporary "savages" to represent prehistoric man in any direct manner. For Werner, the modern-day "primitive" is characterised by special adaptations to the environment. Such adaptations, however, are not truly progressive in an evolutionary sense, rather indicating a kind of premature specialisation which forms an obstacle to true progress.[31] This view is certainly a profoundly non-Darwinian one. Recapitulation for Werner is limited to a hierarchy of formally defined levels of thinking. This is therefore a weak version of recapitulation, one aspect of this weakness being the looseness of the connection between adjacent levels. At the same time, however, Werner was emphatic on the nature of overall trends in development. Early stages are undifferentiated wholes, with all component parts of equivalent function and status. In later stages, components are organised in strict hierarchies of super- and sub-ordination. In this context Werner referred to the work of von Baer, noting correctly (as Piaget did not) that von Baer's position was inconsistent with the strong, ancestral version of recapitulation. Von Baer had in fact refused to accept Darwin's claims, and so did Werner. Werner also rejected the Darwinian position on continuity in mental functioning between man and the animals. For Werner, this position is too mechanistic: It reduces complex and integral wholes to points on a single continuum.

Werner's theoretical claims came to centre on his notion of an "orthogenetic principle of development," defined as the claim that "wherever development occurs it proceeds from a state of relative globality and lack of differentiation to a state of increasing differentiation, articulation and hierarchic integration." This Spencerian formulation was seen by Werner as applying generally to organic phenomena, such that ontogenesis is but one manifestation of it. As Werner recognised, the formulation is inherently a directional one, according to which developmental change is intrinsically progressive; and moreover, the orthogenetic "law" is, "by its very nature, . . . an expression of unilinearity of development." Werner argued that his unilinearity was an "ideal" one, so that "the *ideal* unilinear sequence signified by the universal developmental law does not conflict with the multiplicity of *actual* developmental forms" (emphasis added). This distinction between ideal forms and actual manifestations indicates the strongly idealist cast to Werner's thinking.

Werner's approach, like Piaget's, was thoroughly non-Darwinian. In some respects it reached back to 18th-century thinking: Werner's greatest praise is reserved for Goethe, as the first proponent of what Werner describes as the "organic" model of development. Goethe, as well as being a founder of the Romantic movement, was steeped in the classicism and rationality of the Enlightenment. He was concerned with formal properties of both organic and inorganic matter, with symmetry and order. Werner's analysis of levels of thought is characterised by the same approach. In his outright rejection of Darwinism Werner is perhaps an extreme case with which to conclude these two chapters. But as we have seen, even developmentalists who claimed adherence to Darwin distorted and misapplied his views to a serious extent. The biology by which developmental psychology has been influenced—on which, in a sense, it has been built—is primarily pre-Darwinian. And this reliance on ancient doctrines in biology is matched, as we shall now see, by an adherence to equally venerable notions of a more philosophical nature: Doctrines of sensationism and associationism according to which the child can be considered a "*prisoner of the senses*."

NOTES TO CHAPTER FOUR

[1]On Watson, see Logue's chapter in Buxton (1985); also Harris's in Eckardt et al. (1985). Cohen's biography (1979) is useful although not entirely reliable. Logue (1985, p. 171) suggests that Watson's early writings reveal a commitment to the inheritance of acquired characters.

[2]Gesell (1952/1968, p. 126).

[3]More is said on the I.Q. tradition in Chapter Eight.

[4]Several histories of child development research are focused on such centres (Sears, 1975; Senn, 1975).

[5]On Claparède, see Ash (1985b, p. 353); Claparède (1905/1911; 1930).

[6]The work of Wilhelm Wundt has recently undergone a major re-evaluation, as a consequence of the work of Blumenthal (1980; 1985) and others. Wundt's approach is portrayed in standard texts of the history of psychology as a narrow application of associationist principles, but this appears to be completely erroneous. Since the Gestalt movement has usually been presented as a "progressive" response to Wundt, it too requires some re-evaluation (Ash, 1985a; 1985b). The treatment of the Wundt-Gestalt history has been somewhat "Whiggish," that is, over-interpreted by reference to modern evaluations of these schools. Also see Leichtman (1979).

[7]The work of Karl Bühler is discussed by Kessel and Bevan in Buxton (1985, p. 285), where Bühler's role as a founder of cognitive psychology is evaluated.

[8]Stern (1914/1923, p. 298). In 1930 Stern (p. 375) described Darwin's theory of descent as "the mushy progress by minimal variations." In place of the Darwinian "origin of species" Stern proposed the "birth of species." "The biological species possesses . . . a tendency to self-development, which drives it at certain times to the genesis of new species." Stern's career and influence have been explored by Hardesty (1976a; 1976b) and by Eyferth, both in Riegel and Meacham (1976).

[9]*Thought and language* has recently received a new translation (Vygotsky, 1986) which has now revealed its coherent Marxist framework to the English-speaking audience. Vygotsky's work is explored comprehensively in Wertsch (1985); see especially the chapters by Zinchenko and by Davydov and Radzikhovskii. Also see Rahmani in Riegel and Meacham (1976) and Valsiner (1988). A critical account of Vygotsky is in preparation by J. Valsiner and R. van der Veer.

[10]Engels (1876) cited in Gould (1977, p. 136). The Marx-Engels view on man's relation to the animals is a very complex one, so that a narrow recapitulationism would certainly be a distortion of Marxist thinking on human development (see Sève, 1974/1978; also Riegel's chapter in Buss, 1979; and Chapter Ten, following).

[11]Vygotsky (1978, p. 57).

[12]Ibid., p. 55.

[13]Scribner (1985).

[14]For background information and critiques of Piaget, see Atkinson (1983); Evans (1973); and Rotman (1977). A comprehensive work on Piaget's early sources of influence is J. Ducret (1984). *Jean Piaget, savant et philosophe* (Genève: Librairie Droz), to which I have not had access. Several biographies are reported as being in preparation. The compilation edited by Gruber and Vonèche (1977) contains valuable background and biographical information and is indispensible for its coverage of the early Piaget.

[15]Vidal, Buscaglia, and Vonèche (1983).

[16]Ghiselin (1986, p. 19) argues that Piaget misunderstood Darwin ("[Piaget] never was able to conceive of a taxonomic group as a genetical population . . . This precluded an understanding of natural selection . . . [further] Piaget . . . failed to understand the ecological aspect of natural selection"). Vidal et al. (1983) suggest that Piaget misunderstood the genetic claims

of Mendelism; and Barthélemy-Madaule has noted (1979/1982, p. 159) that Piaget's account of Lamarckism in *Biology and knowledge* is inaccurate (Piaget interprets Lamarck in terms of the body cell/germ cell distinction not introduced until Weismann).

[17]In formulating his own vitalist position Bergson exploited the mistaken interpretation of Lamarck as having based evolutionary progress on effort (Barthélemy-Madaule, 1979/1982, p. 137).

[18]On French anti-Darwinism, see Bowler (1983); Corsi and Weindling in Kohn (1985); and Moore (1977). Felix Le Dantec (see footnote 20 following) observed in 1907 that Darwin's theory "still encumber[s] the field of biology and . . . owing to errors of method, still weigh[s] heavily on the student's shoulders."

[19]Piaget (1918a/1977, p. 40) ("Biology and war").

[20]Le Dantec, who had earlier studied in Pasteur's laboratory in Paris, was one of a group of French neo-Lamarckians of the very early years of the present century (Barthélemy-Madaule, 1979/1982, pp. *x*, 83, 166). Le Dantec's writings are something of a goldmine for the student of Piaget, as indicated for example by the subtitle to his *La philosophie zoologique de Lamarck* of 1903: "Introduction aux limites du connaissable" [Introduction to the limits of the knowable]. The influence on Piaget included metatheoretical claims on life processes, as noted in Chapter Nine, footnote 13).

[21]Bringuier (1980, p. 42).

[22]Piaget (1952/1968, p. 242).

[23]Russell (1916).

[24]Piaget (1967/1971, p. 83).

[25]Piaget (1967/1971, p. 332).

[26]Piaget (1970a/1972a, pp. 18–19).

[27]Piaget (1967/1971, p. 81).

[28]For a recent statement of the continuing Werner tradition, see Kaplan (1983) and the collection of Wapner and Kaplan (1983).

[29]Ash (1985b, p. 342).

[30]Konrad Lorenz makes frequent (although not uncritical) reference to von Uexküll in such recent works as Lorenz (1973/1977; 1978/1981). Lorenz' influence on developmental psychology has arisen from his ethological studies (see Chapter Ten, and especially footnotes 3–5).

[31]Werner (1957, p. 126). Also see Kaplan (1983); Kaplan disputes that the orthogenetic principle is in any way a Spencerian formulation, since it relates to an ideal, not an actual concept of developmental change (see footnote 1 to Chapter Eleven following). Werner's treatment of specific adaptations as being nonprogressive deviations from a general trend recalls that of Lamarck (Chapter Two, footnote 7).

5 "The Prisoner of the Senses": Sensationism in Developmental Thinking

"PRISONER OF THE SENSES"

The preceding chapters, and those which follow, focus on the influence of biological assumptions on the thinking of developmental psychologists. The present brief chapter sketches the historical background to a set of broadly philosophical assumptions closely bound up with the biological ones.[1] These philosophical or psychological assumptions concern the role played by the senses and sensation in the mental life of the child. They gave rise to the view that the infant and child are especially constrained by sensory experience, and that early cognition is thus limited to the "here and now." A related assumption has been that knowledge must be built up from information which is initially tied to one or other sensory channel. This chapter outlines the ways in which a philosophical interest in the role of sensation and perception gave rise to some quite precise assumptions concerning cognition in childhood. It represents a necessary digression into the history of psychological theory, without which an analysis of formulations on infancy, for example, would be inadequate.

Early and influential accounts based on the role of sensation included that offered by Jean-Jacques Rousseau, writing a century before Darwin. "Sensationist" accounts of early child development were updated during the 19th century with the aid of associationist approaches to psychology. These accounts, in their turn, became synthesised with contemporary ideas on evolution. The bridge between the two was the new version of Lamarckism, claiming that individual experience—derived initially from sensation—might become incorporated into the hereditary material. Thus the mind of the child was seen as a reflection of the *experience* of ancestors. The aim of this chapter is to indicate something of the background to the sensationism which has dominated developmental thinking. The point to be made is that the sensationist doctrines antedate the scientific enterprise of developmental psychology. They derived from accounts of the nature of knowledge—that is, epistemology—accounts which were themselves intertwined with claims relating to biology. Thus the issue of continuity or discontinuity between man and the animals is of crucial importance for both the epistemological and the biological enterprises.

One of the most basic assumptions in developmental psychology has been that prototypical experience relates to things present to the senses, any other form of cognition being seen as "higher." The origins of this assumption, and of others with which we are concerned, can be traced back directly to the philosophical writings of the 17th century, to the traditions established by René Descartes, Pierre Gassendi, Thomas Hobbes, and John Locke. The emphasis on direct experience as the source of knowledge is generally associated with empiricist forms of philosophy such as that initiated by John Locke at the end of the 17th century. Locke is conventionally taken to have defined his own position in opposition to that of René Descartes (writing some 50 years earlier):[2] But an emphasis on the role of sensation, at least in the child, is found in Descartes too. Since most modern traditions in Western philosophy derive (if not ultimately) from the work of either Descartes or Locke, the presence of such an assumption in both sources is of considerable significance. Even those who reject one tradition, such as the associationism derived from Locke, may inherit the assumption through the rationalist route instead.

Descartes' position on the relationship between mind and body was that the two are distinct but are able to interact in the human being. The essential characteristic of mind is thinking (whereas the essential characteristic of matter is extension). Therefore, whenever mind exists, thinking must be taking place. For Descartes, the soul is united with the body at *conception*; soul is a kind of mind; therefore some primitive kind of thinking must be present in the unborn child. What form could this thinking possibly take? For Descartes[3]:

> if one may conjecture on such an unexplored topic, it seems most reasonable to think that a mind newly united to an infant's body is wholly occupied in perceiving or feeling the ideas of pain, pleasure, heat, cold, and other similar ideas which arise from its union and intermingling with the body . . . This does not mean that I believe that the mind of an infant meditates on metaphysics in its mother's womb.

The awareness of sensation then, is the ealiest form of thinking. The *freedom* to think of "higher" things is a developmental achievement.

Thus: "In an adult and healthy body the mind enjoys some liberty to think of other things than those presented by the senses, we know there is not the same liberty in those who are sick or asleep or very young; *and the younger they are the less liberty they have*".[4]

In Descartes' account the child is bound by sensation: Limited, essentially, to the here-and-now. This developmental picture was endorsed by John Locke, for whom "reflection" on sensation was a process only reached at maturity. In the early years, according to Locke[5]: "Men's business . . . is to acquaint themselves with what is to be found without; and so growing up in a constant attention to outward sensations, seldom make any considerable reflection on what passes in them, till they come to be of riper years." Locke's account was more systematic than that of Descartes in terms of the processes by which knowledge could progress. The basic mechanism was association:[6] "Their thoughts enlarge themselves only as they come to be acquainted with a greater variety of sensible objects, to retain the ideas of them in their memories, and to get the skill to compound and enlarge them, and several ways put them together." For Locke, as for Descartes, thinking is *necessarily* conscious, even if in only a rudimentary way. The newborn, for Locke, has very little to think about, and *for that reason* is asleep much of the time. With development, however[7]: "As the mind by the senses comes more and more to be furnished with ideas, it comes to be more and more awake; thinks more, the more it has matter to think on."

Such classical accounts of childhood cognition are of interest because of their very extensive influence. One assumption of very great significance has been the emphasis on constraint within the bounds of sensation as a characteristic of primitive cognition. This is expressed clearly by Locke[8] in a discussion on cognition in animals, who can: "in certain instances reason . . . but it is only in particular ideas, just as they received them from their senses. They are the best of them tied up within those narrow bounds, and have not . . . the faculty to enlarge them by any kind of abstraction." The important issue of continuity is touched on here. For John Locke, then, animals and mankind share certain features of cognition; but only man can form abstract ideas. This position was something of a compromise between the discontinuity of Descartes—according to which animals are reflex automata whereas humans can think—and the continuity proposed by Descartes' contemporary Gassendi, according to which no clear-cut boundary can be established. For Gassendi, and for those who followed him, a path of increasing perfection in reasoning could be traced up through the animal kingdom to man.[9]

Another major assumption concerns the relationships between different sensory systems. Locke and his followers argued strongly that the different senses must start off in isolation from each other. Indeed, this position is implied by the stance on "particular ideas" as in the last quotation. For

Locke, the relating together of "ideas" from one sense (e.g. vision) to another (e.g. touch) can only take place with prolonged experience. Therefore, a man born blind, and given sight, could not tell from sight alone that a cube was a cube and a sphere a sphere. His tactile knowledge of these objects could not immediately be accessed by vision: Experience of the two senses working together is a necessary prerequisite.

Locke took it for granted that objects are real, and that their "primary qualities" (such as solidity and extension) exist objectively and independently of the processes of perception. Objects are conceived of as the source, or the *cause*, of sensation. George Berkeley, who followed Locke's approach in certain respects (but that of the French Cartesians in others) put forward a more radical position.[10] For Berkeley, writing at the beginning of the 18th century, the different senses are distinct and could never become joined up. Each is a distinct language, bearing no relation to the others or to any objective "reality." There are no unitary objects, giving off coherent sensory information to the various sensory channels—this is mere delusion. Sensation, for Berkeley, is all there is; thus, what is *seen* is "no more than colours, with their variations and different proportions of light and shade." Berkeley emphasised the "perpetual mobility and fleetingness of those immediate objects of sight." Such views influenced later developmental thinking but in a distorted form. Berkeley's epistemological approach was put to one side, but the state of perception he had described was taken as a real condition: The original condition, to be outgrown by the developing individual. In a rejection of Berkeley's own claims, the "solipsistic" state he had described was taken as a *distortion* of reality. Berkeley's name thus became attached to a solipsistic kind of perception, in which the sensation itself is taken by the perceiver to be "all there is." Critically, this useage takes such a state to be erroneous and transitory, but a necessary initial stage in the acquisition of knowledge through experience.

Associationism, as originally described by John Locke, was extended by David Hume and David Hartley during the 18th century. Hume's version was more radical in its emphasis that discrete sense-impressions form the basis of all knowledge. The association of ideas is a process by which simple ideas, derived from sense-impressions, can be combined to yield complex ideas. The latter can always be re-analysed into the former. Causality, for example, consists solely of the relationship of *contiguity* between two simple ideas, labelled in retrospect as a "cause" and an "effect." This associationist stance has exerted very considerable influence on developmental thinking. Hume himself did not apply the approach in this context (although Hartley did[11]), but a related remark might be noted[12]: "The common defect of those systems, which philosophers have employ'd to account for the actions of the mind, is, that they suppose such a subtility and refinement of thought, as not only exceeds the capacity of mere animals, but even of children and the common people in our own species." Hume's comment is an early example of the type of analogy which, as we have seen, has played such an influential role in shaping developmental psychology. And it was not a casual remark, for the issue of continuity between man and the animals was, as we have seen, a vital one. Locke had agreed with Descartes that human cognition is qualitatively different from that of animals; but one result of Hume's more radical associationism was to dissolve that boundary. For Hume the mental operations of both animals and man were governed by the same laws, and so both must be fundamentally alike. Hume's influence, on this point among others, was considerable; having a real impact, for example, both on Erasmus Darwin and on Erasmus's grandson Charles.[13]

David Hume's sensationism—the reduction of all knowledge to sense-impressions—was applied to the issue of human development first by the Abbé de Condillac and subsequently by Rousseau. Condillac, Rousseau, and Hume were all close contemporaries, flourishing around the middle of the 18th century. As noted by one commentator,[14] Condillac "advanced the program of sensationalism beyond the limits that would have been tolerated by Lockean common sense . . . propos[ing] to account for all of our psychic powers by the consequences of sensation alone." Again, this claim was closely linked to the assumption of continuity and the "perfectibility" of animals, and the notion of animal "instincts" as originating in actual *habits*. Condillac also incorporated certain of Berkeley's claims, arguing that the natural and original state of human consciousness must be "Berkeleyan," with sensations themselves being treated as the whole of reality. By some means, each individual must work him- or herself out from this solipsism so as to encounter the external world of a body and a physical universe. Each newborn is a tiny George Berkeley who must somehow grow up into a John Locke.

Condillac's analysis of the growth of knowledge employed the model of a statue brought to life. Here he referred back to the Cartesian tradition, since Descartes had compared animals with automata, while rejecting Descartes' qualitative demarcation of human from animal reason. If the theoretical statue were to be endowed with senses it would not, argued Condillac, discover an external world: "sensations belong to the mind only; they can only be modifications of its substance." Thus, the mind "would discover neither that it has a body, nor that there were things outside it." The same process, for Condillac, must occur in the human infant: Passive sensation cannot yield knowledge of an external world, nor even of parts of its body *as parts of itself*.

For this differentiation to be acquired, *movement* is necessary and, specifically, the active touching of other objects. The sensation of solidity on touching another object is taken by Condillac to yield the knowledge that two objects are involved: Hence, that there are such things as other objects. The other senses cannot yield such externality; they are truly Berkeleyan. Thus, on the basis of active touch, the baby gradually discovers the external world of its own body and other objects. The sensationist tradition followed by Condillac, especially after Berkeley's contribution, saw the discovery of an external world as a major problematic for the developing individual. And since Condillac himself, the assumption has often been made that it is primarily through *touch* that such differentiation emerges.

Jean-Jacques Rousseau has had a much broader influence on developmental thinking than Condillac, but his genetic account of the construction of knowledge—his genetic epistemology— is substantially similar. Rousseau was at one time tutor to Condillac's nephews; he was also personally acquainted with Hume and much influenced by him. Rousseau's account of individual development is contained in *Emile, or on education*, published in 1762. In many respects, the book is more a critique of society than a developmental treatise. However, some clear developmental claims are contained in it, especially concerning the early years of life. Thus, for Rousseau, the child's first year involves only a few sensations (mainly of pleasure or pain): There is no consciousness, since the infant's brain is smooth and polished so that nothing may enter it. Following Condillac, Rousseau[15] speculated about a statue, a man-sized baby brought to life. Such a creature would be "a perfect imbecile"; he would: "perceive no object outside of himself, he would not even relate any object to the sense organ which made him perceive it . . . The contact of his hands would be in his brain; all his sensations would come together in a common point."

Thus the world of the baby is one of pure sensation. Subsequent progress involves the gradual acquisition of the "representative sensations which show [children] objects outside themselves." By this process objects "gain extension . . . move, so to speak, farther away from their eyes . . . take on dimensions and shapes." Neither memory nor imagination are yet active, so that attention is directed only to objects present to the senses. Active movement is required for the acquisition of the idea of extension, the knowledge that there are "things which are not us." When the child first reaches, he believes that all visible objects can be grasped: He can imagine no extension other than that involved in his own reaching. Thus, the same objects which he had seen "at first in his brain, then in his eyes, he now sees at the end of his arms".

Rousseau's account of early development is thus a radically associationist one. Sensation is primary, and a knowledge of objects must be constructed "from the bottom up." Or rather, from the inside out: The infant starts with the end point of sensation, gradually working back outwards to the world of physical objects. Even with considerable developmental advance, attention is still limited to current sensation. The child's "limited view cannot extend beyond the present." Childhood is "reason's sleep," working not with ideas but only with images, "absolute depictions of sensible objects." Rousseau's model of early cognition was systematic and coherent. With the exception of language which (with Descartes) Rousseau considered rather a special case, the picture was clear and straightforward. The direction of development was from concrete experience to the manipulation of ideas; from sensation to perception; from the here-and-now to a reality independent of oneself; from pictures to objects. To the extent that subsequent developmental psychology retained such assumptions, the heritage of Rousseau and the sensationist tradition has been great indeed.

As well as specific claims on early cognition, certain more general developmental claims were also made by Rousseau. He suggested that certain aspects of individual development correspond to stages in the progress of culture in the human race. This "cultural recapitulation" was to have a considerable influence on educational theory in the 19th and 20th centuries, the argument being that teaching should be devised in a way appropriate to the child's stage of culture or civilisation. In fact such a proposal had already been made by Condillac. For Rousseau, as for Condillac, this form of recapitulation had no precise evolutionary basis, although it was to receive apparent support from the subsequent development of ancestral recapitulation in the 19th century. It did, however, enable Rousseau to argue that childhood is qualitatively different from adulthood, with its own special forms of thinking. This claim was of great influence on those educators and developmentalists (especially in France and Switzerland) who saw themselves as following his lead. With respect to primary education, Rousseau's influence was transmitted through his follower Pestalozzi and through Froebel, and Maria Montessori, giving rise to a tradition placing emphasis on the child's direct sensory experience of the world.[16] The "child-centred" Pestalozzi-Froebel tradition also retained some adherence to Rousseau's cultural recapitulationism, arguing that the educational syllabus should be derived from the cultural history of "the race."

In Rousseau and in his followers, then, sensationism and associationism were already linked up with a version of recapitulation. The systematic synthesis of these traditions took place a century after Rousseau's death. As previously discussed, the recapitulation theories of such early developmentalists as Preyer were easily amalgamated with sensationism—especially with the help of the Lamarckian mechanism for heredity. By this time, in the late 19th century, associationist approaches to knowledge had themselves been developed further by James Mill and by John Stuart Mill. Such philosophical developments had become closely bound up with the emerging discipline of psychology.[17] Specific laws of association were now proposed, concerning such factors as the contiguity between different stimuli and the frequent repetition of a stimulus in relation to learning. Another important line of thinking was *positivism*, promoted in the early part of the 19th century by August Comte. This approach saw the discovery of lawful relationships among observed events ("positive knowledge") as the highest form of knowledge, to be found especially in the physical sciences. For Comte, "highest" also meant most advanced: Human society was seen as moving through successive stages, characterised by different forms of knowledge (the lower stages being first the theological and second the metaphysical). This progressivism owed much to the arguments of the French Enlightenment thinkers such as Condorcet. For Comte, the development of the individual child repeats the evolution of society to some extent. Thus cultural recapitulation once more emerged, now in collaboration with a philosophical outlook based on the physical sciences.

The same overall approach was brought into combination with evolution theory and associationist psychology by Herbert Spencer. In his hands, laws derived from associationist psychology were applied to evolutionary progress. Thus the effect of frequency of repetition of a sense-impression —taken to enhance learning in an individual—was applied to the repetition of experience across generations. An emphasis on such trans-generational effects of individual experience is of course central to the Lamarckian approach to evolution, and Spencer endorsed this approach wholeheartedly. Without giving direct attention to developmental issues as such, Spencer certainly accepted the basic principle of recapitulationary parallels. Thus[18]: "The intellectual traits of the uncivilized are traits recurring in the children of the civilized." Futhermore, Spencer's approach to education was firmly based on the notion of cultural recapitulation[19]: "The education of the child must accord both in mode and arrangement with the education of mankind as considered historically; or, in other words, the genesis of knowledge in the individual must follow the same course as the genesis of knowledge in the race."

The philosophical traditions discussed here represent only some of those which have exerted influence on the thinking of developmentalists. The influence of Kant has also been considerable, and the Idealism of Hegel has also had both direct and indirect influence. But these latter sources have operated at rather a high level of generality, in the main; their application to ontogenetic development has been somewhat imprecise.[20] The sources of influence discussed in this chapter—the essentially *empiricist* frameworks of sensationism and associationism—have, in contrast, made quite precise and explicit claims about early cognition. These claims have been accepted by many developmentalists. The child has thus been seen as a prisoner of the senses, as a prisoner whose developmental liberation must be achieved piecemeal. Empiricist assumptions on early cognition were applied with especial vigour to the first years of the child's life: It is to the various theoretical accounts of infancy that we now turn.

NOTES TO CHAPTER FIVE

[1]The close connections between philosophical-psychological traditions and the origins of evolutionary thinking have been thoroughly examined by Robert J. Richards (1979; 1982; 1987). As Richards has concluded (1982, p. 243): "Evolutionary ideas developed in response not only to . . . problems in zoology, but also to critical difficulties in the epistemological and psychological doctrines of sensationalism . . . [this demonstrates] the central importance of conceptions of intelligence, habit and instinct for the first formulations of evolutionary principles." The sensationalist-empiricist background to Darwin's thinking is noted by Vidal et al. (1983, p. 82).

[2]On the relationships between Locke's thinking and French intellectual traditions, see Wade (1971, p. 483). Hirst (1975, p. 183) has noted that Descartes is in many respects an empiricist (also cf. Hirst's discussion of sensationalism). Contrariwise, Locke himself is no longer regarded as a straightforward empiricist (Farr, 1987; Leahey, 1986).

[3]Cited in Loeb (1981, p. 153).

[4]Loc. cit.; emphasis added.

[5]Locke (1689/1964, p 93 [2.1.8]).

[6]Cited in Loeb (1981, p. 85).

[7]Locke (1689/1964, p. 97 [2.I.22]).

[8]Ibid., p. 130 [2.XI.11].

[9]On perfectibility, see Richards (1979, p. 91): "Sensationalism provided a conceptual framework for detecting an evolutionary continuity between man and animals." The implications of continuity were explored by many thinkers. Pierre-Jean Cabanis, approximate contemporary of Lamarck, noted that (cited in Richards, 1979, p. 97): "the brain, after a fashion, digests impressions and organically secretes thought." As Richards (1979, p. 94) notes, Cabanis was a direct influence on Lamarck, expecially in his emphasis on "an inherent tendency toward perfection" and on "habit as the means by which animals structurally accommodate[] themselves to the environment." "In [Darwin's] first formulations of evolutionary theory, the idea of perfection played much the same role as it had in the theories of Cabanis and Lamarck."

[10]On Berkeley, see Morgan (1977). It is conventional in histories of psychology to locate Berkeley firmly within a British empiricist tradition. As with Locke also, however, French (rationalist) sources must also be recognised—for example that of Descartes' follower Malebranche (McKim, 1987).

[11]Danziger (1985). Hartley's formulations on individual development are also discussed by Coveney (1957/1967, pp. 74–75) in the context of a discussion of the poetry of Wordsworth. Hartley's observations were first published in 1749, as a component of a thoroughly associationist philosophy of knowledge. For Hartley, much more straightforwardly than for Locke, the newborn infant is a blank slate [*tabula rasa*] on which life's experiences come to be written. For Hartley, infancy is a time of "absolute sensation." Further, Hartley was committed to what J. Wordsworth (1982, p. 428) describes as a "millenarian" version of the perfectibility thesis: A quasi-religious belief in "the ultimate happiness of all mankind." For J. Wordsworth, as well as for Coveney (op. cit., p. 38), Hartley's progressivism was very closely related to his associationism: Processes of learning through association being seen as the means to the progressive end. William Wordsworth's reference to Hartley is "close and

unmistakable" (Coveney, 1957/1967, p. 74), and the influence of Wordsworth's writings on 19th-century sensibilities concerning childhood was immense (op. cit., p. 68). One complicating factor is that certain of Wordsworth's writings were inspired by the children of his friend Samuel Taylor Coleridge; one of whom was called Hartley, and another Berkeley. It might also be noted that both Wordsworth and Coleridge were influenced, in content as well as in style, by Charles Darwin's grandfather Erasmus, who wrote in verse form on evolutionary topics (King-Hele, 1977, p. 267). Lamarck (1809/1914, p. 363) himself was committed to sensationalism: "Every idea of any kind originates either directly or indirectly from a sensation."

[12]Hume (1739/1969, p. 227).

[13]Richards (1979, p. 89).

[14]Ibid., p. 90. For a detailed account of Condillac's proposals see M. Morgan (1977). The supposed primacy of touch over vision in early experience is expressed in modern psychobiological terms by Gottlieb (1983, p. 20), who appears to be mistaken, however, in describing this claim as in opposition to that of John Locke (p. 21).

[15]Rousseau (1762/1979, p. 61). Also see Coveney (1957/1967) for a discussion of Rousseau's account of childhood and its influence.

[16]The tradition of sensationism/empiricism in early education is documented by Compayré (1887/1909, pp. 126, 133), who traces it back to Comenius in the 17th century. Compayré brings the account up to Froebel and Pestalozzi, and the Herbartians, all working in the 19th century. The tradition is continued this century by Montessori, among others (Kramer, 1976).

[17]For more detail on the formulations of the Mills, and on their influence, see Buxton's Chapter 4 in Buxton (1985); also, in general, Manicas (1987).

[18]Spencer (1895); cited in Gould (1977, p. 128).

[19]Spencer (1860/1896, p. 122).

[20]However, reference should be made to the accounts of Atkinson (1983); Russell (1978; 1987); and Wartofsky (1983), which all focus on the philosophical background to developmental psychology.

6 Infancy

INTRODUCTION

This is the first of three chapters which focus on specific segments of the lifespan. Here we are concerned with infancy, defined broadly as the period before combinatorial speech (that is, the first two years or so). Infancy has been of interest to developmentalists for a number of reasons. Not least, it has been assumed that the infant is less affected by her or his cultural environment than is the case with the child. For this reason, universal aspects of individual development may be taken to be especially well defined in infancy. A related assumption has been that the infant's state of cultural nakedness allows a more direct access to evolutionary ancestry. The infant is thus seen as trailing a phylogenetic inheritance.[1] This issue is perhaps most pertinent in the context of the newborn period, the topic of the first section.

The second section of the chapter discusses the infant's discovery, or construction, of a physical universe. The relationship of such developments to developments in the interpersonal sphere—the topic of the third section—has been of major theoretical significance. Most writers have argued for cognitive or intellectual primacy, an understanding of the physical world being treated as a prerequisite for social interaction. The final section discusses psychoanalytic accounts of infancy: That is, accounts derived directly or indirectly from the writings of Sigmund Freud. The claims of John Bowlby, who attempted to synthesise psychoanalytic formulations on infancy with ethological theory, are discussed in this context. Some of developmental psychology's most central questions have been posed in the context of infancy. With its biological significance, together with the associationist emphasis on the role of sensation in early development, infancy becomes a crucial arena for the central doctrines of developmental psychology.[2]

THE NEWBORN

This section discusses the most influential and authoritative accounts of the behaviour and competence of the newborn. Here, the newborn period will be taken as the first two weeks of extra-uterine life. It is often taken to be a truism that the newborn represents the "starting-point" of individual development. One impact of Darwin, however, was to emphasise the extent of the ancestral inheritance with which the newborn must be endowed, if only in the form of reflexes. The status of the newborn was thus in a sense reduced: The neonatal period was but one phase in a continuous developmental process stretching back into evolutionary history. Even if the status of developmental acquisitions was rather low, in comparison with ancestral legacies, a description of the newborn was generally considered essential as a baseline. Authoritative accounts were given by adherents of forms of recapitulation and Lamarckism, such as Wilhelm Preyer. Later workers retained many of the earlier assumptions; even those developmentalists, such as Piaget, who wished to place more emphasis on the role of learning and experience.

Because of this conservatism in developmental accounts of infancy, this section begins with a consideration of the contribution of Preyer. It should be noted, however, that detailed accounts of the behaviour of the newborn had been presented long before Preyer's. The earliest was the report of Dietrich Tiedemann in 1787, which included observations on co-ordinated eye movements in the newborn (the eyes moving "from the first as though they were in search of objects") and on learning within the first few weeks.[3] In general, Tiedemann's account was a sensationist one (here, and in other writings), sense-impressions being described as "not yet differentiated" by the newborn. The functioning of the senses was also the focus of attention for Adolf Kussmaul, whose account of newborn activity was published in 1859.

Preyer's own research with newborns involved a substantial number of subjects (where his reports on later development were largely based on his own children). He was also concerned to bring together the findings of the not inconsiderable literature on the newborn which had accumulated by the 1880s, now including Darwin's own observations. Preyer's account of the newborn is subdivided into two areas: the senses, and the will (that is, voluntary movement). For Preyer the newborn is capable of certain "single, distinct sensations" and thus can discriminate between the presence and absence of certain stimuli. In general, however, there is as yet no perception, no "idea of what has been perceived." Perception is ruled out on the basis of physiological evidence: The requisite brain centres are considered to be not yet functional. The physiological argument should not, however, conceal the fact that this developmental distinction between sensation and perception is fundamentally a philosophical one. The primacy of sensation is a central assumption of associationist epistemologies and Preyer's appeal to physiology (here and elsewhere) is an appeal for corroboration, not for independent arbitration. Preyer's account of vision in the newborn[4] is an orthodox one, in that tradition which can be traced back through Rousseau and Descartes: "A considerable time elapses before the child is capable of *interpreting* the coloured, light and dark, large and small, disappearing and reappearing mosaics . . ."

Preyer agrees with what he takes as the prevailing view, namely that the newborn sees "all objects as if painted on a flat surface". The baby[5]: "has as yet no conception of anything external, existing outside of his eye; at any rate, no suspicion of anything external, toward him; . . . the finger appears to him only as a dark patch in a bright field of vision, and does not project in relief from the surface of the picture." It should be noted that Preyer applies this picture—elsewhere referred to by him as "Berkeleyan"—to the newborn, although not to the three-month old. The critical assumption is that the *starting-point* of perceptual and cognitive development must be characterised by such a state.

The newborn's capacity for distinct vision is described by Preyer as severely limited. To a large extent, the infant "can not rightly separate his sense-impressions, especially those of sight." Preyer's more precise observations here should not be neglected. The following passage[6] should be quoted in full, since Preyer follows it immediately with a very careful disclaimer concerning the "quite erroneous results" which would follow from the acceptance of the observations at face value:

> I saw my child before the close of the first day of his life turn both eyes at the same time to the right, then to the left, frequently, hither and thither, his head being still; then, again, he would do it moving the head in accord . . . only five minutes after his birth, when I held him in the dusk toward the window, an associated movement of the eyes took place. And when I began to observe new-born children, it happened that I saw a child thirty-five minutes after birth . . . move his eyes only as an adult is accustomed to do, in accord.

Such co-ordination in eye movements must, for Preyer, be *accidental*. It is a testament to the power of the theoretical assumptions that such striking and personal observations could thus be overturned. Again, Preyer reports that the one-day-old infant can turn to fixate an object. But this is not true fixation, which involves an act of will: Will is not yet present. Rather it is a case of "desire in a primitive form." The object is not yet "a recognised cause of sensation." Such directed turning of the eyes, or of the head, simply results from the fact that the preferred position is associated with pleasure. This argument is theory-driven: That which appears to be voluntary simply cannot be.

With respect to hearing, Preyer states that the newborn is deaf, although only perhaps for a matter of hours. Thereafter, the infant[7]: "hears individual sounds indistinctly, then hears much indistinctly, and very gradually hears distinctly an individual sound out of the number of those indistinctly heard, finally hears much distinctly . . ." This sequence takes the infant beyond the newborn period. As noted for vision, the doctrine of increasing clarity of sensation arises as much from associationist thinking as from empirical evidence. With respect to the "will," Preyer defines volition in terms of the baby's erect balancing of the head. According to this criterion, for Preyer, voluntary movement does not appear during the first three months. Lateral movements of the head do not count in this respect. Thus Preyer is committed to the view that only involuntary movement is present in the newborn (and young infant). As he explains elsewhere, deliberate movement requires prior representation of that movement. This, in turn, requires that "he who acts must already have perceived very many movements of others and have felt very many movements of his own." A period in which movement is purely involuntary is therefore built into the theory. Further, will is taken to presuppose discrimination of the desirable from the undesirable and this, again, demands experience which the newborn does not yet have.

Against the background of these general claims, Preyer divides newborn movements into three kinds: impulsive, reflexive, and instinctive. Impulsive movements arise simply from the overflow or discharge of "accumulated motor impulses": Thus they are purposeless and not co-ordinated with any other movement. Impulsive movements are not a response to environmental events and hence cannot be adaptive. Whereas impulses are unco-ordinated, Preyer's conception of reflexes does allow for co-ordination. Reflexes are adaptive, involving (for example) the warding-off of unpleasant stimulation. In later infancy reflexes are to demonstrate acquisition through experience, with transfer and generalisation; thus for Preyer, as later for Piaget, reflexes are seen as vehicles for learning. In the newborn period, however, they remain "just" reflexes. Comparisons with the newborn of other species are frequent in Preyer's description and, in concluding the section on reflexes, he gives a reminder of the recapitulationary thinking which underlies his account[8]: "A thorough-going comparison of new-born chimpanzees and orangs with new-born negro children in regard to the reflexes would perhaps disclose no differences." The casual racism, so typical of the time, needs no comment. The third kind of infant movement, the instinctive, is for Preyer the least numerous. An example in the newborn is sucking. Unlike reflexes, instinctive movements do not simply respond to specific events; unlike the impulsive movements they are co-ordinated and adaptive. Essentially, instincts represent habits practised by evolutionary ancestors. The Lamarckist reasoning is explicit here. Preyer quotes with approval some remarks of the zoologist Spalding[9]: "The instinct of present generations is the product of accumulated experiences of past generations . . . Why should not [the] modifications of the substance of the brain . . . pass on from parents to their offspring just like any other physical peculiarity? Instinct is inherited memory." This last sentence neatly expresses the prevailing view of instinct in the latter half of the 19th century.[10] As Preyer makes clear, moreover, what is remembered is an association of ideas: "the inherited association of the sensuous recollection with the motor recollection." Preyer's account represents the clear application of Lamarckism and recapitulation in combination with associationism.

In terms of specific observations of instincts one again finds tendentious argument in Preyer. Thus the newborn's clasping of an adult's finger cannot be true (intentional) seizing. As with the instinctive mechanisms in general, "deliberate movements are simulated." What looks like seizing in the newborn must either be impulsive and nondirected or a reflexive clasp. In contrast, "[true] seizing presupposes the perception of an object desired and, in addition, a control of the muscles, both of which are wanting in the first days." Similarly, sucking is instinctive since it is adaptive (not an impulse) and requires a general disposition, not just a specific stimulus (not a reflex). Such instincts are inherited wholesale from evolutionary ancestry. Preyer's observations that initial sucking is imperfect, and that the newborn seems actively to search for the nipple (by head movements, with eyes open) are not seen as contradictory of his claim. Finally, some points should be made on expressive movements. Preyer detects smiling-like expressions in the newborn, in that the mouth is put "exactly into the form of smiling." As Preyer notes, we might "choose to call this a smile." Wrinkling of the forehead cannot yet be expressive since "the psychical states are as yet wanting." At the same time, the newborn's turning away of the head from the breast is accepted as expressive of a refusal to nurse.

Several such inconsistencies occur in Preyer. In connection with learning, for example, the association between the touch of the nipple and the taste of milk is recognised as being established during the newborn period. Still within the first two weeks, Preyer notes that crying is stilled initially by any suckable object but very soon comes to require the breast. The baby has already had "a useful experience." Thus Preyer's account is rich in observation but is highly interpreted in terms of his preferred theoretical stance. Subsequent workers seem to have had the choice of drawing one of two contrasting accounts of the newborn out of Preyer. One alternative was a newborn endowed with some hereditary instincts, many reflexes, and much unco-ordinated impulsive movement. Another was of a well-co-ordinated infant already learning from its own active experience. The unanimous decision seems to have been for the former.

Preyer's account was published in 1882. The next major version to be discussed is that of Piaget, published in the 1930s. Some comments should, however, be made on intervening accounts. A good early example is *The biography of a baby* published in 1900 by Millicent Shinn. Shinn gave general endorsement to the theory of recapitulation although she urged caution in its application.[11] With respect to the newborn, Shinn substantially supported the conclusions of Preyer, noting for example that newborn vision could discern no more than "blurs of light and dark" (and as yet "no colored blurs"). Thus the baby's turning of the head or eyes towards a person or to the light "must be regarded as entirely instinctive or reflex." A Lamarckian mechanism is proposed[12]: "the habit of looking towards any dark moving mass runs far back in animal history and may well have become fixed in the bodily mechanism." In general, there is "nothing that could give the baby any feeling of inner or outer, of space or locality." With Preyer, voluntary effort is strictly ruled out in this period. Apparent attempts to lift the head on the first day, as noted by another observer, are attributed by Shinn to a "drafting of surplus energy into the neck muscles" partly due to the pleasure at the improved visibility achieved by the posture. According to this model, nerve-energy is directed by pleasurable sensation, thus "deepening" certain channels. This associationist-hedonist approach is also applied to the development of vision. For Shinn, association is "that great law . . . by which the raw material of the senses [is] wrought up into an orderly mental life."

William Stern's *The psychology of early childhood* went through a number of editions following its initial publication in 1914. For Stern, all that could exist in the early days was "a dull, undefined foreshadowing of consciousness" in which sensorial and emotional elements are "inextricably intermingled." Movements must in general begin unco-ordinated, although for eye movements co-ordination could take place very quickly—"even at the very moment of birth." Stern found such early co-ordination puzzling: "Strange to say, we have not been able . . . to notice any unco-ordinated movements." At five days, Stern observed the visual following of a moving object and at nine days, turning of the head to fixate a bunch of keys visually. At this time he also observed the selective turning of the head in the direction of the breast (presumably guided by smell). None of these observations, however, were allowed to challenge the overall picture. As Stern noted, instinctive actions are puzzling since their complexity and adaptation to different circumstances appears similar to that manifested by conscious voluntary movement, "and yet any participation, whatsoever, of thought, will, decision, or any form of consciousness is out of the question." Little of substance changed in newborn accounts of the 1920s, such as those presented by Karl and Charlotte Bühler. For the latter,[13] impulsive movements predominate in the newborn: "individual separate movements of all the limbs of the body occurring, as they do, in motley confusion, in inimitable array, and in an unrepeatable succession." The state of the literature was essentially true to the Preyer tradition when the first of Piaget's three children was born in the late 1920s.

Piaget's account of the newborn forms part of a complex theory of infant and child development. In general, however, it succeeds in retaining the chief characteristics of the classical Preyer account. Piaget's first writing on infancy was *The first year of life of the child* (1927) which, however, contains no newborn material. This is to be found mainly in *The origin of intelligence in the child* (1936) in which observations on Laurent Piaget's first two weeks are presented. Some other comments, mainly of a more general nature, are to be found in *The construction of reality in the child* (1937) and in *Play, dreams and imitation in childhood* (1945). The layout of *The origin of intelligence* comprises a chapter for each of six stages in infancy. The first two chapters are headed respectively "the use of reflexes" and "the first acquired adaptations and the primary circular reaction." These two age-related formulations define development in the first few months, since the reflex is taken as the essential feature of the newborn, and the circular reaction (a term taken from Baldwin) as characterising the two- or three-month old. These two points are pre-established for Piaget. Thus features relating to the second (circular reaction) stage are automatically excluded from the newborn period. In Piaget's words[14]:

> It is self-evident that "circular reaction", in Baldwin's sense of the term, could not yet be involved, that is to say, the repetition of a behaviour pattern acquired or in the process of being acquired, and of behaviour directed by the object to which it tends. Here it is only a matter of reflex and not acquired movements, and of sensibility connected with the reflex itself and not with the external objective.

For Piaget, the newborn period is a time of reflex. Even the spontaneous impulsive movements of Preyer are de-emphasised in favour of reactive movements. However, it should be noted that Piaget distinguishes reflexes into a kind that is of psychological interest and a kind that is not. The latter includes sneezing and yawning, which are "unsubordinated to the need for use or experimental trial as a function of the environment." Use is an important issue here: thus[15] "the physiology of the organism furnishes a hereditary mechanism which is already completely organised and virtually adapted but has never functioned. Psychology begins with the use of this mechanism." Such "use" serves to strengthen the mechanism, not to change it. This strengthening is essentially a physiological process. Indeed, considerable appeal to physiology is made throughout Piaget's account. At the same time, it should not be forgotten that the role of use is a central one in the Lamarckian argument: It is use which initially enlarges an organ preparatory to any genetic transmission. Piaget appears to reject the doctrine of the inheritance of acquired character in his introduction to *The origin of intelligence*. However, in his account of newborn reflexes, he remarks that "in so far as the reflex is a hereditary mechanism it perhaps constitutes a racial utilisation of experience."

Piaget's own observations of newborn behaviour focus on sucking. For Piaget, sucking is a reflex, or an instinct (Piaget distinguishes these terms less precisely than did Preyer). However, Piaget does report several observations which seem to cast doubt on the reflex status of sucking. During the newborn period, Laurent searches for the nipple, and rejects substitutes offered in its place. Onset of search becomes earlier as the days go by (by day 12, as soon as the cheek touches the breast) and sucking movements are observed in the situation preparatory to feeding: Ostensibly an *anticipation* of feeding. All of these observations would appear to suggest that the newborn is changing his feeding behaviour as a result of experience.

For Piaget, however, none of these phenomena call for explanations involving learning. Instead[16]: "All these facts admit a physiological explanation which does not at all take us out of the realm of the reflex." The reflex, once in use, can "adapt itself . . . it is capable of gradual accommodation to external reality." Apparent recognition of the nipple—in rejecting substitutes—cannot be true recognition:[17] "Of course there could be no question . . . of the recognition of an 'object', for the obvious reason that there is nothing in the state of consciousness of a newborn child which could enable him to contrast an external universe with an internal universe." This assertion is clearly a priori. Further, recognition of the nipple[18] "does not involve recognition of a thing or of an image but rather the assimilation of one sensori-motor and postural complex to another." Thus the reflex, for Piaget, demonstrates all three basic intellectual functions: accommodatory change to environmental contingencies; the assimilation of a range of appropriate objects; and organisation, in that "the sequential uses of the reflex mechanism constitute organised totalities." These early behaviour patterns, for Piaget, "transcend pure physiology only to [a] very slight extent" and he adds, in parentheses, "to the point where it could seem almost metaphorical to characterise them as 'behaviour patterns' as we have done here."

Piaget is at great pains to rule out the possibility of true learning in the context of the apparent anticipation of feeding. He notes that Bühler's colleagues had made similar observations and had concluded that training was taking place. For Piaget, however, attempting to feed is itself an impulsive behaviour, but one which is usually suppressed in most situations (by crying, or by being carried). Preparations for the feeding situation merely release this impulsive behaviour. The tortuous nature of this argument illustrates the importance with which Piaget viewed the ruling-out of learning in the newborn.

Some more observations of newborn behaviour are discussed by Piaget in his account of Stage II. Thus the seeking of bright objects is attributed to reflex function[19]: "Light is an excitant (consequently a functional aliment) for visual activity, whence a tendency to preserve perception of light (assimilation) and a groping to rediscover it when it vanishes (accommodation)." Piaget makes no attempt to explain any fixation of gaze on dark objects such as persons. With respect to hearing, he notes that his own voice made Laurent cry from day four, and that the newborns in a clinic appeared to imitate the crying of others. Neither case may be taken at face value. For Piaget the relationships are accidental, or attributable (in the first case) to the newborn crying on being woken. His interpretation is cautious: "Let us therefore conclude nothing." Thus Piaget is resolute in insisting that newborn behaviour is essentially reflexive. Contrary observations are shown by Piaget to be in fact consistent with this interpretation. In doing so, of course, the notion of reflex becomes considerably extended, and Piaget's reflex is essentially a learning mechanism. But Piaget, it appears, wishes to retain the authority of the physiological concept of a reflex.

In concluding this account of Piaget's newborn formulations, some comments should be made on his more general views. Thus[20]: "the nursling's psychic activity is at first only simple assimilation of the external environment to the functioning of the organs." Similarly, the first months of life are characterised by "undifferentiated and chaotic assimilation and accommodation." Thus[21]: "at first the universe consists in mobile and plastic perceptual images centred about personal activity." For Piaget, the state of consciousness during the first weeks of life is "protoplasmic." Such a stance represents a simple continuation of the classical tradition of Preyer. Piaget's newborn is a most conservative one.

KNOWLEDGE OF THE WORLD

This section is concerned with the infant's relationship with the physical world. It focuses on some topics which have been of longstanding interest to developmentalists, such as the development of reaching and the retrieval of hidden objects. As with the newborn, the work of Preyer will be discussed first since it exerted considerable influence and was not radically criticised until recent times. For Preyer, the ways in which the infant finds out about the world are determined by the nature of the sensory apparatus. Most significantly, the different sensory channels start off independent of each other[22]: "At the beginning . . . the centres of sight, hearing, smell and taste in the brain are still imperfectly developed, each of these perceives for itself, the perceptions in the different departments of sense having as yet no connection at all with one another." Thus, for Preyer, development must involve the co-ordination of the separate "departments," as well as certain changes within the departments. The development of reaching exemplifies this process. For Preyer, quite simply, effective reaching requires that the senses of sight and touch become "united." But this can take place only after seizing itself has become voluntary, and this requires an apprenticeship of "many hundreds" of involuntary seizings. The voluntary, or intentional, requires time to emerge not because it is "maturational" in a simplistic way but because the relevant nerve-fibres have to be taught by experience first. For Preyer, intentional reaching emerges from a background of the involuntary seizing of objects touched accidentally, or placed on the palm by an adult.

More generally, willing or intention presuppose the "formation of ideas": But this process is not available during the first three months (so that the young infant is "will-less, like an animal without a brain"). Further, a period is required for the association of the idea of the desired object with the idea of the appropriate movement. Thus, as in the newborn, what appeared in week 12 "just as if the child had purposely seized the finger" *must* have been due to reflex instead. Within this associationist framework, Preyer's account of reaching emphasises the motor rather than the visual component. With respect to visual perception, Preyer insists that the situation is "Berkeleyan" at least for the newborn and young infant: Up till three months of age consciousness is "of colours only, not of objects." Objects are only seen as such after things touched have had time to become associated with the colours seen. Reaching itself is required to teach a knowledge of distance. Later (towards the end of the first year) the infant is observed to look after objects falling, or thrown to the floor. This achievement is seen as the culmination of the development since birth of the ability to track visual objects. In general, and fundamentally, Preyer's account emphasises that the infant's perceptual world attains an objective nature only gradually and laboriously. The perception of a world of objects, rather than "coloured, light and dark, large and small, disappearing and reappearing mosaics" is arrived at as the result of exercise and experience, most of it involuntary.

James Mark Baldwin published his first accounts of infant development a decade after Preyer. Several reports were published in the early 1890s and were gathered together, and expanded, in *Mental development in the child and the race* (1895). This book contains rather little experimental material —in marked contrast to Preyer's book—except for some studies on handedness and colour preference. But Baldwin's experimental method is noteworthy. He terms it the "dynamogenic method" and it is based on the claim that the infant is especially under the control of external stimulation. This suggestibility means that the child's movements represent a direct index of sensory discrimination and the attractiveness of external objects. Thus[23]: "the child's reactions are for a long time quite under the lead of its sensory life. It lives so fully in the immediate present and so closely in touch with its environment, that the influences which lead to movement can be detected with great regularity." It must be emphasised that this suggestibility is taken to relate both to the physical and to the social environment. Thus the child's reaching to a bottle (at around four months) is seen as the result of suggestion: It takes place, for Baldwin, as soon as the "clear visual presentation of objects" has been achieved. Baldwin emphasises that what is going on here is the direct suggestibility of movement, rather than the association of ideas as such ("as current atomistic doctrines of association would lead us to expect"). Despite Baldwin's rejection of associationism in this context—a rejection in line with his idealist sympathies—he retains the more general tenets of the sensationist view of infant development.

Baldwin saw early infancy as "totally organic." The newborn is limited by neurology, with an absence of associative connections between lower centres and the cortex. The first six weeks are dominated by physiology. There are as yet no ideas: Consciousness is only in the form of affective states, and even this only in connection with immediately given sensations. The major feature of the first six months is what Baldwin calls simple imitation. This refers to pure repetition of a movement, not the imitation of a model. For Baldwin it is the prototype for subsequent intellectual development, for the volitional, persistent "imitation" of a perceived goal—that is, for purposeful adaptation. It should be noted here that the concept of "simple imitation" in early infancy—fundamentally, "circular" behaviours—was taken into the literature in a way that most of Baldwin's account was not. Finally, it should be re-emphasised that persisent imitation (beginning at around 6–8 months) gave for Baldwin the first indication of intention in infant behaviour.

The approach of Preyer, rather than that of Baldwin, was followed in its major features by such turn-of-the-century writers as Millicent Shinn. For example, intentional reaching for an object was seen as requiring the "coalescence" of two distinct components (the "sight-motor" and the "touch-motor" series) "all welded together by voluntary movements, growing out of involuntary ones." For Shinn, the young infant probably does not see the world "as a world of THINGS—solid objects, visible and tangible." Her niece "had never blended the feel of a thing and the look of a thing into the perception of the thing itself." Not only the various sensations associated with an object, but also the various aspects of the one object (for example, as seen from different locations) needed to become associated together. Thus "to the baby each side of an object must have looked like an entirely new thing." Shinn's account thus remains solidly in the associationist tradition. Some interesting observations should perhaps be noted: For example, the nine-month-old playing peekaboo (peeping from behind a cloth); and pulling at a cloth in order to obtain an object placed on it. More generally, appeal is made in a rather ad hoc manner to the processes of recapitulation. Thus, for Shinn, babies must lose much normal activity as a result of wearing clothes since "they are retracing a stage of human history in which clothes had no part."

During the early decades of the present century, several new schools of psychology emerged to challenge the supremacy of the well-established methods of Wundt. One of these was the Gestalt movement led by Wertheimer, Koffka, and Köhler. Some developmental work was carried out by the Gestalt workers themselves, but the first attempt to incorporate this approach by a major developmentalist was that made by William Stern. Stern's *The psychology of early childhood* was first published in 1914. In it Stern[24] outlined what he saw as the error of associationist empiricism—the view that: "the child has . . . to receive all materials of experience from outside, to allow sense-impressions full play in his sense-organs, and to combine the originally isolated impressions with each other by association, thus creating complicated images, perceptions, ideas and thoughts." For Stern, this picture ignores the active role of the child and also the structured, holistic nature of perception and ideation. In both respects Stern, like the Gestalt workers themselves, was appealing to the philosophical tradition of Kant as an alternative to the formulations derived from empiricism and associationism.

For Stern, active choice must be recognised even in early development, such that "the young creature selects and retains separate elements from the original confused chaos of outer sensations." The elements gradually become perceptions[25]: "It is a long journey from the first stage, in which a sense-stimulus has an immediate effect . . . to the moment when a person, a thing, an objective happening is really experienced and 'perceived'." The departure from the Preyer tradition is clearly only partial. Certainly the emphasis on the child's own activity is relatively new; thus the child's perceptual image of "mother" or "rattle" is taken to include the representation of his own actions in relation to the object. But the fundamental role of sensation remains. Perceptual forms begin as "undefined and indistinct," requiring repeated experience for clarification. Similarly, initial impressions from different senses are non-differentiated[26]: "in the original perception-form of 'the mother's breast' impressions of smell, sight, touch and taste [are] united with sucking movements to form one indivisible whole."

As well as attempting to work out the implications of Gestalt theory for early development, Stern was especially interested in the development of the awareness of space in infancy. In line with the Kantian philosophical tradition, with its emphasis on the organised nature of perception and experience, it was the infant's *concept* of space with which Stern was concerned. For Stern, space is not just a visual phenomenon: Forms of space can be centred on the mouth or the hand, since mouthing or grasping are also spatial activities. However, and despite the theoretical shifts from Preyer, Stern's account of the development of reaching differs rather little. An early stage is involved in which associations are formed between vision and touch, with only the latter sense being capable of yielding three-dimensional information. The co-ordination is achieved by "continuous repetition of these double impressions." A subsequent stage involves the empirical experience of happening to put the hand to a point occupied by an object and this for Stern needs to happen in "innumerable cases." Thus "some time elapses before the fumbling, uncertain attempts develop into direct and certain movements of the hand towards the object seen." Like Preyer, also, Stern notes the interest of cases in which objects are visible but not tangible (as when the child attempts to grasp a mirror-image or a soap-bubble). With respect to the infant's understanding of objects, Stern shows more interest than Preyer in the infant's search for hidden objects. The earliest searching for one object hidden behind another is given as six months and by nine months the infant can overcome "by very practical efforts of his own, all hindrance to sight." Now, also, the infant throws objects out of his pram and looks over the side to see them again.

Both Karl and Charlotte Bühler published extensive accounts of infant development in the period following World War I. Karl Bühler was critical of Preyer as Stern had been, and endorsed Gestalt principles in somewhat the same way. In fact he had himself played a part in the emergence of alternatives to Wundtian psychology in Germany. Bühler was able to employ specific experimental techniques derived from the Gestalt movement. Wolfgang Köhler, one of the leaders of the movement, had studied the problem-solving capacities of chimpanzees using such techniques as placing fruit out of the animal's reach, but obtainable by some intelligent action. In Bühler's experiments, rusks were placed out of reach of the infant, either behind a glass plate or with a string attached. The infant succeeded in retrieving the rusk under these conditions towards the end of the first year. For Bühler,[27] this represented "technical thinking," the "realisation of mechanical connections and the invention of mechanical means for mechanical ends." He considered the analogy with Köhler's chimps to be sufficiently close for the appropriate period of human infancy to be designated by Bühler "the chimpanzee age." Charlotte Bühler became especially interested in the mental testing of infants and established a series of test items for each month of age. Looking for a lost toy was placed at 5 months; reaching around a glass plate, and removing a cloth over a toy, at 10 months. Pulling a toy by means of a string was placed at 10–11 months. Towards the end of infancy, at 18 months, a typical test included the switching around of two inverted boxes under one of which a cracker had been placed[28].

Such systematic variation on the hiding of objects was to be carried much further by Jean Piaget, whose first comments on infancy were made in 1927 in *The first year of life of the child*. Piaget's first child was two years old when the paper was given, and some observations are included. Piaget sets out to examine the implications for infancy of his theory of *egocentrism*—already established by him in the context of childhood. Childhood egocentrism, for Piaget, is a state in which cognition and perception are distorted by subjective features. The child's language, in particular, appears to be socialised but is really just private language "out loud." Piaget's concept of egocentrism was derived from the psychoanalytic concept of *autistic thought*.[29] This latter concept is used throughout the 1927 paper. Piaget argues that the equivalent of childhood egocentrism is infant *solipsism*: a state in which the subject treats the world as an extension of itself. For Piaget, "the baby experiences the universe as himself." Thus, and here agreeing with Baldwin, the baby "has no sense of self." Thinking in the infant "resembles a sort of perpetual waking dream, with all the characteristics of unadulterated autism." But for Piaget there is a paradox here. Alongside the assimilatory process involved in this "autism"—that is, the distortion of reality—there is also some degree of adaptation of movements to the outside world. There is accomodation as well as assimilation. For Piaget this "dualism" is central to the nature of infancy. Thus the infant's thinking is not directed, or intelligent; but at the same time it exhibits "something like an animal's practical intelligence." Piaget struggles to reconcile two inconsistent viewpoints on infancy, both of which predate his own research, and projects this theoretical struggle onto the empirical field itself.

The observations contained in the 1927 paper are mainly concerned with causality. Piaget notes that spatial or mechanical connection are not necessary for the infant to perceive causality; thus the baby will often just repeat her own movements in order to try to cause an object to restart its motion. Considerable appeal is made here to Baldwin's account of the "circular reaction." More generally it is emphasised that the young infant's universe consists of "pictures." Thus[30]: "The baby is submerged in a chaos of interesting impressions without there being any distinction between his internal states and things outside. He is limited to associating nonlocalised sensations of muscular effort and other actions with movements he sees in the universe around him." At least in his initial writing on infancy, then, Piaget remains rather close to the tradition of associationism.

Piaget's detailed account of reaching is given in *The origin of intelligence in the child* (1936) where it makes up part of the description of Stage II. Five steps are outlined, starting with the reflexive or impulsive reaching of the newborn. Next comes the stage in which movements are "prolonged" (a form of circular reaction) with some regard of the hands. In the third stage, grasping and sucking are co-ordinated so that objects grasped nonintentionally are carried to or retrieved from the mouth. Next, objects are grasped only when hand and object are seen simultaneously; and finally, the infant reaches for a visible object irrespective of the location of the hand. Piaget's emphasis throughout this account is on the role of *co-ordination*: The "schemes" of grasping, of sucking, and of looking start off in isolation from each other, and developmental progress is achieved by their coming to be linked together. Such formulations remain firmly within the Preyer tradition. Even where Piaget is more novel, as in the claim that object and hand must be simultaneously visible at a certain point, the picture remains an associationist one. The fortuitous co-appearance of hand and object is an association, a contiguity of sense-impressions.

Piaget's observations appear to be interpreted according to the constraints of theory. Thus when Laurent grasps Piaget's hand at three months this is not true reaching, but merely the "assimilation" of Piaget's hand to Laurent's own, setting off hand-clasping. Even the last stage of reaching does not, for Piaget, achieve intentionality, since it remains within Stage II (and intentionality comes in with Stage III). What is achieved by reaching, for Piaget, is objectification of the world: Objects have become more substantial since they have become simultaneously visible and graspable. Except, to some extent, for the role of the infant's own activity (as we saw in Stern), this formulation is really an application of classic associationism in the tradition of Preyer. Piaget's claim that his account represents an advance on the associationist formulation must be questioned.

Having looked briefly at Piaget's relatively self-contained account of reaching, an attempt will be made to give a critical summary of some of the major claims of the two infancy books. This will be highly selective; Piaget's is the most comprehensive and systematic account of infant development yet formulated. However, some basic claims and assumptions may be identified, and there are numerous points of continuity with the theories and findings of previous workers. It should also be emphasised that Piaget came to infancy research after extensive experimental work with older children and even more extensive theoretical work on the nature and development of knowledge. Piaget's account is formulated in terms of six stages running from birth to eighteen months or two years. *The origin* describes stage-related changes in what Piaget calls "formal" aspects of intelligence; *The construction* is concerned with changes in specific areas of competence such as the nature of objects, space, causality, and time.

The basic format of the stage account predated Piaget's own observations. Stage I is the use of reflexes, Stage II the formation of reflexes into early habits (with the "circular reactions" of Baldwin). Stage III follows the emergence of reaching and prepares for the onset of intentional behaviour at Stage IV. This criterion of intentionality is defined by Piaget, as for previous workers, in terms of goal-directedness and the use of means to achieve ends. Like previous thinkers, Piaget took the emergence of intentionality to represent the major transition point within infant development. Claparède, who had taught Piaget, had defined further developments in intentional behaviour through empirical to systematic forms. These two developments constitute Piaget's Stages V and VI respectively. As well as much of the stage-analysis as such, most of Piaget's tasks were applications or derivatives of tasks in the literature. The tenacity and ingenuity of Piaget's exploitation of these tasks was, however, wholly original. If Piaget had a genius, it was for experimentation.

Stage I has already been discussed, and Stage II is well represented by the development of reaching. During both stages, for Piaget, the infant is solipsistic; all that exists is what is currently perceived, and that is not seen as distinct from the self. A vanished object "is a mere image which re-enters the void as soon as it vanishes, and emerges from it for no objective reason." No true searching is yet possible, and looking towards the source of a sound does not count: "discovery of the visual picture announced by the sound is only the extension of the act of trying to see." The level of understanding of spatial relationships, and of causality, are explicated on the basis of this state of knowledge of objects. Because of the primitive state of object perception there can as yet be no conception of three-dimensional space. A moving object must be seen as a continually re-created image, with change of position not yet distinguished from change of state. With Stern, Piaget argues that specific and localised forms of space exist, centred on the mouth and on the eyes, co-ordination of which is the task of Stage III. Prior to this co-ordination, space is merely "practical": A direct but uncomprehending accommodation to external things. Perception by itself, for Piaget, cannot yield an understanding of space. Causality is primitive in Stage II because neither stable objects nor a unified space yet exist. There is merely "a diffuse feeling of efficacy" accompanying activity, a feeling which would "fill the little child's whole universe or rather would be localised in each familiar centre of perception." Objects, space, causality (and time) are bound up with personal activity.

Stage II is completed with the achievement of true reaching at around four months of age, and activities based on reaching and grasping dominate Stage III. This stage is described as being transitional between the purely repetitive and conservative activities of Stage II and the new combinations to be achieved in Stage IV. The (primary) circular reactions of Stage II were performed simply for their own sake; the "secondary" circular reactions of Stage III are performed for the sake of the result (but not yet *in order* to produce the result). The infant is trying at most to make interesting sights and events last. With the achievement of reaching, the world has become rather more solid[31]: "A visual objective, for example, is much nearer the actual [real] 'object' if it is simultaneously a thing to see, to hear and to touch than if it is only an image to contemplate." This is straightforward associationism, as we have seen.

In Stage III major advances have been made in the retrieval of objects. A partially concealed object can be retrieved, and the infant can search on the floor for a dropped object and return to the place where an object was left. But these are not yet true searches. The search merely extends accommodation, and the nature of the object is still bound up with the appropriate actions performed. There is no "substantial permanence." For Piaget[32]: "The child's universe is still only a totality of pictures emerging from nothingness at the moment of action, to return to nothingness at the moment when the action is finished." With respect to space, such activities as returning to an object's previous location demonstrate some progress. Piaget's description is in terms of a "group" (a complete, self-contained set) of movements or displacements. Here, as yet, the group is "subjective" in that it is centred on the infant's own activity. Space has not yet been objectified in terms of the *possibility* of such sets of movements. Because of these limitations in objects and space, causality remains at the level of efficacy.

Stage IV, occupying the final part of the first year, represents for Piaget the beginning of truly intelligent behaviour. Means and ends are now separate: An obstacle can be pushed away in order to reach an object. For Piaget, the advance in the understanding of objects does not relate specifically to visibility: It is not the fact that an object can now be completely hidden and still retrieved that is of most significance, but rather the fact that two distinct schemes of action must be brought together for retrieval. Here, an original observation of Piaget should be noted: The tendency of the Stage IV infant to search for an object where it had previously been found. For Piaget, this indicates that the permanence of objects, still incomplete, retains intimate connections with personal action. This error is related for Piaget to the fact that this stage is to some extent transitional between Stages III and V. Similarly, space here is transitional in that some interrelationships external to the self are comprehended (the infant can herself hide and find objects). Causality is likewise transitional, in that objects are allowed some autonomy (independence from the subject's own involvement in their movement) and spatial contact is beginning to play a part (an adult's hand is placed on an object to make it move). In general, however, "the universe and the activity itself still form a symbiosis or a global whole."

Stage V, starting from the beginning of the second year, manifests advances in objects, space and causality. Tasks relating to this stage come in the main from the Gestalt tradition of problem-solving in primates. Some, such as the rotating of a stick to get it through bars, go back to the work of Lloyd Morgan on animal intelligence towards the end of the nineteenth century. Many of these tasks had already been investigated in infants by the Bühlers and others. For example, a support or string is pulled in order to obtain an object, or a stick is used to retrieve a distant object. Much empirical trial-and-error ("groping") is described by Piaget and this is important since sudden solutions of similar problems will be the hallmark of Stage VI. For Piaget the infant is now "experimenting," attempting "to ferret out new phenomena." These behaviour patterns "constitute the highest forms of intellectual activity before the advent of systematic intelligence which implies deduction and representation." With respect to objects, permanence in Stage V is no longer restricted to single locations. Objects are independent of actions—clearly a theoretical rather than an observational conclusion. Invisibility can still cause problems: For example, if a change in location of an object is itself carried out non-visibly (the object being transferred, while out of sight, from inside a box to under a cloth). Spatial groups are now objective, with sequences of possible movements including personal activity but not being tied to it. New routes may be used to retrieve an object and the nature of containership is understood. But the comprehension of space is still limited to the perceptual field: Displacements outside of this, as with the object-concept task, are not taken account of. In parallel, causality has become objectified and spatialised. Thus Stage V represents the culmination of the practical, empirical form of infant intelligence and hence, in some respects, the culmination of infancy itself.

The transition to the final stage of infant intelligence, Stage VI, consists in a transformation of the *means* by which problem-solving takes place. Representation now emerges—defined, in the associationist/empiricist tradition, as "the evocation of absent objects." Now the behaviour of objects can be represented in advance and representational processes may even become overt. Thus Lucienne opens and shuts her mouth before opening up the slit of a matchbox to retrieve an object. Solutions are rapid and smoothly executed, a criterion taken directly from the Gestalt tradition. Complex series of non-visible displacements are held by Piaget to require representational processes. Detours in space, including ones involving the whole body (locomotion), can now be invented. Space is now a "motionless environment" within which the subject is located. Likewise, causality has been objectified: Causal sequences not directly given can be represented, and causes reconstructed from effects. The child has risen to a new level of comprehension of the world.

Some general comments should now be made. Piaget's formal account of the development of intelligence, presented in *The origins of intelligence*, focuses on the co-ordination of schemes. Primary schemes such as looking and grasping, themselves derived from reflexes, are co-ordinated in Stage III to yield secondary schemes. Secondary schemes, such as visually directed reaching, are co-ordinated in Stage IV. This account of developmental change is wholeheartedly associationist. Even though an emphasis on personal action also plays a part—an emphasis deriving from different philosophical sources—the overall framework is an associationist one. The state of consciousness attributed to the young infant, from which developmental progress proceeds, comprises a chaos of sensory images. At the start of infancy, then, the ruling epistemology is an empiricist-sensationist one. However, at the end of infancy, the epistemology has become essentially Kantian. The young child is now operating in a universe of real, objective, substantial objects, contained within a unified three-dimensional space and subject to strict causal laws. For Piaget, it appears, infant development involves a change in epistemologies: It is not surprising if theoretical difficulties emerge from such a stance.

Piaget's style of theory-building was a most conservative, assimilatory one. He preferred to incorporate rather than to confront earlier traditions. In the case of infancy, Piaget remained faithful to the associationism of mainstream child study. He was happy to agree that early awareness must be limited to sensations present to the senses. At the same time he wished to insist on the rich and complex nature of cognition in the two-year-old, a complexity which associationism could not comprehend. The fact that even Piaget could not cut himself off from associationist thinking is a testament to its power.

KNOWLEDGE OF PEOPLE AND KNOWLEDGE OF THE SELF

All theorists of infant development have recognised that social aspects of behaviour call for explanation just as much as cognitive or perceptual ones. Where developmentalists have primarily differed is on the issue of primacy: Does social development depend on cognitive development, or vice versa? This section discusses the various claims for the origins of sociability with other persons, including such issues as smiling and imitation, and claims concerning a social knowledge of the self. We should again look to Preyer for a classic account. The first true smiles in his son occurred at one month: What looked like smiles earlier could not be. The newborn could express satisfaction by lifting the corner of the mouth, and a sleeping ten-day-old "put his mouth exactly into the form of smiling" (and the same, awake, two days later). But these movements "lacked the consciousness that is required to complete the smile." Imitation, for a movement well established in the infant's repertoire, was first seen at three-and-a-half months: Imitation of a new movement was not observed until around one year of age. This issue of novelty also involves recapitulation, since movements never performed by ancestors "are never, under any circumstances, imitated correctly at the first attempt." Thus the experience of ancestors *prepares* the infant for imitation.

Comprehension of a self emerges, for Preyer, as the result of several processes. For the first three months at least, internal and external sensations are not distinguished. The child does not know that parts of its body belong to itself. For Preyer, sensory exploration of one's own body has to be painful (as in biting one's arm) in order to be effective in this respect: Hand-sucking is not sufficient. A second contributory process is the connection discerned between changes brought about in the external world and one's own movements. Thirdly, for Preyer, the sensory apparatus must gradually habituate to the body through constant exposure: Arms and legs no longer giving rise to separate, distinct ideas but beginning to conglomerate. A dim feeling of "I" would thus begin to emerge. This last, highly associationist process is explained further by Preyer elsewhere. All sense departments start off in isolation, with separate "I's." Thus:[33]

> Only by means of very frequent coincidences of unlike sense-impressions, in tasting-and-touching, seeing-and-feeling, seeing-and-hearing, seeing-and-smelling, tasting-and-smelling, hearing-and-touching, are the inter-central fibers developed and then first can the various representational centers, these "I"-makers, as it were, contribute, as in the case of the ordinary formation of concepts, to the formation of the corporate "I", which is quite abstract.

For Preyer, then, the "I" is never more than the organised totality of the egos of the separate departments of sense. This unification requires wakefulness and attentiveness, in the absence of which temporary disintegration occurs.

Those who followed Preyer, towards the end of the 19th century, although in general less systematic and comprehensive, altered little in his account. James Sully thought he detected "an attempt at a smile" on his son's third day but this *must* have been merely mechanical and not a true smile. Millicent Shinn noted possible smiles at around three weeks, but[34]: "being forewarned of the 'colic smile' which counterfeits so exactly the earliest true smiles,—fleeting as these are, just touching the mouth and vanishing —I . . . never dared to record the expression till it first occurred for unmistakeable pleasure." Some of Shinn's observations on the role of the mother's face should also perhaps be noted. Shinn[35] writes:

> Nature has provided an educational appliance almost ideally adapted to the child's sense condition, in the mother's face, hovering close above him, smiling, laughing, nodding, . . . in the thousand little meaningless caressing sounds . . . that proceed from it . . . the patting, cuddling, lifting, and all the ministrations that the baby feels while gazing at it, and associates with it, till finally they group together and round out into the idea of his mother as a whole.

Thus, for Shinn, it was the mother's face "which gave the baby her first idea, so far as I could detect." This terminology of "ideas" in Preyer and Shinn may seem quaint, but the substance of their claims is not dissimilar to that of claims made up till very recently.

A final quotation from Shinn will lead us to one of the major innovators in the area of sociability and selfhood, as well as providing a sidelight on his reception by his contemporaries. Shinn writes[36]: "Professor Baldwin has written a solid book, mainly to show from the development of babies and little children that all other people are part of each of us, and each of us is part of all other people, and so there is really no separate personality, but we are all one spirit, if we did but know it." James Mark Baldwin may not have recognised this resumé of his claims, but Shinn's remarks do at least indicate that his position was considered a radical one by his contemporaries. Even so, Baldwin's position on early smiling was orthodox. Thus, apparent smiles of the newborn towards himself and his wife probably represented "a purely reflex indication of agreeable organic sensation." On imitation, Baldwin's criterion was stringent (imitation had to be repeated several times), and he did not observe this until nine months.

Baldwin's theoretical position focused on the development of suggestion. For Baldwin, its first form is "physiological." For example, the one-month-old could be induced to sleep by being placed in a specific posture. Next, "sensori-motor suggestion" includes the elicitation of reaching by an object. Early "efforts" therefore—such as attempting to lift the head at two months, or attempting to raise oneself at four months—are for Baldwin simply sensorimotor suggestions, not involving intention. Preyer had been too bold, for Baldwin, in taking the first raising of the head (four months) as a sign of volition. It is, instead, simply "a matter of native inherited tendency." Of more importance, for Baldwin, is the role of suggestion in the infant's nascent awareness of persons. Such "personality-suggestion" involves the stimulus to activity received from other people. A perceived distinction of persons and things is of central importance here. First, the distinction is based on movement in association with pleasure and pain. Thus:[37] "It is movement that brings him his food, movement that regulates the stages of his bath, movement that dresses him comfortably, movement that sings to him and rocks him to sleep." Next, in the second half of the first year, the irregularity and unpredictability of the behaviour of persons is noticed. Persons are thus further distinguished from things, but still essentially on physical criteria.

A sense of agency, or of actuation attached to others, is now forming. This situation leads to the emergence of attempts to imitate persons. Apparent imitation before this is explained in other terms. Baldwin had observed his five-month-old crying at a picture of a crying man, but this was simply due to "the assimilation of new material to old schemes"—in this case to the memory of personal suffering. (An alternative explanation is also offered by Baldwin: That the sight of the outward expression of sadness directly suggests the same expression to the infant. The appropriate emotional state is then triggered.) At this early stage, the infant's knowledge of other people is of an observational or contemplative nature. In a sense it is a stage of objective knowledge, involving no reference to *selves*. Baldwin's term for this level of knowledge is the "projective" stage. Persons are distinguished from things in terms of what they do rather than what they are. Essentially, persons are still special kinds of objects. The next stage, commencing at around seven to nine months, arises from the infant's volitional imitation of other persons. The effort of imitation gives rise to the separation off of a primitive sense of self, focused on the experience of agency. In the earlier stage, agency was essentially a feature observed in others. Now, in what Baldwin terms the "subjective" stage, various attributes of persons acquired by observation of others in the projective stage come to be applied to a self. This acts as a nucleus for the assimilation of all other elements which differentiate the infant's own body from the outside.

During the subjective stage a self is gradually built up out of experience which is both personal and observational. Finally, towards the end of infancy, this subjectivity is applied back to those other persons whose attributes had previously been observed in a rather cold and objective manner. Other people become selves too, "other me's." Thus it is not until this last, "ejective" stage that other persons are known *as* persons. It is important to note that it is only at this third stage that the child acquires a relatively complete sense of its own self. Thus[38]: "The *ego* and the *alter* [other] are born together . . . both ego and alter are thus essentially social; each is a *socius*, and each is an imitative creation." In fact much development has still to occur, but the elements are now there and the ego and the alter "get purified and clarified together" by mutual interaction. For Baldwin it is the *process* of development that is social, not its starting point as such. Baldwin's intellectual sources for this stance included idealist philosophy in general and the ideas of his contemporary Josiah Royce in particular. The social nature and social origins of mind were emphasised by the idealist philosopher Hegel in the early part of the 19th century, and both Royce and Baldwin took part in a major revival of interest in Hegel at the end of the 19th century. Royce himself had made specific proposals about the social origins of mind in the development of the individual, as Baldwin acknowledges.

A discussion of the contribution of William Stern brings us back to a more empirical tradition, and one which has represented the mainstream in the history of developmental psychology. For Stern, the earliest form of imitation is self-imitation—that is, repetition of movements (and here Stern incorporates Baldwin's "circular reaction"). Imitation of a model is seen as an extension of self-imitation. Thus the earliest such imitation is of sounds which the infant has heard himself make but which are now presented by an adult. Imitation of movements in the repertoire, but never observed by the infant—such as facial expression—is a subsequent achievement. The baby's experience of self-observation is thus crucial. Finally, towards the end of the first year, imitation of truly novel movements emerges and such imitation may be either immediate ("direct") or delayed ("indirect").

Piaget's account of imitation follows Stern's closely. His major formulation is presented in *Play, dreams and imitation in childhood* (1945), which is concerned with the development of representation. Piaget makes strenuous efforts to show that his account of imitation is consistent with his six-stage scheme for infant development. Thus, in Stage I, apparent examples of imitation are explained away. Laurent's crying in chorus with other babies, or in response to Piaget's imitation of Laurent's *interrupted* crying, illustrates "merely the starting off of a reflex by an external stimulus." In Stage II, repetition of the infant's own movements or vocalisations takes place, essentially an example of circular reaction. Such repetitive imitation becomes more systematic in Stage III but imitation is still only of self-observed behaviour: Of actions one can see oneself performing. Imitation of behaviour *not* seen in oneself—such as tongue-protrusion—occurs for Piaget in Stage IV, towards the end of the first year, together with the imitation of novel stimuli. Both become systematised during Stage V and in Stage VI the emergence of representation enables imitation to be "deferred" or indirect, and to yield success immediately rather than by successive approximation.

Throughout Piaget's account, imitation is seen as an indicator of intellectual function rather than as a social activity per se. In general, for

Piaget, people are special kinds of objects, sometimes with special privileges. Thus[39]:

> Just as people doubtless constitute the first permanent objects, so also they are very probably the first objectified sources of causality because, through imitating someone else, the subject rapidly succeeds in attributing to his model's action an efficacy analogous to his own. Imitating someone else, as Baldwin has shown, is the source of both *alter* and *ego* . . . it represents one of the principal occasions for distinguishing between the external world and the self and consequently a factor in the substantiation and spatialisation of the world.

Although Piaget's account might indeed seem consistent with Baldwin's, it is important to stress that, for Piaget, the personal efficacy which the subject attributes to the model is itself personal in origin. Essentially, Piaget has adopted the second and third of Baldwin's stages—the subjective and the ejective—but, critically, has omitted the first "projective" stage. Piaget emphasises that personal efficacy is not a primitive, directly given function, but that it emerges from a diffuse awareness of causal relationships in which one finds oneself. Fundamentally, however—and in contrast to Baldwin—such efficacy is an intellectual, not a social construction. Developmentally, for Piaget, a general awareness of causality differentiates out into an awareness both of external causal relations and of an "internal" intentionality.

Piaget was taken to task on the issue of sociability by his Marxist contemporary, Henri Wallon. For Wallon, middle infancy is intensely social. Wallon was highly orthodox in his view of early infancy, viewing the first months of life as dominated by physiological needs and by reflexes. From four to six months onwards, however, the infant for Wallon is bound to adults in a kind of "affective symbiosis" dominated by the expression of emotion. During this period what looks like imitation is really "participation," a kind of fusion of oneself with another. Real, intentional imitation involves choice and spontaneity, indicated by delay (imitation in the absence of the model). For Wallon, this form does not fully emerge until the age of three years, when it plays a part in lifting the child from a practical, sensorimotor level to a symbolic level.[40]

Wallon's insistence on the primacy of social-communicative factors certainly differs radically from Piaget's position. To some extent, it relates more closely to Vygotsky's proposals about infancy. For Vygotsky, social communication of a low-level kind is a biological "given." Wallon's account focuses on the direct communicability of emotion, not of intellect; a kind of fusion with the group on an affective level. This approach relates quite closely to the classic assumption of greater "suggestibility" or weakness of will in the child, supported as we have seen by Baldwin. In some respects Wallon's approach converges with the formulations of psychoanalysis, in its concern with emotional factors in infancy. It is to a brief review of these that we now turn.

THE PSYCHOANALYTIC TRADITION

Psychoanalytic thinkers from Freud onwards have been interested in infancy, and yet their formulations do not fit neatly into either of the previous two sections. Their claims concern the infant's relations both with the physical and the social world. In some respects, neither aspect is treated as primary: Rather they are twin features of developmental change. Certainly it would be a mistake to treat Freud, for example, as being primarily concerned with interpersonal behaviour in the infant: In many respects his model is a very impersonal one.

Freud's early and fundamental position was that the first two years of life are dominated by "primary process" thinking, consisting mainly of hallucinatory wish-fulfilment. This account focuses on the satisfaction of instinctual needs. Subsequently, Freud began to develop more systematic accounts of stage-like changes in the localisation and expression of instinctual energy, culminating in a sequence of oral, anal, and phallic stages of early psychosexual development. Earlier versions of the developmental account, presented for example in the first (1905) edition of *Three essays on the theory of sexuality*, are simpler. Here, sexuality in the under two-year-old is described as autoerotic: Sexual types of pleasure are obtained by the infant through such activities as feeding. Sexuality is not directed at an outside object. The mother's breast is the nearest thing to an object known to the infant, but it is not treated as part of a person. It is only later, Freud notes, that "the child is able to form a total idea of a person to whom the organ that is giving him satisfaction belongs." Freud's infant, then, is dominated by the hedonic factors of pleasure and discomfort. In *The interpretation of dreams* Freud describes this account as a "fiction," a term which is clarified in a paper 11 years later. A state of *pure* primary process (in the infant) is not a possible state, *because* no evolutionary ancestor could have existed in this state: Primary-process thinking cannot lead to survival and reproduction. The theory of recapitulation thus plays a major role here. For Freud the "fiction" of pure primary process is justified on practical grounds, since[41]: "the infant—provided one includes with it the care it receives from its mother—does almost realise a psychical state of this kind. It probably hallucinates the fulfilment of its internal needs; it betrays its unpleasure . . . by the motor discharge of screaming and beating about with its arms and legs . . ."

When this state of primary process gives way to reality-testing, which involves acting on the world in order to change it, a number of consequences arise. In addition to pleasure and "unpleasure," sensory qualities can now also be comprehended. Attention now "meets the sense-impressions half way, instead of awaiting their appearance." The language here is broadly consistent with associationist thinking. Subsequent to the emergence of reality-testing, the pleasure principle is left in control of a restricted sphere—that of fantasy and of sexual activity. The latter, for Freud, "remains far longer under the dominance of the pleasure principle, from which in many people it is never able to withdraw." The general trend for the sexual instincts is reiterated: "from their original auto-erotism through various intermediate phases to object-love in the service of procreation." In the 1915 edition of *Three essays*, pregenital (pre-adult) sexual development is formulated into clear-cut stages for the first time. The first stage is oral or cannibalistic, the main activity being incorporation (of milk or food). For Freud, this incorporative activity represents the prototype of later identifications with people. The second pregenital stage is anal or sadistic, arising from the infant's gaining of control over the anal sphincter and from pleasurable sensations associated with this achievement. The sadistic element arises from the feeling of mastery. At the same time, external constraint is experienced since other people attempt to control one's excretory behaviour. Here Freud emphasises the recapitulationary parallel: In embryogenesis, according to Freud, the anus is derived from the mouth. These two stages occupy approximately the first two years of life, during which no true object-choice has taken place (sexuality remains focused on bodily activities, not external objects). The first true object is the phallus, which Freud takes to be the focus of attention for the three- to five-year-old child of either sex.

Significant although highly theoretical changes were introduced by Freud in a paper on instincts in 1915. These changes concerned Freud's picture of the initial state of consciousness of the infant. What he did was to introduce an initial reality-state before the pleasure-state which he had previously taken as the starting-point. Thus[42]: "The antithesis ego—non-ego (external), i.e. subject-object, is . . . thrust upon the individual organism at an early stage, by the experience that it can silence *external* stimuli by means of muscular action but is defenceless against *instinctual* stimuli. This antithesis remains, above all, sovereign in our intellectual activity . . ." The distinction of self from the world is thus a very early achievement, and the very young infant is in a reality state rather than a pleasure state governed by hallucination. The emergence of the pleasure state itself now calls for explanation. For Freud, it results from the caretaking activities of adults. Ministering to the baby's needs allows the continuation of delusions of hallucinatory wish-fulfillment since, indeed, the baby does not actually have to take action itself. This new pleasure state now also involves the "introjection" into the self of pleasurable aspects of the world and the "projection" into the world of unpleasurable aspects of the self. For Freud these processes are intimately related to the origins of love and hate. Throughout the developmental sequence then, from this point in Freud's theorising, there was posited a primitive distinction of self from the world.

One process which grew considerably in theoretical significance for Freud was *identification*. As noted, this had first been seen as a kind of generalisation of oral-cannibalistic activity. As such it had been given a recapitulationary basis in *Totem and taboo* (1912/13), in which the devouring of the primeval father by his sons had been described as identification. The process of identification assumed a central role in *The ego and the id* (1923). Now, identification was treated as a primary function[43]: "it is a direct and immediate identification and takes place earlier than any object-cathexis." This "first and most important identification" is with the parents. It is not specifically with either mother or father, since the child does not yet, for Freud, distinguish them in such terms. The effects of this first identification are described as being "general and lasting." This position probably represents Freud's most extensive theoretical recognition of the importance of other persons to the infant.

In many ways the publication of *The ego and the id* in 1923 was a turning-point for the theory of psychoanalysis and for the thinking of Freud's followers. The theory of conscious and subconscious processes was now formulated in topographical terms, with a quasi-spatial model of the mind consisting principally of ego and id. Ego (Freud's *das Ich*, the "I") represents the interface between the id (*das Es*, the "it") and the outside world. The id is the store of instinctual impulses. Developmentally, id is primary[44]: "at the very beginning . . . the ego is still in process of formation or is still feeble." The id, and hence the pleasure principle, dominate early life. Freud's emphasis on the ego was quite new, but this applied to much later aspects of development. The general picture of infancy had not changed.

Some brief comments should now be made on Freud's influence, especially on his followers, in the context of infancy theory. It might first be noted that Piaget's paper of 1927 in which infant thought was described as "one long, completely autistic waking dream" was, if not up-to-date on Freudian theory, at least broadly consistent with it. Freud's direct psychoanalytic followers extended and challenged Freud's infancy account in various ways from the 1920s onwards. His own account had been almost completely free of empirical observation of any kind, the actual analysis of (school-age) children being pioneered by Freud's daughter Anna. The emphasis was coming to be on the functions of the ego, with coping mechanisms, rather than exclusively on the unconscious processes of the id. In line with this emphasis, but extending it in ways unacceptable to Freud, the analysis of preschool children was carried out in the 1920s by Melanie Klein.[45] After leaving Germany, Klein became the most influential child analyst operating in Britain up till the arrival of father and daughter Freud shortly before World War II. For Klein, the young infant learns that the mother's breast can be a "bad" object (when dry) as well as a good object. Hence the infant learns that good and bad can coexist in one and the same object. Despite this focus on the breast, the account was quite impersonal, as Freud's had been. A sequence of positions or phases was identified, resulting from such processes as the projection of "bad" parts of the self. Klein's analyses recovered the same kind of material from the very young child as Freud's did from the five- or six-year-old: Material relating to Oedipal conflicts and to superego functions. Such findings on the precocity of psychic development pose a major challenge to Freud's own account. More generally, it should be noted that Klein's formulation attributes considerably greater cognitive sophistication to the infant than Freud's had done.

Another strong influence on postwar British psychoanalysis was Ian Suttie, for whom a relationship with the mother is at the heart of individual development. Play, competition, and cultural interests were for Suttie later substitutes for the "mutually caressing relationship" of the "primal attachment-to-mother." Such emphasis on personal and not primarily sexual relationships was opposed to Freudian theory, although less so to later than to earlier accounts. The emphasis on interpersonal processes had become widespread in psychoanalytic circles in the 1930s, especially among a group sufficiently divergent to be labelled as "Neo-Freudians". This group included Karen Horney and Erich Fromm from Germany and Harry Stack Sullivan from the U.S.A. Of the three, Sullivan was most concerned with infancy. Influenced to some extent by the thinking of George Herbert Mead, his emphasis was on the social origins of adult personality. Following the first few months, a period dominated by physiological functions, infancy was dominated for Sullivan by an emotional empathy with caretakers, an "emotional contagion or communion." By this means, for Sullivan, the infant becomes aware of the mother's emotional states through sharing them. The similarity of this empathy position with that of Baldwin on suggestion, and that of Wallon on imitation, should not be overlooked.

Something should also be said on the early thinking of a psychoanalyst who is currently of considerable influence, Jacques Lacan.[46] Lacan has attempted to synthesise Freudian thinking with structuralist accounts of language. In his formulation, the unconscious is treated as a language. In his original writings on infancy, Lacan's major emphasis is on the "mirror stage"—a period apparently lasting from around 6 months to 18 months.

In this stage, the immature and motorically incompetent baby sees itself in a mirror, and takes the image as a more mature and competent self with which to identify. Lacan refers to Baldwin in this context, and also to the work of Köhler on problem-solving in chimpanzees: In which regard he notes that the infant "is for a time, however short, outdone by the chimpanzee in instrumental intelligence." Even in esoteric psychoanalysis, then, the human infant is compared to the adult animal and the spectre of recapitulation is thus encountered.

Perhaps the most influential of psychoanalytic versions of infancy has been that of John Bowlby. In terms of social policy (particularly regarding childcare), Bowlby's influence was very considerable in the decades following World War II.[47] With respect to theory, Bowlby's innovation was the attempt to incorporate the ethology of Konrad Lorenz into the Freudian account of infant development. The points of convergence seemed considerable to Bowlby: Both Freud and the ethologists were concerned with innate, instinctual behaviour, with fixed patterns of action, including action related to parent-infant relationships. Both were concerned with sensitive periods in early development, periods during which certain kinds of learning must take place for normal development to proceed.

Bowlby therefore formulated an account of infant development in the terms favoured by ethology, an account focusing on fixed signal systems by which early development was guided and directed. The attachment of the infant to its parent became the central theme, with attachment being defined in terms of behaviour directed at maintaining proximity with the adult.[48] Models and formulations from the study of nonhuman animals were used freely. The various biological components of Freudian theory were thus overlaid with a more explicit layer of biological interpretation. This new biology was derivative of that of Lorenz himself, and Darwinian claims have played a minor role in the development of Lorenz's own biology.[49] The kind of evolutionary argument that Bowlby found in Lorenz, and which he applied to human infancy, tended to focus on the presumed adaptiveness of certain kinds of signal or action. Thus, for Bowlby, smiling in infancy is claimed to be so strong a signal that babies who smile more should in general benefit from a higher survival rate.

Attachment behaviour is, in general, taken to have such a strong connection with survival that its universality can only be explained by evolutionary selection. In spite of the substantial discrediting of many of Bowlby's more specific claims—especially concerning the dire effects of maternal separation—the more general emphasis on biology remains widely endorsed. Moreover, a vigorous programme of experimental research became established in which an infant's strength of attachment is measured in a standardised setting.[50] The methodological sophistication of this programme, and its success in the production of data, has enabled the biological presuppositions of the definition of attachment to go "underground."

The theoretical positions discussed in this chapter—many of them legacies from the 19th century or earlier—remain influential in developmental psychology if only in a covert manner. In some areas of research—newborn competence being the best example—very substantial revisions have been made to the classic positions; and yet such revisions have tended to be piecemeal. Extensive empirical research, beginning in the 1960s, gave rise to major re-evaluations of the capacities of the newborn but such "competence" was accepted most readily when it related to the functioning of specific sensory or perceptual systems. Suggestions that competence might stretch to co-ordination between the senses, or between the senses and voluntary movement—as proposed by such pioneers as T.G.R. Bower—were resisted. Similarly, a revival of interest in early social interaction tended to reinstate such biological notions as the natural, adaptive harmony of communication between mother and baby.[51] The technical sophistication of micro-analysis of videotaped interaction has allowed much more finely grained description of such situations, but it has not encouraged the scrutiny of underlying assumptions and definitions. The success of data-generating procedures such as these—and in such terms, infancy research has been a major success story of recent developmental psychology—has seemed to overwhelm the more fundamental issues. In general, the classic formulations on infancy are straightforwardly biological ones. This biology is not, by and large, Darwinian. And formulations on infancy have exerted a major influence much further into the lifespan: In developmental psychology, the baby is very much the father to the man.

NOTES TO CHAPTER SIX

[1]Wordsworth: "Our birth is but a sleep and a forgetting:/ The soul that rises with us, our life's star,/ Hath had elsewhere its setting/ And cometh from afar:/ Not in entire forgetfulness/ And not in utter nakedness,/ But trailing clouds of glory do we come/ From God who is our home./Heaven lies about us in our infancy; . . ." (The "Intimations Ode"). As emphasised by Coveney (1957/1967, pp. 75, 77), Wordsworth's account of infancy here is at odds with his general commitment to Hartleian associationism and the *tabula rasa* (see footnote 11 to Chapter Five). Wordsworth here made deliberate use of a Platonic formulation (of pre-existence) for poetic purposes. Wordsworth's Ode became (Coveney, 1957/1967, p. 80) "one of the central references for the whole 19th century in its attitude to the child." The context for such early-19th-century formulations, and their impact on subsequent thinking, is discussed in Bradley's forthcoming *Visions of infancy* (Cambridge: Polity Press).

[2]Indicative sources for recent investigations of infancy are Bower (1982); Bullowa (1979); and Butterworth (1987).

[3]Tiedemann (1787/1927); more details may be found in the chapter by Jaeger in Eckardt, Bringmann, and Sprung (1985, p. 70). Lamarck himself makes a comment on newborn functioning (1809/1914, p. 364) in his discussion of the principle of the sensory origin of

knowledge. The child is described as trying to suck, and seeming to look for the breast, "a few minutes after birth." For Lamarck, the explanation follows from a recognition of the inheritance of acquired characters. The newborn is acting "in the direction of an acquired propensity without any previous experience . . . by a transmitted propensity evoked by its inner feeling." The work of Kussmaul is discussed by Bringmann et al. in Eckardt et al. (1985); and that of Preyer, throughout the same book.

[4]Preyer (1882/1914, p. 61); emphasis in original.

[5]Ibid., pp. 60–61.

[6]Ibid., p. 35.

[7]Ibid., p. 96.

[8]Ibid., pp. 233–234.

[9]Ibid., p. 238.

[10]The instinct-as-memory formulation, including the version of William Butler, is discussed by Gould (1977).

[11]Numerous examples may be found of recapitulation-based accounts of the newborn at around this time. W. Drummond (1908, p. 53) describes many of the same characteristics as Romanes had done (Chapter Two, footnote 22): Kirkpatrick endorses the recapitulationary explanation for finger- and toe-clasping and notes (1903/1922, p. 103) that: "the tendency to bring the hands to the mouth, so prominent almost from the first, may be the result . . . of an instinct which was useful in the earlier history of the race."

[12]Shinn (1900, p. 42).

[13]C. Bühler (1927/1930).

[14]Piaget (1936/1977, p. 46).

[15]Ibid., p. 53.

[16]Ibid., p. 44.

[17]Ibid., p. 49.

[18]Ibid., p. 54.

[19]Ibid., p. 78.

[20]Piaget (1937-1971, p. 247).

[21]Ibid., p. 396.

[22]Preyer (1882/1892, p. 205).

[23]Baldwin (1895/1903, p. 45).

[24]Stern (1914/1923, p. 101).

[25]Ibid., p. 106.

[26]Ibid., p. 107.

[27]K. Bühler (1919/1930).

[28]C. Bühler and H. Hetzer (1935). This "switching" task was later introduced into neo-Piagetian research in infancy (see Bower, 1982, p. 200). Such research has more generally focused on Piaget's "Stage IV" (perseverative search) error, perhaps because it fits closely with established methods in comparative psychology. One common claim has been that eight-month-olds do not seem to make the Piagetian perseverative error nearly so much as Piaget predicted. One reason may be that such subjects are too old, and that six to seven months would be a more appropriate age. Some promising experiments of my own on a seven-month-old of my acquaintance were unfortunately interrupted by an earthquake.

[29]Piaget's derivation of egocentrism from autism is discussed at the beginning of Chapter Seven. It is difficult to respect chronology here, since Piaget's detailed study of infancy post-dated his foundational work with young children.

[30]Piaget (1927b/1977, p. 207).

[31]Piaget (1936/1977, p. 197).

[32]Piaget (1937/1971, pp. 46–47).

[33]Preyer (1882/1892, p. 205).

[34]Shinn (1900, pp. 62–63).
[35]Ibid., p. 76.
[36]Ibid., p. 77.
[37]Baldwin (1895/1903, p. 121). Also see Danziger (1985).
[38]Ibid., p. 321; emphasis in original.
[39]Piaget (1937/1971, p. 360).
[40]On Wallon, see Voyat and Birns (1973).
[41]Freud (1911; S.E. XII, p. 220).
[42]Freud (1915; S.E. XIV, p. 134); emphasis in original.
[43]Freud (1923; S.E. XIX, p. 31).
[44]Ibid., p. 46.

[45]Post-Freudian viewpoints on infancy—with especial reference to mother-child relationships—are summarised by Bowlby (1969/1971, Appendix). On Melanie Klein also see the interview with Segal in J. Miller (1983). A recent extension of the psychoanalytic theory of infancy is the work of M. Mahler (Mahler, Pine, & Bergman, 1975); also Bettelheim (1967). It should be noted that Bettelheim's discussion of convergences between Piaget's infancy theory and that of psychoanalysis nowhere mentions the direct connections between them.

[46]For a contemporary view on Lacan, see Urwin's chapter in Henriques, Hollway, Urwin, Venn, and Walkerdine (1984). The chronology of Lacan's "mirror stage" paper is somewhat problematic (Gallop, 1985, p. 74). It appears that the paper was written in 1949 but retrospectively dated 1936 for rhetorical purposes.

[47]Bowlby's work and its practical influence are discussed by Riley (1983).

[48]Bowlby saw his approach as a revision of that of Sigmund Freud; where Freud had taken attachment to be a secondary or derivative phenomenon Bowlby (and the object-relations school in general) treated attachment as a primary drive or instinct (Bowlby, 1969/1971, Appendix). Bowlby seeks evidence that Freud himself may have been moving in this direction in his last years. His supportive quotation from Freud is a claim for the over-riding of "personal accidental experience" by phylogenetic ancestry (p. 428). It should be noted that Anna Freud (1969) considered Bowlby to have misunderstood her father's theoretical position (and hence her own), to have made misleading comparisons between the Bowlby and the Freud views, and to have proposed an over-simplistic account of early attachment. From a very different perspective, a corroborative judgment on Freud's writings is made by Marcuse (1955, Epilogue). For Marcuse, Freud had put forward an uncompromisingly impersonal theory of early development (op. cit., p. 231) ("the decisive relations are thus those which are the *least* interpersonal"). The "revisionists"—Fromm, Horney, Sullivan—are accused of emasculating the theory by rendering it into an interpersonal account.

[49]See Chapter Ten, footnotes 3–6 and text.

[50]A major contributor to the experimental investigation of infant attachment, Mary Ainsworth, worked alongside Bowlby at London's Tavistock Clinic in the early 1950s.

[51]See Harris, *The rationalisation of infancy* in Broughton (1987).

7 Childhood

INTRODUCTION

This chapter discusses theoretical assumptions which have been central to accounts of middle childhood—that is, the period following infancy and prior to adolescence. Early sections discuss the emergence and early development of language, the relationships between language and thinking, and the nature of reasoning in childhood. Next, the interrelated areas of drawing and of spatial cognition are discussed. Finally, some accounts of social and moral development in childhood are considered: In particular, the accounts of Freud and of Piaget which focus on the child's relationship to the society of adults.

The range of issues discussed is very wide, but some formulations are common to many of the accounts. In particular, the notion of "primitive thought" has exerted considerable influence on concepts of childhood. Much of the empirical investigation of the nature of children's cognition—the work of Piaget, for example—has started off with the assumption that similarities are to be anticipated between the thought of children and that of "primitives". As we have seen, this assumption is derived from recapitulationary logic. To a large extent, this derivation becomes concealed in the detailed accounts offered by Piaget and his contemporaries. The influence of this doctrine is not, however, lessened by its low profile.

The single most influential account of child thought has been that of Piaget. One of Piaget's central claims is that the young child should be thought of as "egocentric": A formulation first applied by Piaget to language-use and social cognition, and subsequently to spatial representation. The concept of egocentrism, which served in some respects as Piaget's equivalent of "primitive thought," was derived by him from psychoanalytic writings. These accounts, in turn, were firmly based on biological doctrines. Therefore, before turning to accounts of the nature and functions of early language—a topic which involves direct continuity with the material from the last chapter—it is important to clarify the origins of Piaget's concept of egocentrism.

FROM AUTISM TO EGOCENTRISM

At the beginning of the present century there was broad agreement on certain aspects of child thought. It was seen as reflecting, in the main, the operation of nonconscious processes: Its nature was contrasted sharply with the conscious, rational thought of the adult. In the years just before World War I, several precise formulations of these "two kinds of thinking" were presented. They derived in part from Freud's formulation of primary and secondary processes of thought and were, likewise, concerned only rather incidentally with ontogenetic development. Their major concern was psychopathology. One formulation, however—that of Eugen Bleuler—did give some consideration to developmental implications. Bleuler's account together with some aspects of Jung's, served as the starting-off point for Piaget's theory of childhood egocentrism. A third version was Freud's own updated account of the two kinds of thinking, published as *Two principles of mental functioning* in 1911.

Eugen Bleuler (1857–1939), an almost exact contemporary of Freud, was director of the Burghölzli psychiatric hospital in Zürich. His major interest was in the severe thought-impairment characteristic of the condition then known as "dementia praecox." Bleuler renamed the condition "schizophrenia" and offered a detailed and sensitive account of its symptoms. Chief among these was what Bleuler called "autism": A detachment from reality in which the schizophrenics live (in Bleuler's words) "in a world of their own." Autistic thinking, for Bleuler, obeys its own laws, being characterised by the use of symbols and analogies, fragmentary concepts, and accidental connections. The autistic world is real for the patient, who is therefore subject to delusions and hallucinations. In general there is a "loss of the sense of reality." For Bleuler, autistic thinking competes in the schizophrenic with "realistic" thinking. Moreover, some degree of autistic thinking is present—but under control—in the normal person. Autistic thinking makes a contribution to poetry, myth, and fantasy. Further, a considerable degree of autistic thinking was seen as normal for a young child. Thus a child pretending that a thermometer is a boat "ignores reality in a high degree, he only uses just so much of it as is necessary for the part he is playing."[1] The implication was that the autistic-realistic model is a developmental one, with the former giving way to the latter in the development of the normal person. In the child, fantasy and reality might not always be differentiated: A characteristic on which the child, for Bleuler, was like the "savage."

One of Bleuler's appointments at the Burghölzli was, in 1900, the 25-year-old Carl Gustav Jung. Jung undoubtedly contributed to the theoretical development of the concept of autistic thinking, although he was later to describe Bleuler's formulation as "shallow." A major early responsibility of Jung's was the experimental investigation of thought patterns in the patient population. Here he employed the available methods of experimental psychology, especially the technique of word-association. Types of response were categorised under a number of headings, one of which was "egocentricity." This label implied that the association seemed excessively subjective and personal. For each patient, or for each type of patient, the percentage of responses falling in each category was recorded. But Jung's experimental work increasingly gave way to clinical investigation and theoretical speculation on the underlying causes of the symptoms he observed. He first adopted, and then rejected, Freud's formulations on unconscious motivation, the final break being signalled by Jung's publication of *Symbols of transformation* in 1912. This book, a wide-ranging account of symbolism and nonconscious processes, included his formulation of what he termed the "two kinds of thinking."

Jung's two kinds were first, "archaic" and second, directed or reality-thinking. The term archaic emphasised for Jung—as against "autistic"—the nonpathological nature of such primitive thought. It also highlighted the ancestral nature of this kind of thinking, for Jung was committed both to recapitulation theory and to the Lamarckist account of heredity (as exemplified in Jung's concept of the "collective unconscious" or race memory). For Jung[2]: "All through our lives we possess, side by side with our newly acquired directed and adapted thinking, a fantasy-thinking which corresponds to the antique state of mind." Jung's account brought in material on myth, ritual, and religion, as well as on psychopathology, to demonstrate the universality of archaic thinking. Jung's own summary[3] of the two kinds should be quoted:

> We have, therefore, two kinds of thinking: directed thinking, and dreaming or fantasy-thinking. The former operates with speech elements for the purpose of communication, and it is difficult and exhausting; the latter is effortless, working as it were spontaneously, with the contents ready to hand . . . The one produces innovations and adaptation, copies reality and tries to act upon it; the other turns away from reality, sets free subjective tendencies and . . . is unproductive.

Jung himself did not explore the developmental implications of this dichotomy. It was Jean Piaget who did so. Piaget studied at Zürich in 1918–1919, where he was taught by Bleuler and also encountered Jung's writing. (An autobiographical recollection of having attended Jung's lectures must be mistaken: Jung gave his last lecture at Zürich some years previous to Piaget's arrival.) After Zürich, Piaget went to Paris and here he presented a lecture on "Psychoanalysis in its relations with child psychology" (published in 1920). The purpose of this address was to inform the Paris audience of recent developments in the Zürich school of psychoanalysis, which was dominated by the ideas of Bleuler and Jung. Piaget strongly endorsed the Bleuler-Jung model of the two kinds of thinking, and emphasised its developmental implications. Autistic thinking, for Piaget, is personal and incommunicable; it is "the thought of the child, of the neurotic, of the dreamer, of the artist, the mystic." He summed up the developmental picture in two short sentences[4]: "In the child, autism is everything. Later, reason develops at its expense." Spoken just before he embarked on his research programme, this succinct claim might be seen as having guided much, if not all, of what Piaget was to do over the next 60 years of his productive career.

After Paris, Piaget returned to Switzerland. In Geneva, in 1921, he underwent a training analysis with Sabina Spielrein, ex-pupil (and ex-patient) of Jung.[5] Spielrein had also spent time in Vienna, there making important contributions to Freud's theory of psychoanalysis. The impact of this experience on Piaget is hard to evaluate, but it certainly did not weaken his adherence to the model of autistic and realistic thinking. Indeed, his first discovery in child development, the theory of egocentrism, was a triumphant vindication of that model. The discovery was announced in Piaget's first book, *The language and thought of the child* (1923), which also contains references to Spielrein's theoretical formulations on language. Here, as well as in the companion volume *Judgment and reasoning in the child* (1924), egocentrism is defined *in terms of* the two-stage model. Egocentrism is an intermediary stage between autism and scientific thought. It shares the basic structure and content of the former, but also exhibits certain motivational (communicational) features of the latter. Egocentrism is transitional; it is autistic thought *trying* to be social. Thus[6]:

> . . .between autism and intelligence there are many degrees, varying with their capacity for being communicated. These intermediate varieties must therefore be subject to a special logic, intermediate too between the logic of autism and that of intelligence. The chief of those intermediate forms, i.e., the type of thought which like that exhibited by our children seeks to adapt itself to reality, but does not communicate itself as such, we propose to call *Egocentric thought*.

Not only the theory, but also the methodology for egocentrism was derived from Jung and Bleuler. Piaget's experimental method was to record and categorise young children's utterances. This categorisation was carried out in essentially the same manner as Jung had done with word-association. Indeed, Jung himself had explicitly linked his own useage of the term egocentricity—as a reference to particularly idiosyncratic or subjective associations—to autism. Thus Piaget's first major discovery in child development, and the cornerstone of much of his subsequent thinking, derived directly from psychoanalytic thinking. More generally, it derived from the widely held assumption that the thought of the child is archaic and primitive: An assumption highly consistent with the recapitulationary logic which dominated the times.

THE ORIGINS AND FUNCTIONS OF LANGUAGE

This section discusses viewpoints and assumptions concerning early language, with especial reference to Piaget and Vygotsky. The issue of language and of its development has long been central to discussions of the relationship between man and the animals. Language was taken to be a uniquely human competence by a number of influential linguists in the latter half of the 19th century. Charles Darwin, in contrast, saw in language an example of the continuity between man and the animal kingdom and was very aware of the importance of developmental evidence for this claim. Darwin's publication of the *Biographical sketch of a baby* in 1877 was prompted by an ongoing debate on this issue. The Darwinian continuity approach to language[7] was taken considerably further by Darwin's protégé George Romanes, who set out to obtain direct evidence of continuity from developmental observation.

Combinatorial speech was identified by Romanes as emerging at around two years of age. Romanes also studied the nonverbal methods of communication, such as signs or gestures, used by the young child. Critically for Romanes, the "late-developing" two-year-old—one who has not yet achieved combinatorial speech—does not simply stand still in developmental terms, but instead develops more systematic and powerful systems of signing. Thus signing and speech are to some extent alternatives, able to subserve similar functions at least to a certain degree. The existence of such alternative routes demonstrated for Romanes the falsity of setting any single cut-off point between animal and human attainment: The overlap itself is strong evidence for continuity. Romanes published his account in 1888. In general, little more of substance was added by his contemporaries. One extension, however, was in the exploration of recapitulationary parallels to the development of language in the child. Thus James Sully compared the language of the young child with that of the "savage." The single words of the child could be seen as an abbreviated sentence or "sentence-word" as in the simplest known stage of adult language: "As with the race so with the child, the sentence precedes the word" (and the recapitulationary origins of the concept of "holophrase" should therefore be noted).

The next major theorist of the development of language was William Stern, who was writing in the second decade of the present century. Stern placed emphasis both on imitation and spontaneity. Pure repetition, for Stern, could not explain the acquisition of adult forms: Imitation must be *indirect*, and must include the production of similar but independent expressions. The child's language production must involve analogy, as in the incorrect application of "ed" to past forms ("runned"). With respect to actual stages of development, Stern argued that speech involves the coming together of three components: active babbling, which has built up associations between feelings and sounds; impulsive, unintelligent imitation; and comprehension. Single-word utterances for Stern amount only to "unconscious speech for particular occasions." As yet, words refer only to transient aspects of objects or events. These first utterances represent whole sentences, more specific categories not yet being "differentiated from the primitive embryonic form." A single word can have multiple senses. As yet, words do not signify the idea of a single thing, since this would require a comparison of occasions of use and the observation of identity across occasions. Nor do single words refer to a *class*, since this would require, again, a comparison across occasions with the rejection of variant elements to arrive at that which is common. In either case, comparison would involve memory; and only an associative form of memory is as yet available[8]: "the child offers a purely associative reaction to a present experience with one word only, because, at an earlier period, this or that point connected with the experience had appeared connected with the same word."

As noted before, then, Stern's account retained an adherence to associationism. For Stern, the first uniquely human advance is taken at 18 months, at which time the child discovers that "everything has a name." This is the child's first general thought, and is the impetus for subsequent development. No longer is the child dealing simply with "perceptions and their associations." Single words are now put together and structured sentences begin to emerge. This lowest level of human language use is taken by Stern to characterise some human languages, languages in which sentences are constructed by the juxtaposition of unchanging words. The (European) child of the "educated classes," however, soon acquires inflections to indicate tense and so on. Recapitulationary processes are strongly implicated with the suggestion that the "racial" (evolutionary) development of syntax is paralleled in the development of the individual child.

Lev Vygotsky's account of early language was worked out in the 1920s, the decade following the publication of Stern's. The account of the emergence of language presented by Vygotsky has several points of continuity with previous authors. Vygotsky was, however, especially critical of Stern's claim for the importance of the child's "discovery" of the name-property of objects. This discovery, for Vygotsky, had been taken by Stern to transform word usage into an *intentional* activity, since now words meant things. But, argued Vygotsky, intentionality could not emerge fully fledged in this manner: Intentionality must itself develop. And, moreover, Stern's interpretation of this level exaggerated its level of complexity. For Vygotsky, the two-year-old child does not, like an adult, treat the word as a conventional *sign* for an object but rather as an attribute of that object. The child "grasps the external structure word-object earlier than the inner symbolic structure." Stern's account was, for Vygotsky, "intellectualistic" and anti-developmental; it assigned to intellect "an almost metaphysical position of primacy as the origin, the unanalysable first cause of meaningful speech." Stern's theory, in Vygotsky's words, claimed that "personality generates language out of the goal-directedness of its own essential nature." For Vygotsky this was the outcome of an "idealistic, 'monadic' conception of the individual person [which] naturally leads to a theory which sees language as rooted in personal teleology."[9]

Despite the attack on Stern, Vygotsky's actual developmental account is not all that radical. The account is concerned with "the genetic roots of thought and speech" and in this context, close parallels between phylogeny and ontogeny are discussed. Vygotsky's major claim is that thought and speech have distinct and independent origins, and that these independent roots remain distinct both in animals and in the pre-verbal child. Only in the human child, at a certain point, do they come together to yield verbal thought and intellectual language. Vygotsky thus claims that both a pre-intellectual (but communicative) form of language *and* a pre-verbal (practical) form of thought co-exist in the young child. He credits Stern for having noted this co-existence (and indeed, Preyer had also done so). Thus in both higher animals and in the preverbal child expressive (but thoughtless) vocalisation co-exists with practical (but word-less) intelligence.

The vocalisation of the infant, from crying to babbling and the first words, has an emotional, release function but also a communicative function. The response to the human voice is an example of this communicability, and reference is made here to the work of Charlotte Bühler. At the same time, but independently, the pre-verbal infant demonstrates practical intelligence in problem-solving situations. Here reference is made to Karl Bühler's work which applied to children the tasks devised for chimpanzees by Wolfgang Köhler. Like Romanes and Stern, Vygotsky treated the first single words as of rather little significance. They are communicative but nonintellectual vocalisations. It is the coming together of the two roots of language which interests Vygotsky. Not only does this transform the development of the individual, it transforms the nature of the developmental process itself, "from biological to sociohistorical." For Vygotsky,[10] "Verbal thought is not an innate, natural form of behaviour but is determined by a historical-cultural process . . . we must consider it subject to all the premises of historical materialism [ie, Marxism] which are valid for any historical phenomenon in human society." Thus the "roots" themselves are indeed biological functions. Before the child enters human society he is essentially animal; Vygotsky's position here is quite orthodox.

The final topic in this consideration of the claims of Vygotsky is the language of the preschool child. In this context, Vygotsky was responding to the findings and claims of Piaget on egocentrism in child language (to be discussed next). For Piaget, much of the language production of the preschool (kindergarten) child is only superfically social. This kind of speech Piaget labelled "egocentric." Vygotsky accepted Piaget's observations but disputed his developmental interpretation. For Piaget, egocentric speech represents a transition stage between private, "autistic" thought and true socialised language. It is "on its way outwards." For Vygotsky, however, egocentric speech is a transition state *en route* to verbal thought, and deriving from communicative vocalisation. Hence it is "on its way inwards." Pre-intellectual speech is, for Vygotsky, profoundly social; privacy is a characteristic of the adult use of language, as an "inner speech" with which to regulate action. Thus, for Vygotsky,[11] "Egocentric speech emerges when the child transfers social, collaborative forms of behaviour to the sphere of inner-personal psychic functions." Vygotsky's criticisms of Piaget are included, together with a number of penetrating comments on the origins of Piaget's theoretical assumptions, in his preface to the Russian translations of Piaget's first two books. These books, *The language and thought of the child* (1923) and *Judgement and reasoning in the child* (1924) contain the reports of Piaget's first major research programme. Vygotsky notes that Piaget's conception of egocentric thought "though never presented by Piaget in a coherent, systematic fashion, is the cornerstone of his whole theoretical edifice." As we have previously noted, Piaget's egocentrism was derived from and defined in terms of the psychoanalytic notion of autistic thinking. In Vygotsky's words,[12] "[Piaget's] conception of the development of thought is based on the premise taken from psychoanalysis that child thought is originally and naturally autistic and changes to realist thought only under long and sustained social pressure."

Piaget's *The language and thought of the child* is largely concerned with the description of egocentric speech. The first, key study was carried out by Piaget in 1921/1922 at the *Maison des petits* of the *Institut J.-J Rousseau* in Geneva. The speech of two six-year-old boys was recorded over a one-month period (a total of some 1500 utterances) and categorised into two major types. "Socialised speech" was that in which direct adaptation to the needs of a listener could be shown; "egocentric speech" was that in which it could not. For both children, egocentric speech made up just under half the total. This category of egocentric speech included several different kinds of utterance. In repetition, "words thrown out [by another] are caught on the bounce, like balls." Repetition for Piaget is an unconscious form of imitation, involving "a confusion between the I and the not-I, between the activity of one's own body and that of other people's bodies." Reference is made to Baldwin in this context. Second, in the monologue or thinking out loud, words serve merely to accompany action or perhaps to promote it in a magical way. "For the child words are much nearer to action and movement than for us . . . The child is impelled . . . to speak as he acts." Third, the *collective* monologue involves an audience for the same process as in the (solitary) monologue: Other people serving merely as a stimulus.

Piaget's novel claim was that young children's language is often not truly social even when it appears to be. The child[13]: "does not know what it is to keep a thing to himself. Although he talks almost incessantly to his neighbours, he rarely places himself at their point of view." The emergence of social language use is a result of a new "verbal continence." At the same time, other points of view begin to be taken into account. Here the concept of "point of view" should be clarified. At this point, Piaget uses the term to refer to a position in an argument; a stance or standpoint. The role of argument between persons is critical in Piaget's theory since for him true argument is socialised interaction *par excellence*. The ability to participate in a true argument, with the necessary justification of one's assertions and adaptation to those of one's antagonist, represents the acme of socialisation. At this stage, then, "point of view" for Piaget is quite metaphorical: It certainly does not refer to a physical vantage-point in space. For Piaget, then, the young child's thought—as indicated by language—is concerned rather little with a collective reality. Here Piaget refers to the accounts of language given by, among others, such psychoanalytic thinkers as Sigmund Freud and Sabina Spielrein: Accounts which compare the language of "savages, imbeciles and young children." For Piaget, the young child may be intelligent in certain ways, but is not *logical*. The inconsistent nature of child thought is taken as given; the new findings on egocentric speech merely corroborate this.

Piaget discusses the emergence of logic in the young child in terms of the systematisation of beliefs and the attempted avoidance of contradiction: Again, the centrality of *argument*. Here referring to the writings of Pierre Janet (close colleague of James Mark Baldwin in Baldwin's Paris exile), Piaget assigns this achievement to the age of seven or eight years. According to Janet, the emergence of this systematisation of thought, or "reflection," derives from the reproduction of attitudes to *oneself* which one had previously adopted towards others. Such a formulation is, of course, very much a Baldwinian one. In Piaget's words, "logical reasoning is an argument which we have with ourselves, and which reproduces internally the features of a real argument." Piaget presents evidence to show that it is not until this critical age of seven to eight years that children become capable either of true argument *or* of true collaboration. With the decline of egocentrism, argument emerges from mere assertion, and collaboration from mere association. Thus social interaction prepares for the achievement of logic. This last point was seized on by Vygotsky, for it is much more consistent with his general viewpoint than it is with Piaget's.

This discussion has taken us away from the development of language as such. This is only appropriate, since for both Vygotsky and Piaget language is inextricably bound up with thought. Piaget's own account of the acquisition of language is somewhat sketchy, being contained within a general account of the development of representation. With respect to the functions of early language, the claims of both Vygotsky (who emphasised its communicability) and Piaget (who emphasised its incommunicability) lead directly to the issue of reasoning and logic in child thought.

REASONING AND LOGIC

The most detailed and systematic analysis of children's reasoning has been that of Piaget, and for this reason Piaget's account is the major topic for this section.[14] It should be emphasised, however, that Piaget's account formed an extension and an application of orthodox viewpoints and that his analysis has much in common with both antecedents and contemporaries. In this connection, some aspects of the accounts of both Vygotsky and Werner will also be discussed. Piaget published four highly influential books on child thought topics during the 1920s. In terms of content, as well as publication date, these four may be thought of as two pairs of related works: *The language and thought of the child* (1923) and *Judgment and reasoning in the child* (1924); *The child's conception of the world* (1926) and *The child's conception of physical causality* (1927).

In these volumes Piaget explores the form and content of children's thought from the standpoint of his theory of egocentrism. The developmental decline of egocentrism—with the associated socialisation of thought—is seen as the fundamental process at work. The overall transition is from autistic, incommunicable thought to scientific, communicable thought. As already indicated, the age of seven to eight years is identified with the major transition in this developmental course. Childhood egocentrism is now in steep decline; thought and language are becoming socialised. *The language and thought of the child* has already been discussed. Its companion volume *Judgment and reasoning* includes a general discussion of both books. Here Piaget argues that the thought of the child should be evaluated in its own terms, not simply as an inferior version of adult thought; he refers to Rousseau in this context. However, Piaget also proposes that child thought should be placed "on the same level in relation to adult, normal and civilised thought" as the "primitive mentality" described by Lévy-Bruhl and the autistic or symbolic thought of Freud. These two claims appear inconsistent. It is the latter—child thought as primitive—which dominates Piaget's account. Thought is now described as moving with development from disorder and unstable equilibrium towards ordered complexity. For Piaget "the mind always begins in chaos." Early thought is unconscious and tied to action; it seeks pleasure rather than truth (and here reference is made to Freud); it flows in one direction in a succession of images.

Up to the critical point of seven to eight years child thought is self-contradictory, syncretic (working on nonanalysed wholes) and transductive (working from one particular to another). Such characteristics arise, for Piaget, from a reliance on immediate perception, treated as absolute. Immediate perception is itself *distorted*. The child's thought is egocentric not because of being limited to personal perception, as if this were veridical but incomplete, but because the perception is erroneous. For Piaget,[15] "Things are schematised in accordance with the child's own point of view, instead of being perceived in their intrinsic relations." The child's perception is incorrect: The "contents" of perception are not analysed. Similarly, transductive reasoning arises from the child's inability to comprehend generalities or universals. Difficulties thus emerge with any problem involving sets and subsets. In general, Piaget's claims are familiar ones: Moreover, they are consistent with recapitulationism. According to Piaget, the child, like the "savage," is "impervious to experience." The emphasis on sense perception indicates the associationism built into Piaget's account. Thus the child is described as being limited to taking in one piece of information at a time and hence is unable to make comparative judgments. The child, for Piaget, has a "narrower field of attention."

The third and fourth books are concerned mainly with verbal investigations of specific areas of child thought, such as the origin of the night, of mountains, or the mechanism of the bicycle. *The child's conception of the world* (1926) describes child thought as being realistic, animistic, and artificialistic. Realism includes the treating of an object's name as a part of that object (as also described by Vygotsky): Animism refers to an inadequate differentiation of living from nonliving matter. (Piaget distinguishes this usage from the anthropological one which is seen as involving a more sophisticated level of reasoning: James Sully, to whom Piaget makes frequent reference, had made the same point.) Artificialism refers to the attribution of human manufacture to such natural phenomena as mountains. The term itself appears to have been taken from a commentary on the physics of Aristotle. Defining an object by its use is seen as a form of artificialism ("a mountain is for climbing up") and such "human sense"—to use a modern term—is taken as a constraint on thought.

In *The child's conception of the world* Piaget makes frequent reference to what he calls the "prelogical mentality of primitive races." Animism, artificialism, and "precausality"—for example, magical or finalistic forms of causality—are straightforwardly "prelogical." As well as such analogies with the "primitive," Piaget is greatly concerned with parallels between the child's development and the history of science. For example[16]:

> It may very well be that the psychological laws arrived at by means of our restricted method can be extended into epistemological laws arrived at by the analysis of the history of the sciences: the elimination of realism . . . the growth of relativism etc., all these are evolutionary laws which appear to be common both to the development of the child and to that of scientific thought.

This rather grandiose prospect is presented early on in Piaget's research career, when his empirical work had only just begun. The assumptions it reflects are influenced profoundly by the theory of recapitulation.

Before continuing the discussion of Piaget's account with an analysis of his formulations on later childhood, something should be said on the ways in which Piaget's contemporaries made use of notions of "primitive thought." Both Vygotsky and Werner, in different ways, explored the implications of this comparison. For Vygotsky, a key term was *syncretism*. Piaget, and others, had already described children's thinking as syncretic: Holistic and nonanalytical. For Piaget, syncretism is a manifestation of egocentrism and is fundamentally *pre*-logical, like primitive thought in general. Up till the age of seven or eight, syncretism characterises both verbal and perceptual processes which rely on analogy and image. Syncretism in language use is still observed after the decline of egocentrism, for example in the child's understanding of proverbial sayings.

For Vygotsky, syncretism is to be observed in the context of the development of conceptual thought. Thus, the young child's classification of a group of objects will employ only such superficial criteria as spatial contiguity. The analysis and employment of systematic criteria based on common features of objects is a subsequent achievement. Vygotsky, however, considered syncretism somewhat more positively than did Piaget; "the syncretic schemata . . . [can] lead the child toward adaptation." More generally, Vygotsky accepted the validity of the concept of primitive thought and of its application to the child. Thus, taking an object's name to be an integral part of that object was, for Vygotsky, "characteristic of primitive linguistic consciousness" in either modern child or prehistoric man. The relating together of objects or phenomena on subjective, non-logical grounds—called "participation" by Vygotsky—was observed to characterise the child (from Piaget's findings), the schizophrenic, and the modern-day "primitive."

Werner's work is perhaps the most extreme application of the concept of "primitive thought" among all the developmentalists. For Werner, a *formal* identity in thinking can be demonstrated between children, "primitives," schizophrenics, and adult "defectives". In his *Comparative psychology of mental development* (1926), which sets out to investigate the nature of primitive mentality, examples and conceptual formulations are drawn from all these areas. With respect to the anthropological evidence, Werner exhibits what can only be described as a radical ethnocentrism, more typical of the 19th than of the 20th century. A rigid distinction is maintained between European and "lower forms of civilisation." The former is characterised by abstract, universalist, reflective thinking, an independence from immediate concrete reality, and a scientific world-view based on general laws. The latter gives rise to thought that is concrete, diffuse, pragmatic, nonsymbolic, perceptual, imaginative, accepting of contradiction, and recognising no lawful necessity nor causality. Werner applies this dichotomy with great thoroughness, and the characteristics of primitive thought are taken to apply ipso facto to the thought of the child. For Werner, the thought of the child is illogical, unsystematic, and incommunicable: It works by images and global perception rather than by analysis.

Where Vygotsky and Werner tended to discuss the nature of child thought in general, Piaget sought to delineate qualitative changes *within* childhood. Certainly, the transition point set at 7–8 years was of central importance to his argument. For Piaget, however, this critical age does not give rise to true logical reasoning, and hence another transition point—at 11–12 years—was introduced. There was now a tripartite scheme, defined by the two major transition ages. This scheme remained central to Piaget's subsequent thinking. Following the work on infancy, published in the 1930s, an initial period was separated off at the beginning, but within the same overall framework. The account now consisted of four stages or periods: the sensorimotor (infancy), the pre-operational (early childhood), the concrete-operational (late childhood) and the formal-operational (adolescence and beyond). Progressively, the role of logic came to be emphasised more and more in Piaget's descriptions and definitions and in the 1940s the language of mathematics became dominant. Later still, cybernetics played a similar role in the redefinition of stages. But the basic developmental picture was to remain essentially as first described circa 1924.

Many fundamental Piagetian notions are introduced in *Judgment and reasoning*. "Operations" and "reversibility" are defined by reference to logic. Logic is also now used to describe early cognition, which is said to manifest a "logic of action." One unconscious act *entails* another without the involvement of conscious awareness. The contradictory nature of child thought is seen as arising from the antagonistic effects of the twin processes of assimilation (distortion of reality) and imitation (self-distortion to fit reality). These processes do not really collaborate until thought becomes socialised at age seven to eight. Throughout *Judgment and reasoning* social processes are seen as primary. Thus, at the seven to eight year transition, the advance depends on social contact: "We become conscious of ourselves to the extent that we are adapted to other people." There is a "shock of contact" which leads to a need for verification. When the child[17]: "seeks to adapt himself to others, he creates between himself and them a new order of reality . . . where speech and argument will henceforth hold their sway."

It would be hard not to detect the influence of Baldwin here, perhaps refracted through the writings of Janet. Not only the first but also the second transition (at 11–12 years) appears to depend on social interaction. "Here again" notes Piaget, "it is social intercourse . . . that modifies the structure of thought." Thus 11–12 year-olds have[18]: "a marked impulse to form themselves into groups, and . . . the respect paid to the rules and regulations of their play constitutes an important feature of [their] social life." Argument therefore becomes more intricate, and more directed toward agreement and co-ordination. *Both* of the major intellectual advances arise primarily from social interaction. The whole development of thought is characterised by its inexorable socialisation, before which egocentrism increasingly gives way.

The fourth of the child thought books, *The child's conception of physical causality* (1927), reports semi-experimental studies. The child is now asked questions about a concrete physical demonstration, such as the flotation of a boat. This situation leads on to an exploration of the child's knowledge of weight and density. Piaget outlines a developmental sequence in which boats are first seen to float because "that's what boats do," or because they are moving; next, because they are light (or because they are heavy). But, in this context, weight is seen as a simple correlate of size: A pellet rounded out into a bowl is seen as having become lighter. In a footnote, children of under ten years are reported as saying that a long sausage rolled from a ball of plasticine is lighter than a short cylinder rolled from an identical ball. Piaget comments that "the child would appear to be ignorant of the principle of the conservation of weight." The context in which the important issue of *conservation* is introduced should be noted. Fundamentally the child's difficulty is seen as one of dealing with relationships. The comprehension of flotation, for example, requires that lightness and heaviness are thought of in relative terms: A floating boat is light for the water (from the point of view of the water).[19] Similarly, transitive judgments are difficult, as in the sequential ordering of the three girls given "Edith is fairer than Suzanne and darker than Lili". For Piaget, the young child's realism or absolutism precludes a girl being both fair (to a dark one) and dark (to a fair one) simultaneously.

The overall change Piaget now discerns is from realism to objectivity, from realism to reciprocity, and from realism to relativity. Objectivity, for Piaget, involves the separation off of the internal from the external world, and thus the ability to free cognition from its subjective elements. Awareness of one's own subjectivity is a prerequisite for this. Piaget explains that every thought is the product both of sensorial elements and the organism's own activity in organising such material. These two contributions are initially undifferentiated by the organism. The whole, rather than the "real" (external) part alone, are treated as objective. For Piaget, development consists in becoming sufficiently aware of oneself to exclude oneself from one's experience. Subjective features are eliminated in this intellectual mortification. What remains after this process has been carried out must be "objective."

This developmental process depends on social interaction, but this is not sufficient: Reason must transcend the social environment. The young child's thought is, paradoxically, both closer to and further removed from reality than that of the adult. The child may adopt "crude forms of actuality as they are presented in observation: One boat will float because it is light, another because is it heavy, etc." Logical coherence is sacrificed in such cases in favour of fidelity to raw fact. The causality which results from "phenomenism" of this kind is not unlike that which is found in primitive races. At the same time, the child "is farther away from reality in his thought than we are." His reality is "overgrown with subjective adherences": The world is filled with forces. "In evolving an adult mentality [the child] both advances towards reality and recedes from it."

The four child thought volumes supply the foundation for Piaget's later work. In them, Piaget welds together a mass of theoretical material, much of it rather derivative, into a systematic whole. A formalised account of development emerges, containing two major turning-points at 7–8 years and at 11–12 years. The general transition from autistic-incommunicable thought to socialised-logical thought remains at the heart of the system, although the developmental sequence is now more complex. In the next decade, the 1930s, Piaget published his account of moral development in childhood and his two major infancy volumes. The infancy research exerted considerable influence on his subsequent thinking about childhood, when he returned to this area. As he noted in the foreword to *The child's conception of number* (1941), his aim was now[20]: "to investigate how the sensory-motor schemata of assimilating intelligence [in the infant] are organised in operational systems on the plane of thought [in the child]." More particularly, the infancy research had demonstrated the importance of experimental methods. Such methods, necessary in the context of the speechless infant, had exposed intelligent action of much greater complexity than Piaget had anticipated. More work, especially of an experimental nature, was now required on childhood. Even more specifically, the infancy work had led to a greater interest in the topic of conservation. A major topic in *The construction of reality in the child* (1937) was the developmental acquisition of the concept of the permanent object. For Piaget, again writing in *The child's conception of number*, object permanence represents "the most primitive of all [the] principles of conservation." Conservation was now a central issue: "conservation is a necessary condition for all rational activity." Similarly, "the need for conservation appears then to be a kind of functional *a priori* of thought."

In the context of the development of arithmetic, Piaget argues that a set or collection is only conceivable as such if its basic character is seen as invariant over changes in spatial distribution and so on. The first experimental version of conservation is an example of this: The contents of one of two equally filled beakers is poured into two smaller beakers. Do the two small ones now contain the same as the large one? Essentially, it should be noted, this test is an extension of the earlier tests of wholes and parts. For Piaget, the younger child—up to six-and-a-half or seven years—takes immediate perception as the basis for judgment, and moreover centres this perception erroneously on only one factor such as the width of the beaker. "Centring" here means roughly the same as "taking the point of view" of the width, as Piaget might have expressed it in his earlier writings.

The psychology of intelligence (1947), first delivered as a lecture series in 1942, is primarily a theoretical work which systematises earlier claims. Conservation is now taken as a defining achievement for the period now termed "concrete operations" (7–8 to 11–12 years). This period involves operational groupings of thought with respect to concrete materials. As well as the terminology of concrete and formal operations, the book introduces the terminology of "groups" and "groupings." A system of operations is an internalised set of actions. "Group" is a mathematical term, referring to a set of (mathematical) operations which form a closed sequence: "grouping" is Piaget's term for the analogous set of *psychological* operations. A grouping will demonstrate equilibrium (stability). For Piaget, at this point, the grouping is actually more fundamental than the group, since "logic is the mirror of thought . . . the axiomatics of reason."

Developmental change is now expressed in terms of "stages in the construction of operations." The period between infancy and concrete operations is thus termed "pre-operational." This period involves a repetition of infant development at the higher level, an internal recapitulation of the sequence of development. The achievement of concrete operations, such as conservation, corresponds to the *infant's* achievement of object permanence (conservation of the object). The earlier definitions of developmental periods are thus reformulated. Purely verbal features of pre-operational thought—such as animism and artificialism—are now played down in favour of experimental features such as failure on conservation or class-inclusion tasks. The framework, however, is the same as that laid out in the early 1920s.

The final period of thought is now termed "formal operations" (instead of just formal thinking). In this last period, "formal thought is perfected and its groupings characterise the completion of reflective intelligence." Concrete-operational thought is seen as being completely transformed by the new advance. Mental actions now work on signs detached from reality, not on reality itself or on signs still "attached" to it. Piaget emphasises that concrete operations still provide the content of thought while formal operations transform its structure. For this reason, formal logic alone is seen as inadequate to describe thought. With the advent of formal operations, the individual transcends reality[21]: "The world of the possible becomes available for construction . . . Mathematical creativity is an illustration of this new power."

Concrete operations can embrace reality as it is, providing a detailed "plan" of reality allowing flexibility of routes from point to point. Prior to this, the information provided in the preoperational period relies on discrete images or "stills." The sensorimotor intelligence of infancy does not represent reality at all, the detours of which it is capable being only within the direct field of action. And at the very start, "perceptual assimilation and accommodation involve merely a direct and rectilinear form of interaction." This formulation starts from the assumption that initial interaction with the world is direct but superficial, and that developmental progress consists of placing greater distance between oneself and the world. This position had been worked out in detail in *The construction of reality in the child* (1937). Although this version is a sophisticated one, with more than a dash of idealism, the assumption that representational distance must be acquired gradually is in fact quite consistent with classic associationist epistemology. From this viewpoint, *presentation*—dealing direct with "superficial" sensory information—must precede *re*presentation.

We have emphasised the role attributed by Piaget to social factors in his early works, partly because his later writings tend to neglect this issue in favour of greater formalisation. In *The psychology of intelligence* a dual relationship between social interaction and logical thought is put forward. Discussion and the exchange of ideas are, as before, prerequisites for the internalised discussions characteristic of reflective, logical thinking. But social interaction does not simply trigger such logical advance: Logic itself is and remains social. It "requires common rules or norms." Logic is "a morality of thinking imposed and sanctioned by others" (and here reference might be made to Baldwin, who, quoting Royce, discussed the "social deduction of the category of universality"). For Piaget, noncontradiction is as important for interaction and co-operation as it is for reflective intelligence, and "the child first seeks to avoid contradicting himself when he is in the presence of others."

The role of the social is now, if anything, greater than before. But here Piaget takes the crucial step of subsuming *both* individual and interpersonal processes under the formal system of groupings. The formal analysis, for Piaget, accounts for[22]: "both the equilibrium of interindividual interaction and that of the operations of which every socialised individual is capable when he reasons internally." For Piaget, the state of affairs described by groupings in equilibruim represents an ideal state both for individual thought (when it no longer distorts the thought of others) and for society as a whole (when it "no longer exerts distorting constraints on the individual"). Piaget's claims are on a grand scale and relate closely to his long-standing interests in part-whole harmony as a phenomenon of very wide applicability. For Piaget, the development of reason in the individual cannot meaningfully be separated from the individual's place in a social world. This issue is explored in more depth in the final section of this chapter.

DRAWING AND SPATIAL REPRESENTATION

This section is concerned with two closely related topics. Developmental psychologists have long been fascinated by children's drawings; for a number of reasons, including the use of drawings as an index of cognition. One major aspect of this exploration concerns the child's representation of spatial relationships between objects in the environment. More direct investigations of spatial cognition have also been carried out, the single most influential being Piaget's explorations of a spatial form of egocentrism. Central to both drawings and the issue of spatial egocentrism is the concept of a *point of view.*[23] An additional layer of complexity is thus added to this ambiguous term. One of the earliest systematic accounts of children's drawings is that of James Sully. With his contemporaries of the late 19th century, Sully placed child drawings in a recapitulationary context, making comparisons with "savage" and with prehistoric art (such as cave-paintings). However, he considered such comparisons imperfect and used them in a flexible manner. The features Sully noted in young children's drawings were subsequently reported by numerous later commentators. For example, the five-year-old child would include both eyes in a profile face, and would show hidden parts such as an arm seen through the body.

As noted by Sully, the child draws "what he knows"—on the basis of knowledge about the world—rather than what he sees. The human figure might, for example, be drawn with the trunk in front view, head in side view and legs in side view; what Sully called a "mixed scheme." As Sully pointed out, this arrangement "displays much that is characteristic and valuable in the human form." Sully explained these features in terms of cognitive factors (not, for example, in terms of graphic incompetence). The drawing represents "a diagrammatic scheme [rather] than an imitative representation of a concrete form." The child, in drawing, is bent on "a linear description of what he knows." The process of drawing, for Sully, is "controlled by knowledge of things as wholes and not by representations of concrete appearances or views." The child[24]: "is not in the least troubled about the laws of visual appearance, but setting perspective at naught compels the spectator to see the other side, to look through one object at another, and so forth." What the child has access to in drawing is "a mass of generalised knowledge embedded in words, *viz.*, the logical form of a definition or description."

Sully's account exposes the inadequacies of a "sensationist" analysis of young children's drawings: That is, one described in terms of the straightforward representation of transient optical viewpoints. William Stern, writing some 20 years later, was also acutely aware of the limitations of the sensationist or associationist account, and his description of children's drawings followed Sully closely.[25] For Stern, the child draws "what he means, thinks, knows—not what he sees." Thus knowledge cannot start off from the passive reception (or "contemplation") of observed reality, as associationism would predict: Otherwise children's drawings would be visually (optically) realistic from the start. Instead, early drawings are "schematic," while the reproduction of what is apparent to vision comes later. The young child produces a square with four legs for a table, irrespective of whether a real model or a perspective drawing is presented. The young child, also, tends to ignore orientation (a point previously noted by Sully). In terms of age, Stern reports an observation on his son at just under five years which suggests the achievement of an awareness that drawings should involve one specific vantage point. Alongside this developmental trend, Stern noted an increase in "synthetic capacity," the power to perceive and represent parts as constituents of wholes.

Similar phenomena were reported by Karl Bühler, who appealed to language to explain the fact that "the child draws from his knowledge."

For Bühler, thinking in terms of concepts must have *replaced* thinking in terms of concrete images. Thus the associationist account is saved, by pushing it back into earlier childhood. For Bühler, the child draws essentially from memory, and hence portrayed objects receive only "their most constant and essential attributes." Thus, "the most important and most familar aspect of the hand is the front view, which allows most of its structure to be seen." The emphasis on familiarity and, as is implied, frequency of observation of one view of the object, again effects a compromise with the associationist emphasis on the cumulative experience of specific forms. In general, for Bühler, the fault in children's drawings[26]: "lies not so much in a chaotic mind, as in *errors* of translating from knowledge—formulated in language—to the spatial order of pictorial representation." Bühler is insistent that the young child's drawings are *wrong*. The cause is language: The civilised child has been corrupted by language from a more natural state which would have given rise to realism. The drawings of prehistoric man, and of the Eskimos and the Australian aborigines, are said to be realistic. The simplest explanation for this might seem to be the adulthood of these artists—that is, adult aborigines and Eskimos draw like adult Europeans. But this is rejected by Bühler. These people "belong to the culturally lowest type"; hence their realist drawings derive from their primitive natural state, a state uncorrupted by civilised language. Their drawings are not yet even at the level of the civilised child: A claim which demonstrates the great power of recapitulationary arguments.

By the time Piaget became interested in drawings, in the 1920s, a considerable literature had accumulated, including both empirical and theoretical material. Piaget's own most direct source was Luquet, who had published an extensive account in 1913. Luquet's observations were similar to those of previous and contemporary workers, but his theoretical account was more systematic. Luquet outlined four stages: first a "fortuitous realism" associated with early scribbling; second a "failed realism" associated with a "synthetic incapacity"—an inability to put graphic elements together correctly—which characterises the child up to about five years of age. From then until the age of eight or nine, drawings manifest "intellectual realism": The child drawing what is known rather than what is seen, and employing transparency, multiple viewpoints, and so on. Finally, the mature stage was labelled "visual realism," with visual perspective now being employed in a systematic manner.[27]

Piaget adopted Luquet's terminology and drew parallels with other aspects of child thought. "Synthetic incapacity" was examined by Piaget in the context of drawings of bicycles: Correct parts being shown by young children, but not their correct connections. This Piaget related to the young child's lack of understanding of the causal mechanisms in the bicycle, correct explanations of which are said to co-emerge with correctly connected drawings. A paper of 1922 included an attempt to extend the term "intellectual realism" to child thought in general. Thus young children's drawings show isolated "absolutes," in which details are "juxtaposed" rather than synthesised—as with child thought in general. For Piaget, then[28]: "the early stages of children's drawings are not characterised by visual realism, i.e. by a faithful copy of the model in question, but by intellectual realism, such that the child draws only what he already knows about things and copies only an 'inner model' . . . *Intellectual realism is the picture of the world that is most natural to ego-centric thought.*" Thus Piaget incorporated Luquet's system into his own.

During the 1920s Piaget's accounts of drawings and of thought in general were mutually supportive. Egocentric thought took immediate perception as "absolute," but this certainly did not mean that such perception was veridical. *Au contraire*, immediate perception was fragmentary, imbued with subjective factors, incoherent, and self-contradictory. The emergence of visual realism in drawings—giving rise to representations of arrays from one specific vantage-point—paralleled the emergence of socialised thought and the demise of egocentrism at the critical age of seven to eight years. Visual realism, for Piaget, required an awareness of subjectivity, and this was not available to the young child. This neat picture was disturbed, however, by the results of Piaget's work with infants, starting in the late 1920s. As described in the concluding section of the second infancy volume, *The construction of reality in the child*, spatial development in the *child* should be seen as a repetition, at a higher level, of spatial development in the infant. There is thus recapitulation within individual ontogeny. According to this approach, the spatial achievements of the two-year-old—the location of oneself in a spatial universe—correspond to the achievements of the seven- to eight-year-old in overcoming childhood egocentrism. There is a *décalage* or shift from one level to the next: The higher level includes and extends the lower. (For Piaget, this process also occurs in the history of science—from Aristotle to Newton to Einstein.) Piaget's studies of infancy brought to his attention characteristics previously thought limited to later childhood: The theory of internal repetition being his solution to this problem.

As in much of Piaget's earlier writings, social factors are given considerable prominence here in seeking to explain these developmental patterns. If a practical understanding of space has been achieved by the two-year-old, why should an advance to a higher level take place at all? For Piaget, this level is demanded by social communication. Thus "pure representation detached from personal activity presupposes adaptation to others and social co-ordination." Such social co-ordination involves the points of view of others. Now, however, *for the first time*, these points of view are said to be spatial (optical) ones[29]: "If it is possible for the child to imagine himself as occupying several positions at one time, it is obvious that it is rather by representing to himself the perspective of another person and by co-ordinating it with his own that he will solve [spatial] problems." "Co-ordination" here means the co-ordination of the *veridical* points of view of oneself and others. The implication is that one's own cognition is incomplete merely from being partial, not from actually being distorted, as Piaget had previously insisted. Egocentrism is now a spatial phenomenon.

In the context of this discussion, in *The construction of reality*, Piaget gives his first, brief report of an experiment carried out by an assistant, Edith Meyer. This experiment was the original of the subsequently well-known "three mountains" task. Meyer carried out and reported the study (published in 1935) while Piaget was working on *The construction of reality*, and reference is made by Meyer to Piaget's work in progress. Meyer's introduction makes it clear that the three mountains task is designed as a test of the repetition theory of spatial development. Will children regress to infantile levels of spatial cognition in certain situations, hence indicating the developmental continuity between infancy and childhood? The experiment itself involves a model landscape with three mountains, distinguished by colour, size, and certain features. The child subject is required to match up pictures of the array, taken from different vantage-points, with specific locations of a toy doll on the landscape. Meyer's first two experimental conditions consisted (first) of the child selecting a picture, with the doll at a given location, and (second) the child placing the doll on the display in accordance with a picture presented to the child. A third condition involved the child constructing a representation of what the doll would "see" from a given location (as in the first condition), but now apparently using cut-out cardboard pieces to represent the mountains.[30]

The first two conditions yielded two kinds of error in younger children. Some of these four- to seven-year-old children treated different positions as equivalent to each other, and different pictures also as equivalent to each other. They appeared concerned with the whole display, not with specific viewpoints of it. As Meyer put it, "It is the whole of the display which matters to them". This finding would seem consistent with Luquet's intellectual realism: That is, specific perspectives are not something with which the young child is concerned. However, others of the young subjects made a very different kind of error: When asked to find the doll's view from (for example) the side of the display, they picked out their own current view instead. Older subjects increasingly took account of left-right and back-front relationships of the various mountains, success being reached by around nine to ten years. The third experimental condition—with the cut-out pieces—is reported as having elicited own-view responses from *all* the younger children (who are therefore described as manifesting "an almost pure egocentrism"). The oldest subjects are now described, in comparison, as being entirely disengaged from their own point of view.

In Meyer's report, then, egocentrism consists of the adherence to one's own spatial perspective, a viewpoint veridical in itself but erroneously employed. This usage was consistent with Piaget's newly developed standpoint. Piaget's own description of the study, in *The construction of reality*, placed emphasis on the own-view errors. For Piaget, simplifying the results somewhat, the young child "always considers his own perspective as absolute"; he "reproduces his own view of things." Fundamentally, this practice was seen by Piaget as a regression to infantile ways of thinking. It represented a point in the infant's spatial development *prior* to the achievement of practical space: the spatial awareness of the four- to six-month-old. At this stage, as described in an earlier part of *The construction of reality*, the baby exhibits "optical realism": He or she "substitutes for the physical relations of bodies the visual relations corresponding to the apparent data of perception." Optical realism "consists of considering things as being what they appear to be in immediate perception." In the baby, this practice constitutes "integral egocentrism."

Thus the errors of the four- to six-*month*-old are repeated by the four- to six-*year*-old. The young child's own-view response to the three mountains task is a form of optical realism: A regression, under the demands of the task, to an infantile level. This finding was a vindication of Piaget's new picture of individual development as involving repetition or recapitulation within the course of ontogeny. Now, crucially, immediate perception was being treated as veridical in itself. The primitive state involved the taking of immediate perception as real. Essentially, this was the classic picture of the child or infant as a "Berkeleyan," endorsed by developmentalists since Rousseau. It is perception of the here-and-now that is fundamental: A claim central to associationist accounts of early development.

Piaget re-reported the Meyer study in *The psychology of intelligence* (1947). On this occasion, the report is set in the context of a discussion of egocentrism (rather than a context of spatial awareness). Here, Piaget makes it clear that *infant* egocentrism is basically perceptual and motor: Thus learning how to reverse an object manually requires a "progressive decentralisation from the egocentric point of view." Exactly the same process is held to apply to the child's learning to reverse an object *in thought*: But now, the decentralisation is representative, rather than merely perceptual-motor. "Representative decentralisation" is illustrated by Meyer's study. The focus is on own-view errors; "small children still remain dominated by the point of view that is theirs at the moment of choice." An important change has now been made, however. The child's response is no longer regressive, but appropriate for his or her age. The own-view errors are *characteristic* of childhood egocentrism. The young child "cannot see another point of view, either socially or geometrically." For Piaget,[31] "there is nothing here that is not perfectly natural; the primacy of one's own point of view . . . is merely the expression of an original failure to differentiate, of an assimilation that distorts because it is determined by the only point of view that is possible at first."

In these "post-infancy" books, Piaget has formulated egocentrism in spatial or geometric terms, rather than in the social-cognitive terms of the 1920s. It is the concept of "point of view" that links egocentrism with drawings, and the final book to be discussed here brings both issues together. *The child's conception of space*, co-authored by Barbel Inhelder, was published in 1948. It sets out a systematic theory of the development of spatial representation from infancy onwards. It employs a range of experimental evidence, including the Meyer study and results from drawings. Its basic theoretical claim is that of *The construction of reality in the child*: Development during childhood constitutes a systematic repetition, at a higher level, of development in infancy. What is new in theoretical terms is the terminology by which Piaget categorises different systems of spatial awareness. Both infant (sensorimotor) and childhood (representational) development involve progress through three stages: topological space, projective space, and Euclidean (metric) space. Topological space recognises only such features as proximity and separation, and for Piaget, constitutes the kind of practical understanding of space found in the first two stages of sensorimotor development. The next two sensorimotor stages, for Piaget, include the achievement of size and shape constancies which indicates primitive forms of both projective and Euclidean systems of space. This achievement becomes extended and systematised in various ways during the remainder of infancy. But the *child* has to start all over again: The achievements of infancy are only at the level of perception and action, not of thought.

Thus the young child's first systematic understanding of space is as a topological system: Knots and intersections are comprehended (the child distinguishing, for example, two loops which intersect from two which do not). The drawings of the young child are brought in here: Proximity is correctly represented "even where [it] runs counter to perspective" and enclosure relationships are conserved, if in rather a bizarre fashion. Thus[32]: "The relationship of surrounding or enclosure assumes very great importance, since in many situations the interior of things is represented by means of transparency. Thus, food in the stomach, a duck in its egg . . . potatoes in the ground." The stage of intellectual realism in drawings corresponds, for Piaget, to the domination of topological space. Projective and Euclidean features are only just beginning to emerge[33]: "Representation is still essentially topological, consonant with flexible and deformable objects . . . As a result one finds in one and the same drawing evidence of a jumble of irreconcilable points of view." The clear implication here, and one consistent with the already extensive literature on drawings, is that the emergence of single, coherent viewpoints in drawing must be an important developmental achievement.

This indeed is Piaget's claim. Elsewhere in *The child's conception of space*, empirical findings are reported which show that young children have difficulty representing the *apparent* shape of an object held in an unusual orientation—for example, a pencil held end-on to the child will be drawn as if from the side. The achievement of the ability to draw as seen in this way co-emerges with the ability to line up a set of objects by "sighting" along the row. This skill is indicative for Piaget of the projective level of space, in that it involves imposing a straight line onto an array of objects. Seeing what things look like from a specific vantage point appears to be a major developmental achievement—as had been noted by Stern. For Piaget, indeed,[34] "The discovery that he has a particular viewpoint, even the child's becoming aware that he occupies one momentarily, is far more difficult to come by than might at first be supposed." Fundamentally it is the inclusion of a single, coherent vantage-point which distinguishes the projective from the topological system of space. Thus[35], "Projective space . . . begins psychologically at the point when the object or pattern is no longer viewed in isolation, but begins to be considered in relation to a 'point of view'."

The account so far is consistent. Young children demonstrate intellectual realism: They "are not in the least concerned about which aspect they view the pattern from." Such characteristics are consistent with some of the findings in Meyer's study: Many younger subjects treated different pictures as equivalent (as long, presumably, as all three mountains were shown). But Piaget's report on the three mountains experiment in *The child's conception of space*—still Meyer's study—highlights the own-view responses, as his previous reports had done. Achievement of success on this task now, for Piaget, indicates a transition to the final, Euclidean system of space: One that involves an objective system of orthogonal, three-dimensional co-ordinates. Errors in the younger child mean that the child is[36]: "rooted to his own viewpoint in the narrowest and most restricted fashion so that he cannot imagine any perspective but his own. Indeed he cannot imagine any perspective but that of the passing moment." This conclusion represents an archaic assumption on the nature of child thought, one closely bound up with associationism in its various forms. This account by Piaget sits uneasily within the theoretical framework developed in *The child's conception of space* as a whole, and it might be considered unfortunate that this one chapter (on the three mountains task) has greatly outweighed the influence of the rest of the book.

This section has discussed a range of issues unified by the ubiquitous concept ot "point of view." In previous sections, we have seen how Piaget first developed a theoretical framework in which egocentrism was a failure or distortion in social cognition—a failure to take account of the cognitive points of view of others. The present section has described how this position became transformed into one which focused on the visual-spatial points of view of oneself and others. It has been suggested here that this latter development ran counter to the long-established findings on children's drawings, themselves recognised by Piaget. Piaget himself would certainly claim to have achieved a synthesis. Synthesis or syncresis, it has been the spatial form of egocentrism which has generally been taken to represent the most central feature of child thought. As a version of the assumption that the child's cognition is limited to the "here and now," itself related to similar claims for "primitive" cognition in general, spatial egocentrism can be seen as being in the long tradition of recapitulationism and sensationism.

CHILDREN, PEERS, AND THE ADULT WORLD

This section is concerned with the child's relationships with other people, including parents and peers. Attention is focused on two influential approaches: that of Freud, for whom all human relationships are deeply sexual, and that of Piaget, whose special interest was the development of moral judgement. These two approaches are more closely connected than might at first appear. For Freud, the development of morality in the individual is an outcome of psychosexual development within the family setting, and Freud's concept of the Oedipus complex was for him central both to sexuality and to morality. Like Freud, but without Freud's concern for sexuality, Piaget took as primary the situation in which child behaviour is constrained and controlled by adults. Both Piaget and Freud saw a process of detachment and distancing from adult constraint—and hence an increasing involvement with one's age peers—as an important developmental achievement.

As early as 1900, in *The interpretation of dreams*, Freud noted that the first object of desire for a child of either sex must be the opposite-sex parent. The same-sex parent must therefore be treated as a rival. Although this early statement proposed symmetrical positions for the boy and the girl, Freud's major interest was in the fact in male development. The boy's predicament, involving love for mother and rivalry with father, was compared by Freud to the legend of Oedipus who, in Sophocles' play, unknowingly murdered his father and then married his mother. Again for the male, the mother's breast was considered by Freud the first sexual object, lost by him during development but regained by the adult man as a mature sex object. This position is set out in the first edition of *Three essays on the theory of sexuality* (1905) where, also, the importance of a period of latency is emphasised. Latency refers to a period between childhood psychosexual stages (oral, anal, phallic) and adult (genital) sexuality emerging at puberty. For both sexes, Freud argues, latency serves as a barrier to incest since it disrupts the original love-choices (for the parent of the opposite sex) and allows the choice of a more appropriate person.

The focus on male development was carried futher in *Totem and taboo* (1912–1913), in which an historical origin was described for male psychosexual development. For Freud, early man lived in "primal hordes" in which a strong male dominated a group of wives. The strong male drove his sons away from the horde (to set up their own) as soon as they became old enough to challenge him and to threaten his right of sole access to his wives. "One day," as Freud tells us, the brothers joined forces and slew the father. Then they ate him. For Freud[37]: "This memorable and criminal deed . . . was the beginning of so many things—of social organisation, of moral restrictions and of religion." In the devouring of the father the sons attained an "identification" with him; "each one of them acquired a portion of his strength." This ancient crime was for Freud the prototype of modern men's own development: Rivalry with the father for the sexual favours of the mother (sisters playing no part in Freud's account), resolved by an intense identification with the father, a taking of the father into oneself. Freud's proposal of this event as the source for modern changes was certainly serious. Lamarckian processes were appealed to[38]: "An event such as the elimination of the primal father by the company of his sons must inevitably have left ineradicable traces in the history of humanity."

Similarly, the barrier against incest is described in the 1915 edition of *Three essays* as "probably among the historical acquisitions of mankind." The two broad periods of individual development separated by latency were described by Freud as very similar to each other, except for the actual person chosen: opposite-sex parent in the first (phallic) and opposite-sex nonparent (exogamous choice) in the second (genital). Otherwise, the phallic stage of early childhood is not much different in basic organisation (at least for the boy) from the genital stage of adolescence and adulthood. Repetition or recapitulation is clearly implied here, and Freud was later to make the related claim that an early human ancestor must have reached sexual maturity at five years of age. Modern pregential sexuality is a recapitulation of this ancient five-year-old maturity; and modern *adult* sexuality a repetition within development—with minor changes—of modern pregenital sexuality. The Oedipus complex is the culmination of pregenital sexuality. As Freud notes in the 1920 edition[39]: "It represents the peak of infantile sexuality which, through its after-effects, exercises a decisive influence on the sexuality of adults. Every new arrival on this planet is faced by the task of mastering the Oedipus complex . . ." A process founded on recapitulation must be universal.

Freud sometimes used the term Oedipus complex to refer to the female as well as to the male situation, at least when he was treating the two as broadly symmetrical. Such symmetry is assumed in *The ego and the id* (1923), which introduces the concept of the "superego" which for Freud links sexuality with moral judgment. For Freud, the superego emerges following the dissolution of the Oedipus complex. It is an outcome of the taking-in or identification with the father, by which paternal authority, with its moral implications, is assimilated. It happens no more by chance than does the Oedipus situation itself, and "the differentiation of the superego from the ego . . . represents the most important characteristics of the development both of the individual and of the species." The superego gives "permanent expression to the influence of the parents." For Freud, then, the influence of the parents is not in general a contingent, environmental effect. Its overall character and consequences are determined just as much by evolutionary history as is the psychosexual development of the individual. Human development in general is a matter of biology. In the formation of its superego the child reaches back into its "archaic heritage." The superego forms an unbroken continuity with ancient life, since each son acquires from his father that which his father acquired from *his* father. The tradition of patriarchy is unbroken. Freud explains the process as follows[40]:

> The experiences of the ego seem at first to be lost for inheritance; but, when they have been repeated often enough and with sufficient strength in many individuals in successive generations, they transform themselves, so to say, into experiences of the id, which is capable of being preserved by heredity [Lamarckism] . . . when the ego forms its superego out of the id, it may perhaps only be reviving shapes of former egos and bringing them to resurrection.

For the boy, the dissolution of the Oedipus complex leads to "an intensification of his identification with his father." The result is a consolidation of masculinity in the boy. A symmetrical process occurs in the girl, but for Freud the girl's motivation in setting up a superego is much less than the boy's. The boy had feared castration at his father's hands, and hence a severe authoritarianism forms the nucleus of the superego when the father is identified with. The girl, however, does not fear castration (believing it to have already been carried out). This concern with castration emphasises the theoretical link between the Oedipus situation in either sex and the phallic psychosexual stage with which it is associated. The issue of female sexual development was finally faced by Freud in 1925. Up to this time, he had attempted to treat it as basically symmetrical to male development, with some minor deviations. But now an implicit paradox in his earlier accounts had to be faced. If the Oedipal state required an attachment to the parent of opposite sex, how did this arise in the girl? For, surely, the first attachment of both sexes was to the mother—a female. How were girls turned away from females as love objects preparatory to the Oedipal situation? For Freud it was now axiomatic that attachment to the opposite-sex parent must be present during the phallic stage.

The answer for Freud revolves around penis envy. First, the little girl blames her mother for sending her into the world so ill equipped. Second, she gives up clitoral masturbation—a *masculine* form of the practice in that it involves a protruding organ—on finding herself again much less well endowed with the relevant anatomical apparatus than boys. For Freud, penis envy dictates the little girl's relationships to male peers. Clearly, the penis has a lot to answer for. In boys, fear of its loss triggers the dissolution of the Oedipus complex and hence the reconstruction of paternal power in the superego. In girls, envy of it brings on the Oedipal state. Because of this developmental history in the girl, however—the Oedipal being a late acquisition, not the original state of affairs as in the boy—its subsequent dissolution is slower and less sure. For Freud, therefore, the superego is less well developed in women; it is "never so inexorable, so impersonal, so independent of its emotional origins as we require it to be in men." Thus women "show less sense of justice than men . . . they are more often influenced in their judgements by feelings of affection or hostility." The male superego is pure: A representation of paternal authority as manifested in the history of the race. From a contemporary perspective it is hard not to see the "weakness" of the female superego rather as a weakness of Freudian theory, and as an inevitable consequence of Freud's male-centred approach. But the moral superiority of the male in Freud's account should not be written off as mere chauvinism. In Freud's system, the moral authority of the man derives from evolution, from the power of ancestry. The relationships of child to parent and of child to peer are biologically predetermined.

As we have already seen, Freud's views exerted considerable influence on the early thinking of Jean Piaget, whose main discussion of adult-child relationships occurs in *The moral judgment of the child* (1932). Before examining this account, something should be said of a quite different tradition concerning social interaction in childhood, that represented by the philosopher George Herbert Mead in America and by Lev Vygotsky in the Soviet Union. Mead (1863–1931) had broad interests in the social sciences and has had most impact in sociology, although this impact has been a diffused one. Mead's philosophical stance was a form of pragmatism, and as such his interests in psychology were in its functional aspects (in common, to some extent, with William James and John Dewey). Mead's pragmatism was a *social* one, in which the communicative aspects of behaviour were taken as fundamental[41]. His thinking has much in common with that of James Mark Baldwin in this respect, and Baldwin was certainly familiar at least with the earlier writings of Mead. Mead's psychology (which others have called a "social behaviourism") was worked out during the 1920s at the University of Chicago. His most important work is of a philosophical nature, but a collection of students' lecture notes was made up into the influential volume entitled *Mind, self and society* in 1934. Here Mead presents an account of individual development in which self-consciousness is seen as emerging from the experience of social interaction. Language, peer interaction, and social role-playing are presented as being absolutely central to human development.

As noted, this position of social primacy converges to some extent with the position of Baldwin on the emergence of self, and also with that of Vygotsky. The latter was working in Moscow while Mead was at Chicago and, through experimental studies, coming to the conclusion that "intrapsychic" (mental) processes are always derived from "interpsychic" (interpersonal ones.[42] Vygotsky was very much concerned with interpersonal situations in which some form of cultural instruction was taking place. Thus, for Vygotsky, individual development should be seen as being defined within interpersonal contexts. What the child can do with help becomes of central importance: For Vygotsky, such assisted achievements are more profoundly and more directly "developmental" than unassisted performances. Such considerations gave rise to Vygotsky's concept of the "zone of proximal development," defined by him in the following way[43]: "The zone of proximal development . . . is the distance between the actual developmental level as determined by independent problem solving and the level of potential development as determined through problem solving under adult guidance or in collaboration with more capable peers."

For Vygotsky then, as for Mead, social interaction is absolutely central to a conceptualisation of individual development. It is on this point that these thinkers differ from the more orthodox tradition of Freud and Piaget, for whom social interaction of a co-operative nature—most particularly, interaction with peers—is a developmental *achievement*. For Vygotsky and Mead, interaction with others is at no point as assymetrical as the orthodox position takes the starting-point to be. Piaget's account takes it for granted that the child's early experience is of *constraint* imposed by adults or by older children and that more equal relationships have to be constructed with development. This assumption should be noted when discussing Piaget's claims for the developmental significance of social interaction, as presented most clearly in *The moral judgment of the child*. As in the "child thought" books of the 1920s, social interaction (and especially equalitarian discussion with peers) is taken here as a prerequisite for the emergence of *mature* forms of reason. In Piaget's words, "reason . . . is a collective product." The nature of social interaction, and its implications for moral judgment, are examined in detail. Piaget's fundamental claim is that an *autonomous* form of morality gradually emerges in the child as a result of social interaction. The early form of moral thought in the child is seen by Piaget as deriving directly from the young child's relationship with adults. The relationship is quite simply one of constraint or coercion. The inequality between child and adult is seen as exerting a real *pressure* on the child. The young child is suggestible, because "the younger the child, the less sense he has of his own ego." Thus[44]: "The adult and the older child have complete power over him. They impose their opinions and their wishes, and the child accepts them without knowing that he does so."

As Piaget acknowledges, this picture of constraint is a traditional one. His own more original claims concern the later, autonomous form of morality. For Piaget, the constraint or "heteronomous" state closely resembles the position described by the sociologist Durkheim for whom, however, such conformity characterised moral development in general (throughout the lifespan). Certainly Freud would have agreed with its basic tenets. For Piaget, the state of adult constraint and unilateral respect relates closely to childhood egocentrism. The young child is suggestible and lacks awareness of his or her own ego. Constraint by adults—or by older children whose constraint "evokes adult authority"—gives rise to a *realist* kind of thinking in the young child. Rules are seen as unchanging, as emanating from all-powerful adults. Piaget makes it clear that adult constraint is inevitable in the family situation, even in a liberal household such as his own. Heteronomous morality sees punishment as connected in a direct and mystical way with delinquent acts: Punishment makes retribution, not restitution. The motivation for the delinquency is not relevant.

The form of morality seen by Piaget as deriving from adult constraint is fundamentally a *primitive* form. Piaget appeals to anthropological and sociological literature in describing it. Further, the developmental progression from heteronomy to autonomy is seen by Piaget as paralleling an historical, evolutionary progression in human society. Cultural recapitulation plays an important role in *The moral judgement of the child*. Comtemporary primitive societies are seen as being characterised by the kind of morality which results from adult constraint, in which tradition, custom, and the authority of elders is all-powerful. Similarly, for Piaget, the young child is "traditional." Analogies are drawn between the world of the child and the primitive state of society, as described by Durkheim. In both, for Piaget,[45] "The individual does not count. Social life and individual life are one. Suggestion and imitation are all-powerful . . . The traditional rule is coercive and conformity is demanded of all." In accord with the recapitulationary logic, the ontogenetic transition to a higher state of morality is seen as paralleling the historical advance in human society. A model for the latter is taken from Durkheim, for whom societal progress involves the differentiation of roles and the rise of individuality.[46] The primitive state involves collective identity, the advanced form true personality. Similarly, for Piaget, the social world of children changes from an amorphous whole into a regulated unity with division of labour; from simple, mutual imitation, and suggestibility to discussion, the interchange of ideas, and the formation of true personality. The direction of developmental change, and the characteristics of much of the course, are the same in the child as in the race.

According to Piaget, the impetus for change in the child is social interaction with peers. Just as constraint is fundamental to heteronomous morality, *co-operation* is fundamental to autonomy. "Co-operation . . . constitutes the deepest and most important social relation that can go to the development of the norms of reason." Co-operation involves mutual respect, not mere assent. A sense of solidarity with one's peers is now experienced[47]: "Solidarity between equals appears once more as the source of a whole set of complementary and coherent moral ideas which characterise the rational mentality." Co-operation emerges in opposition to constraint; the latter gives rise to an unstable equilibrium, which must inevitably give way to "the state of co-operation which constitutes the normal equilibrium." In play, for example, co-operation emerges at around seven to eight years (in the case of marbles). For Piaget, competition to win must presuppose a basis of co-operation. Autonomous morality, involving an understanding that rules are socially constructed and subject to negotiation, develops as a result of the experience of co-operation. Piaget emphasises the parallels between the development of reasoning and of morality, with co-operation being seen as "the one determining factor in the formation of the rational elements in ethics and in logic."

Piaget's account of mature, autonomous morality sees it as founded on social interaction rather than biology. But the early stage is quite simply a *primitive* morality, and the overall trend in development is seen as an evolutionary one. Durkheim's analysis of the evolution of society—focusing on the gradual increase in differentiation of roles and personalities—is endorsed in the description of contemporary maturity[48]: "The civilised adult of today presents the essential character of co-operation between differentiated personalities who regard each other as equals." For Piaget, the same evolutionary trend applies to the history of thought in general[49]: "There exists in European thought a law in the evolution of moral judgments which is analogous to the law of which psychology watches the effects throughout the development of the individual." Thus the recapitulationary point is made once more. Piaget's interest in the constitutive role of society is a real one. But the nature of that society itself, especially in its interpersonal features, is seen as a consequence of evolutionary processes: The very same processes at work in the development of every individual. The conditions under which the child lives, no less than the nature of the child's mind, reflect the operation of biological processes. For Piaget, and for developmental psychology in general, childhood is a biological phenomenon.

NOTES TO CHAPTER SEVEN

[1]Bleuler (1913). Bleuler, Jung, and their intellectual background are discussed by Ellenberger (1970). Jung consistently devalued the influence of Bleuler, and the Freud-Jung correspondence contains many slighting references from both authors. Jung's autobiographical *Memories, dreams, reflections* (1963) presents a distorted and self-serving view of the Burghölzli approach as having been solely classificatory. Students of Jung lack a balanced and critical biography, those available tending to the sycophantic. (At the other extreme, perhaps, is the attitude of Marcuse [1955, p. 218] for whom Jung's work comprises the "right wing" of psychoanalysis and consists of "obscurantist pseudo-mythology.")

[2]Jung (1912/1956, p. 28).

[3]Ibid., p. 18.

[4]Piaget (1920/1977, p. 59).

[5]Spielrein's training analysis of Piaget is noted by McGuire (1974, p. 228) and by Carotenuto (1982). Sabina Spielrein is one of the most fascinating figures in the history of psychoanalysis. A Jewish Russian, she was a medical student at the University of Zürich when she became a patient of Jung (c.1904–1907). Her case was discussed by Jung at the First International Congress of Psychiatry and Neurology in 1907 (Jung, 1908/1961, p. 20). Subsequently Jung's pupil, she went on to collaborate with Freud and to make major contributions to psychoanalytic theory. The nature of her relationship with Jung is not clear, but certainly there was a very strong romantic attachment between them (see Carotenuto, 1982). Spielrein had been discussed between Jung and Freud as a clinical case (Jung to Freud, 23.10.06; 6.7.07; Freud to Jung, 27.10.06: all Freud-Jung correspondence cited may be found in McGuire, 1974). When Jung complained that Spielrein was jealously hounding him and spreading malicious rumours Freud took Jung's side (Jung to Freud, 7.3.09; 11.3.09; 4.6.09; 21.6.09; 10.7.09; Freud to Jung, 9.3.09; 3.6.09; 7.6.09; 18.6.09; 30.6.09). Brome's biography of Jung does so also (1978, p. 112). Spielrein and Freud also communicated about these matters during this period (Carotenuto, 1982: The source for all letters to or from Spielrein).

Later, after Spielrein had joined Freud's group at Vienna (in 1911—after gaining her M.D. in Zürich) and when Jung had seceded from Frued, Freud came to take Spielrein's part. Spielrein had confided in Freud her earlier fantasies of bearing a son ("Siegfried") to Jung, and in 1913 she wrote to Freud of her pregnancy. Freud replied (28.8.13) "I am, as you know, cured of the last shred of my predilection for the Aryan cause, and would like to take it that if the child turns out to be a boy he will develop into a stalwart Zionist . . . We are and remain Jews. The others will only exploit us and will never understand or appreciate us." After hearing that Spielrein's child was a daughter (Renate), Freud wrote to Spielrein (29.9.13): "It is far better that the child should be a 'she.' Now we can think again about the blond Siegfried and perhaps smash that idol before his time comes."

Spielrein's relationship with Jung is considered by Carotenuto (1982, p. 211) to have played a major role in Jung's development (around 1914) of the concept of anima (cf. Jung, 1963,

p. 210). Spielrein played a part in developing the Freudian notion of "thanatos" or death instinct (Carotenuto, 1982), especially through her 1912 paper 'Destruction as the cause of coming into being.' Later she wrote on aspects of early development in the child, including a paper of 1922 (published in *Imago*: Spielrein, 1923a) on conceptions of time and duration. According to Carotenuto (1982, p. 194) this paper is conceptually related to Piaget's experimental work.

Spielrein also published accounts of her daughter Renate's early language. One of her language papers—a comparison of thought in the child, in the aphasic, and of the unconscious—runs consecutively with an early paper of Piaget's in the *Archives de psychologie* (Piaget, 1923a; Spielrein, 1923b). Piaget's own paper had originally been delivered at the Seventh International Congress of Psychoanalysis in 1922. Spielrein was in Geneva from 1921 to 1923, in which year she returned to her native Rostov-on-Don in the U.S.S.R. No records have been traced since 1937 (Carotenuto, 1982). It is possible that the I.N. Spielrein mentioned by McLeish (1975, p. 146) as having been a Soviet psychologist around 1930 was related to Sabina.

[6]Piaget (1923b/1959, p. 45); emphasis in original.

[7]A contemporary example of the Darwin-Romanes continuity tradition on child language may be found in Bruner (1983). Bruner's emphasis is on the continuity of communicative functions across the language-acquisition watershed.

[8]Stern (1914/1923, p. 150).

[9]Vygotsky (1962, p. 32).

[10]Ibid., p. 51.

[11]Ibid., p. 19.

[12]Ibid., p. 13.

[13]Piaget (1923b/1959, p. 39).

[14]Recent and contemporary research on child reasoning is indicated in Carey (1985). Carey explores parallels between processes of developmental change in the child and historical changes in science (p. 197). For an analysis of Piaget's early "child thought" volumes see Sugarman (1987).

[15]Piaget (1924/1928, p. 249).

[16]Piaget (1927a/1930, p. 240).

[17]Piaget (1924/1928, p. 213).

[18]Ibid., p. 72.

[19]Thus, in a tall building, what is the floor for one level is the ceiling for another: An observation made spontaneously by a five-year-old of my acquaintance.

[20]Piaget (1941/1952, p. *vii*).

[21]Piaget (1947/1964, p. 151).

[22]Ibid., p. 165.

[23]Cox (1986) reviews recent work on children's drawings, and on perspective-taking in language and in spatial cognition, against the background of the Piagetian claims. Also see Morss (1987a).

[24]Sully (1895, p. 295). Groos (1898/1901, p. 316) cites Lukens as having noted in 1897 that children "object to drawing from Nature . . . They prefer to make the absent present in their art."

[25]Stern (1914/1923).

[26]K. Bühler (1919/1930, p. 116); emphasis in original.

[27]Luquet's work is discussed by Cox (1986) and by Freeman (1972). Cox's version describes three stages (p. 104), Freeman's four.

[28]Piaget (1924/1928, p. 249); emphasis added.

[29]Piaget (1937/1971, p. 415).

[30]Meyer's study, which has never been translated into English, is discussed in Morss

(1987a). There is some uncertainty over the materials in the crucial third experiment: The English translation of "*cartons*" is given as 'boxes' in Piaget (1937/1971) but as "pieces of cardboard" in Piaget and Inhelder (1948/1956).

[31]Piaget (1947/1964, p. 161).

[32]Piaget and Inhelder (1948/1956, p. 50).

[33]Ibid., p. 50.

[34]Ibid., p. 165.

[35]Ibid., p. 153.

[36]Ibid., p. 242.

[37]Freud (1912–1913; S.E. XIII, p. 142).

[38]Ibid., p. 155.

[39]Freud (1905/1920; S.E. VII, p.226).

[40]Freud (1923; S.E. XIX, p. 38).

[41]Mead and the pragmatist movement in sociology is discussed in Lewis and Smith (1980); Mead himself in more detail by Joas (1985). James Mark Baldwin refers to some early work of Mead in Baldwin (1904).

[42]Vygotsky's notion of "interiorisation" is discussed in Morss (1988). The formulation has been further developed by Leont'ev, and criticised by Rubinstein, both within a Marxist framework (Rahmani, in Riegel & Meacham, 1976; also see Chapter Ten).

[43]Vygotsky (1978, p. 86).

[44]Piaget (1932/1977, p. 87).

[45]Ibid., p. 98.

[46]On Durkheim, see Hirst (1975). Manicas (1987, p. 159) observes that for Durkheim, "society is an organic unity which, like an organism, is capable of living, dying, changing and evolving. Indeed, its 'evolution' is unilinear, as in Comte."

[47]Piaget (1932/1977, p. 313). The notion of mature morality as essentially rational has been developed further by L. Kohlberg (see Kohlberg, Levine, & Hewer, 1983) in what has become the most influential stage theory of the development of moral judgement. Kohlberg's early (childhood) stages remain close to the Piaget formulation.

[48]Ibid., p. 81.

[49]Ibid., p. 384.

8 Adolescence

INTRODUCTION

This chapter completes the group of three chapters concerned with specific segments of ontogenesis. Its focus is on theoretical accounts of adolescence.[1] To take adolescence as the effective end-point of individual development may seem inadequate, but the focus of developmental psychologists has traditionally been on pre-adult stages. It is therefore important to recognise the significance with which adolescence has been viewed in the classical formulations of developmental psychology. As contemporary advocates of lifespan developmental psychology point out, this historical focus on pre-adult development is itself tied to theoretical assumptions, basically of a biological nature. There has not been a coherent tradition of interest in adulthood or lifespan development, this very lack perhaps testifying to the strength of the biological ideas.[2] However, accounts of adolescence inevitably bring with them certain assumptions on the nature of adulthood (if only by default). Some adolescence theories are embedded in systematic formulations of the lifespan, that of Erik Erikson being the best example.

The first section discusses conceptions of adolescence as the culmination of *intellectual* development. Piaget's account of "formal operations" is the most systematic version of this claim. The assumption that "mental development" reaches some kind of peak in mid-adolescence is, however, also to be found in the psychometric tradition, the curve of mental growth being held to stabilise or decline after this time. Thus the qualitative and the quantitative approaches agree that, at least as far as intellect is concerned, it is during adolescence that the individual is at the peak of his or her powers.

The next section discusses various formulations of the "turmoil" or disequilibrium often held to characterise adolescence. Theories of adolescence have been dominated by a concern with emotion and affect, under the influence of the concept of "storm and stress" as promulgated by Stanley Hall and others. Sigmund Freud's account of adolescence has been the most influential of such theories, with its claim that adolescent development consists fundamentally in the individual's response to biological (physiological) events. Sigmund Freud's account was extended and modified by his daughter Anna Freud, who explored the cognitive as well as the affective consequences of these presumed biological events. As we will see, the "affectivist" accounts agree in many respects with the claims of the intellectualist accounts.

The third section is concerned with theories of the influence of culture on development. In the work of Margaret Mead and of Erik Erikson, adolescence is a major focus but not an exclusive one. With their concern for cultural differences, and hence for differences in the final (adult) outcome of ontogenesis across cultures, both authors set adolescence within a lifespan context. The early work of the anthropologist Margaret Mead was to some extent motivated by a criticism of Stanley Hall's claims concerning the inevitability of adolescent "storm and stress." However, as will be discussed in the third section, Mead came to accept a great deal of the psychoanalytic account of human development. Mead's examination of the influence of culture on development led her to make claims concerning *universal* features of human development, claims which were explicitly biological and highly convergent with the psychoanalytical account. Mead's later work was greatly influenced by the child psychoanalyst Erik Erikson, author of an influential account of lifespan development as well as being a major influence on recent developmental thinking on adolescence. Erikson's own account of the cultural impact on development is a firmly psychoanalytic one. Erikson's eight-stage account of lifespan development—an expansion of Freud's theory of psychosexual stages—is now one of a number of attempts to extend developmental psychology beyond childhood.

ADOLESCENCE AND THE ACME OF INTELLECT

It has generally been assumed that the years of adolescence manifest the first appearance of adult ways of thinking. Adult thought has been defined and measured in various ways, but its basic format has generally been held to have been attained by the late teens or so. Qualitative changes in thinking have therefore come to an end, and quantitative changes still to come are held to be relatively trivial ones. To a considerable extent, the adolescent years have been taken as essentially equivalent to adulthood as far as "mental growth" is concerned, so that accounts of intelligence in adolescence represent theoretical views of intellectual maturity. A classic account may be found in Rousseau, who defined the period of 12 to 15 years as the "third stage of childhood." This stage is characterised by a "surplus of faculties and strength" in comparison to the child's actual needs. For Rousseau, this period manifests the lifetime peak of such a superabundance of strength. "Strength" for Rousseau includes the intellectual powers, and it is in this stage that he places the emergence of adult reasoning (as described at one point, "*formal* reasonings"). Rousseau's Emile is brimming over with intellectual curiosity in this period and is hence led, through the experience of real-life problem solving, to the personal discovery of numerous natural laws.

The viewpoint of adolescence as cognitive maturity is most clearly expressed in the psychometric tradition. Systematic attempts to measure intellectual growth can be said to have commenced with the work of Alfred Binet, in Paris, at the beginning of this century. Binet devised a set of varied test items and subsequently established average attainment for children of different ages (originally up to 13 years). Although a considerable theoretician—in the associationist tradition—of cognition and individual differences, Binet's intentions for his measuring instrument were largely pragmatic. The demand from the education authorities was for the improvement of the accuracy and efficiency with which schoolchildren needing special attention were identified. Binet's solution was to define such children in terms of retardation in achievement and to devise a practical instrument for the diagnosis.[3]

Binet himself was concerned with mental "levels" rather than the more narrowly statistical mental "ages" which were later to become key features of the psychometric approach. However, his preparatory studies on intelligence, carried out in the first years of the century, had focused on measurements of head size and in this context he had assembled precise age norms against which to compare individuals (with a view to diagnosing retardation). The method was termed by Binet, and his collaborator Theodore Simon, the technique of "anthropometric frontiers": The "frontier" being a figure taken as a cut-off point for the demarcation of significant retardation. Though never applied by Binet to intelligence as such, this statistical technique was a clear anticipation of later developments. Binet did not live to see the full extent of the English-speaking extensions of his work, although Simon has been reported as having considered the I.Q. formulation as a "betrayal" of the original aims[4]. In the context of the intelligence tests, Binet and Simon tended to see actual test *items* as "frontiers" (that is, as particularly clear indicators of qualitatively different levels of functioning). This approach was carried forward by Piaget—working initially in Simon's laboratory, after Binet's death—in his devising of critical tests of transition in cognitive development.

The Binet-Simon work on the measurement of intelligence gave rise to a first test in 1905, and 3 years later to a revised version which was standardised on about 300 children. Versions of Binet's 1908 revision were introduced into the U.S.A. by Henry Goddard and Lewis Terman, both of whom were concerned with the intelligence levels of adults (such as the retarded and the genius) and of different populations of adults (such as European immigrants to the U.S.A.). In England, Cyril Burt translated and adapted the Binet test. Burt also developed further reasoning items, an examination of which was the topic of Piaget's first experimental research in the Simon laboratory. Goddard, Terman, and Burt incorporated Binet's methodology into quite a different theoretical framework: One which focused on the genetic fixedness of individual differences between adults.

Early work in the individual-differences tradition, and especially that of Francis Galton in England, had included such measures as muscular strength. Goddard and Terman conceived of intelligence as in a sense analogous to strength: As a kind of mental *power*, having a fixed level in the individual. Moreover, the adult's level of such mental power was taken (with Burt) to be determined largely by heredity. This viewpoint on the nature of intelligence was associated with assumptions on the relative status of different races and classes, assumptions interconnected with the evolutionist thinking of the time[5]. It was taken that a single scale of achievement could be seen as underlying such relative status: At once a scale of individual development and a scale of racial comparison. Binet's method supplied the only missing ingredient: The measuring instrument. For Goddard and Terman the test instrument measured something quite unitary and precise, namely mental growth. The psychometric tradition, developing from the work of Burt, Goddard, and Terman, engendered such issues as the comparative intelligence of different races; but also raised less provocative questions such as the age at which mental growth comes to an end in the average individual.

It must be emphasised that the issue of "the age of cessation of mental growth" is not simply an empirical one. Its determination depends on the kinds of problems selected as definitive of adult competence. Lewis Terman, working in Stanford, California, published his revision of Binet in 1916, together with data on the performance of 1000 children aged from 3 to 18 years. This was the first version of the massively influential "Stanford Binet" I.Q. Instrument. For Terman, normal adult achievement was defined by reference to the performance of the 16-year-old. The performance of the 18-year-old represented the "superior adult." Writing at around the same time, other psychometric workers suggested slightly earlier (e.g. 13 years) or slightly later as the "age of cessation." In England, Cyril Burt advocated 15 years. Consensus was to settle on the early 20s as the age at which "mental growth" reaches its apex in the individual. It was, however, also agreed that *rate* of increase peaks at around 16 years so that mental "power" is indeed at its greatest during the late teens. Thus the psychometric tradition presented the view that *adolescence* gives rise to a high point in intellectual ability.

This adolescent peak of the psychometricians is itself replete with qualitative connotations, although such aspects have always been rather poorly defined in comparison to the numerical precision of the quantitative account. The most systematic and influential formulation of *qualitative* differences in adolescent thinking has been that of Piaget. Although differing very greatly in important ways, Piaget's qualitative account is not inconsistent with the quantitative tradition. Indeed, it could be argued that Piaget's account consists of a qualitative reinterpretation of a finding based on psychometric methods, for the age which Piaget set for the initial emergence of adolescent thinking (11 to 12 years) was obtained from the employment of the verbal reasoning tests of Binet, Simon, and Burt.

As well as adapting the Binet tests for English use, Cyril Burt had devised his own. His intention was to improve on Binet in one particular way: In the detection of intellectual superiority. The Burt test focused on verbal reasoning and logical argument, requiring its subjects to combine sets of if/then statements and to understand problems of transitivity. The most similar test in Binet was the detection of absurdities ("I have three brothers, Jack, Tom, and myself") for which Binet found average achievement at 10 to 12 years, Burt at 11 years. Such were the items with which Jean Piaget worked in Paris in 1920 and to which he referred throughout his career as indicators of adolescent thinking. Moreover, the age of 10 to 11 became a fixed point in Piaget's chronology of intellectual development. *Judgment and reasoning in the child* (1924) discusses the changes occurring at 11 to 12 years. Piaget had earlier, in 1922, identified this age as the time of onset of formal reasoning, basing his decision on experiments with tests taken from the literature. Formal reasoning, for example, enables the young person to understand the absurdity statements of Binet. For Piaget, it is the logic of *relations* that is not understood by the child. With the "three brothers" test, for example, the child has to distinguish between the point of view of the total set of three brothers and the point of view of the fraternal inter-relationships between the brothers. "Point of view" is used here in a very broad and metaphorical sense, as a topic or feature. The 9- or 10-year-old, for Piaget, treats "brother" as an absolute, invariant across the two "points of view" (as it would be correct to treat the word "boy," being nonrelational). What emerges after 11 to 12 years, for Piaget, is an awareness of logical *necessity*. Formal thought, as it is called in *Judgment and reasoning*, seeks verification and noncontradiction. The child is freed from immediate beliefs of the moment. Assumptions and hypotheses can now be entertained. Where the younger child will dispute the premises of an hypothetical question ("What would happen if there were no air?" "There's always air!"), the 11- to 12-year-old accepts the premise for the sake of argument. The achievements of the 11- to 12-year-old are seen as constituting the mature level of logical reasoning. This mature level works with relationships, rather than with the single, absolute objects of "egocentric immediacy".

Philosophical claims play an important part here. For Piaget, the immediate data of the external world form a "flux." However[6], "A certain number of fixed points stand out in contrast to this flux, such as concepts and the relations subsisting between them, in a word, the whole universe of logic." This standpoint appears close to such idealist philosophies as Plato's. For Piaget, logic is independent of time and hence in a state of equilibrium (in other words, it is perfect). It has no temporal structure; it is "reversible." *Psychological* structures attain a similarly exalted status only when mental operations can return freely from an end-point to a starting-point. Piaget's account of the end-point of cognitive development is thus couched in terms of a logico-mathematical idealism. The 11- to 12-year-old is apparently making contact with eternal truths.

In later writings, and especially during the 1940s, Piaget became concerned with the formalisation of his developmental theory. One aspect of this concern was the introduction of the terminology of "operations." Thus the thought of the (older) child was now termed "concrete operational" and that of the adolescent "formal operational." Another aspect was the reinterpretation of child and adolescent thinking, as previously identified, in logico-mathematical terms. Piaget's longstanding interest in mathematical logic gave rise to publications in the area around the late 1940s. The co-authored *The growth of logical thinking from childhood to adolescence* (1955) is heavily influenced by this work. In this book Piaget presents his logico-mathematical account of adolescent thinking, with illustrations from a number of empirical studies. The experimental work involves the presentation of some physical apparatus, such as a pendulum, a balance, or communicating vessels filled with water, with the subject essentially being required to work out the basic physical principles involved. That is, the subject must establish what it is (weight of bob, length of string) that causes a pendulum to swing fast or slow; and so on. The subject's task is the "discovery of the law" in each case.

Piaget's developmental analysis comprises two concrete-operational stages (in the child) and two stages within the formal-operational thought of the adolescent. Concrete-operational thought is hence to some extent redefined, and formal thought is divided into a preparatory and a consummatory ("equilibrium") stage. The first of the formal stages emerges at around 11 to 12 years, as in Piaget's previous accounts; the second at around 15 years. Piaget's attention is focused on the ways in which subjects attempt to establish the factors controlling the particular system. The child's attempts are described as unsystematic, whereas those of the adolescent are increasingly controlled by the techniques of experimentation: The testing out of all possibilities and the varying of one factor at a time. Such systematic experimentation emerges in the *second* of the formal-operational stages, the first exhibiting only preliminary versions of this behaviour. Indeed, there is considerable continuity between the second concrete-operational and the first formal-operational stage (that is, the stages either side of 11 to 12 years). In this sense, the data might seem to support a starting-point of around 15 years for formal operations as here defined. However, Piaget appears committed to the transition point of 11 to 12.

Piaget's theoretical account is based on an analysis of the protocols of the oldest subjects. For Piaget, these formal-operational subjects are working with a fully integrated system of logical operations. This system is described in terms of two kinds of logico-mathematical structure, the *group* and the *lattice*. The group features relate to a closed system of operations, realised most clearly in problems relating to dynamic equilibrium in physical apparatus (water in communicating vessels). Here the adolescent's thinking is taken to model and to reflect the set of self-cancelling and counterbalancing relationships operating in the apparatus. The lattice features relate to an exhaustive system of propositional logic (of "if p then q" relations) such that all possible combinations of implication are available for inspection. Those problems in verbal reasoning which Piaget still takes as indicative of formal thought are now interpreted in terms of this propositional framework.

The new account of formal thinking is linked to a reinterpretation of thinking during the concrete operations of later childhood. The "group" structure of formal thought is now contrasted with the less totally integrated "groupings" of concrete thought. These "groupings" refer to the rather limited kinds of logical treatment available to the child in dealing with classes (especially the inclusion of one set in another) and with relations (especially transitivity). Likewise, the lattice structure of formal thought is contrasted with the kinds of classificatory scheme available to the child. Further, Piaget argues that concrete thinking involves two distinct kinds of "reversibility," one connected with classes and one with relations. His group structure for formal thinking (referred to as the I.N.R.C. group) combines and integrates these two forms of reversibility.

Piaget's account of intellectual development from approximately seven to eight years upward is now, therefore, couched in somewhat abstruse logico-mathematical terms. But this formulation should be seen as a direct extension of earlier versions, which still provide the framework. Even the more general characterisations of the developmental change can be seen as extensions of earlier claims. In *The growth of logical linking* the formal thinker is characterised as operating with *possibilities*; what is actually the case being treated by the subject as fitting into a broader framework of what might have been. This is entirely consistent with the conclusions of Piaget's earlier work in which children were described as over-attached to actual reality and hence unable to work with hypotheticals ("Suppose there were no air?"). Piaget's adolescent is centrally concerned with the hypothetical: "If such and such is the case, then . . ."

As far as the structure of intellect is concerned, Piaget's account of formal operations in late adolescence essentially represents an account of adult competence. Thus, "this general form of equilibrium can be conceived of as final in the sense that it is not modified during the lifespan of the individual." Here it might be noted that recapitulationary parallels with the history of science play a part in Piaget's account. Thus, the Greeks are considered not to have achieved the experimental methods observed in the modern adolescent (and therefore "it is probable that the Greek children were behind our own"). Similarly, the suggestion that certain aspects of mechanical equilibrium are intrinsically *difficult* is backed up by the note that its "late appearance in the history of science . . . [being] unknown to the Greeks, is evidence that such a difficulty exists." Finally something should be said on Piaget's more general claims concerning adolescence. Piaget's emphasis is on the intellectual changes seen to characterise adolescent development. However, he has also attempted to give some causative status to affective and social factors. In the concluding chapter of *The growth of logical thinking* Piaget argues for a reciprocal relationship between social demands (the requirement to fulfil adult roles in society) and the affective and intellectual changes in the individual. This qualification of the role of the intellect seems rather out of context in this book, although the emphasis on social relationships in fact continues directly from the books of the 1920s and from *The moral judgment of the child* of 1932. (In fact, much of this chapter appears to be a rewritten version of a paper first published in 1940.)[7]

For Piaget, the adolescent is above all concerned, and *able* to be concerned, with the future, and hence with planning. The logico-mathematical *means* of thought are tied to social and personal *ends*. The working out of a personal life-programme is for Piaget the epitome of adolescence (after all, he did it himself). The adolescent is idealistic, grandiose, even Messianic. Intellect is over-valued; thought and "Ideas" are believed to be capable of changing the universe. The adolescent is in possession of mature intellectual structures but has yet to apply them in an adult way (the world of work playing a major educative role in this respect). These claims concerning the characteristics and concerns of adolescent thought are of considerable antiquity; idealism and a concern for the future having been noted in the adolescent by Aristotle, for example. Similarly, Eduard Spranger's influential *The psychology of youth* (1924) had described the adolescent as concerned with formulating a life-plan and selecting a system of values.[8] More of the background to Piaget's *general* claims on adolescence will be outlined in the next section.

Piaget's position on the lifespan status of adolescent thinking is expressed with more consistency in the 1940 paper (noted earlier) than in the 1955 book. In 1940, adolescence is presented as a period of disequilibrium, to be resolved by an equilibrium state in adulthood. In 1955 adolescent thinking itself represents an equilibrium state: A *formal* equilibrium in the formal-operational mechanisms. Piaget attempts to disavow a position of intellectual primacy, according to which cognitive change must precede any advance in affectivity or in social co-ordination. However his commitment to the role of logico-mathematical structures makes such a position unavoidable. In spite of himself, perhaps, Piaget's account of adolescence bases itself on the emergence of adult reasoning: A position quite compatible, at least in broad terms, with a straightforwardly biological view of "mental growth."

ADOLESCENCE AND TURMOIL

As we have seen, Piaget attempted—perhaps unsuccessfully—to outline a theory of adolescent development which gave equal weight to intellect and to affect. In doing so, he acknowledged the longstanding tradition by which adolescence is seen as a period of emotional turmoil, of "storm and stress." This account of adolescence as the high-point of the emotions is to be found in Rousseau's *Emile* and in the influential writings of Stanley Hall. In between, the Romantic writers produced creative works extolling the virtue of the passions and the potential of youth, popularising the term "storm and stress" (*Sturm und Drang*) itself. However it has been psychoanalytic theory, starting with Sigmund Freud and continuing with his daughter Anna, which has incorporated the concept of adolescent turmoil in the most systematic way.

As noted in the previous section, Jean-Jacques Rousseau had located the peak of intellectual curiosity in his third stage of 12 to 15 years. Already in this period, he notes that "the passions are approaching . . . as soon as they knock on the door, your pupil will no longer pay attention to anything but them." The next stage begins with the sudden emergence of the sexual passions: It is a "moment of crisis," a "second birth"[9]: "A change in humor, frequent anger, a mind in constant agitation, makes the child almost unmanageable ... His feverishness turns him into a lion. He disregards his guide; he no longer wishes to be governed." Such characterisation already reflected received wisdom, and was to remain the orthodox view of adolescence. The account promulgated early in the present century by Stanley Hall, some 150 years after Rousseau, can be said to have done little more than reformulate this received wisdom into evolutionary terms. For Hall, the "second birth" became a great leap in developmental progress, corresponding to the phylogenetic emergence of a new stage in man's ancestry. "Storm and stress" was the inevitable result in the young individual retracing this catastrophic evolutionary event. Edmund Sanford —colleague of Stanley Hall, research supervisor of Gesell and Terman— outlined a lifespan account of human development in which adolescence was described as a period of maladjustment and disturbance, arising from its transitional nature (age seven to eight being another major transition point). The adolescent transition is initiated by accelerated physical growth and by puberty. For Sanford, the adolescent's increased powers of reasoning are unbalanced and still immature; interests are unstable. This is the time of ideals, of altruism, of a concern for religious and moral questions. As far as sexuality is concerned, it is the time of attachments of the male youth to the older woman or of young girls one to another.[10]

Sigmund Freud's accounts of adolescence, starting with the *Three essays on the theory of sexuality* (1905), emphasise the psychological tasks faced by the young person and examine some of the possible variations in individual development. For Freud, the adolescent has to move toward a genital-based sexuality involving an opposite-sex partner from outside the immediate family (exogamy). Relationships such as homosexual or age-incongruous ones are, for Freud, immature and should be merely transitory. The latency period of middle to late childhood, which emerges from a resolution of the Oedipal conflicts (including fear of the father), is a relatively tranquil one. But latency is upset by the onset of biological puberty; many of the early childhood conflicts break out again, demanding resolution even more urgently than before. For Freud, the latency period is an evolutionary device which has enabled mankind to establish adult, exogamous sexuality and hence to construct civilisation itself. There is a correspondence between early childhood and adolescence, which are both periods of conflict, and between latency and adulthood, which are both periods of relative calm.

Freud's correspondence theory of adolescence was based on recapitulationary logic, but it did not explore the notion of a systematic repetition in adolescence of early childhood events. This approach was investigated by Freud's colleague and biographer, the psychoanalyst Ernest Jones, who published his "recapitulation" theory of adolescence in 1922. For Jones,[11]

"Adolescence recapitulates infancy, and . . . the precise way in which a given person will pass through the necessary stages of development in adolescence is to a very great extent determined by the form of his infantile development." Jones' "recapitulation" theory, referred to as such in later psychoanalytic writing, is a theory of repetition within the lifespan. It is derived, however, from Freud's theory of *ancestral* recapitulation. More generally, adolescence was coming under the attention of an increasing number of psychoanalytic thinkers in the 1920s and early 1930s. Anna Freud's first and most influential account of adolescent development was presented in *The ego and the mechanisms of defence* of 1936. Sigmund Freud's books of the 1920s had placed increasing emphasis on the role of the ego (that part of the psychic apparatus including consciousness) in comparison to his earlier focus on the unconscious id. Anna Freud developed this line of investigation, treating the ego as a component of the individual personality possessing a degree of autonomy, and going through important changes in the lifespan (whereas the contents of the id were treated as largely invariant through life). For Anna Freud—whose therapeutic work focused on children rather than adults—adolescence constitutes a period in which the ego can be studied with some precision and she therefore used adolescence for examples and evidence in documenting her general theoretical claims.

Anna Freud's account of the ego and the id at puberty begins with a summary of the established phenomena of adolescence as noted in *non*analytic writings. These claims are indeed common to many theoretical formulations on adolescence; moreover, Anna Freud's own statements have been very influential. Further, the very *style* of the account plays a role in its message. For all these reasons, this passage (and several following) justify being quoted at length. According to Anna Freud, nonanalytic writing had accurately described[12]:

> the disturbances in the psychic equilibrium, and . . . the incomprehensible and irreconcilable contradictions then apparent in the psychic life. Adolescents are excessively egoistic, regarding themselves as the centre of the universe and the sole object of interest, and yet at no time in later life are they capable of so much self-sacrifice and devotion. They form the most passionate love relations, only to break them off as abruptly as they began them. On the one hand, they throw themselves enthusiastically into the life of the community and, on the other, they have an overpowering longing for solitude. They oscillate between blind submission to some self-chosen leader and defiant rebellion against any and every authority. They are selfish and materially minded and at the same time full of lofty idealism. They are ascetic but will suddenly plunge into instinctual indulgence of the most primitive character. At times their behaviour to other people is rough and inconsiderate, yet they themselves are extremely touchy. Their moods veer between

> light-hearted optimism and the blackest pessimism. Sometimes they will work with indefatigable enthusiasm and at other times they are sluggish and apathetic.

Anna Freud endorsed these claims and attempted to formulate a psychoanalytic explanation. Adolescence was, for Anna Freud, the indirect response to puberty; the organism's attempt to cope with an essentially *physiological* event. In her rephrasing of Sigmund Freud's account[13]:

> The latency period sets in, with a physiologically conditioned decline in the strength of the instincts, and a truce is called . . . But the breathing space provided by the latency period does not last long. The struggle between the two antagonists, the ego and the id, has scarcely ended in this temporary truce before the terms of agreement are radically altered by the reinforcement of one of the combatants. The physiological process which marks the attainment of physical sexual maturity is accompanied by a stimulation of the instinctual processes . . . The relation established between the forces of the ego and the id is destroyed, the painfully achieved psychic balance is upset, with the result that the inner conflicts between the two institutions blaze up afresh.

For Anna Freud, "the quantity of instinctual energy has increased," thus reviving the dormant id; "there are very few new elements in the invading forces. Their onslaught merely brings once more to the surface the familiar content of the early infantile sexuality of little children." The embattled ego attempts to keep its grip. Were it to be overwhelmed, then entrance into adult life "will be marked by a riot of uninhibited gratification of instinct." The ego does, however, have some defensive processes available to it, and it is the description of these which constitutes Anna Freud's theoretical contribution. Two of these defence mechanisms are *intellectualisation* and *asceticism*. Anna Freud's "intellectualisation" is a mechanism by which instinctual demands are resisted by a kind of intellectual detachment. For Freud, the adolescent becomes "more intelligent" with "the accession of instinctual energy." As she notes, this result is a reverse of the usual situation in which "the storms of instinct or affect [bear] an inverse relation to the subject's intellectual activity."

Where the interests of latency had been "concrete"—focused on things which have "an actual, objective existence"—those of the adolescent are in "abstractions." Some adolescents have "an insatiable desire to think about abstract subjects, to turn them over in their minds, and to talk about them." They[14]: "will argue the case for free love or marriage and family life . . . or discuss philosophical problems such as religion or free thought, or different political theories, such as revolution versus submission to authority . . ." In intellectualism, if not perhaps in intellectualisation as such, Anna Freud's adolescent is a close relation of Jean Piaget's. The relationship consists in the main of common ancestry: Of common background assumptions. However, Piaget does in fact make reference to Anna Freud in his concluding chapter to *The growth of logical thinking*. Like Piaget's, Anna Freud's adolescent fails to live up to his (or her) intellect[15]:

> His empathy into the mental processes of other people does not prevent him from displaying the most outrageous lack of consideration toward those nearest to him . . . The fact that his understanding of and interest in the structure of society often far exceed those of later years does not assist him in the least to find his true place in social life, nor does the many-sidedness of his interests deter him from concentrating upon a single point—his preoccupation with his own personality.

Again, the final comment here converges with Piaget's notion of a peculiarly adolescent form of egocentrism.

The second major kind of defence mechanism is "asceticism." Here, the adolescent attempts to repress all kinds of sensory and physical drives in order to prevent the incursion of the forces of the id. For Anna Freud, this general kind of repression is more primitive than the more specific kinds found in adult neurotics. It reflects[16]:

> a disposition to repudiate certain instincts, in particular the sexual instincts, indiscriminately and independently of individual experience. This disposition appears to be a phylogenetic inheritance, a kind of deposit accumulated from acts of repression practised by many generations and merely continued, not initiated, by individuals.

Like Sigmund Freud, Anna Freud appeals to the Lamarckian formula of inheritance in proposing this recapitulationary explanation for adolescent asceticism. Although much more narrowly focused, with an almost exclusive concentration on issues relating directly to therapy, the daughter retains the biological determinism and the non-Darwinian framework of the father.

Anna Freud's account of adolescence has been of very great influence, stimulating the work of such psychoanalytic students of adolescence as Peter Blos and, more importantly, Erik Homburger Erikson. Where analysts such as Blos remained within mainstream psychoanalysis, Erikson attempted to synthesise the Freudian account with more anthropological considerations (as discussed in the next section). But the general features of the Freudian account—the set of phenomena taken as fundamental facts of adolescent behaviour—are also common to a much broader range of theories. As we have seen, even the highly intellectualist account of Piaget agrees on many points. This orthodoxy or received wisdom treats adolescence as in large part a psychological unbalancing or "disequilibrium" resulting from sexual maturation, a viewpoint which is straightforwardly biological.

THE ADOLESCENT IN CULTURE

As we have seen, adolescence has been considered a period in which the individual is especially aware of his or her own place (both present and future) in a society and a culture. The general relationships between individual development and culture have been of long-standing interest to developmental psychologists. Perhaps the most influential accounts of these relationships have been those of the close contemporaries and colleagues, Margaret Mead and Erik Erikson. Both authors—the first an anthropologist, the second a psychoanalyst—have had an especial interest in adolescence, partly because of a concern with the varying characteristics of the adult worlds into which young people were seen as entering at that stage. In addition, however, both authors set adolescence firmly within the lifespan, relating adolescence to earlier and to later phases of development. Of the two, Erikson has retained more of a special interest in adolescence and his account remains of very considerable influence.

As we have seen, the notion that adolescence is an intrinsically stressful period is an old and pervasive one. The most direct challenge to this assumption came from comparative anthropology, with the proposal that adolescence is only stressful in certain cultures (and hence only because of certain culture-bound factors). This cultural-relativist form of anthropology was championed early this century by Franz Boas as an alternative to the predominantly biological-evolutionary character of classical anthropology. It was a student of Boas, Margaret Mead, who produced the first, and in many ways the most influential, document arguing the cultural-relativist case in the context of adolescence: *Coming of age in Samoa* (1928). Margaret Mead's introduction to this book states its aim very clearly. The book's objective is to challenge the notion that adolescence is *inevitably* a period of "difficulties and conflicts" as argued by Stanley Hall and others. For Mead, such disturbances do in fact emerge in her contemporary America but they are a cultural product, not a biological necessity. Franz Boas himself, in his preface to Mead's book, outlines a broader target: The view that "the difficulties of childhood and of adolescence" are unavoidable. As he notes, "the whole psycho-analytic approach is largely based on this supposition."

Mead's empirical evidence came from Samoa where, she claimed, adolescence was experienced as a relaxed and not a stressful period.[17] Mead did not question that adolescence was indeed a time of disturbance in contemporary America. Hence she retained a modified version of the "storm and stress" approach. Her more detailed argument was that adolescent problems in Western society arise from the complexity of that society and from conflicting demands which are thus made on young people. The Samoan society was a "primitive" one: It was simple, making clear-cut requirements of its youth. Its simplicity was held to enable swift and accurate study: "a trained student can master the fundamental structure of a primitive society in a few months." This picture of the relationships between societies is essentially an evolutionist one, with the implication that more "advanced" cultures are more "complex." The implication of Mead's argument is that adolescent disturbance is indeed inevitable *in an advanced society*. Despite the cultural determinism, then, and perhaps underpinning it, biologistic assumptions may be discerned. That such a reading is not merely tendentious is supported by more historical considerations. Mead's Samoa book is essentially in a long tradition of South Sea romances on the peacefulness of the "primitive," and such accounts had been assimilated easily into late 19th-century evolutionist thinking.

Whatever the status of biological thinking in Mead's early work, her mature statements certainly came to be increasingly biological. The reasons for this change probably include the influence of Mead's one-time husband Gregory Bateson, who came to anthropology from zoology, and the influence of Erik Erikson who began writing on developmental issues in the 1930s and 1940s. *Male and female* (1950) is representative of the mature Mead. With empirical material drawn from seven Pacific Island cultures, including Samoa, Mead attempts to establish the "basic regularities in human sex development." Perhaps inevitably, such regularities turn out to constitute a set of biological constraints which over-ride any cultural variation. Mead admits a "new willingness to come to grips with our biological past . . . [with] the limitations imposed by our mammalian nature" and refers to "our biological ancestry that we dare not flout."

Such a change of tone is substantive, not merely stylistic. Mead's account of the origin and nature of sex differences is very closely tied to psychoanalytic accounts of human development and shares their attachment to biological argument. For Freud, and in general for Freudians such as Erikson, the course of human development shares certain universal and essentially biological characteristics. The centre of the child's psychic world moves from the mouth (first sucking, then biting) to the anus (retaining or releasing the faeces) to the phallus; activities relating to these stages (taking in, holding on, letting go) remaining fundamental to the individual personality. Developmental differences between the sexes are basically caused by assymmetry in early experience—the fact that a *female* mother is encountered both by a son and by a daughter. Subsequently, it is the presence or absence of a penis that is all-important.

Margaret Mead endorses all of these psychoanalytic claims as representing *universals* of development. Thus[18]:

> the girl finds that the reinterpretation of impregnation and conception and birth fits easily into her early experience with the intake of food, while the boy with the same initial experience . . . will find himself heavily confused if he attempts to use it to interpret his own (role). The girl-child who has received her mother's breast happily need make no new or structurally different adjustment to accept an adult sex relationship. Inception is a form of behaviour that fits *the essential biological rhythm of her being.*

Again, on weaning (and again universally), the break from the mother-child relationship is in a sense temporary for the girl since "she will some day repeat it" (as a mother); while the boy "leaves it forever, reliving it only inasmuch as intercourse may express symbolically re-entry into the womb." Mead's whole argument in *Male and female* is psychoanalytically influenced in similar ways. In concluding her chapter on "basic regularities" she notes that, whereas the male *must* be enabled (in some cultural fashion) to reach "a solid sense of irreversible achievement," in the case of women "it is only necessary that they be permitted . . . to fulfil their biological role, to attain this sense of irreversible achievement." Mead's position on early development and on sex differences is straightforwardly Freudian, in its basic assumptions.

From cultural determinism, as apparently espoused in *Coming of age in Samoa*, Mead has now reached biological determinism. The newly written introduction to the 1962 edition of *Male and female* states that she now considers herself to have *under*estimated the role of biology and evolution in that book. Mead now notes that she would wish to include the hypothesis that the relationship between son and father is based on evolutionary history. That is, she would now wish to propose that the son's need to "discipline his impulses towards a very much larger, stronger, male parent" was developed "as a biologically given pattern in earlier human forms, when men matured much earlier, before the establishment of the learning period which separates childhood from adulthood today [Freud's latency]." This is straightforward Freudian recapitulation theory. In fact, with its appeal to early-maturing ancestors in explaining the behaviour of modern *children*, it could well have been written by Stanley Hall himself.

In the sense that Freudian theory has always formed the basis of his thinking, biology has played a more explicit role in the writing of Erik Erikson. Although only one year younger than Mead, and a close colleague, Erikson's influence has been more recent (largely since the publication of *Childhood and society* in 1950). Erikson came to Vienna in the late 1920s as an itinerant art student to take up a school-teaching post associated with Freud's psychoanalytic movement. He underwent analysis with Anna Freud alongside training as a child psychoanalyst, and also graduated from the Montessori training programme. On his arrival in the U.S.A. in the 1930s, Erikson's research interests focused on play in children and young adults—a topic influenced by both his Freudian and his Montessori background.[19] Just prior to and during World War II Erikson became interested in the culture and childrearing of the native American Sioux and Yurok. At this time also he wrote an article on Nazi Germany which included some discussion on the nature of adolescence.

While retaining his commitment to orthodox Freudian theory, Erikson was already moving well beyond the usual traditions of "applied psychoanalysis." He accepted that the Yurok people presented characteristics justifying the category "anal" (that is, "personality" traits related in Freudian theory to the anal stage of development) but took this as a starting-point rather than a finishing-point in his investigation. His analysis of Adolf Hitler was essentially sociological and political rather than a case history, and his comparison between Hitler's Germany and adolescence was hedged with cautions.

Erikson's interests were increasingly in social, cultural, and historical issues, topics quite antithetical to the biological individualism of orthodox Freudian theory. However, Erikson took this conflict to demand synthesis, not a choice between the disciplines. The synthesis was attempted in his 1946 paper *Ego development and historical change*. Here Erikson attempted to formulate a notion of "group identity," comprising the perceived goals and values common to a group or a nation, within the framework of Freudian theory. His focus was on the importance of social organisation in the development of the individual ego. The historical and geographical awareness of a community was thus brought to centre stage in a manner quite foreign to orthodox Freudian theory. For Erikson, however, the two approaches could be brought into agreement by means of Freud's notion of the superego.

According to Freud, the superego is the representative in the individual of the line of paternal authority, stretching back into prehistory. It provides for the continuity of moral control across the generations. The internalisation of moral restraint is held by Freud to have come to be hereditary by Lamarckian principles, and Erikson extends this Lamarckist mechanism by claiming that aspects of cultural history may also come to be transmitted directly after many generations. Hence, for Erikson, the superego comprises not only the personal qualities of the parents but also "the characteristics and traditions of the race from which they spring." Erikson's account of cultural transmision is, then, a highly biological one. It enabled Erikson to pursue his interests in social organisation without having to abandon the Freudian framework.

For Erikson, "group identity" is complementary to the "ego identity" of an individual. The concept of "ego identity" is a straightforward application of the ego psychology developed by the Viennese psychoanalysts with whom Erikson had studied. Ego psychology, to some extent initiated by Anna Freud herself, involved a shift of emphasis from the instinctual processes of the id to the more conscious and adaptive activity of the ego. Later, Erikson was to propose that ego identity is a major and particular concern of the developing adolescent—a claim upon which his whole account of adolescence would be based.

Erikson's *Childhood and society* (1950), which includes much reworked material of an earlier date, makes it clear that Freud's account of psychosexual development is to be the starting-off point. Erikson endorses Freud's "id" as "the oldest province of the mind, both in individual terms . . . and in phylogenetic terms, for the id is the deposition in us of the whole of evolutionary history." For Erikson, psychoanalysis cannot "remain a workable system of enquiry without its basic biological formulations"; thus he is prepared to speak "of biologically given potentialities which develop with the child's organism." More specifically, Erikson argues that "the Freudian laws of psychosexual growth in infancy can best be understood through an analogy with physiological development in utero." This is not the recapitulation theory of embryology as such, but a related notion: What Erikson terms the "epigenetic" theory of development. Epigenesis for Erikson consists of a programmed sequence of development, by which each of a set of organs emerges at the right time. Any disturbance of "proper rate" or "normal sequence" gives rise to pathology. The appeal to biological arguments is explicit here, as a substantial quotation from Erikson should make clear[20]:

> Still a "precerebrate" bundle fit only for a slow increase of limited kinds and intensities of stimulation, the infant has now left the chemical exchange of the womb for maternal care within the training system of his society. *How the maturing organism continues to unfold by developing not new organs, but a prescribed sequence of locomotor, sensory, and social capacities* is described in the literature of child development. Psychoanalysis has added to this an understanding of the more idiosyncratic experiences and conflicts by which an individual becomes a distinct person . . . it is first of all important to realise that in the sequence of significant experiences *the healthy child, if halfway properly guided, merely obeys and on the whole can be trusted to obey inner laws of development*, namely those laws which in his prenatal period had formed one organ after another and which now create a succession of potentialities for significant interaction with those around him. *While such interaction varies widely from culture to culture, in ways to be indicated presently, proper rate and proper sequence remain critical factors guiding and limiting all variability.*

As this quotation demonstrates, Erikson's biological assumptions on preprogrammed sequences of growth play a central part in his articulation of the role of culture in development. Having noted that some of the later Mead might almost have been written by Stanley Hall, it could be observed that some of Erikson might almost have been written by Arnold Gesell.

Childhood and society contains two pictorial accounts of developmental stages. The first (and earlier) diagram is simply an expansion and reinterpretation of Freud's account, a chart comprising "zones"—oral, anal, genital—and "modes"—incorporative, retentive, eliminative, intrusive. Erikson's reformulations reflect a greater concern for the positive outcomes of the various stages, such as "basic trust" resulting from the oral experience. Elsewhere in *Childhood and society* Erikson presents a second chart of lifespan development in which these outcomes are taken as the key features of what he now terms "psycho*social* stages." Here, each of Freud's four psychosexual stages up to latency are re-labelled, and Freud's final (adult, genital) stage is expanded to four stages, from youth to old age. The result is Erikson's "eight stages of man."

Both of Erikson's charts in the revised edition of 1965 show developmental progress as ascending the page; for the first chart this is a reversal of orientation. Erikson now notes that he has "accepted the repeated recommendation that a chart of growth should ascend [the page], like family trees and pictorialisations of evolutionary descent." In a similar vein, he notes (with reference to some comments by Konrad Lorenz) a "feeling that the relation of modes and zones points to a biological and evolutionary principle." It should perhaps be noted at this point that Erikson elsewhere does reject the claim that "primitive" adults can usefully be compared with "civilised" children. Erikson states, with irony, that "primitive societies are neither infantile stages of mankind nor arrested deviations from the proud progressive norms which we represent." Erikson's brief summary of his eight-stage theory has been of considerable influence. "Youth" or adolescence—the fifth stage—is characterised in terms of a need for the achievement of (ego) identity. The biological emphasis should be noted, however[21]: "But in puberty and adolescence all samenesses and continuities relied on earlier are more or less questioned again, because of a rapidity of body growth which equals that of early childhood and because of the new addition of genital maturity. The growing and developing youths [are] faced with this physiological revolution with them . . ."

Erikson's brief account of "identity vs. role diffusion" has since been expanded with considerable clinical detail. Essentially, this stage represents a preparation or transition into the mature "genitality" described by Freud, which is now located by Erikson in "young adulthood." Like Freud's, Erikson's mature young adult should be looking for mutuality of orgasm in a *heterosexual* relationship. The final two stages of life are characterised by "generativity vs. stagnation" and finally by "ego integrity vs. despair." Erikson's lifespan account could be considered a developmental-stage theory of the ego, where Freud's was a developmental-stage theory of the id.

What then should be said of the ostensive culture-sensitivity of Erikson's account of adolescence? As the long quotation (earlier) makes clear, the variability available to cultures is severely constrained. In his conclusion to the chapter on "infantile sexuality" Erikson notes that cultures "elaborate upon the biologically given." Erikson's theory remains, like Freud's, a biological one in its essentials. Erikson's adolescent, like at least the later Mead's, grows up in a manner determined much more by biology than by society. Like the baby and like the child, the adolescent has been seen by developmentalists as approaching adulthood only by obeying the dictates of biology.

NOTES TO CHAPTER EIGHT

[1]Early theories of adolescence are discussed by Muuss (1968). Recent and contemporary approaches are outlined in Coleman (1980) for whom theory in adolescent development remains dominated by "classical" formulations, especially the notion of turmoil. A more innovatory approach is indicated by Youniss (1983a).

[2]Lifespan approaches are examined in Chapter Ten.

[3]The work of Binet is discussed variously by Gould (1984), by Voyat in his chapter in Riegel and Meacham (1976), and by Wolf in her biography (1973). The important work by Flynn on massive secular increase in measured I.Q. is most recently summarised in his chapter in Olssen (1988; also see Olssen's chapter. The cover illustration to this collection is particularly striking.)

[4]Wolf (1973, p. 203).

[5]Relations between racism and evolution theory are discussed by Gould (1977). As observed by Sève (1974/1978, p. 216) "where biologism flourishes racism is never far away."

[6]Piaget (1924/1928, p. 171).

[7]Piaget (1940/1967). ("The mental development of the child," reissued as part of *Six psychological studies*.)

[8]Spranger's 'interpretive' approach to adolescent development is discussed by Muuss (1968) and by Thomae in Riegel and Meacham (1976). In the Preface to his *Types of men* Spranger (1928, p. XII) writes:

> The supplement to [my] type psychology would be a developmental psychology emphasising on one hand structural transformations in the different ages of individuals and on the other, structural changes in the human soul itself during its thousand-year-old history. So far I have only attacked the first part of this problem in my *Psychologie des Jugendalters* . . . It is also necessary to study the mental structure of primitive people or earlier cultural epochs, and a few attempts have been made in this direction. To Stanley Hall's well-known book *Adolescence* I owe many suggestions. And Spengler . . . [has] shown an especially fine psychological sense in this direction . . . We must bridge the gap between soul and soul, and if possible in the same way between group and

group. This is, as it were, the conscious re-establishment of the divine total context of life from which our modern culture has drifted away but without which a higher culture in the long run cannot last.

[9]Rousseau (1762/1979, p. 211).
[10]Sanford (1902).
[11]Cited in A. Freud (1958/1969, p. 138).
[12]A. Freud (1936/1968, pp. 137–138). Reproduced by permission of the estate of Anna Freud by arrangement with Mark Paterson and Associates.
[13]Ibid., pp. 144–145.
[14]Ibid., pp. 159–160.
[15]Ibid., p. 160.
[16]Ibid., p. 157.
[17]Margaret Mead's early Samoan work has been severely criticised by Freeman (1984) who suggests that Mead was misled by an over-reliance on the accounts of adolescence presented to her by the young girls who were her informants. Sexual license does not appear to have existed in the way reported to, and by, Mead. Freeman should also be consulted for a summary of the conflicting viewpoints (evolutionist and relativist) in the anthropology of the early years of this century.
[18]M. Mead (1950/1962, p. 144); emphasis added.
[19]Erikson's early interest in children's spatial representation, and the connection with Montessori training, are noted by Coles (1970/1973). General relationships between Freudian psychoanalysis and Montessori training in the Vienna of the 1930s are discussed by Kramer (1976, p. 319) who emphasises the role of Lili Roubiczek in trying to bring the two traditions together. On Montessori, also see Walkerdine in Henriques et al. (1984).
[20]Erikson (1950/1965, p. 61); emphasis added.
[21]Ibid., pp. 252–253.

9 Models and Processes

INTRODUCTION

The previous three chapters have been concerned with theoretical positions relating fairly narrowly to subdivisions of the lifespan. In the present chapter we are concerned with issues which transcend these boundaries: Issues of overall explanatory frameworks and of general developmental processes. Assumptions concerning such factors have to a considerable extent determined the definition of the boundaries themselves. It should also be noted that the criterial ages themselves have a history: That is to say, certain ages have been taken by many authors as transition points, independently of extensive theorisation or empirical research. The ages of 7 years and 14 years have an especially long history. For example, classical divisions of the lifespan noted by James Sully in his *Teacher's handbook of psychology* include those of Beneke (0–3; 3–7; 7–14); Pfisterer (0–2; 2–7; 7–14); and Crichton Browne (0–1; 1–7; 7–14). Each also proposed a final pre-adult division, defined by age only in the last version as 14–21. The number 7 has been described as a "magical" number in psychology in several senses, and its role in theoretical subdivisions of childhood certainly has a ritual quality. The age of 7 years is of course a critical one in such theories as Piaget's.[1]

As with most of the preceding chapters, the major focus here is on the influence of biological ideas on the thinking of the developmentalists. As will be seen, issues of overall models of development and issues of general developmental process are closely interrelated.[2] Perhaps the most fundamental assumption concerning an overall picture of individual development is that of *progress*. Derived from, or at least legitimised by biological sources, the notion that the individual gets better and better as time passes has been central to most developmental thinking. Such an assumption is in many ways an inheritance from the evolutionism of the last century, although of course the general notion of human progress has deeper roots. Stage theories of individual development generally constitute concrete realisations of the doctrine of progress. That is, stages are usually defined as stages *toward* an end-point, normally the adult state. More generally, therefore, stage theories assume the presence of an in-built directionality in development: This assumption is sometimes explicitly formulated, sometimes not. Stage theories, of various kinds, have probably been the most enduring and most influential of the developmentalists' overall models of their subject matter.

Any stage theory of development, however precisely or loosely those stages are defined, leads to questions concerning the mechanism of change from one stage to the next. Other kinds of developmental theory must also give some account of the processes of change. The nature of such postulated mechanisms may simply reassert the assumption of progress: Change happens *because* the subsequent state is more satisfactory than the earlier one. In addition to such circular arguments, formulations of specific processes may also be offerred. One of the most general of such postulated processes has been that process by which new experience is incorporated into the present structure or state of the organism: That is, *assimilation*. To differing extents, it has been felt necessary to balance up such a process with a mechanism for the positive adaptation to such novelty. "Balance" itself has indeed been seen as a developmental process. The most systematic version of this is found in Piaget's theory in the form of "equilibration," a superordinate mechanism responsible for the balancing of such processes as "assimilation" and "accommodation." As will be noted, the concept of a superordinate balancing mechanism is one derived in part from psychoanalytic thinking.

Finally, the overall pattern of developmental change within the individual may be considered as exhibiting such features as "differentiation" or "integration," or some combination of the two. Consideration of the meanings and implications of these terms uncovers some of the interrelationships between the biological influences and the more epistemological influences discussed in Chapter Five. Thus, notions of differentiation as a developmental process have been influenced by the work of the Gestalt psychologists in the early decades of this century. The Gestalt movement was explicitly opposed to atomistic and elementalist interpretations of consciousness: Such interpretations being, as the Gestaltists were aware, direct derivations of empiricist and associationist philosophies of knowledge. The Gestalt emphasis was on structures and wholes. In this emphasis it converged, to some extent, with holistic doctrines originating from idealist versions of biology. For such reasons, the developmental impact of the Gestalt movement was somewhat diffused and perhaps distorted. For example: Heinz Werner, whose developmental theory gives the most prominence and status to a process of differentiation, was influenced jointly by the Gestaltists and by the idealist biology of von Uexküll.

Notions of integration are, similarly, of mixed biological-philosophical parentage. Integration may refer to the synthesis of isolated sense-impressions, or the "co-ordination" of separate bodily parts. The term may be applied in the context of neuromuscular control patterns, as in the theoretical claims of Arnold Gesell. All of these issues concern individual development as a whole, or rather individual development as a general (perhaps universal) phenomenon. Such an orientation is closely bound up with the biological approach to individual development and to the practice of looking to evolutionist biology for a theory of development.

The aim of this chapter is to explore the ways in which developmental psychology has applied such biological theory in defining itself and in constructing problems for empirical research programmes to tackle. It is a working assumption of this book that, in the main, theories determine empirical projects rather than the reverse. This chapter thus brings together much of the earlier material in presenting an outline of the origins of the major viewpoints on models and processes of individual development. Because of the range and the nature of the topics discussed, chronology is respected rather less as an organising principle in this chapter than in previous chapters.

PROGRESS AND DIRECTIONALITY

The assumption of progress in individual development is probably the most fundamental of the presuppositions of developmental psychology.[3] In general, theories address themselves to how and why progress takes place rather than *whether* progress takes place. The influence of evolutionary biology has certainly only been one among many in the installation of this assumption within developmental thinking. However, evolutionary arguments have certainly given structure and legitimacy to otherwise vague formulations. In general, the kinds of evolution theory to which appeal has been made in this context have not been Darwinian ones. Darwin's theory attributes a subtle and complex role to what might be termed progress or direction in evolution; by and large, his account provides a formulation free of such high-level, ordering principles. Non-Darwinian theories, in contrast, place considerable emphasis on such principles. These have been conceptualised in various terms, such as purpose, direction, or as a cohesion inherent in the evolutionary process. As we have seen, most developmentalists were influenced far more by non-Darwinian than by Darwinian formulations, so it is not surprising that assumptions concerning direction and progress play such a major part in their thinking.

The interrelated assumptions of progressive change, and of the ascent of a hierarchy, are of course fundamental to the concept of recapitulation. Even a fairly flexible version of recapitulation, like that of Baldwin, brings with it the implication that some overall scheme of progress is at work[4]: "The determination of the direction of evolution has been found to follow that of development . . . The determination of the individual's development is by a process of adjustment to a more or less stable environment. The evolution of the race is throughout, in its great features, a series of adaptations *to the same bionomic conditions*." Similar points are made by Piaget, for whom, again, the tasks of ontogeny and of the development of science (in this case) are in some respects the same.[5] "[Epistemology] will clearly have to aim more at analysing the 'stages' of scientific thought, and at explaining the intellectual mechanisms employed by the various fields of science in the conquest of reality. *The theory of knowledge is therefore essentially a theory of adaptation of thought to reality* . . ." Similarly, in *Adaptation and intelligence* (1974), Piaget notes that[6]: "If it were not for the multiple problems raised by the environment or the outside world, both organism and subject would remain conservatively oriented, and incapable of new invention (like . . . some human societies—or even some human adults)." Progress is an inherent presupposition of such general recapitulationist parallels.

Darwin's major claims on evolutionary mechanisms, especially as strengthened in neo-Darwinism, concern the *unplanned* and certainly unpredictable nature of phylogenetic change. Accounts based on, or flirting with, notions of progress or direction in evolutionary change thus represented the most fundamental alternative to Darwinism. This category should be seen as including the vitalistic formulations of Henri Bergson, for whom *both* Darwin and Lamarck were too mechanistic. Bergson's approach to evolution was of considerable influence on Piaget.

More significant, perhaps, was the issue of directionality: Some of those thinkers who focused their attention on this were in many ways sympathetic to the Darwinian claims. This group included several biologists with interests in human development and, most importantly for our purposes, it included James Mark Baldwin. Arguing from a number of cases, but especially from the evolution of social behaviour, Baldwin attempted to show that evolutionary change could be steered by the adaptations or "accommodations" of individuals and groups. This was "organic selection" (discussed in Chapter Three). For Baldwin and his co-workers in this area, C. Lloyd Morgan and H.F. Osborn, the process was seen as a refinement or improvement of Darwinism. The deficiencies in the radical neo-Darwinism of Weismann (with its exclusive advocacy of natural selection) were seen to centre on this issue of direction. Natural selection might operate as a weeding-out mechanism, but how could it take a species forward? If, however, animals' own accommodations and adaptations might somehow prepare the way for more permanent congenital variations then directionality would have a place. It should be emphasised that the directionality proposed here is of a low-level kind; Baldwin and his colleagues were not discerning grand plans for macro-evolution in this sense (although the commitment to recapitulationary parallels does itself have such connotations). The *extent* of directionality was perhaps no greater than in orthodox Darwinism: Positive responses to environmental change are by definition directional. But the *mechanism* for directionality was very different. For Darwin (in general) progress was a by-product, a consequence of the general mechanism which was itself essentially "blind." Organic selection allowed the mechanism some sight, albeit of restricted range, of the road ahead.

It is true that Darwin himself did propose, in Chapter VI of the *Origin*, that new habits might be seized on by the mechanisms of evolution to the extent that mutation of species might occur. Darwin's example was of a bear learning to swim in water and catching insects in its mouth, with the eventual descent after many generations of a whale-like animal.[7] Here Darwin is suggesting that a species' extension of its habits can alter selective pressures and hence give *natural* selection a grip on the reproductive success of variations. It is implied, I think, that the extension of habit is itself in some respect related to constitutional (heritable) factors. Darwin's general comment is that it is difficult to tell *and "immaterial"* whether habits or structure change first in a given situation; and "both probably often change almost simultaneously." In stark contrast to this cautious position is the claim of Baldwin[8]: "This position [organic selection] is the general one that *it is the individual accommodations which set the direction of evolution*, that is, which determine it; . . . .*Organic selection becomes, accordingly, a universal principle, provided, and in so far as, accommodation is universal*." For Baldwin, the leading role of accommodation—of adaptive habit—was of central importance. Natural selection was very much a secondary and a minor process. Short-term directionality, of the kind represented by an animal's adaptive response to environmental change or opportunity, was seen as the key to evolutionary progress: As Piaget was to put it, behaviour is to be seen as the "*motor*" of evolution.

James Mark Baldwin's version of genetic epistemology was expressed most comprehensively in the several volumes of *Thought and things* (1906–1911). As in his earlier writing, but with immensely greater detail and structure, Baldwin's mature theory described stages of development leading up to an intellectual and aesthetic ("pancalist") pinnacle.[8] Baldwin's *Thought and things* had rather little impact on developmental psychology, due partly to its philosophically technical nature and partly to the unusual course of its author's own career. Baldwin's contemporary, Stanley Hall, achieved much greater prominence. A developmental theory like Hall's, based on the doctrine of recapitulation, must necessarily possess a strongly progressivist character. One point should perhaps be noted, however: Developmentalists have had a certain amount of leeway in defining the high point of development, the point up to which the course leads generally upward. For Hall, the highest point was reached in late adolescence rather than adulthood. Much less explicitly, and perhaps only by default, Piaget's emphasis on the cognitive achievements of the adolescent presents a somewhat similar picture.

The process of directed evolution plays a major role in the later theoretical formulations of Piaget, for whom (as the theory of the "phenocopy") it represents a central phenomenon of development and evolution (*Adaptation and intelligence*, 1974; *Behaviour and evolution*, 1976: the latter's original title translates as "behaviour, the motor of evolution"). Piaget's mature thinking in these areas is influenced by the somewhat unorthodox biology of the embryologist Conrad Waddington, as well as by systems theory. What is of interest here is the way in which Piaget's mature account of individual development is buttressed by the biological presuppositions. For Piaget, ontogeny—like evolution—consists of the internalisation of external conditions, a transmutation of the exogenous into the endogenous. In both cases, development is inherently and essentially progressive. With respect to the individual, development involves the progressive conquest of environmental conditions such that intellectual activity can become free from the immediate situation. To some extent, the arguments of Lev Vygotsky could be read in a similar way, such that external (inter-individual) processes increasingly come to be "internalised" and hence "intra-psychic." Vygotsky was more concerned with the interpersonal conditions of development than with formulating an account of progress (a general stage theory, for example). However, his position on the relative status of infancy vis-à-vis childhood, and his claims concerning "interiorisation"—together with his commitment to a kind of recapitulation—all presuppose a general progression in individual development. The "orthogenetic principle" of Heinz Werner, of course, takes progress and directionality as an axiom.

Jean Piaget's own project is a description of the growth of knowledge, and the fact that such growth takes place is therefore taken for granted. "Genetic epistemology" is inconceivable without the assumption of progress and directionality. One mechanism described by Piaget should be discussed in slightly greater detail. The notion of *equilibrium* was central to

Piaget's thinking from his very earliest writing and in his later work was extended to yield the concept of *equilibration*. Equilibration refers to progressive equilibrium; to a tendency toward more complete, more systematic, and more logically coherent equilibrium states. Independent of the status of the equilibrium formulation itself (discussed at greater length in the next section), equilibration as a process is straightforwardly progressivist. It constitutes the "search for better equilibrium," and the "higher cognitive operations" are thus described as being "completely equilibrated." Similarly, in *Biology and knowledge* we read that[10]: "the autoregulatory function of the cognitive mechanisms produces the most highly stabilised equilibrium forms found in any living creature, namely, the structures of the intelligence, whose logico-mathematical operations have been of inescapable importance ever since human civilisation reached the stage of being consciously aware of them."

In general, Piaget's account of individual development presupposes the kind of progressive pattern unavoidable in any theory which appeals to recapitulationary analogy. Thus, for Piaget, what he terms an "evolutionary" account of cognition in the individual is corroborated by four sources of evidence: the history of (scientific) ideas; comparative psychology and cultural ethnology; cognitive development in the individual (a kind of "mental embryology"); and genetics, with its concern for the "phylo- and ontogenetic processes of cerebralisation." Again, reference is made in *Biology and knowledge* to Waddington's account of directionality in embryogenesis and the concept of "homeorhesis." This term refers to a tendency for developmental processes to maintain a trajectory: To return after perturbation not to a steady state (as in homeostasis) but to a steady channel or course. Whether focusing on biological or epistemological issues, Piaget's genetic epistemology was firmly based on the notions of progress and direction.

The position of Freud and his followers is less clear-cut in some important respects. As we have noted before, the notions of regression and the return to earlier states are very important to Freud. The rather simple-minded description of the child "getting better and better" with ontogeny, while not inaccurate when applied to Piaget, requires much more qualification with Freud. The concept of regression often indicates that some very basic characteristics of an individual never really change; and that what *does* change does not therefore constitute the whole of ontogenesis. The individual, like the species, becomes civilised with development, but this process of civilisation is itself something of a tactic or coping mechanism. Freud is in many ways thoroughly pessimistic, and the term "progressive" is thus somewhat inappropriate for his account. Certainly, however, individual development is taken as directional.

Freud's stage theory per se does to some extent constitute a progressive scheme, a gradual ascent toward adult forms of sexuality, even if the context within which the stage theory is set cannot easily be described as progressivist. Further, those of Freud's followers who have been especially influential as developmentalists have generally shed the metatheoretical pessimism. In moving closer to the mainstream of developmental thinking, such post-Freudian accounts fall in with the progressivism of this mainstream. The best example of this process is the stage theory of Erik Erikson. Erikson's reformulation of the Freud account focuses attention on the outcomes of particular stages. Thus Freud's four pre-genital (pre-adult) stages are now characterised in terms of trust/mistrust, autonomy/shame, initiative/guilt, and industry/inferiority. The outcomes of Erikson's newly defined stages of adolescence and adulthood concern the achievements of identity; the capacity for intimacy; the feeling of generativity; and eventually integrity. While noting the negative outcome possible at each of the eight stages, Erikson makes it clear that the positive sequence represents the desireable pattern. The theory is straightforwardly progressivist, even if so much attention is given to the possibilities of deviance. Indeed, the latter concern makes sense only within the context of a pattern of development defined as "correct."

Erik Erikson's account is highly derivative of Freud's, and hence carries over certain biological influences from that source. In addition, however, Erikson appeals to embryology in his formulations of early childhood stages, with especial emphasis on the role of *proper rate* and *normal sequence* (as previously noted). The concept of a correct, prescribed sequence of developmental changes is central to Erikson's account. As quoted elsewhere, "the healthy child, if halfway properly guided, merely obeys and on the whole can be trusted to obey inner laws of development . . . proper rate and proper sequence remain critical factors."

This quotation demonstrates that Erikson's stage theory is founded on the assumption of a *correct* sequence. For Arnold Gesell, also, individual development was a process driven naturally along a correct path as long as nurture was adequate (compare Erikson's "if halfway properly guided"). Gesell's own stage theory has been of too little scientific influence to merit detailed discussion here, consisting of summary descriptions of "the" three-year-old, "the" four-year-old, and so on. It should be noted however, that Gesell's age/stage theory also includes an account of cyclic variations in temperament—from "ingoing" to "outgoing" and back again—a thoroughly biological notion. For Gesell, as for more sophisticated theoreticians, directionality and progress are features inherent in development itself. It may be that such assumptions are indeed necessary components of any theory of development. Certainly, these assumptions have much more to do with non-Darwinian accounts of evolution than with any of Darwin's own arguments.

PROCESSES OF CHANGE AND PROCESSES OF STABILITY

Given the general assumption of progress in individual development, it becomes necessary for developmental thinkers to attempt a formulation of some of the processes supporting this progress. To a considerable extent, this attempt focuses on the ways in which the developing organism exploits and incorporates the environment in which it finds itself. Unless a narrowly defined version of learning theory is adopted, by which generic learning processes are seen as of sufficient explanatory power, some account must be given of processes essentially "internal" to the organism. Such processes are often conceived of as of great generality, perhaps as "invariant" processes, and as governing the organism's interaction with its environment in a manner largely independent of specific conditions. For some theorists, processes concerned with the balancing and regulation of a postulated internal economy are of central significance without which developmental change cannot be described or explained. Piaget's emphasis on processes of equilibrium is a good example.

The accounts with which we are concerned here are essentially accounts of change, but of change conceived within a *structural* framework. It is possible to locate theoretical positions in terms of a continuum, defined in terms of the extent to which the *organisation* of behaviour is taken into consideration. Generic theories of learning per se, such as those of John B. Watson and his behaviourist followers, might be seen as representative of one extreme of this continuum. Such learning theories pay little regard to structure or organisation in behaviour. The opposite extremes of the continuum would be represented by theories focusing exclusively on organisation itself: On postulated structures of cognition or affect considered as superordinate to actual behaviour. The best examples of such formal accounts of process in development are found in the writings of Piaget, but the emphasis on organisation is one common to many developmentalists.

A concern for organisation "within" the individual tends, perhaps necessarily, to give rise to an emphasis on the ways in which material (however defined) is incorporated into a pre-existing structure. This was certainly a concern of James Mark Baldwin, whose account of "assimilation" was expressed in quasi-neurological terms. For Baldwin, assimilation of something new meant that a new stimulus comes to elicit the same motor discharge as some "old" stimulus. Such neurological accounts were commonplace among the early developmentalists and must be thought of as attempts to articulate certain assumptions concerning structural and organisational properties of behaviour. These neurological accounts were driven by such theoretical concerns rather than by advances in anatomy and physiology per se. For example, Preyer's formulations on infant development appeal to neurology in quite a similar way to Baldwin's, although Preyer was much better qualified in terms of the physiological background. Similarly, Freud's early psychology (as in his *Project* of 1895 and in *Studies on hysteria* of the same year) employed a neurological framework in an attempt to explain the mechanisms of repression. Freud's general concern here is how the organism *deals with* "stimuli": How the environment is negotiated with. Above all, the concern is with the organism's ability to maintain stability and integrity in the face of an unpredictable environment. Such a concern is in many ways a biological one, for it is the problem of how animals maintain themselves and reproduce their kind while remaining adaptively responsive to outside events. From certain perspectives this is indeed the central problem of evolution itself.

James Mark Baldwin and Jean Piaget, among others, were concerned to find a formula which balanced conservative forces (habit, assimilation) with progressive ones (accommodation, imitation). Baldwin made the most serious attempt before Piaget to give equal weight to these two kinds of developmental processes. His account may even be considered the more successful of the two in that Piaget consistently emphasised assimilatory processes, such as egocentrism. Baldwin's favoured terms were "habit" for the conservative repetition of worthwhile actions and "accommodation" for the adaptive response to new situations. Occasionally Baldwin used the term assimilation ("the mind's digestion") for the former. His term for the balanced interplay of the two processes was "imitation," meaning activity which is goal-directed and purposeful (the goal is steered towards or "imitated"). Imitation in this sense is most clearly exhibited in middle to late infancy when the child is observed to keep on trying to achieve something in spite of early failure. The behaviour is repetitive but also open ended. Earlier forms of imitation, for Baldwin, are essentially "organic" and "subcortical." The young infant responds to a stimulus simply by sensorimotor suggestion, and habitual behaviour is simply repetitive. Consciousness is not involved here: It will arise with the volitional component of the later, "persistent" imitation. For Baldwin, intention and volition emerge developmentally out of organic activity.

One influential model for the conceptualisation of stability and change in living systems was that of the French physiologist Claude Bernard. Writing in the middle years of the 19th century, Bernard argued that bodily systems should be seen as maintaining a dynamic kind of equilibrium, by which external disturbance would be automatically compensated with the effect of restoring the system to its former state.[11] Such a formulation was very much in line with the physicalist and mechanistic kind of thinking being applied to many aspects of the life sciences around the middle of the 19th century—an intellectual milieu profoundly influential on, among others, Sigmund Freud. Within psychology, related formulations concerning forces and the distribution of energy were promoted by Herbert Spencer in the latter half of the century. The notion that mental processes involve some kind of energy, and that energy systems must maintain a balance, was taken as axiomatic: What was at issue was the mechanism by which balance was maintained.

This assumption of balance and equilibrium in mental processes remained central to Freud's thinking. It is the disturbance of a steady state that motivates behaviour: Most generally, disturbance arising from external stimulation. Such external demands, for Freud, constitute *pain*; it is the satisfactory compensation for these demands—not something more positive—which constitutes pleasure. Prototypically, the excess energy supplied from the external source is channelled away by an appropriate reflex (hence a *discharge*). In more highly evolved organisms, surplus energy is derived from instincts as well as from external sources. The Freudian account of adolescence, for example, is based on the claim that *increases* in libidinal (instinctual) energy take place at puberty. To compensate for the extra demands of the instincts, however, mankind also possesses a greater range of discharge mechanisms including such representational processes as dreaming. It is assumed that unitary mechanisms underly all such discharge processes, whether behavioural or representational. Post-Freudian analytic theory pays little attention to such quasi-neurological processes. However, it still defines its field of enquiry in terms derived from this conceptual framework. "Dynamic" psychologies (that is, psychologies of unconscious processes) necessarily involve assumptions concerning energy and motivation even if these assumptions are unexamined. The general notion of balance remains a central one. Thus, in the developmental context, Erik Erikson argues that the successful outcome of a psychosocial stage consists in a satisfactory *ratio* of such polarities as trust and mistrust.

This notion of balance in affective components of mental life has, at least in its more general applications, a very long history. Ancient Greek and mediaeval formulations on personality referred to the relative strength or quantity of various "humours," sometimes associated with such bodily substances as blood and bile. Jean-Jacques Rousseau employed the notion of balance in the developmental context, proposing that the relative strength of an individual's needs and powers change with age with important consequences. Adult maturity indicates a final balance or equilibrium. As we have seen, Jean Piaget's theory defines the end-point of development in a basically similar way. Piaget certainly considered himself to have been influenced by Rousseau. More directly, notions of dynamic equilibria and their developmental implications were derived by Piaget from the work of Pierre Janet and Edouard Claparède. Pierre Janet, a close contemporary of Freud's, was a French psychiatrist and psychologist who established a theoretical system similar in many ways to that of Freud.[12] For Janet, psychopathology was seen to result from the disturbance of equilibrium states in the mental apparatus. Claparède was the founder (in 1912) of the *Institut Jean-Jacques Rousseau* in Geneva at which Piaget's research programme was carried out. A psychologist and educationalist, Claparède also maintained close links with the psychoanalytic thinkers based in Zürich (including Bleuler and Jung). For Claparède, child behaviour exhibits the results of an antagonistic relationship between energy for physical growth and energy for intellectual activity. Claparède was also particularly interested in children's problem-solving, and argued that adaptive behaviour in this kind of situation arises from a disequilibrium: A failure to surmount an obstacle by currently available means. For Claparède, such disequilibrium creates a need, giving rise to action which, if successful, restores equilibrium. Moreover, the emergence of mental process into consciousness was also seen by Claparède as resulting from the original state of disequilibrium.

Piaget's employment of equilibrium concepts drew on all of the traditions described here. In his very early writing such as the *Recherche* of 1918, equilibrium was treated in a somewhat mystic fashion, in such contexts as the equilibrium between parts and wholes. At the same time, Piaget was exploring the relationships between "assimilation" and "imitation" in organic life, under the influence of the biological writings of Felix Le Dantec.[13] A little later, and partly through Claparède's influence, Piaget encountered the writings of Baldwin. By the 1930s, in the context of his studies of infancy, Piaget had developed a formulation in which the two processes of assimilation and (now) accommodation were held to be in equilibrium.

This balanced account is first described in the introduction to *The origin of intelligence in the child* (1936). Despite their formal symmetry, processes of assimilation in fact play a much greater role in Piaget's infancy theory than do processes of accommodation. (At one point Piaget confesses a "risk of sacrificing precision to a taste for symmetry"). This is partly the result of Piaget's strenuous efforts to distance himself from an empiricist position, with its over-emphasis on the direct role of the environment. The centre of Piaget's infancy theory is the *assimilatory scheme*. Assimilation is always prior to accommodation; thus, "the primary fact is . . . the assimilatory activity itself without which no accommodation is possible." Again, assimilation "constitutes the primary fact whence analysis must proceed." Looking ahead, Piaget notes that "this primacy of assimilation is expressed [on the rational plane] by the primacy of judgement." Infant development is to be explained chiefly in terms of the vicissitudes of assimilation: "we have shown, stage after stage, how the progress of the assimilatory mechanism engenders the various intellectual operations." Assimilatory schemes themselves may be assimilated one to another (but not accommodated one to another). Piaget's concluding section to *The origin of intelligence in the child* is concerned with arguing the case for assimilation as the central process in intelligent behaviour (especially as contrasted with *association*). The equilibrium or complementarity between assimilation and accommodation announced in Piaget's introduction to this book remains unsubstantiated except in the most general terms.

In general, Piaget's account of developmental process in the infant consists of an amalgamation of Baldwin with Claparède. Claparède had outlined some of the ways in which problem-solving emerges in infancy, from trial-and-error or "groping" to systematic forms. Piaget reformulated this account to arrive at the latter half of his six-stage theory. Baldwin's account supplied the foundation for the first three stages. Neither Claparède nor Baldwin had Piaget's predilection for rigid stage theories, both having been more centrally concerned with functional issues. In addition to the points noted earlier in this section, Baldwin had coined the term "circular reaction" to refer to the repetitive (but potentially progressive) activity of the infant. Piaget's "primary circular reactions" are, like Baldwin's, repetitive behaviours involving the child's own body but which go beyond reflex activity (hence distinguishing Stage II from Stage I). Piaget's "secondary circular reactions" involve prehension and hence external objects (Stage III) and his "tertiary circular reactions," active experimentation (Stage V). There is however little substance to the generic term "circular reaction" in Piaget's theory, and little explanatory force in its supposed developmental transitions. The circular reaction is basically an assimilatory mechanism, its accommodatory features emerging only slowly: "It is only in the fifth stage that accommodation is definitely liberated."

Piaget's basic claims for infant development again endorse Baldwin and Claparède. Piaget's claim is that intelligent, intentional behaviour emerges gradually out of *organic* responses. Intentionality for Piaget is a function of the extent of mediation between stimulus and response (and the behaviourist terminology does less disservice to Piaget's theory than might be imagined). In the young infant (Stages I–II) activity is set in motion directly by external stimuli; "by directly perceived sensorial images." This is simply sensorimotor *suggestion* as in Baldwin. Again, for Piaget, there is as yet no conscious awareness, "this awareness being itself a function of the number of intermediary actions necessitated by the principal act." The Stage III infant demonstrates "momentary hierarchies of ends and means" and *hence* some glimmerings of conscious awareness. Means and ends come to be firmly dissociated from Stage IV onwards.

As we have seen, the notion of an equilibrium between two symmetrical processes was little more than a general claim within Piaget's infancy theory. However, as he became increasingly concerned with *structures* of cognition, and developmental changes in such structures throughout childhood, the concept of equilibrium re-emerged. Notions of disturbance, compensation, reversibility and balance came to be central to his increasingly formalised account of intellect and its development.[14] The logico-mathematical structures held to characterise the high-point of individual development were described in terms of virtual disturbances and virtual compensations. Piaget was eager to embrace cybernetic theory, with its feedback loops and similar equilibrium formulations. At the other end of the scale, phenomena of perception were explained in terms of balance and compensation. Alongside this increasingly formalised account of equilibrium processes—reaching its culmination in *The development of thought* (1975)—Piaget also maintained that development involves a general improvement in the *quality* of the equilibrium attained. This developmental trend was termed "equilibration," as discussed in the previous section. Equilibration is a rather general and not very precisely defined process in Piaget's theory. We now turn to a consideration of some postulated processes which, for Piaget and others, have been formulated in rather more precise terms.

DIFFERENTIATION AND INTEGRATION

In addition to, or in place of, such general processes as assimilation and equilibrium, appeal has frequently been made to certain overall trends or patterns in developmental change. In many respects such an appeal represents the attempt to give more precision to general claims concerning progress and direction. That is to say, the assumption that developmental change is an orderly process leads to the attempt to characterise the overall trend of that process. A number of developmental thinkers have employed the concept of *differentiation* in seeking to provide an overall picture of ontogenesis. Differentiation implies that some function is becoming more definite, more specified, or more systematically subdivided. The term has been interpreted in a variety of ways, in some of which processes of *integration* are seen as closely related. In such formulations, functions or entities are seen as separating out from a more general earlier state and hence becoming capable of interrelation. The differentiation processes are generally taken as primary, however, and some accounts place little or no emphasis on integration. At the other extreme are theoretical positions founded exclusively on integration and synthesis: Theories derived essentially from empiricist and associationist frameworks with their emphasis on discrete sensations and on the constructive nature of knowledge.

Differentiation theories derive at least in part from biological considerations. During the 19th century the embryologist von Baer presented an account of development based on the process of specification. For von Baer, general and common forms become (during embryogenesis) increasingly differentiated into species. Although this theory effectively ruled out ancestral recapitulation—which relies on the repetition of adult forms of specific ancestral species, not general forms—it did agree that development was essentially progressive. Von Baer's account was taken up later in the 19th century by Herbert Spencer, for whom all organic change was to be seen as a movement from homogeneity to heterogeneity. Spencer did not attempt to apply this formula in any precise way to individual development, but his general picture was certainly an influence on the thinking of many subsequent developmentalists; most notably, if perhaps indirectly, on that of Heinz Werner.

Spencer was one of the many 19th century thinkers whose work James Mark Baldwin considered himself to be synthesising. The theoretical accounts of both Baldwin and Freud contain aspects which could be considered as differentiation. The description of a separating-off of the individual from the world (subject from object), found in different versions in both accounts, represents a general differentiation. The stage-sequence in Baldwin's genetic epistemology might be considered a differentiation account, with each stage a refinement of the last; however the notion of differentiation per se should probably not be seen as carrying much explanatory weight here. Freud's account of the initial "individuation" of the child has been reworked by his followers in various ways. The concept of differentiation remains largely tied to the context of identity rather than being applied to development as a whole. Again, Freud's account of early psychosexual development suggests the replacement of a diffused sensitivity by specific erogenous zones: A differentiation theory but rather a context-specific one.

The most systematic attempts to apply the concept of differentiation to developmental change can be found in those writers most strongly influenced by Gestalt psychology. The emphasis of the Gestalt thinkers, whose work was carried out in the early decades of this century, was on holistic aspects of perception and cognition. Hence they vigorously opposed accounts based on elementary sensations or images. Such elementalist accounts were associated with the assumption that developmental change involves integration or the putting together of disparate units. The holistic emphasis of the Gestalt thinkers gave rise, in contrast, to the description of behaviour as organised and structured. Developmental change, it was implied, must involve changes *in* organisation rather than the creation of organisation out of nothing. If it was to be assumed that such change in organisation must be progressive, then differentiation appeared to represent a strong candidate as the major developmental process. Developmental change must be change in *detail*.

Four thinkers—Kurt Koffka, William Stern, Heinz Werner, and Kurt Lewin—formulated Gestalt-influenced differentiation theories of one kind or another. All four were German nationals and all four emigrated to the U.S.A. in the early 1930s. Only one of the central contributors to the Gestalt movement, Kurt Koffka, attempted to outline its implications for developmental psychology. However, William Stern's thinking was considerably influenced by the Gestalt movement and its precursors, as was that of Stern's younger colleague Heinz Werner. Werner's contemporary, Kurt Lewin, developed his thinking alongside the Gestalt movement and arrived at his own differentiation theory. Not surprisingly, perhaps, it was Koffka's account which carried the implications of Gestalt thinking the furthest, whereas both Stern and Werner attempted to synthesise it with older traditions. Lewin, for his part, concerned himself with developmental issues only as one feature of a general account of human behaviour.

William Stern's account was the earliest of the four under consideration. Stern made an explicit attempt to excise the associationist and empiricist assumptions underlying orthodox theories: Assumptions such as the passivity of early experience, the atomistic nature of early consciousness, and the mechanical nature of the association of elements during development. For Stern, the initial state should not be thought of in terms of discrete sensations or images, but rather "a general condition of blended sensibility": A "confused" or "diffuse" state, "indistinct and shapeless like a veil of mist." This state was essentially the "one blooming, buzzing confusion" described by William James in 1890. For Stern, development involves not the association of independent particles but the "raising [of] certain impressions out of the general undifferentiated state." Consciousness thus comes to contain "spots distinguished by a certain quality (colour, noise, hardness), by certain boundary lines . . ."; and "amongst these we should find such complex impressions as arise from the mother's face, voice and gentle touch, or from the shape and noise of the rattle." Differentiation for Stern means the emergence of order from chaos: From "the original confused chaos of outer sensations." As Koffka himself was to make clear, Stern's account was only half-heartedly a Gestalt one. Certainly Stern emphasised that images were "whole" from the beginning, but this wholeness was diffuse and global. Gestalt-type "forms" were seen as gaining in definition, distinctiveness, and clarity, an assumption of early developmental change more usually associated with sensation-based accounts (and in this context to be traced back to the writings of Descartes, for example).

Stern's *The psychology of early childhood* was first published in 1914 when Wertheimer, Köhler, and Kurt Koffka were already establishing the Gestalt movement. Koffka's *The growth of the mind* first appeared in 1921. Koffka, although making some appeal to parallels between the child and the "primitive," took a very cautious stance with respect to recapitulation per se. He rejected the mechanical, ancestral form of recapitulation, but also the neo-Darwinian proposal of Thorndike that all development was characterised by random variation followed by selection. Koffka suggested that ontogenesis might resemble phylogenesis in certain respects as a result of the operation of similar, general processes. The most general of such processes was a Spencerian differentiation, such that "the primitive and more roughly-hewn precedes the more complicated." Koffka noted that Stern's support was for a similar, "correspondence" picture, although as he also noted Stern himself was not entirely consistent.[15]

Koffka gave careful consideration to the world of the newborn, and here he dissented from Stern's account. With Stern, Koffka rejected empiricist assumptions concerning a mass of separate sensations but his alternative focused on the *organised* nature of initial consciousness. For Koffka, "a certain order dominates experience from the beginning." Thus, the newborn infant may be aware of a distinctive figure against a background—one of the forms of perception held by the Gestalt psychologists to be basic. Similarly, although in reference to later infancy, Koffka argued that an awareness of relative features—brighter than, larger than—precedes an awareness of absolute values and that the "absolute" size of a perceived object—its retinal projection—is of less importance than its real size. These findings pressed the anti-empiricist case very much harder than Stern had done. For Koffka, then, it is *configurations* which are primitive in consciousness, not sensations or qualities. Koffka noted that it is apparently complex stimuli, such as a human face, to which the infant responds most readily; even though the "sensation" aspects must be constantly changing (light and dark and so on.) Friendliness in a face must be considered as a "phenomenal fact" in infant perception. Koffka's account was therefore a radical one, in which the anti-elementist claims of the Gestalt tradition were applied rigorously. Although he does not use the term, Koffka is essentially claiming that infant perception begins with *abstract* features and works towards more specific ones.

Before discussing the differentiation theory of Heinz Werner, which essentially develops Stern's account, something should be said of Kurt Lewin. Lewin's general theory was a *field* theory, employing such constructs as force, relative position, and valence with respect to psychological entities. Lewin postulated a "lifespace" which he described as increasing in size and in differentiation (that is, in the subdivision of its regions). For example, individual development was seen as involving the extension of a time perspective both forward and backward from the present, but also of the increasingly fine subdivisions of, for example, levels of reality-irreality. The general developmental trend is to an increase in scope, in differentiation, in organisation, and in flexibility. Divisions in the lifespace in the infant and child were taken to be quite rigid. Measured intelligence was taken as a correlate of differentiation (that is, as correlated with the rate of increase of subdivisions and the related characteristics). It was thought that there might be regressions in which disorganisation and de-differentiation might temporarily take place. Lewin's thinking was greatly influenced by the Gestalt thinkers, such as the findings of Köhler on structural features of perception in problem-solving and the general emphasis on holistic characteristics. However, the outcome of the influence was more like the case of Stern than that of Koffka. It is revealing that Lewin gives a quite misleading reference to Koffka in claiming that "the life space of the newborn child may be described as a field which has relatively few and only vaguely distinguishable areas."

Heinz Werner's differentiation theory of development was a direct, if more systematic, extension of Stern's account. Werner's most influential book *The comparative psychology of mental development* (first published in 1926) presented an analysis of "primitive" thought as represented by thought in the child, in the "savage," and in psychopathology. Werner's concept of differentiation was essentially a Spencerian one, development being seen as moving from homogeneous to heterogeneous. However, his explicit appeal was to the writings of Goethe. Werner, following Goethe, characterised developmental change in morphological terms: As the increase in dissimilarity and subordination of body parts. For Werner, differentiation is associated with an increasingly hierarchical organisation: An holistic kind of integration process. With Goethe, the evolution of *segmentation* was taken as a general example of these processes, the evolution of the nervous system being another. For Werner, developmental change in general is characterised by a movement from syncretic to discrete; from diffuse to articulated; from indefinite to definite; from rigid to flexible; and from labile to stable. Clearly, Werner's account has much in common with that of Lewin.

An interrelated dimension of developmental change is from immediate to mediate. Primitive states in general are taken by Werner to be characterised by a directness of contact between organism and environment: A pragmatic kind of negotiation, "intimately bound up with the concrete situation." Above all, primitive consciousness reveals a lack of differentiation between subject and object. Development gives rise to a polarity and a distancing between the two; to means, instruments, planning, and the separating off of an objective world of reality from a subjective and internally motivated personality. One of Werner's summaries should be quoted here[16]:

> Naive, concrete thought is very close to the perceptual-imaginative level; primitive reflection always means concrete configuration. Typical European reflection is universal in nature, abstract; it functions more or less independ-

ently of the immediate, concrete reality, and is governed by an awareness of general laws. The thought of primitive man is pinned down to the reality of the thing-like world, and is therefore pragmatic, concrete, individual.

The case of the newborn is of special interest to Werner, as it was for Stern and for Koffka. Here immediacy is absolute. The newborn is completely subordinated to "the vital global situation"; its activity is unco-ordinated, "a mere floundering about with happy or unhappy results." Unco-ordination is with respect to the outside world, since the newborn's activity is integrated in itself; but this integration is a global and rigid one. Newborn consciousness is to be thought of as "a total situation," in which "motor-emotional and sensory factors are blended into one another." For Werner, this situation is an example of the *syncretic* nature of primitive thought process. In general, primitive thought manifests a lack of differentiation between feeling and activity, and hence an absence of objectivity. In the area of emotion, for example, emotional states are not clearly defined and detached from action as in "higher mental life," so that the noncivilised adult will "thrash about" and "jabber in heated, broken language." In the child, emotional expression is seen as differentiating out from a general affect of "excitement."

For Werner, a special case of syncretic thinking relates to perception. *Synaesthesia* refers to the evoking of a specific quality in one sensory modality by a specific quality in another (for example, a specific tone associated with a specific colour). Werner argues that synaesthesia must play a greater role in "primitive and archaic peoples" and in childhood, since for him it results from a lack of differentiation. Werner discusses "the primordial unity of the senses" but his claims must be carefully distinguished from the position implied by Koffka. Werner's account follows Stern and the sensationist tradition by assuming that consciousness is comprised of sensory qualities, even if these are not initially differentiated by the subject. Objects of perception are represented to the subject as conglomerations of such sensory qualities and the images of personal activity. For Koffka, it is *relative* qualities (bigger than, brighter than) which are primitive: Such qualities being more general than mere sensations. For Werner, differentiation with respect to different sense modalities is analogous to discrimination "within" one sense: Again, the discrimination of specific sense qualities. For Werner, again, experimental situations can be devised which parallel or simulate the ontogenetic trend. In both the macro (developmental) and the micro (experimental) contexts, tones and melodies emerge for the subject from a "blurred tonal ground," "as if by a process of crystallisation." Despite the holistic Gestalt influence, Werner remained attached to the sensation-based tradition of Stern.

Piaget distanced himself somewhat from Gestalt psychology, considering it to have emphasised structure at the expense of developmental change ("structure without genesis"). Certainly, however, considerable influence might be traced: For example, in the derivation of the tasks Piaget employed in his investigation of infant problem-solving. More generally, certain features of the Gestalt tradition appeared to converge with other sources of influence. Thus an emphasis on wholes and structures, and on the equilibrium between parts and wholes, was central to Piaget's thinking but derived from philosophical biology rather than from psychology. Piaget's version of differentiation in fact agrees in the main with that of Werner for whom, despite a closer adherence to the Gestalt tradition as such, holism also derived essentially from the influence of biology.

Processes of differentiation and of integration both play a role in Piaget's theory of assimilation. "Integration" for Piaget is to some extent primary as far as explanation is concerned; for integration consists of the co-ordination of separate schemes of action, a co-ordination guaranteed by the process of assimilation itself. The differentiation of schemes—the adaptation of action patterns to more specific constraints of the environment—is a secondary result of the attempted generalisation of these schemes. Generalisation, again, is fundamentally a conservative (that is, an assimilatory) process. The diversity of objects and the amount of accommodation consequent on this diversity is not sufficient, for Piaget, to explain the specification of schemes. Assimilatory schemes are the driving force for developmental change, and differentiation is a result more than a causative process. Thus, for example, visual images become differentiated by the application of discrete schemes such as prehension, sucking, and so on.

More generally, and here very much in agreement with Werner, Piaget proposes that developmental change proceeds from an initial state of indifferentiation between organism and environment. Assimilatory activity does not in itself recognise a boundary between the subject and the object of action. The external world is confused with the sensations of a self unaware of itself. As expressed with most clarity in the concluding section to *The construction of reality in the child* (1937), early interaction is direct and immediate, between the surface of the subject and the surface of things. Gradually, and in a correlated way, the polarity between a self and an objective environment is established. The increased awareness of the nature of physical reality develops in tandem with an increased awareness of the subject's own intellectual operations. For Piaget, it should be noted, such a dual process is also to be observed in the history of science.

This general picture of differentiation is seen by Piaget as an outcome rather than as a process as such. With Werner, developmental progress is seen as involving the emergence of planning and other forms of mediation between the self and the world. Lack of differentiation is a characteristic of primitive states. Thus egocentrism in the young child is described as a form of nondifferentiation: The world and the self are insufficiently distanced from each other for the subject to be aware of anything other than the results of his or her assimilatory processes, and such processes do not recognise a boundary between what is subjective and what is objective.

In this most general context, differentiation for Piaget refers to the joint creation of objectivity and subjectivity out of chaos. The earliest forms of consciousness, as in the newborn baby, are taken to be blurred and confused as in the sensationist tradition. Such an account is perhaps not wholly consistent with the emphasis on discrete action schemes as the raw material for developmental progress. This latter account fits more easily into a straightforward integration theory. Perhaps, therefore, Piaget's attempt to include both differentiation and integration within the same overall framework is necessarily misguided. The two kinds of process may be incompatible so that an adequate theory of the one must preclude the other. If this is the case then all those developmentalists who have claimed some kind of synthesis of the two—including Werner and Gesell, as well as Piaget—must be considered to have been mistaken.

NOTES TO CHAPTER NINE

[1]Gesell described 4 stages of 6 years each (0–6; 6–12; 12–18; 18–24). The appearance of 6-year molars is identified as a key indicator of the first major transition (Gesell et al., 1940, Preface). Also see the discussion by Vonèche (in Broughton, 1987, p. 78) where the coincidence of developmental transitions and institutional boundaries is noted (for example, "the stage of concrete operations corresponds with the age of schooling children at the elementary level.")

[2]Some explanation should perhaps be given for the decision not to employ the influential distinction of Reese and Overton (1970) concerning "mechanistic" versus "organismic" models of development. The major reason for putting this formulation to one side is its lack of precision. Thus the term "organismic" has been taken to cover virtually all theories of development which are not behaviourist ones. The dichotomy prevents the recognition of positivistic aspects of the organismic approach—the search for unified laws of development—since positivism-reductionism is ascribed to the mechanistic side. It is therefore quite misleading to state that "the biological model is . . . rooted in a model of man as spontaneously active" (Reese & Overton, 1970, pp. 130–131). The dichotomy also seems to be a highly evaluative one, with the organismic approach being clearly favoured. This evaluation is also a reminder of the relationship of the mechanistic-organismic dichotomy to Wernerian theory, from which it would seem to derive. Further (ibid., p. 127), "The organismic definition has the advantage that it can [also] be applied to . . . the development of music, art, literature, science, philosophy and history."

Finally it should be noted that the dichotomy has itself been employed in a quasi-recapitulationary manner. Thus Reese and Overton claim that the path of individual development may be described first according to mechanistic, and then according to organismic principles (this is a "'good' kind of eclecticism" (ibid., p. 123). They write approvingly of a general practice of "implicitly assuming [the mechanistic model] in accounting for at least prenatal and infant behaviour, and often child behaviour in general, and assuming another model—often organismic but sometimes contextualistic . . . in accounting for adolescent and adult behaviour. A circle is completed by many of the accounts of behaviour in old age, which again becomes mechanistic." (Also see Labouvie-Vief & Chandler, 1978 on such "thematic horse switching" and its implications.) The practice is further exemplified in Lerner (1986, p. 53). Now if theoretical accounts were equally balanced between those which posit a mechanistic view of earlier development, and those which posit an "organismic" view of it—switching to the other as appropriate, with adolecence and adulthood—then the label of "eclecticism" might be justified. But this is not the case. The order in which the approaches are seen to apply in ontogenesis is always the order in which they are considered to apply to phylogeny. Overall, the Reese and Overton dichotomy is misleadingly imprecise and has perhaps outlived its usefulness.

[3]According to Gergen (1982, p. 152), "the ordered-change orientation in general . . . has become the guiding paradigm within contemporary developmental psychology." The evaluative nature of this ordered-change assumption is also noted (ibid., p. 171). Again, the notion of progress is noted by Gollin (1981, p. 233) as being central to the developmental theories of Piaget, of Werner and even of contemporary behaviourists. This issue is further discussed by Toulmin in the same book (*Does mental development have a unique destination?*; p. 256); also see Toulmin (1985, p. 20). Kagan has noted that descriptions of the child over the past 100 years have shared many presuppositions, including the assumption of gradual, purposive, cumulative progress. This core assumption is for Kagan a biological influence (Kagan, 1983, p. 553). According to Kagan, the end-point or goal of development has been defined in terms of *freedom*. The end-point of development plays a crucial role in the moral-judgment theory of Kohlberg. Kohlberg's final (sixth) stage of moral reasoning is characterised by an appeal to a rational and coherent moral philosophy. As Kohlberg makes clear (Kohlberg, Levine, & Hewer, 1983, p. 60–64), the end-point is required to make sense of the whole sequence, even though there is no empirical support for the so-called final stage. General issues relating to progress in developmental change are discussed in Bever's *Regressions in mental development* (1982) and in Strauss' *U-shaped behavioural growth* (1982).

[4]Baldwin (1902, p. 41); emphasis added. The "internalisation of external events" is identified by Kagan (1983) as a developmental process presupposed by a wide range of theoretical positions.

[5]Piaget (1970a/1972a, p. 18); emphasis added.

[6]Piaget (1974/1980, p. 79).

[7]Darwin's comments on bear habits are made in Chap. VI of the *Origin*, "Difficulties on theory." In the Variorum text this is VI/97–98 (the general comment on habit vs. structure is VI/93). Darwin had made a similar proposal much earlier, in the Transmutation Notebooks of 1838; here it was suggested that the jaguar might come to be transformed into an otter-like creature, as a consequence of fish-hunting habits (Grinnell, 1985, p. 69).

[8]Baldwin (1902, pp. 37–38); first set of emphases added.

[9]For an analysis of Baldwin's *Thought and things* see Russell (1978).

[10]Piaget (1967/1971, p. 37).

[11]Bernard's approach to science is discussed by Hirst (1975). According to Hirst, Bernard's *milieu intérieur* was intended to be a precise physiological formulation, not a formal description of balance, of "equilibrium" or of "system," all of which descriptions would be in themselves compatible with approaches Bernard rejected (especially vitalism) (Hirst, 1975, p. 67). However, the emphasis on function is not the same as an emphasis on adaptation. As Toulmin (1985, p. 21) notes,

> Jean Piaget was more at home in the physiological tradition of Claude Bernard, with his essentialist views about *individual* organisms, than with English naturalists like Charles Darwin, or their dynamic vision of *populations* of organisms

> . . . [thus for Piaget] intelligence is not an "adaptation" in the dynamic Darwinian sense, in which entire populations of organisms change in response to changes in the habitat, but rather in the sense of Bernard's static "adaptive systems" which enable each individual organism to respond appropriately to changes in its immediate situation [emphasis in original].

It might also be noted that Wilhelm Preyer spent some time working in Bernard's laboratory.

[12]On Janet, see Ellenberger (1970); also Sève (1974/1978, p. 203); and Wertsch and Stone, in Wertsch (1985, p. 165).

[13]Equilibrium and reversibility processes were especially emphasised in the writings of Felix Le Dantec (1907, p. 24): "Effects become causes and causes become effects . . . The existence of this reversibility" said Le Dantec "rules all biology." On both reversibility and equilibrium, Le Dantec employed quasi-mathematical formulae as Piaget was to do. Equilibrium was modelled on physical-chemical processes, and (ibid., p. 138) "in the living animal the phenomenon of equilibrium takes a particular form that is characteristic of life—habit." Further (ibid., p. 210), "explanations based on equilibrium are very satisfying when we study the adaptive evolution of living species." Le Dantec's commitment to Lamarck was total; his (ibid., p. 89) law of "functional assimilation" was "the literal translation of Lamarck's principle 'the function creates the organ'." Recapitulation is a consequence of the inheritance of acquired characters (ibid., p. 246): "'the embryology of an animal reproduces its genealogy' [Müller] . . . in other words, the series of individual characters appears in the same order as the series of corresponding ancestral characters."

[14]On Piaget's mature position regarding the metatheory of structures, equilibrium and function see the fine series of technical papers by Broughton (1981) in *Human Development*, Volume 24.

[15]On Koffka see Ash (1985b); also Gould (1977). The more general philosophy-of-science objectives of the Gestalt psychologists are discussed by Leichtman (1979).

[16]Werner (1926/1948, p. 299).

10 Biology and Alternatives to Biology in Contemporary Developmental Psychology

INTRODUCTION

Earlier chapters have made the case that the basic formulations of developmental psychology are unsound. The whole discipline, it has been argued, is constructed on insecure foundations. Thus far, this claim has been supported by an analysis of the early development of the discipline, few of the formulations discussed being more recent than the 1950s. It has been assumed that such classic or foundational formulations must still exert influence on contemporary discussion and research. The influence will be exerted most of all, perhaps, as a result of the institutionalisation of research methods. Rather than attempting to document such influence in sufficient detail—which would require an analysis of 30 years of intense, diverse, and large-scale scientific activity—an alternative route has been taken. An attempt is made to indicate the "extremes" of contemporary thinking—with reference to the role of biology—rather than all its intermediary positions.[1] This chapter is thus concerned with those contemporary approaches which are most, and those which are least, biological. This is intended to facilitate an appraisal of the claims made in this book, and also to make it possible to highlight any genuinely new directions in the discipline.

In the first section, attention is focused on those approaches to human development which make a direct appeal to biology: Namely, the ethological and the psychobiological approaches. It would seem important to examine such contemporary formulations quite carefully. Have they succeeded in transcending the influence of the outdated biologies on which this book has focused? If earlier developmental psychology had been led astray, that is to say, it may be that formulations based on appeals to *contemporary* biology may provide the discipline with its best hope for the future. On the other hand, this contemporary biology itself—at least insofar as it relates to matters of development—may retain significant elements of the earlier formulations. It need not be assumed that developmental applications of what is currently taken to be Darwinian or post-Darwinian biology necessarily escape from the old pitfalls, if such they were.

The four sections which follow discuss a range of approaches which might be seen as "alternatives" both to explicitly biological traditions and also to those approaches which merely perpetuate earlier orthodoxies. The first of the alternative approaches is the "*lifespan*" orientation which emphasises that development is a lifelong process, not one which stops at the attainment of adulthood. Rather little has been said about lifespan issues in previous chapters. Although many antecedents have been identified, the lifespan approach—more accurately, lifespan approaches— have only recently become formulated with any degree of clarity. In certain respects the lifespan orientation has presented itself as an alternative to biology, it having been argued that treating the attainment of adulthood as an end-point is an assumption derived from a biological view of maturation.

Despite this anti-biological stance, however, some at least of the many versions of lifespan theory do retain certain of the presuppositions discussed in this book. Some versions, for example, adopt a measurement-oriented, psychometric methodology. Others employ the same kind of cognitive-experimental approach familiar in research with infants and children. The latter represent "information-processing" versions of the lifespan orientation. Information-processing in its childhood context is discussed in the next section, together with other approaches which could be described as "*formal*" ones; derivations of the rule-based linguistics of Chomsky, developmental applications of J.J. Gibson's "ecological" approach to perception, and the closely related formulations of T.G.R. Bower. Formal theories place emphasis, in different ways, on abstract or systemic features of developmental change and would seem to give rise to substantial alternatives to a number of the more orthodox positions.

In apparent contrast to the formal theories, with their somewhat impersonal flavour, the third and fourth groupings of alternatives are characterised by a concern for social aspects of development. This concern has been defined and operationalised in a variety of ways. Some approaches have consisted of rather minor revisions of Piaget; some, like that of Bronfenbrenner, might be seen as converging with the lifespan orientation. These formulations are discussed as versions of a concern with the "*social context*" of individual development. Stronger versions of the social emphasis are discussed in the final section under the heading of "*social construction*." This term is taken rather loosely as covering not only such approaches as those of Rom Harré but also applications of Marxist theory, according to which individual development must be seen as constructed, or constituted, or produced, within a framework of social relations. Such approaches appear to present themselves as the most radical alternatives to biological thinking currently available.

BIOLOGICAL THEORIES: ETHOLOGY AND PSYCHOBIOLOGY

The major claim of this book is that non-Darwinian forms of biology have exerted a determinate influence on the development of developmental psychology. It is therefore important to examine those contemporary approaches to development which seek to apply modern biology to the area. Such approaches, if any, might be expected to demonstrate a more valid employment of the biological standpoint: If for no other reason than that they may be assumed to have a closer contact with recent and contemporary trends in the biological sciences themselves. Both the ethological and the psychobiological approaches set out with an appeal to processes of (broadly Darwinian) evolution as one set of causative factors in individual development, with appeals to the evolutionary past playing an especially prominent role in ethology.

For both approaches, the major thrust of the Darwinian argument is taken to be that behaviour, like anatomy, is *adaptive*. Any significantly general phenomenon of development must therefore have been shaped, if not created, by natural-selective pressures. Such arguments, however, run the risk of treating adaptation, and hence postulated evolutionary history, as somewhat of a catch-all: As a means of explaining why everything is now observed just as it is. The breadth of the explanatory framework then works against precision, and the result may be vacuous. This tendency has been subjected to cogent criticism in its wider biological context by Gould, for whom the "adaptationist programme" collapses the distinctions between different kinds of adaptation and is unable to recognise instances where features are nonadaptive.[2] It should also be pointed out that an important step in Darwin's own theory-building was the formulation of an account of imperfections, of sub-optimal fits between animal and environment. An account based on perfect harmony is vulnerable to translation into theological, and other nonevolutionary, explanatory frameworks, and should certainly be classified as pre-Darwinian. The role played by appeals to "adaptation" in contemporary biologies of development should therefore be scrutinised carefully.

Ethology was founded by Konrad Lorenz and Niko Tinbergen in the 1940s, on the basis of detailed naturalistic observation and of certain key assumptions on the nature of biology. The biology was of an originally anti-Darwinian kind, although natural selection came to be seen as compatible with the ethological perspective. Thus Lorenz's own introduction to Darwinian theory was through the writings of Wilhelm Bölsche, student and biographer of Haeckel, and for whom Haeckel's work was a consistent development of Darwin's.[3] Again, Lorenz's most frequent reference to Darwin is to *The expression of the emotions*, which is based on the inheritance of acquired character. In recent writings, Lorenz has attempted to explicate the ways in which ontogeny influences the course of evolution and here he is following a well-worn path by seeking ways *around* the Darwinian mechanism. Like James Mark Baldwin and Jean Piaget, Lorenz seeks to delimit the role of natural selection to a "weeding-out" process; which would be to return it to its pre-Darwinian status.[4] Again, Lorenz's search for "innate releasing mechanisms" has been guided in part by appeals to Kant, as well as to von Uexküll, neither of whom sit easily with Darwin.[5]

One of ethology's major concerns is with the "natural" life of animals, including mankind (so that scientific study should be naturalistic rather than experimental). This principle is not merely a methodological one, but is itself based on certain biological-philosophical assumptions. Lorenz's concern with the "natural" life of animals is closely related to some general convictions over the nature of civilisation and of domestication. Both, for Lorenz, lead to *deterioration*: To the disruption of instinctive patterns and hence to pathology. This concern with the decline of "civilised man" has been Lorenz's most constant theme. It has been pointed out that such an orientation was, at least, highly compatible with certain elements of Nazi ideology in pre-war Germany and Austria.[6] Such pessimistic and even apocalyptic viewpoints on the nature of human aggressiveness and so on have only the most tenuous connection with the work of Darwin.

Lorenz is still regarded as the "founding father" of ethology, although (human) developmental applications begin most systematically with Bowlby. Here attention will be focused on the recent, authoritative account by Hinde of the ethological contribution to the study of child development. *Attachment* has been of major interest to ethologists, partly because of the comparative possibilities presented by its generality in the "higher" animals. In a discussion of the findings on attachment behaviour, and following an evaluation of Bowlby's contribution, Hinde notes that "we now know more about the selective forces acting on parent-infant relationships than was the case 20 years ago" and that[7]: "Infants are presumably adapted to cope with mothers who reject them. Thus, although Bowlby was right that natural selection would favour protective mothers, it is also the case that it favours mothers who promote their infants' independence. In turn, infants must be adapted to emerge from such relationships adjusted to the society in which they live." The notion of adaptation is being applied so broadly as apparently to lose all explanatory value or Darwinian legitimacy. Surprisingly, hints at recapitulationary argument may also be found here. Hinde notes the developmental progress in learning made by laboratory rats, "from a stage at which learning . . . occur[s] without cognitive intermediaries to a stage in which goal anticipation plays a crucial role" and endorses the proposal that[8]: "this ontogenetic change is comparable to the phylogenetic difference in capacity between the fish-reptile and bird-mammal phylogenetic levels, cognitive intermediaries becoming important in the learning process." Recapitulationary parallels still, it seems, have a part to play in contemporary ethological thinking.

It should also be noted that the ethologists' attempt to study the "natural" situation (the animal in its habitat) has sometimes given rise to a simplistic view of development and of the range of choices in development. The "ecological" notion of balances between organism and environment is a most important one, but is always in danger of reducing to a simplistic notion of harmony or "preadaptation": Of a *perfect* match between animal and world.[9] To this extent, at least, ethology and its developmental manifestations tends to the idealist, this tendency being in line with the origins of the approach. Again, the notion of species-specific behaviour—that is, of behaviour universal within a species, but unique to that species—is one which is not inherently Darwinian. Von Uexküll's exploration of species-specificity was carried out within a framework which stressed the radical uniqueness of species, not their family relationships as a result of descent.

Preadaptation is itself a complex notion, and one with a long history in biological theory. Its relevance has always seemed greatest in the earliest phases of ontogenesis, so that its employment may be thought of as an extension (perhaps a disguised one) of the concept of instinct. To be sure, instinctive behaviour of various kinds was explained by Darwin as being due to natural selection (a key example being certain behaviour of neuter, that is nonbreeding, social insects). But Darwin did not endorse a blanket appeal to instinct or to preadaptation as a general solution to apparently adaptive behaviours in the very young organism. Gould's "adaptationist programme" in general biology is perhaps matched by a "preadaptationist programme" in developmental ethology.[10] In any event, when applied to human subjects, ethology has had to combine forces with such traditions as behaviourism or psychoanalysis (as the work of Bowlby demonstrates) and its theoretical presuppositions have thus become admixed with those of its host. Ethology cannot yet therefore be said to have provided an adequate Darwinian (or post-Darwinian) alternative to classical developmental psychology.

The ethological approach to human development derives from the study of animal behaviour, and attempts to apply methods appropriate for the latter to the human case. The psychobiological approach, similarly, represents an attempt to extend the applicability of techniques well established in a separate enterprise: In this case, techniques relating to the function of the genes and of the central nervous system. The psychobiology of development thus approaches the topic from a position which emphasises the explanatory role of physiology, biochemistry, and evolutionary biology. Indeed, it appears that the interest in developmental phenomena is essentially a strategic one: It is held that the behavioural sequelae of neurological processes do in fact become manifest only over time and must hence be studied in the context of a developing (growing) organism. For the psychobiological approach, development is a means to a neurophysiological end. It is because of this motivation that the psychobiological influence has been most felt on studies of early (including foetal) development. In this respect, indeed, the approach represents a direct continuation of the embryological-physiological tradition of Wilhelm Preyer.

A recent summary statement by Gottlieb tackles the issue of recapitulation head-on, in a discussion of the extent to which psychobiology has transcended this "outmoded conception."[11] For Gottlieb, it is the *explanatory* pretensions of Haeckel's law which have been most misleading in the past: Individuals may indeed show some repetition of ancestral features, and may well go through universal sequences of behaviour, but "phylogeny" as such cannot explain such phenomena. Explanation must be sought in mechanical and physiological processes. Moreover, for Gottlieb, Haeckel's claim was wrong in its assumption of "terminal addition" as the way in which evolutionary progress is registered (new adaptations being added to the end of a chain): For early stages are not stable (as this would predict), and ancestral features may in fact often drop off the adult stage. This introduces the complex issue of neoteny (the evolutionary prolongation of early features to become adult features), a process also explored by Gould in his attempt to formulate a non-recapitulationist framework for development and evolution.[12] More fundamentally, however, Gottlieb is still working with a picture of individual development as a single track, a sequence of states, so that his rejection of Haeckelian recapitulation remains incomplete. In many ways it is the notion of "phylogeny" itself—a linear series of states—which is most fundamentally "wrong" with Haeckel; but Gottlieb retains it. Thus, rather than ontogeny being based on phylogeny, "phylogeny is based on ontogeny," and the notion of the phylogenetic scale certainly underlies Gottlieb's comments on "what we take to be our advanced psychological development compared to other primates, other mammals, and other vertebrates."

The issue of a fixed sequence of stages in development is a key one for Gottlieb. It is one of a set of "exceptionally well-founded principles of development" and examples include the maturation of sensory systems (such as in the human foetus) and the Piagetian account of cognitive development. Another principle of development is that of "differentiation and hierarchical organisation." Thus, as Gottlieb emphasises,[13] "a descriptive hallmark of all developing systems, whether organ or organism, is that they differentiate, which means that they progress from a relatively homogeneous to a relatively heterogeneous state." Herbert Spencer would of course have agreed; and in his discussion of differentiation, Gottlieb refers to the work of Heinz Werner as having been "able to frame a rather comprehensive comparative account of psychological development in humans and animals based entirely on the notions of differentiation and hierarchical integration." The notion of "differentiation," given such a central role by Gottlieb is not, therefore, a new and more technical one (derived perhaps from neurophysiology) but the one with which we are familiar. For Gottlieb, as for Werner, this differentiation is complemented in developmental progress by hierarchical organisation. An example of the latter is the layered structure of the brain, as manifested by the release of "earlier" connections (foetal reflexes) when outermost layers are interfered with. As we have seen, this is Hughlings Jackson's evolutionist picture, as employed 100 years ago by Freud and others. The latest application of biological science seems to lead back to square one.

Gottlieb stresses the importance to the psychobiological enterprise of causal relationships *within* ontogenesis, that is, the developmental consequences of earlier events and experiences on later outcomes. This emphasis on plasticity[14] relates to Gottlieb's notion of "probabilistic epigenesis" as an overarching theory of development. For Gottlieb the stronger position of "predetermined epigenesis"—by which developmental change is the result of simple maturation—is not generally adequate as ignoring the role of plasticity, *but* it "may be correct for the very earliest stages of embryonic and larval development." Straightforward maturation therefore retains an important role, and it is characteristic that it is with respect to *earlier* stages that such a determinate formulation is maintained. Again, the importance of within-ontogenesis effects is exemplified by the *repetition* in later development of movement patterns first employed earlier (for example, the repetition by the newborn of embryonic or foetal movements). As we have seen, the appeal to repetition as a form of explanation in development has close ties with recapitulationism. These ties have certainly been lost in Gottlieb's account, as they have in various psychological formulations of such repetition. But such claims have not arisen *de novo*, simply from empirical findings. The concept of repetition in the developmental course has itself a history which cannot easily be erased.

As with much of the Gottlieb position, which I think can be taken as an authoritative one, the very real sophistication of technique with respect to neurophysiology and related contexts is wedded to a set of presuppositions on the nature of development which derive from quite venerable and certainly unfashionable notions of biology. The biology itself has philosophical sources (here, idealism) of which Gottlieb demonstrates no awareness. In particular, the notion of species-specific forms of perception derives from the view that each organism has a special and unique relationship with the environment—a pre-established harmony or balance.

Neither psychobiology nor ethology can therefore be said to have applied a fresh and modern biological perspective to the phenomena of developmental psychology. Indeed, these approaches have themselves been influenced by the theoretical presuppositions which underlie the definition of those developmental phenomena. This reciprocal interaction —this feeding back of developmental assumptions into the biological source—is not the only way by which assumptions come to be held in common. The developmental presuppositions themselves derive from 19th-century biology, and modern biology derives from that same source. For a combination of reasons, therefore, related to the historical intertwining of biology and developmental psychology, it might be unreasonable to expect totally fresh viewpoints on development to emerge from an appeal to contemporary orthodoxy in biology. Neither ethology nor psychobiology have yet provided such fresh viewpoints.[15] Rather, their arguments serve to demonstrate the tenacity of those classic, 19th-century formulations whose influence is the theme of this book.

ALTERNATIVES: LIFESPAN THEORIES

Advocates of a "lifespan" approach to human development have argued that this orientation represents the most radical alternative to biologically derived developmental theories. Indeed, the approach is often seen as radically different from all previous formulation. The lifespan orientation de-emphasises the traditional boundaries between pre-adult development and maturity: Individuals of any age, it is argued, have very much more in common (in learning and development) than they have as fixed consequences of chronology. Changes during adulthood must be seen just as much as developmental phenomena as changes during childhood. This orientation to the whole life course, rather than just to the pre-adult years, has been advocated by a number of workers for a number of reasons and has given rise to a diversity of formulations. There is no single lifespan approach: Most derive from the linking together of the lifecourse orientation with some more orthodox tradition or methodology. In many respects, where the lifecourse orientation itself may well be quite novel, the associated theoretical frameworks frequently preserve the more established doctrines.[16]

It has been argued by lifespan advocates that the definition of development as excluding adulthood is a narrowly biological one. That is to say, when development is defined by close analogy with physical growth, the developmental period is terminated by the attainment of a stable adult size. Of course, growth models of development have exerted very great influence over ontogenetic formulations, particularly in the measurement-oriented traditions of intelligence and other psychometric approaches; but a major subdivision within the lifespan camp adopts this very psychometric framework: Adult development being defined as a lifelong continuation of childhood development, to be studied by the highly orthodox means of intelligence-type tests.[17] For example, a major contribution to the lifespan literature has come from studies of intellectual performance in old age. This research has given rise to advances in methodology, particularly with respect to the teasing apart of cohort (year-of-birth) effects from age effects. But the basic methodology remains that of psychometrics, which itself brings with it certain presuppositions on the nature of development (discussed, for example, in Chapter Eight). The extension of traditional approaches into the adult years does not in itself constitute theoretical innovation: It may indeed serve to conceal the need for such innovation.

Not all lifespan researchers employ psychometric methodologies, and some certainly take the need for new methodology as quite urgent.[18] Even here, however, the rejection of biological models seems incomplete. It is noted by Baltes, for example, that growth models—involving assumptions of continuity and gradual upward progression on a fixed course—must be incorporated as special cases within a broader framework. Such models are thus seen as one of a number of patterns which development may take. That is to say, the "growth" model from biology "has some features that are inappropriate or too restrictive for the study of ontogenetic change in a lifespan framework." It is implied that the growth model applies quite well to circumstances dominated by "normative age-graded influences." Examples of such influences are "biological maturation and socialisation when the latter is viewed as consisting of the fairly universal acquisition of a series of age-correlated roles or competences."[19]

For Baltes, developmental change is the result of the interaction of three types of influence: the age-graded (just discussed) and the history-graded, both of which are essentially normative; and the non-normative or idiosyncratic. Baltes notes that the universal or "fairly universal" age-graded normative influences—essentially, those which are modelled on biological growth—might be expected to dominate development in childhood and in old age. Baltes comments that this fact may explain "why much work in child development has been focused on age-graded influences." If the general claims of this book have any validity, and developmental research has in fact been *driven* by the presupposition of such features, then Baltes' comment would have to be considered somewhat naive.

The issue of old age has been mentioned as being of particular relevance to lifespan study. Theoretical accounts of old age have not been discussed in this book, since those falling into the appropriate chronology have not been sufficiently related to the major themes under discussion except in rather general terms. It is certainly the case that many descriptions of old age have been quite straightforwardly biological in their postulation of a terminal state of senility or decay. As far as research programmes into ageing are concerned, this viewpoint has been combined almost exclusively with a test-oriented methodology derived from the psychometric tradition. One exception to this is the approach of Klaus Riegel, who came to the lifespan area from a background in gerontology research.[20] Riegel's own theoretical orientation is to a "dialectical" interpretation of development.

One trend in the lifespan movement has been towards pluralistic or multivariate explanations.[21] The attempt has been made to articulate a system in which very many variables are at work, and are interacting, in order to produce developmental effects. Lifespan theorists have made a virtue of recognising the range of *kinds* of influences at work: maturational influences, historical influences, and so on. To a certain extent, however, the lifespan theorists have dealt with this problem by recourse to methods designed to cope with multiple factors *of the same kind*. Appeal has been made, that is to say, to methodologies designed for experimental situations in which many variables are manipulated. Such theorising thus presents developmental change in the lifespan as a massive psychological experiment, with the researcher seeking for patterns and, above all, "lawful relationships."[22] This approach has been substantially assisted by the development of computer programs for the causal analysis of multivariate, correlational information. It has been suggested, however, that despite the undoubted sophistication of the techniques themselves, the "logico-philosophical underpinnings" of the approach are still in need of attention.[23]

Pluralistic approaches to developmental psychology have usually been tied to an empiricist framework: That is, to a fact-finding orientation to research ("the universe is a series of multidimensional, ever-changing facts").[24] Some advocates have proposed that this connection is not a necessary one, and that interpretive methods of research should also be seen as consistent with the pluralist world view. Whether necessary or not, the connection has been a close one, so that the pluralism advocated by lifespan theorists tends in the main to reduce to a certain kind of statistical determinism: Individual development is the outcome of multiple, independent (but interacting) variables.[25] And as noted earlier, it is usual for biological-universal aspects of development to be separated out as a distinct type which is allowed to retain a privileged status. The choice is presented as being between a "monism" in which "robust, biologically orchestrated irreversible functions" are taken as the general model for development, and a "pluralism" in which the development of such functions manifests only one of many possible trajectories. The pluralism reduces to a dualism of biological functions versus cultural functions. Given that the former are assumed, or explicitly stated to dominate early life, the resulting picture is a classical one: Individuals start off determined by biology but come increasingly to be responsive to cultural effects.

"Lifespan developmental psychology" is very much an umbrella term, covering a very diverse group of theoretical positions. Each such position has its own background, despite attempts to construct a unified history for the overall approach.[26] It is perhaps to be anticipated that more precise formulations of adulthood and old age will emerge from the lifespan school than it has yet achieved. To date, much theorising has essentially consisted of the revision of classical formulations. Thus, as noted earlier, psychometric accounts of childhood are "corrected" by extending their sphere of application into the adult years. Similarly, attempts have been made to correct Piaget by defining new, "higher" stages of cognitive development.[27] Such extensions tend to leave the *childhood* component largely unaltered, suggesting that the classical account is inadequate simply through incompleteness. This kind of procedure must run the risk of importing older presuppositions into the newer context of adulthood. Certainly such notions as order and progress are found to be central in stage theories of adult development.[28]

In many respects, then, the lifespan approach has to be seen as less innovatory than it presents itself to be. The critique it offers of childhood-based theories is perhaps superficial: Such theories are considered inadequate simply because of their limited scope. Much more extensive and radical revisions of childhood theories could in fact be articulated on the basis of the lifespan doctrines: In particular, the role of biology could be subjected to much greater scrutiny than has been the case. Partly due, perhaps, to their awareness of ageing, biology remains the "bottom line" for most lifespan theorists. And it is this general assumption on the *master status* of biology that represents the most tenacious effect of biological thinking on the theory of human development.

ALTERNATIVES: FORMAL THEORIES

One of the major traditions to which the lifespan approach presents itself as an alternative is the work of Piaget. However, there are a number of other approaches which have also been presented as alternatives to

Piaget but which retain the focus on infancy and childhood. Some such alternatives concern themselves rather narrowly with the re-interpretation of Piagetian tasks; some attempt a wider critique of Piagetian theory. Most generally, these approaches reject the global-stage postulates of Piaget, developmental change being seen much more in "domain-specific" terms. The approach usually termed "information-processing" has been considered by some the major alternative to Piagetian traditions, in the contexts both of infant and of child development. In general, the information-processing approach has located itself at the narrower, more operational end of the range of alternatives: Accepting the significance of Piagetian tasks rather at face value, but seeking alternative explanations for children's performance on those tasks.

The information-processing approach to developmental psychology emerged during the 1960s and 1970s, much influenced by advances in computer technology. It consists essentially of the application of cognitive psychology to developmental issues. Cognitive psychology has formulated human performance in terms of the processing of discrete particles of information by channels of limited capacity. The emphasis here is on the sensory, or at least perceptual origin of knowledge, and cognitive psychology certainly remains in the mainstream of associationism from which psychology's experimental methods were derived.[29] Illustrations of this emphasis may be found in a recent summary of the information-processing approach to development in which, for example, it is made clear that the approach is an atomistic or elementalist one[30]: "One objective of information processing psychologists has been to determine the set of elementary information processes from which complex behaviour derives."

Despite considerable success in the description of low-level processes, the information-processing tradition has perhaps been relatively unsophisticated in its attempts to account for developmental *change*. The general assumption has been that children get better and better as processors of information: That they improve in "speed, exhaustiveness, and flexibility of encoding," in the complexity of stimuli which can be processed, and in the fineness of discrimination between alternative stimuli. Such regular, monotonic improvements are often taken to reflect the gradual increase in "capacity" of some kind of storage or working memory system. At the same time it is assumed that the components of knowledge, however described, come to accumulate and cohere into more and more complex structures.[31] These kinds of assumption may amount to little more than a restatement of the classical claims of associationist psychology.

It should certainly be noted that some lines of work have extended the theoretical base of the information-processing approach beyond its usual limits. For example, the investigation of "metacognition" has focused experimental attention on children's use of and awareness of deliberate strategies in problem-solving. Such concerns represent an important departure from the mechanistic framework more usually adopted, in which the child is treated as an essentially passive operator. The metacognition work involves a synthesis of the methodology of cognitive psychology with certain aspects of the Piagetian tradition, in particular the functional, problem-solving theme derived from the influence of Claparède. Somewhat more radical, perhaps, is the version of information-processing recently advocated by Siegler: A version which is formulated in terms of *rules*. For Siegler, children's performance is best described in terms of sets of rules, which articulate specific kinds of error as well as specific kinds of success. Developmental change is thus seen as the replacement of one rule, or of one set of rules, by another.[32]

This version of the information-processing approach would seem to represent a major departure from the mechanistic, channel-capacity model. There is certainly considerable influence from the linguistics of Noam Chomsky, with its emphasis on structural or "grammatical" (that is, rule-bound) aspects of cognition. In some respects, like the metacognition work, the kinds of direction in which theoretical change has taken place have been back toward Piaget rather than further away: Certainly in the emphasis on the importance of specific errors and on the structural nature of explanation. It would perhaps be just as accurate to label Siegler's approach neo-Piagetian as information-processing. The latter term has thus come to refer to a very broad and diverse collection of approaches united by little more than a similar experimental methodology.

Siegler's reformulation of the information-processing approach has much in common with the *computational* approach to human cognition. Like the information-processing approach, but in a more thorough and comprehensive way, the computational approach is influenced by the linguistics of Noam Chomsky. However, the orthodox cognitive psychology which underlies the former approach has included the study of mental imagery, of analogic representations of objects in the world. For the "computational theory of mind" representation has to be seen as digital or symbolic: Of exactly the same nature as representation within a computer. Cognition involves the manipulation of symbols, that is, the rule-bound or grammatical transformation of states in the "machine language." The approach is therefore above all a *formal* one. The formal nature of the computational approach has important theoretical implications, at least in the version articulated by Jerry Fodor. Fodor has argued that the kind of description required to capture the richness of human cognition actually finds no place for causal interconnections with the natural world.[33] This claim is radically anti-biological in a very broad sense: It denies the functionality or adaptiveness of cognition. Fodor's claims have not been made in the context of developmental theory, but if they indeed represent the legitimate application of the computational approach then the implications may be profound. Information-processing may be considered quite a conservative tradition, in its adherence to empiricism and associationism: Fodor's computational theory is certainly radical. Its implications for any available formulations on developmental change would be entirely destructive.

One "formal" line of thinking which has had a nondestructive impact on developmental theory is that derived from the work of J.J. Gibson. Agreeing with the Gestalt position to some extent, at least in opposition to a sensation-based account of human perception, Gibson has developed the view that active and meaningful ("ecological") examples of perception involve the subject in picking up information of a quite general kind from an environment: Information concerning movement and events rather than features or elements. In particular Gibson has argued that *invariant* characteristics of stimulation play a central role in perception. This line of argument is present to some extent in the Gestalt writings of Koffka but is worked out with systematic thoroughness by Gibson, especially in *The ecological approach to visual perception* (1979). In contrast to Fodor, the Gibsonian tradition places adaptive perception of a real world at the centre of psychology and hence of development. Gibson's term "ecological" is a considered one.

Gibsonian notions such as invariance and affordance have been applied to a wide range of topics in infant and child development, initially by E.J. Gibson in the investigation of early perceptual learning.[34] Within infancy, the Gibson perspective has allowed a much greater emphasis on the role of perception in early development than had previously been the case. This approach has provided an alternative to the more traditional sensation-based account of infancy. Most dramatically, Gibson's orientation has led to formulations and investigations of "amodal" features of early perception and cognition: Features which are not specific to one or other sensory "channel" as conventionally defined. This line of thinking has been carried furthest in the work of T.G.R. Bower, for whom developmental change consists essentially of "differentiation without loss": Of progress *from* abstract levels or structures *to* successively more concrete and specific ones. It is important that the differentiation is qualified as being "without loss," since the earlier, more primitive frameworks are held to remain in existence as the details are increasingly filled in. For example, the more general amodal forms of perception and cognition come to be increasingly tied down to specific sensory systems.[35]

Bower's line of argument, which is supported by neo-Piagetian experimentation on infant development, is also related to the rule-following and fundamentally formal tradition deriving from Chomsky and Fodor. For Bower, and consistent with such anti-empiricist sources as Fodor, the theory of differentiation-without-loss represents an explicit rejection of the associationism and empiricism which have long dominated psychological theorising. Following the tradition of Koffka and Gibson, the sensationism of earlier developmental theory is overturned. In its detailed attention both to theoretical and to empirical issues, Bower's formulation is certainly the most systematic and comprehensive of the formal alternatives yet to be presented.

ALTERNATIVES: THEORIES OF SOCIAL CONTEXT

Biological, formal, and cognitive-based approaches have all suffered from something of a backlash in the last 15 years or so, being accused in a rather wholesale fashion of ignoring such factors as social interaction and the communicative demands of experimental situations. A number of important contemporary approaches may be defined as different reactions to such perceived deficiencies in the cognitive-experimental mainstream. For example, much recent experimental work, especially with young children, has explored issues of meaningfulness and context in such Piagetian tasks as conservation and class-inclusion. Workers such as Margaret Donaldson have argued that the orthodox Piagetian methodology is in a sense unfair to the young child, in that it demands highly "abstract" or decontextualised performance. The claim is that children's everyday performance is in meaningful and often communicative contexts and hence that any descriptive science must focus on situations representative of this.[36]

For Donaldson and for this tradition, however, the objective is the correction, not the destruction, of Piaget's claims. Much of the empirical literature gives rise to little more than a *recalibration* of Piaget, children now being shown to "pass" Piagetian tasks earlier than previously thought. Such recalibration does not challenge the *meaning* of success on the tasks (accepting rather at face value the postulated significance of conservation, class-inclusion, and so on).[37] Similarly, Donaldson's "human sense" account fails to examine the issue of "abstractness," rather taking it for granted that developmental growth involves increasing distance or detachment from immediate situations. This assumption is, of course, central to Piaget's own account. Indeed, issues concerning "human sense" are not entirely absent from Piaget, who described the child explaining natural phenomena in terms of human manufacture and everyday household experience. One of Piaget's most slighted tasks, the "three mountains" task for visual perspective-taking, was designed to simulate real-life and everyday experience for his young Swiss subjects. Finally it must be remembered that Piaget has attempted to take account of social factors and that there is a strong sociological tradition in his writings, although this is somewhat disguised for English-speaking readers as a result of selective translation.[38]

One line of argument which is closely allied to this, yet points in more innovative directions, relates to the redefinition of "stages" in terms of "strategies." The notion here is that forms of conduct previously assigned a fixed place in an ontogenetic sequence might better be seen as alternatives, determined in any particular case by various situational factors. Such a proposal has been examined, for example, in the context of children's drawings. One well-established formula has been the developmental replacement of intellectual realism by visual realism—the replacement, that is, of the employment of multiple viewpoints by that of a coherent perspective. It has been proposed that the two systems of representation be considered alternatives, whose sequential order is governed by secondary and contingent factors. Here such factors are seen as including communicative aspects of the situation.[39]

Similarly, although perhaps more radically, stages in the development of moral judgement have been re-examined as strategies. As discussed by Harré, the forms of negotiation identified by Kohlberg as discrete, developmental stages might better be seen as alternatives which depend on the distribution of power in the social situation.[40] Stage-like phenomena are therefore seen as being socially *constituted*: A claim which goes beyond the social-context framework being considered here. It should be noted that the strategies position can be formulated in a much *less* social way also, that is in cognitive or information-processing terms.

Another kind of response to perceived deficiencies in orthodox experimental methodology has been that of Urie Bronfenbrenner. Bronfenbrenner has been especially critical of the laboratory-boundness of much developmental research and theorising, and of its related neglect of wider cultural and institutional settings.[41] Against such tendencies, Bronfenbrenner has urged the crucial importance of "ecological validity," which is to say that the setting should be examined as a crucial determinant of what is observed within that setting. Building on such arguments, Bronfenbrenner has proposed a model comprising a framework of nesting "systems" which both enable and constrain developmental change in individuals. This model is described as constituting an "ecology" of human development. This version of ecology is derived principally from the field theory and the "topological psychology" of Kurt Lewin (discussed briefly in Chapter Nine). In this context, but also with reference to such sources as G.H. Mead, it is emphasised that the version of "ecology" is a fundamentally *phenomenological* one. That is to say, the position is one in which "the meaning of environments to individuals" is taken to be fundamental.

Phenomenological approaches to social life have been explored in the work of Alfred Schutz and others. This "social phenomenology" has itself been criticised on several grounds, including voluntarism—the exaggeration of the extent of choice an individual has in social action—and subjectivism.[42] Prior to such technical issues, however, is the question of the consistency or otherwise of Bronfenbrenner's professed phenomenological attitude. The general tone of Bronfenbrenner's programme is a positivist one, in which the search is for general laws, to be uncovered by empirical research. Such laws do not exhibit the kind of relativism which the phenomenological attitude would seem to demand. Nor are they examples of the kind of regularity in individual perception which some forms of phenomenology might seek. An unkind critic might interpret Bronfenbrenner's appeals to the subjective meaning of situations as little more than lip-service to the social constitution of knowledge. This approach is certainly not carried through to the evaluation of literature or to the design of the research programme. The observational and experimental methodology endorsed by Bronfenbrenner is quite orthodox, and derives from intellectual traditions to which the phenomenological attitude is quite foreign.

What, then, is development for Bronfenbrenner? He defines it as follows[43] "Definition 7: Human development is the process through which the growing person acquires a more extended, differentiated, and valid conception of the ecological environment, and becomes motivated and able to engage in activities that reveal the properties of, sustain, or restructure that environment at levels of similar or greater complexity in form and content." With respect to developmental change as such, Bronfenbrenner seems to maintain a rather narrowly progressivist orientation. His concept of individual development is essentially one of "psychological growth" or betterment, usually of a rather poorly defined nature.[44] Again his picture of the young child gaining awareness and control over ever-widening circles of reality—of increasingly remote and intangible forces around it—is a most orthodox one. Throughout his writing, Bronfenbrenner lays emphasis on the theoretical significance of the child's everyday environment: That is, on issues of child care. But this emphasis tends to reduce to a general evaluation of environments as being either "good" or "bad" as facilitators of development. Bronfenbrenner's work cannot be said to exhibit an awareness of the *constitutive* impact of child-adult settings on individual development such as can be found in Vygotsky. For Bronfenbrenner, social contexts influence development but do not constitute development.

Bronfenbrenner's attempt to systematise a developmental psychology of social context appears to be premature. The term "social *context*" may itself be the key to the problem: That which is social, it seems to be implied, is just the background for the developmental phenomena, not the phenomena themselves. The social context position is inherently a weak or compromise position. It represents a dilution, rather than a rejection, of the classical standpoint. Indeed, if some kind of dichotomy is implied as between "social" and "biological," and if it is the context which is social, then the object of study must itself still be in some respect biological. This suggestion is borne out by an examination of the proposals of Donaldson and of Bronfenbrenner, neither of whom doubt that the basic trend in individual development is upward, onward, and outward. In emphasising the communicational and the familial background to individual development, the social context position may have deflected attention from the key issue: Can individual development itself be said to be intrinsically social?

ALTERNATIVES: THEORIES OF SOCIAL CONSTRUCTION

Finally, in this survey of contemporary approaches, we come to a movement which seems to offer the possibility of genuinely novel formulations on individual development. Over the last 20 years or so, an approach has been gathering momentum; according to this approach, developmental change and developmental outcome are seen as *socially constituted*. This approach has been strongly influenced by various more general movements in the social sciences, including: the sociology of knowledge; linguistic philosophy; structuralism and post-structuralism; hermeneutics; ethnomethodology; and various derivative of Marxist thinking.[45] The general emphasis is on the *public* nature of knowledge, so that developmental change is also taken to be a public affair: A matter of "social construction."[46] Although proponents of such an approach would agree on many points, it is also essential to note the range of interpretations given to "social construction" and related terms. The increase in influence and recognition of this approach has been accompanied by something of a fragmentation.

Early versions of these ideas were advanced in the early 1970s by Riegel, who argued the case that developmental theories themselves reflect the socio-historical characteristics of the societies from which they emerge. Thus British and American theories were identified as broadly "capitalistic-mechanistic" and European theories as "mercantilistic-mentalistic." The former see development as "an accumulation of information by . . . passive organisms" and the latter see it as "the spontaneous emergence of new modes of operation for which the environment merely provides the information."[47] Riegel also made specific proposals concerning an alternative, "dialectical" approach which would incorporate both viewpoints. More generally, Riegel's sweeping critique of developmental psychology helped to establish a tradition of the investigation of the cultural setting and cultural definition of development.[48] Such investigations are inherently critical of the role of biology, especially of biological universals in development: However, the history of "cross-cultural psychology" shows that the critique is often rather an inadequate one.[49]

In the U.K., the early explorations were due to Harré and to Shotter, for example in M. Richards' *The integration of a child into a social world* of 1974. Harré has continued to investigate the ways in which human development may be seen as socially constructed, and has developed the approach into its most systematic and formalised version.[50] Shotter has taken something of a hermeneutical or deconstructionist approach to developmental issues (with particular reference to infant development).[51] Both Harré and Shotter have appealed to the writings of Vygotsky, and to a lesser extent to those of G.H. Mead, in attempting to give some precision to the general claims. For Harré, Vygotsky's contribution was the outlining of a process of "appropriation" as the key to individual development. That is, for Harré, Vygotsky demonstrated that ontogenesis involves the "taking in" of public knowledge, of culture in all its manifestations. This account appears to be a radically anti-biological one, although it is possible that some orthodox elements remain. Thus an inherent, non-socially-constructed increase in cognitive capacity is retained; "the ability to deal with more complex tasks and to handle greater masses of material."[52] This factor is highly constrained and overlaid by social negotiation, but represents a quasi-biological core nevertheless.

It could be argued that all these approaches fall short of a truly radical version of social-constructionism, and that for such a version a direct appeal to Marxist traditions needs to be made. Certainly, it was Marx who first argued that human life is defined by an "ensemble of social relations"[53]: Such social relations being taken as including those arising from the production and distribution of wealth. The contribution of Marx's own writings to a developmental psychology is only one line of enquiry. The developmental psychology of the Soviet Union must also be considered, and some attention should also be given to available syntheses of Marxism with psychology. Finally, there are contemporary developmental psychologists who have made serious attempts to adopt a Marxist framework. Somewhere in this set of traditions, perhaps, some indications of a rigorous alternative to biologism may be found.

It is not surprising, in view of the extent of his interests and output, that a variety of interpretations may be given to Marx's own observations on individual development. One clear message appears to have been that the liberation of individual development is itself a major objective, and a major criterion, for the communist revolution. "Self-realisation" can only become possible under such a post-capitalistic society. At least, it is only then that it becomes possible for all citizens, since Marx can be read as implying that the development of a member of the ruling class under a class system is itself already free from constraint. If so, Marx might be said to have provided a model of what makes up true individual development. Alternatively, this version of "self-realisation" can be seen as connected with an early, "humanist" Marx, such that no prescriptive account of proper human development should be extracted from the mature theory.[54] Instead Marx can be said to have described the framework of forces by which human life and human development are produced under any society. Marx would hence be seen as a social scientist of process, describing the ways in which social being is inherently public and inextricably bound up with the division of labour. Such an interpretation might be an extension of a "sociology of knowledge" or might see itself as a development of "mediation" versions of Marxism.[55]

It might be argued here that the approach of Riegel, as noted earlier, is surely a direct application of Marx. Societies have certain basic (that is economic) characteristics; the nature of social life, human consciousness and individual development are all directly determined by that economic base.[56] However, this kind of "base/superstructure" account should not be seen as the definitive Marxism of Marx. It has been described as "economism" or "vulgar" Marxism, as a late 19th-century distortion of Marx, by which Marxism "fell prey to the very positivism which its critique had been at pains to undermine."[57] This issue is a crucial one, for many of those who consider themselves to be true descendants of Marx maintain a most positivistic, scientistic orientation ("the iron laws of historical development"). As far as individual development is concerned, this attitude has always been closely allied to evolutionist argument. Hence it is possible to find Marxist theoreticians appealing to unilinear models of evolution in exactly the same way as "bourgeois" developmental psychology has done.[58]

What then of developmental psychology in the U.S.S.R? The discipline has undergone a series of transformations, as the official version of Marxist-Leninism has been redefined at a political level. Vygotsky's work was guided by a certain form of Marxism, but came to be seen as unsound during the Stalin years. Vygotsky's students and younger colleagues developed his ideas in various ways.[59] Thus Leont'ev saw Vygotsky's notion of "interiorisation" as possibly implying "a pre-existing, internal 'plane of consciousness'" and hence a kind of idealism.[60] Leont'ev's own account focused on the *production* of this plane of consciousness and of its contents, and hence on "activity." Leont'ev's influential "activity theory" has in turn been opposed by Rubinstein, again in a manner related to the interpretation of Marxist theory.[61] Despite these intense debates, however, much of the actual Soviet research appears to have deviated rather little from orthodox Western work. One reason for this has been the continuous presence of the Pavlov influence, which has steered much of the early development research into the study of the conditioning of reflexes. Stage theories of development are also widely applied.[62]

Attempted syntheses of Marxist thinking with psychology have, in the past, been initiated mainly from the Marxist side and have focused on the writings of Freud. Further, it has usually been Freud's therapeutic methods and the related theory—rather than the developmental account as such—on which attention has centered. The most rigorous attempt to draw a psychology (of "personality") out of Marxism has been that of Sève, who is severely critical of the Freud-Marx syntheses. Because of its neglect of social labour, Sève argues, it is impossible that Freud's account could become the basis for an adequate theory of human personality.[63] In general, for Sève, it is a mistake to look for the origins of adult personality in the child; childhood is only the starting-point, and the social activities in which adults are immersed totally transform any personality characteristics they may have formed as children.[64] In some respects such an orientation converges with the life-span approach to development, but Sève's version would be considerably more radical than those currently described by that term. The possibility of a Marxist account of *child* development is in fact also indicated, in a discussion of the role of social labour in parent-child relationships.[65] More specifically, Sève presents an outline sketch of a Marxist theory of human development in terms of the relative distributions of "use-time" at different ages and stages (schoolchild, student, worker, retired). The account is, however, more illustrative than substantive.[66] More generally, Sève makes it clear that a place must be reserved for the "psychobiological determination" of the "growth of capacities." He also endorses such orthodox notions as the "weak organic composition" of the child and, at the other extreme, the "biological reality" of the process of senescence.[67] Sève's full-blooded Marxism is still a little timid when it comes to the "facts" of biology.

It is only in recent years that developmental psychologists in the West have made serious efforts to engage with Marxist thinking on social life. Riegel's specific proposal for a "dialectical" developmental psychology was perhaps the first such contribution, but it now seems somewhat inadequate (especially since it has been readily absorbed into the lifespan-contextualist movement).[68] A more thoroughgoing attempt at a Marxist-conscious developmental psychology has been that of a group associated with the journal *Ideology and consciousness*.[69] In recent years this group has looked more to structuralist and post-structuralist traditions, especially the work of Foucault, rather than to Marxism as such. However the emphasis on the public nature of knowledge and on the interrelations between power and knowledge—all of which are major themes of Foucault—are themselves a part of the legacy of Marx to the social sciences of the present century.

The most co-ordinated account from this group of researchers is the collection *Changing the subject: Psychology, social regulation and subjectivity* of 1984. Critiques of developmental psychology comprise only parts of that book, although in many ways the most successful parts.[70] The authors present a vigorous defence of the *inherently* social nature of individual development, and hence identify orthodox developmental psychology as individualistic and biologistic, especially in its assumption that children grow *from* biology *to* culture. This orthodox viewpoint involves the equation of the biological with the natural, and hence defines the social or cultural as secondary, derived, or artificial. An important related practice is the "naturalisation" of social facts: The taking of facts which are relative to a certain institutional framework as absolute and universal.[71] Reading certain socially constructed practices as "natural"—and, necessarily, other such practices as artificial—is a process which inevitably involves value judgements. For example, the naturalisation of certain kinds of mothering or of intellectual development in childhood must reflect the distribution of appropriate power and knowledge within the society. When such practices are further defined as the source of information for developmental psychology—as providing the phenomena which the discipline must seek to explain—then the science is very definitely being driven by social forces. Social facts are treated as natural facts, and natural facts as biological facts. Childhood is biologised.

One general argument endorsed by the contributors to *Changing the subject* is that the term "social" must be taken in a broad and structural sense; that is to say, as something much more than "interpersonal." Interpersonal relations must themselves be seen as constituted by social structure and the unequal distribution of wealth, power, and knowledge. Some applications of this approach might adopt a "field" theory of social relations[72] in which individual activity is described as the deformation of pre-existing structures and networks. Such an approach might, however, neglect the ongoing production of social forms by personal activity; that is, it might reify or naturalise the social and institutional arrangements that happen to be in place. Some role must, it seems, be found for individual action, including action that seeks to challenge existing power structures.[73]

An issue central to many of the social-construction and social-production writings is gender. Urwin and Walkerdine, two of the authors of *Changing the subject*, discuss the significance of gender across a range of contexts both in that book and elsewhere. Urwin is especially concerned with infancy, the emergence of language, and the social practices of mothering[74]; Walkerdine with the school years, with the construction of rationality, and with the particular case of mathematics learning.[75] Both provide uncompromising critiques of orthodox developmental psychology as it relates to these issues; both relate the critique of theory very closely to the critique of practice. Language is seen as having special connections with women's issues throughout the lifespan, and as playing a crucial role in the construction of individuality as a gendered entity. "Child-centredness"—either in the mother of an infant, or in the model for pedagogy—is analysed as an apparatus for social control, for surveillance, and for the normalising and naturalising of specific social practices. "Normal" development of the child is defined as natural, but at the same time as dependent on certain attitudes in the mother whose needs are (naturally) identical with those of her baby. Female identity can only be either natural or pathological. Hence gender is deeply implicated in any account of developmental psychology: Any claims the discipline might make to be neutral in this regard can only be fraudulent.

The concern with women's issues is central, not peripheral, to the social-construction or social-production approach being explored by these authors. Together with the informed critique of professional and scientific practice—and interrelated with it—this concern gives an urgency and significance to this body of writing which is lacking in versions noted previously. The theoretical issues, some of which are highly technical, are shown to *matter*. These aspects combine to make this version of the social production of development perhaps the most threatening to the existing order. Although still perhaps somewhat programmatic, social-productionism may indeed represent the most genuinely distinct of the alternatives to biology. A focus on the ways in which individual lives are socially produced does seem to offer a way forward. We may perhaps be in a position to make a choice between the old way and a new way: Between the biologising and the *socialising* of childhood.

NOTES TO CHAPTER TEN

[1]Reviews of recent and contemporary work may be found in Bornstein and Lamb (1984) and in the various volumes of the *Handbook of child psychology* (Mussen, 1983).

[2]See Gould (1985); Gould and Lewontin (1979); Gould and Vrba (1982).

[3]Evans (1975, p. 5); Kalikow (1983). Bölsche's work, and its influence on Freud, are discussed by Sulloway (1979, p. 261–263). As noted by Kalikow (1983, p. 45), "Bölsche pictured nature as a romantic, mystical, upward-spiraling life process, in true Haeckelian fashion." Bölsche's biography of Haeckel (Bölsche, 1900/1906, pp. 225–226) argues that recapitulation was endorsed, but not fully exploited by Darwin: "it was reserved for Haeckel to develop its full importance." If Lorenz learned of Darwin through Bölsche then he would have learned of a Haeckelian Darwin. As Ghiselin (1986, p. 15) notes, "Modern ethology developed largely oblivious to Darwin's contribution."

[4]Lorenz (1973/1977, p. 27). Lorenz also makes it clear here that evolution has a clear *direction*.

[5]Lorenz's key article on the contribution of Kant is reprinted in Evans, 1975 (originally 1941). Kant had argued that certain general frameworks for human cognition must be presupposed as prior to specific acts of perception or judgment (hence a priori). He had further drawn a distinction between knowable appearances or phenomena and the source of

such phenomena, the unknowable thing-in-itself or *noumenon*. Lorenz's argument is that the general trend of evolution is toward a closer and more complete acquaintance with this Kantian "noumenon" or thing-in-itself (Evans, 1975, p. 184). Lower species (ibid., p. 213): "achieve a correspondence to the properties of the thing-in-itself less detailed than that of man"; "our perception is true to a higher degree than is the animal's image of the universe." Therefore the limits of the animal's world are themselves *within* the limits of the human world. Hence the total perceptual universe of the lower animal is comprehensible to the higher. Lorenz outlines a systematic research programme based on this account: The comparison of the innate working hypotheses of different species, which in each case indicate the level reached by the a priori for that species (ibid., p. 201). This picture of epistemological evolutionism represents a synthesis of von Uexküll on the species-specificity of perceptual worlds with Kant on the relation between knowledge and the knowable.

A phylogenetic scale is quite explicit here (concrete examples of relative "mental level" including amoeba, water shrew, rat, and human, in that order). As far as a knowledge of space is concerned, the lower animals work by rote and by association whereas the higher ones think in terms of a three-dimensional layout. Parallels between the evolutionary scale and phenomena in the child and in the "primitive" are also noted (Evans, 1975, pp. 208–209). In recent writings, Lorenz makes it clear that the direction of evolution—from "lowest" to "highest"—relates to the *amount of knowledge* inherent in the system (Lorenz, 1973/1977, p. 28). In general, Lorenz's picture of evolutionary progress is one of increasing perfection: As such, Lorenz is a true descendant of Lamarck.

[6]Kalikow (1983); also see Campbell's chapter in Evans (1975). For Lorenz on "the progressive decay of our civilisation" (Lorenz, 1973/1977, p. 18; also p. 176) see especially *The enmity between the generations and its probable ethological causes* (originally 1970; in Evans, 1975). As cited by Brandt (in Buss, 1979, p. 89), Lorenz has described behaviourism as a "doctrine [which] undoubtedly carries a considerable share in the responsibility for the impending moral and cultural collapse of the United States." On behavioural pathology in captive animals see Lorenz (1978/1981, p. 49). Here he notes that one common "disturbance" is the "diminution of intensity" and tendency to incompleteness in instinctive patterns, and "this pathological disturbance of a phylogenetically programmed behaviour pattern is very similar to the normal incompleteness which we observe in the ontogenesis of young animals."

[7]Hinde (1983, pp. 62–63).

[8]Ibid., p. 41. See footnote 5; also footnote 1 to Chapter Nine.

[9]As noted by Lorenz (1965/1966, p. 24), von Uexküll was committed to the notion of pre-established harmony between organism and environment.

[10]The pre-adaptationist interpretation of infant development was clearly indicated by Bowlby (1969/1971, p. 319).

[11]Gottlieb (1983).

[12]Gould (1977).

[13]Gottlieb (1983, p. 6).

[14]Plasticity is a notion also emphasised in life-span accounts; the term seems to retain much of its biological definition in that context.

[15]See, however, P.P.G. Bateson (1987) for a balanced and positive evaluation of the possible contributions of contemporary biology. Detailed arguments for the contribution of the neurosciences to developmental psychology are presented by Crnic and Pennington (1987).

[16]For a general introduction to the lifespan approach, see the chapter by Baltes and Reese in Bornstein and Lamb (1984). A critical evaluation is offerred by Gergen (1982, p. 148) who predicts "a major crisis" in its theoretical base. According to Labouvie-Vief and Chandler (1978) the study of lifespan development has been held back by "a residual form of idealism" according to which intellectual competence is portrayed (ibid., p. 184) "as though it were

moving inextricably [sic] along some nomological path toward an ideal state of mature adult cognition." Thus developmental stages are defined "as imperfect or progressive categories aimed at and only ultimately realised in a fixed ideal goal or end state. Change . . . is inherently directional, growth is understood as progress, and adulthood is regarded as success. Developmental research . . . becomes a kind of ontological ballistics, tracking growth along a unilinear trajectory toward its idealised apogee in maturity."

[17]Schaie (1983).

[18]Baltes, in Lerner (1983).

[19]Ibid., p. 96.

[20]Riegel (1977).

[21]Dixon and Nesselroade (1983).

[22]Schaie (1983, p. 1).

[23]Dixon and Nesselroade (1983, p. 131). This chapter and the general notion of "pluralism" is thoroughly examined by Kaplan (1983). Among other deficiencies, Kaplan (ibid., p. 224) accuses Dixon and Nesselroade of a "loose and superficial treatment of the history of ideas."

[24]Ibid., p. 140. Kaplan's (1983, pp. 193, 197) account is savage but sound. "Enjoining neither a theory nor a concept of development and hence enjoying the obvious advantage of not knowing what it is that they are studying . . . To constitute a life-span developmental psychology in terms of a catalogue . . . of facts garnered from every perspective, utilising every method, and examining the functional relations between every variable and every other variable is not only a vain endeavor; it is an inane one." Similar points are made by Kitchener (1983) on the positivistic and empiricist nature of approaches such as that of Baltes.

[25]Closely related is the notion that early stages of development manifest "plasticity" in ways that later stages do not. Plasticity in human development has been described by Scarr (1986, p. 565) as "a hopeful concept, science's version of human perfectibility." The comment is made in a review of R. Lerner's book on this topic. Scarr continues (1986, p. 566): "Mixed into the plasticity metaphor is the lifespan developmentalists' credo of reciprocal, and ever more complex, determinism of life courses. Everything determines and is determined by everything else . . . is this a research program or just an impressive display of words?" On the same point, see Bateson (1987, p. 19). Lerner's approach is criticised also by Kitchener (1983, p. 18) as adhering to outdated notions of philosophy of science (namely, a logical-positivist view of verification and proof).

[26]Antecedents to lifespan developmental psychology are examined by Baltes, in Lerner (1983); and by Reinert (1979).

[27]As noted by Broughton (1986, p. 157), the normative assumption in stage theories of adulthood serves to define any "resistance" or attempted avoidance of "the various prescribed hurdles" as a sign of immaturity. Such pathology necessitates a therapeutic technology for getting the client "back on the track."

[28]The analysis by Labouvie-Vief and Chandler (1978, p. 200) is of direct relevance here: "Because idealistic theories commonly interpret . . . intellectual development as the derivative consequence of . . . instabilities equilibrated at the level of some 'most mature' form, progressive growth in childhood is explained by constructs intrinsic to the theory, while subsequent lifespan changes are explained away by principles extrinsic to the original theoretical account." As they express this earlier (ibid., p. 185), "children are pictured as swept along toward some inevitable cognitive maturity by powerful, universalistic forces that gradually spend themselves as physical maturity is approached." This viewpoint is necessarily evaluative: In contrast to maturity (ibid., p. 200), "the efforts of the young or culturally alien appear puny and amateurish, while the attempts of the ageing or elderly are seen as hollow caricatures of youth."

[29]The associationist ancestry of cognitive psychology is stressed by J. Russell (1984, p. 118).

[30]Siegler (1983b, p. 164). The information-processing approach to development is commit-

ted to the notion of "monotonic" progress, even when the phenomena seem to suggest the decline or loss of capacities (see the chapters by Klahr, and by Richards and Siegler, both in Strauss, 1982).

[31]A thorough and comprehensive application of this approach may be found in Case (1985). Case's approach is examined by Kuhn (1983) who compares the popularity of information-processing models with the former popularity of Piagetian theory. Kuhn warns that information-processing may simply substitute for Piaget—itself assimilated only as a theory of stages—without the more fundamental issues of developmental change being addressed.

[32]Siegler (1983a). Somewhat related approaches include the cognitive-developmental work of Mehler and of Mounoud (both in Bever, 1982). Mehler discusses ways in which early growth may involve the loss of capacities (cf. footnote 30) and Mounoud presents the case for "revolutionary" changes in developmental organisation, each ensuring "a different type of mastery" of the world. Both authors, however, make it clear that the general trend is toward improvement.

[33]Fodor (1980). For a detailed critique of the "computational theory of mind" see J. Russell (1984). Fodor's anti-naturalistic approach is an extension of that of Chomsky, who has been reported by Toulmin (1985, p. 14) as saying: "Anyone who asks for 'evolutionary precursors' of language doesn't understand what language is." (Also see Chomsky, 1986.) It is important to note that Fodor finds the approach of Gibson just as unacceptable as the more orthodox "representational" theories of mind.

[34]See J.J. Gibson (1979). Developmental applications are discussed by Butterworth (1987); Costall (in Butterworth, 1982); Lee, Young, and McLaughlin (1984); Morss (1987a; 1988); and Russell (1984) (and here also cf. Morss, 1989).

[35]Bower (1979; 1982); also see Morss (1984); and E.J. Gibson (1985). The general issue of whether it is possible to develop from a "weak" to a "strong" state—to "get more out of less"—is discussed in the introduction to Strauss (1982).

[36]Donaldson (1978); also see Bryant (1982).

[37]Cogent criticisms of the Donaldson approach are presented by Light, by Ingleby, and by Urwin, all in M. Richards and Light (1986); and by Walkerdine in Henriques et al. (1984).

[38]Mays in Butterworth, Scaife, and Rutkowska (1985).

[39]Light and McEwen (1987).

[40]Harré (1983, p. 227).

[41]Bronfenbrenner (1979). Also see Bronfenbrenner and Crouter (1983) which is mainly concerned with tracing the historical origins of the Bronfenbrenner approach. (Piaget has carried out the same exercise on a number of occasions, but taking the Piagetian standpoint as exemplifying modernity.) Perhaps inevitably, in view of this objective, the chapter is entirely Whiggish in tone as earlier "stages" and precursors of the contemporary position are examined. The use of the term "evolution" in the chapter's title is quite deliberate and should be examined. Also see Kaplan's (1983) critique of Bronfenbrenner.

[42]The limitations of Schutz's social phenomenology are described succinctly by Rubinstein (1981, p. 74). Schutz's approach is that followed by Berger and Luckmann (1967)—see footnote 46 following.

[43]Bronfenbrenner(1979, p. 27).

[44]This naive progressivism is also to be found in the Bronfenbrenner and Crouter (1983, p. 398) chapter where G.H. Mead is invoked in the context of the "facilitation of psychological growth."

[45]For a clear and concise review, see Ingleby's chapter in M. Richards and Light (1986). Ingleby concludes (ibid., p. 315): "If the idea of progress in developmental psychology means anything at all, the social constructionist movement is at the leading edge of it." *Deconstructionism* could well have been included in the list of social science trends; for a review of its implications for psychology, including developmental psychology, see Kurtzman (1987).

[46]On knowledge as a public phenomenon see Rubinstein (1981); also Toulmin (1985, p. 19) who presents the following epigram: "Our Inner Lives are the 'servants' of manifest, public Outer Minds." Implications for developmental psychology are explored in Morss (1988). The term "social construction of reality" often connotes the approach outlined in the book of the same name (Berger & Luckmann, 1967). It should be emphasised that Berger and Luckmann's is a very specific version: An application of the social phenomenology of Alfred Schutz. This approach has not been particularly influential on developmental thinking. Berger and Luckmann themselves do present some claims on the nature of (early) development, but these turn out to be highly orthodox, biologistic claims. Thus the neonate is to be considered an entirely biological entity—still in effect a fetus (part of the mother) for one year or so (ibid., p. 66). For a discussion of related notions of "symbiosis" see Morss (1988). Konrad Lorenz has found it possible (1973/1977, p. 174) to read Berger and Luckmann as proposing that "the social construction of reality" involves the overlaying of an innate perceiving apparatus by a cultural superstructure. Given that Berger and Luckmann appeal to von Uexküll (ibid., p. 219), and given their deference to biology in the determination of human consciousness, Lorenz's version is less of a distortion than might at first appear.

[47]It might be observed that Riegel's dichotomy is rather similar to that of Reese and Overton (1970): See footnote to Chapter Nine. Riegel's papers are reprinted in Buss (1979; the quotation is p. 340). Also see Riegel (1976). Also reprinted in Buss (1979) is the 1975 paper of Buck-Morss (no relation to myself!) on socioeconomic bias in Piagetian theory; in a similar vein to Riegel but perhaps more rigorous. Buss's own Introduction, originally 1975, gives a good indication of the early contributions to a "sociology of psychological knowledge." For a recent account of these broader issues in psychology see Gergen (1982).

[48]Kessel and Siegel (1983).

[49]On the issues relating to cross-cultural psychology and its assumptions, see Buck-Morss (1975/1979).

[50]Harré (1983; 1986; 1987); also Morss (1987b). For a related approach, see Gergen and Davis (1985); this collection includes some slightly bizarre contributions alongside those of Harré and Shotter and serves to illustrate the breadth and perhaps looseness of the term "social construction."

[51]Shotter (1984). In general, Shotter has eschewed systematisation, preferring to explore such sources of ideas as literary criticism and other textual approaches (Shotter, 1986). On Shotter's infant development work, see Morss (1985b) (and subsequent commentaries). One by-product of the recent appeal to G.H. Mead, by Shotter and others, has been a renewed interest in Mead's more general philosophical claims. As a pragmatist philosopher—following C.S. Peirce in particular—Mead was centrally concerned with practical activity in the world. Mead's discussion of a "co-operation" between organism and environment (G.H. Mead, 1938) amounts to an *ecology*, which might fruitfully be compared with that of J.J. Gibson (Morss, 1988). Shotter himself appeals more to Vygotsky than to Mead. For examples of the "rediscovery" of Vygotsky see Bruner and Haste (1987); some contributors (especially Haste) appearing somewhat uncritical in this regard. Vygotsky threatens, perhaps, to sweep through developmental psychology in a similar way to Piaget (as discussed by Kuhn, 1983).

[52]Harré (1983, p. 225).

[53]Marx (1845/1986).

[54]On self-realisation in Marx, see Sève (1974/1978, pp. 76, 201); also, the clear and careful paper by Mobasser (1987). As cited there (p. 125), David Hume had claimed that "the different stations of life influence the whole fabric [of a person], external and internal . . ."; thus "The skin, pores, muscles and nerves of a day-labourer are different from those of a man of quality: so are his sentiments, actions and manners." The humanist orientation of the early writings of Marx is emphasised by Sève (1974/1978, p. 68).

[55]This "labour process perspective" is explored by Young (Note 4; 1985b).

[56]Marx (Preface to *The critique of political economy*, 1859/1986):

> In the social production of their existence, men inevitably enter into definite relations, which are independent of their will, namely relations of production appropriate to a given stage in the development of their material forces of production. The totality of these relations of production constitutes the economic stucture of society, the real foundation, on which arises a legal and political superstructure and to which correspond definite forms of social consciousness.

But Engels wrote many years later (cited in Young, Note 4, p. 29):

> According to the materialist conception of history, the *ultimately* determining element in history is the production and reproduction of real life. More than this neither Marx nor I have ever asserted. Hence if somebody twists this into saying that the economic element is the only determining one, he transforms that proposition into a meaningless, abstract, senseless phrase.

[57]Young (Note 4, p. 24). The same point is made by Manicas (1987, p. 116) for whom neither Marx not Engels in fact claimed to have discovered determinate laws of history, although their rhetoric did imply such a stance. Neither could "free themselves from the idea that human progress was inevitable." Manicas concludes: "Engels's famous graveside speech must surely have fuelled a positivist understanding of the Marxist 'laws of development.' By the end of the 19th century, especially with the work of Plekhanov, Marxism came to have many of the features of a Comtean positivism joined with a Spencerian monism." An observation by Lenin is relevant here (cited by Cole, in Luria, 1979, p. 3); progress in science Lenin stated is "a development that repeats . . . the stages already passed, but repeats them in a different way, on a higher plane . . . a development, so to speak, in spirals, not in a straight line." For current debate on related issues, see Mouzelis (1988).

[58]Thus Novack (1972) criticises what he describes as "skepticism in sociology" for *denying* that the "typical manifestations of social life can—or even should—be arranged in any determinate order of historical development in which each has its given place from the beginning to the end, from the lower to the higher . . . This [skeptical] view and method is thoroughly anti-evolutionary, anti-scientific and essentially reactionary." The chapter, titled "The long view of history: How humanity climbed to civilisation" is Haeckelian both in style and in substance. The attachment of the more positivist and determinist versions of Marxism to a unilinear account of evolution is also indicated by Young (Note 4, p. 25; 1985b), for whom Kautsky—"leading theoretician of the Second International"—reduced the social-economic base itself to biological evolutionism. Plekhanov (cf. footnote 57) described Marxism as "Darwinism in its application to social science" (cited by Young, 1985b, p. 209).

[59]Soviet developmental psychology is discussed by Rahmani in Riegel and Meacham (1976); by Sutton (1983); by contributors to Wertsch (1985); and by Valsiner (1988). Also see the autobiographical account by Vygotsky's younger colleague Luria (1979) in which useful details of the early developmental work are given. Thus it is noted that children's development was conceived as arising from two kinds of process, natural and cultural. Natural processes change quantitatively with age, including such "mental processes" as memory span. Cultural processes change qualitatively. Now "among young children . . , cultural processes still play a subordinate role." Luria (1979, pp. 83–84) describes a "period where natural processes are dominant (5–7 years)" and a "period where cultural processes are normally dominant (11–13 years)." Although the analysis of the interplay of the two kinds of process

was sophisticated in a Marxist sense, the outcome as a description of children's development was entirely orthodox.

[60]Leont'ev (1981); cited in Wertsch and Stone, in Wertsch (1985, p. 163).

[61]On Rubinstein, see Rahmani in Riegel and Meacham (1976); and, less critically, Riegel in Buss (1979). Where Leont'ev maintained the natural/cultural distinction referred to in footnote 59—dividing human abilities into those shared with animals and those not—Rubinstein argued that all human abilities are of the same, social-productive kind (Rahmani, in Riegel & Meacham, 1976, p. 118). Also see the technical accounts by Zinchenko, and by Davydov and Radzikhovskii, both in Wertsch (1985).

[62]An introduction to contemporary Soviet developmental thinking is given by Sutton (1983), who includes an account of the stage theory of El'konin.

[63]Sève (1974/1978, pp. 148, 345, 353).

[64]Ibid., pp. 214, 322, 344. Sève's devaluation of child development is considered to be excessive by Leonard (1984), for whom feminist theory on childrearing as a labour process renders Sève's more classical Marxism inadequate. Leonard also differs from Sève in wishing to incorporate certain aspects of psychoanalytic theory into an account of human development.

[65]Sève (1974/1978, pp. 157, 214).

[66]Ibid., p. 348. Sève's diagrams—four quadrants, each with a circle of different size inscribed—recall, in different ways, the graphical representations of Harré (1986) and Lewin.

[67]Ibid., pp. 356–357, 361. Sève does however also note the following (ibid., p. 214): "The effort to give the personality considered as a *historico-social* formation a theory *with a biological basis* is itself one of those aberrations the persistence . . . of which should be enough to show that psychology has still not altogether reached maturity" (emphases in original). This use of the term "maturity" could itself be questioned, of course.

[68]See Lerner (1986). The "contextualist" orientation is potentially quite a radical one, at least as defined by Labouvie-Vief and Chandler (1978, p. 201), for whom contextual theories set aside assumptions of directionality and progress. "Contextual theories regard change as simply that, and make no assumptions that such variations are in the service of achieving a particular goal or idealised end state. The omission of this single idealistic assumption is sufficient, according to Pepper [*World hypotheses*] to cause the progressive categories of organismic models to suffer a general revision in the direction of contextualism." But this de-idealising is precisely what Lerner (1986, p. 67) is not prepared to do, although he recognises the strength of Pepper's argument. The Labouvie-Vief and Chandler version is an anti-universalist, relativistic position. For Lerner, however, Pepper's contextualism cannot be adequate (1986, p. 68); "a world view that stressed only the dispersive, chaotic and disorganised character of life would not readily lend itself to the derivation of a theory of development." Lerner's favoured position is a synthesis of contextualism with a (broadly psychobiological) organicism: This amalgam being termed variously "contextual organicism,' "probabilistic epigenesis," and "developmental contextualism."

[69]As well as the manifesto published in the first issue (Adlam et al., 1977), reference should also be made to Riley's (1978) important paper *Developmental psychology, biology and Marxism*. Also see Sinha (1988).

[70]Henriques et al. (1984); also see Morss (1986).

[71]Vonèche, in Broughton (1987, p. 79).

[72]Morss (1988).

[73]Walkerdine, in Steedman, Urwin, and Walkerdine (1985).

[74]Urwin, in Henriques et al. (1984); Urwin (1985; 1986a; 1986b). Urwin (1986a) is one of the most successful contributions to M. Richards and Light, *Children of social worlds* (1986). This collection seeks to "update" Richards' *The integration of a child into a social world* (1974). Despite a social-constructionist theme, some of the other contributors appear un-

aware of the extent to which orthodox developmental theory is challenged by the social-construction approach. Urwin herself has major interests in psychoanalysis, and radical approaches in psychoanalytic theory are probably the most important grouping of alternatives not discussed in this chapter (see various contributions in Broughton, 1987).

[75]Walkerdine, in Henriques et al. (1984); Walkerdine, in Steedman et al. (1985); Walkerdine (1985); Walkerdine, in Broughton (1987); Walkerdine (1987).

11 Conclusions

INTRODUCTION

I have argued in this book that developmental psychology is built on foundations which are rotten. Not only its more classic formulations, but also most of its present-day versions, adhere to outdated notions of a biological-philosophical nature. There are some alternative proposals which may yet transform this situation, but whether the discipline would be recognisable after any such transformation is hard to predict. It may be that the discipline is *constituted* by the appeal to evolutionist logic and the related doctrines, and could have no independent existence. If so, developmental psychology might be seen as a mere hangover from the late 19th century: A blind alley in the onward progress of the social and life sciences.

To speak in such terms might be to fall into the very evolutionist trap which I have identified in the discipline as a whole. This might be a timely warning that my claims are over-stated. However these issues do seem to be important, and the encouragement of debate may be better served by a certain amount of hyperbole than by timidity. The mainstream in developmental psychology has proved itself very capable of assimilating radical proposals. Indeed it is a major part of my argument that the discipline's response to Darwinism was to assimilate it to pre-Darwinian frameworks. Of course any claim for novelty or radicality has a propagandist element, the degree of which it is hard for its author to evaluate. The novel element in my own claim, if judged to be so, concerns the sheer ubiquity of the biologistic influence. This claim has I hope been supported in the preceding chapters. Here the claim is summarised in a more general way and some of its implications considered. What are the basic foundations of developmental psychology? What can be said about the role of Darwin in the self-image of the discipline? And what is the future?

THE FOUNDATIONS OF DEVELOPMENTAL PSYCHOLOGY

The assumptions on which developmental psychology has been said to be based are of two kinds, biological and philosophical. The biological assumptions derive from the evolutionist thinking of the last century, with its single-track view of developmental ascent. The philosophical assumptions relate to the sensory origin of experience, and hence to the nature of the acquisition of knowledge in the individual. These sets of assumptions have always been interconnected and they share many features. The notion of *progress* is central to both: Evolutionist thinking is based on it, and sensationism is meaningless without it. Again, both traditions lay claim to *universality* of application: The sequences of change which they prescribe must apply to all relevant contexts. More generally, both sets of assumptions might be considered empiricist and positivist, at least as they impinge on the study of individual development.

The interconnectedness of the biological and the philosophical doctrines is well illustrated by the role played by Lamarck. For Lamarck himself, as a mechanist, the sensory origin of knowledge was a basic principle. At the same time, developmental change was seen in terms of the ascent of a series of forms, always increasing in organisation and *perfection*. Lamarck's claims, in a reworked version, played a major part in the evolutionist debate stimulated by Darwin. In the most widely influential accounts of the time, the single, universal track of development was given even more status and the mechanism of progress was described in terms of the animal's learning from experience. The "new" Lamarckism placed the inheritance of acquired characters at centre stage, and hence made learning the motor for evolutionary change. The sensationist account of "micro"-development—that is, of learning—was combined with the evolutionist account of "macro"-development. This combination of an overall plan for development with a set of mechanisms for its advance in the individual proved irresistible to psychology.

The most central assumption in developmental psychology is that change with time is fundamentally progressive. The nature of this progress in the context of individual development has been formulated in many different ways. Some accounts have postulated universal laws of developmental change; some have proposed universal sequences of stages. The notion of progress has been combined in various ways with notions of circularity and repetition. Theorists have differed over the degree of cohesion between different aspects of development: Whether the individual moves forward all at once across a broad front, or in a diverse and loosely controlled manner. Some accounts find it easy to accommodate minor anomalies in the forward movement; some find it impossible. But if the general trend is not toward betterment then the more detailed claims are likely to lose all meaning.[1]

All such approaches encourage the seeking of parallel sequences of progressive change across different situations. Comparisons may relate to the development of science, the evolution of animal types or that of early and "primitive" mankind. I have described these parallels as versions of recapitulation theory and have argued that the role of such thinking has been primary, not secondary, in developmental psychology: That recapitulation has had a constitutive role in the growth of the discipline. The very possibility of such comparisons is an indication of the basic presuppositions. For recapitulationary parallels to make sense—for the comparisons to be other than entirely gratuitous—it is necessary for individual development to be conceived of as lawfully progressive. Since the stronger, causal versions of recapitulation are no longer acceptable, the application of the term to what are identified as weaker versions is unavoidably rhetorical. However, any set of laws and any sequence of stages which seeks to describe development "in general" is likely to carry with it the recapitulationary tendency. Such a tendency may certainly have become attenuated, with attention narrowed down to the empirical study of the individual. But the competence remains, even if the performance is suppressed.

A fundamental claim derived from the sensationist tradition has been that information is received by the child in the form of sensations tied to specific sense modalities. It is a task of development to learn to co-ordinate such information, both across sense modalities and across to voluntary action. Many descriptions of early development still use the term "co-ordination" as if it is totally free of theoretical content. There has likewise been considerable resistance to the claim that perception in the infant might relate to information which is general across several modalities, and that it might be a developmental task to separate out the senses rather than to learn to co-ordinate them. Also significant is the associationist assumption that the real world comprises unified objects giving forth streams of coherent sensory information, and that the child must simply find this fact out for him- or herself. Theoretical accounts of early language are still struggling to excise the notion that first words are about concrete *things*. Similarly, the notion that it might be *events* that are salient to the infant (or adult), rather than objects and their features, has been treated with great reserve, although it is now beginning to attain experimental respectability.[2]

The approach which I have labelled sensationism thus has a strong grip on theoretical discourse in the area of early development. Its tenets are indeed built into those experimental methodologies which are given most support by the major agents of research publication.[3] These methodologies are essentially empiricist and positivist ones. The most influential tenets of non-Darwinian biology—those that have determined most precisely the research programmes of developmental psychology—are of the same cast. To view individual development in terms of universal sequences, of a regular progress onward and upward toward adulthood, or as the manifestation of a set of underlying laws, is to take a positivist approach to the subject matter. Positivism in the social sciences is of course a much larger target than the one at which this book has been aimed. It may, however, be the real or at least the more fundamental target.[4]

It might be argued that the historical influence of outdated forms of biology and of associationist philosophy have simply been outgrown: That contemporary thinking, perhaps because of its experimental soundness, has left such problems behind. Even if this were the case, the historical exercise might still be worthwhile in the interests of correcting developmental psychology's self-serving myths concerning its past. However, as must have become clear, I do not believe that such powerful influences can be put aside so easily; and I do not believe that experimental methodologies do away with the influence of presuppositions, assumptions, and other kinds of theoretical baggage. Science can certainly forget its past, and can certainly misrepresent it; but except in very unusual circumstances, it cannot easily escape from it.

THE DARWINIAN MYTH IN DEVELOPMENTAL PSYCHOLOGY

The issue of the influence of Darwin on developmental psychology has been widely discussed. The claims made here concerning the limited impact of Darwin receive support from a number of sources.[5] Generally, however, it is argued that what are taken to be positive aspects of Darwin's claims exceeded in influence such non-Darwinian claims as recapitulation. At least, the Darwin influence is held to have triumphed in the longer term. For example, Cairns writes that recapitulation theory attracted such early developmentalists as Hall, Preyer, Freud, and Baldwin but that it "collapsed shortly after the turn of the century."[6] The influence of Darwin is held to have been of sufficient power and status to have shrugged off the alternatives, evaluated with hindsight as having had little credibility.[7] Historians of developmental psychology therefore feel justified in ignoring non-Darwinian formulations. The influence of 19th-century biology *is* the influence of Darwin; Darwinism is taken as "the prevailing natural science orthodoxy of the middle years of the 19th century."[8]

Now there are a number of difficulties with this emphasis, aside from questions concerning detailed matters of influence on individuals. As previously observed, the tone of this kind of history is consistently "triumphalist": It takes the contemporary scene (or some component thereof) as a high point in the development of the science and asks how history has contributed to this state of affairs. History is employed in order to construct a *developmental* rationale for the eventual emergence of the present.[9] To use such an approach in the context of developmental psychology thus adds another layer of evolutionism to the debate. The past is congratulated insofar as it is seen to have contributed to the present; in so doing the present congratulates itself. Such an approach cannot easily be combined with anything but an uncritical orientation to the current state of the science.

The triumphalist approach to the role of Darwin includes the exaggeration of the status of Darwin himself within his contemporary social and scientific context. There is more than a hint of the "Great Man" orientation in developmental psychology's history of its Darwinian roots.[10] Likewise, Darwin's developmental and behavioural writings tend to be somewhat over-valued and even distorted. For example, much is made of the importance and originality of the *Biographical sketch of an infant* but this judgement may have more to do with a halo effect than with detached analysis. Similarly, *The expression of the emotions* is greatly admired but its reliance on the inheritance of acquired characters is overlooked. More generally, the tone of many evaluations is rather blandly progressivist, as if the (assumed) scientific progress were inexorable. Thus we read that "early developmental psychologists [Baldwin, Hall, Preyer] drew a measure of sustenance from evolutionism and then turned to face the fresh contact of their own social or intellectual milieu."[11] The approach to history is *itself* an evolutionist one: Progress in developmental psychology is perceived as having been steady if not uninterrupted, almost as if the early workers could dimly see the future to which they were contributing.[12]

This description is a caricature, of course; but the tendency to de-emphasise the role of "incorrect" ideas, of work that "got nowhere," is a very powerful one. Darwin's ideas are the epitome of "correct" ideas, and developmental psychology has laid claim to Darwinian authority and status in a quite systematic way. The role of this Darwinian myth—its function in the propagation of the science—can only be hinted at, but is probably very substantial.[13] If Darwin is seen as the epitome of careful, modest scholarship in the life sciences then a Darwinian origin for an insecure discipline might be a very happy discovery.

I have argued in this book that developmental psychology has not been Darwinian. The question thus arises, *should* developmental psychology be Darwinian? Such a question could well get entangled in issues of "what Darwin really said," and the account presented in Chapter Two is far from being definitive in this respect. Alternatively the question might be rephrased as "What would constitute a truly Darwinian developmental psychology?" This issue has never yet, I would propose, been satisfactorily addressed within the discipline: not, that is, without presupposing the answer. More to the point, perhaps, the question might be posed in terms not of Darwinian but of post-Darwinian biology. Biology in the 1980s is not the same, even in certain very basic ways, as Darwinian biology in the 1880s or even as the Mendelian synthesis worked out in the early decades of this century. In many ways the present time in biology is as lively and as open to innovation as at any time since Darwin.[14] Some well-argued positions in current biological debate might appear to converge with positions I have labelled "non-Darwinian" and I would certainly not wish to be seen as dismissing such biological theories per se.[15] My argument is that developmental psychology is fundamentally *pre*-Darwinian in its biological presuppositions, so that it should certainly become post-Darwinian in some sense. Being post-Darwinian might well mean the assimilation of modern biology and the excising of the 19th-century baggage. Alternatively, it might mean the excising of biology altogether. For the whole of this debate—and if only as a ground-clearing exercise—the subject-matter of this book (if not this book itself) is vital.

THE FUTURE

The characteristics of developmental psychology which this book has sought to examine are in essence empiricist and positivist characteristics. This book is thus part of a wider movement against empiricism in psychology. It has certainly been strongly influenced by this movement. The kinds of alternatives to empiricism thus far offerred in this wider literature include versions of realism, versions of social-constructionism, and versions of Marxism. It is possible that the future progress of the discipline of developmental psychology—if future progress it is to have—is dependent on the articulation and further definition of these general orientations. Developmental psychology may inevitably represent the application of ideas from an alien discipline: If not from biology, then from philosophy or social science. Even if this is so, it should not be assumed that developmental psychology will necessarily be "rescued" by advances in other disciplines. A variety of formulations from other disciplines have been assimilated into the mainstream of developmental psychology in the past, and empiricist research practices may still be too strongly entrenched for any significant theoretical accommodation to take place.

A current example of this ability to absorb new ideas is the response to social-constructionism. In this case, the process of absorption has been facilitated by the looseness of definition of the approach. The wide range of versions of social-constructionism has led to its synthesis with a diverse set of social-science traditions, not all of which are consistent with each other. Names like Foucault, Habermas, Gramsci, and Derrida may be equally unfamiliar to many developmental researchers, but this does not mean that their ideas can be amalgamated into an instant alternative. If the role of biologistic argument has been as pervasive as this book proposes, then it will only be eradicated by some highly disciplined thinking.

Perhaps disciplined thinking is especially to be sought in Marxist traditions. Contemporary Marxism, as relevant to the development of the individual, is both diverse and exciting. It too is attempting to free itself from a legacy of 19th-century positivism and empiricism. Social-constructionism has tended to be a microsociological enterprise; a Marxist social-*productionism* might offer something with more scope and more power. It may be that contemporary feminist critiques of orthodox Marxism could play a major role here. Again, the issue of gender and of its production in the individual could well become a central and paradigm case for the social construction of human development.

The kind of approach I am endorsing has been described in previous chapters as radically different from what is available in the orthodox programme of developmental psychology. In this respect, for example, contemporary attempts to find a place for a "social context" have been seen as rather half-hearted, and the lifespan orientation has been seen as deeply committed to biological standpoints. Surprisingly, perhaps, it is in certain versions of the "formal" orientation that some trends can be identified which seem to converge with social-constructionist formulations. This possibility is surprising because formal approaches have been castigated by the social-constructionist camp, especially for ethnocentrism in various aspects of theory. However, in its stronger versions, the formal orientation to human development is profoundly anti-empiricist; its mode of analysis is descriptive rather than causal. With social-constructionism, although in a very different way, it sets aside the interpersonal domain in favour of a more structural or procedural analysis. Social-constructionist approaches set the interpersonal in a wider context of social relations, of networks of power, knowledge, and responsibility. The formal side emphasises rules, the social side human practices. These emphases are not diametrically opposed. It is possible that some kind of alliance could be forged here, and this possibility should at least be investigated.

In general, it is essential that the scope and the limits of the new, social approaches be thoroughly explored. Biology has had a very good run as the dominating discipline in developmental psychology. A place must certainly be found for it: Biology is itself, it could be argued, a social science. But this would be a new biology. For the present, social formulations must be allowed to take precedence. Only in this way will developmental psychology be enabled to transcend the 19th-century biology and the 17th-century philosophy which have imprisoned it for so long.

NOTES TO CHAPTER ELEVEN

[1]The tradition least committed to progress in individual development is perhaps that of Freud, for whom such progress is in a sense superficial. This orientation has, however, been perceived by others as a "pessimistic" one and has been revised by various post-Freudian movements (Marcuse, 1955). Freud's account might be read as one alternative to progressivism, but there are others. Ontogenetic change might be seen as a process of decay, of deterioration, or of corruption. Or orderly change might itself be denied, the apparent connectedness of the individual life-course being treated as illusory. Some applications of post-structuralist or deconstructionist thinking might point in this direction (Kurtzman, 1987). Less drastically, change and development might be located entirely outside the individual so that child-adult differences would be seen as differences in social practice (Harré, 1983; Morss, 1988). A different kind of alternative is that proposed by Kaplan (1983), for whom "development" is an inherently evaluative description which must be detached from ontogenesis as such. For Kaplan, that is to say, there is nothing inherently "developmental" about the individual life course, but it can be described as orderly and progressive if such an orientation is favoured. This explicitly idealist approach has the merit of highlighting the ideological nature of the term "development" and of its application.

[2]On "event perception" and related issues see Butterworth (1987).

[3]Richards in M. Richards and Light (1986, p. 3); also Morss (1984, pp. 265–266).

[4]The general impact of positivism is described by Manicas (1987) and the positivist dominance within developmental psychology by Kitchener (1983). As Kitchener (1983, pp. 23–24) notes, "positivistic views, implicit in developmental psychology, either have been abandoned by the positivists themselves or have been successfully challenged and criticised by non-positivistic philosophers of science." A number of alternatives to positivism have been discussed by these and other authors. Thus Kitchener describes some non-positivist philosophies of science which might be more appropriate for the analysis of developmental phenomena. For Manicas, the alternative to positivism is realism. Implications of this "new" realism for developmental psychology have not yet been fully explored (however, see Margolis, Manicas, Harré, & Secord, 1986). Toulmin (1985, p. 29) has appealed to a range of research methods "that are now available for studying how human personality and culture work together in our practical conduct and experience." Youniss (1983b) has discussed the possible contribution of the "critical theory" of Habermas (which he finds compatible with some aspects of Piagetian theory). More generally, Youniss (1983b, p. 49) observes: "The single most important issue facing developmental psychology stems from the demise of positivism . . . In adopting positivism, developmentalists severed themselves from intellectual traditions that offer insights that cannot be achieved from online observation of here-and-now behaviour." Broader yet is the analysis of Reiss, for whom the scientific thought of the last three centuries has been "analytico-referential," thus displacing the previous discourse of "patterning." According to Reiss (1982, p. 379), "patterning" came to be classified "as a 'form of thought': 'ancient,' 'primitive,' 'mythical' . . . 'pathological' . . . 'prescientific' thought . . . the analytico-referential eclipsed the discourse of patterning, naming it as an object of abuse."

[5]For example, Reinert (1979, pp. 217–218) notes that Darwin did not have a great impact on the origin or progress of developmental psychology. Reinert cites two German authors "among many others" and it is likely that uncritical deference to Darwin is less among Continental scholars than among the English-speaking. Vidal et al. (1983, pp. 90–91) note the

extent to which developmental psychology's early use of Darwin "impoverished the original conceptual and metaphorical structure of the Darwinian discourse, and narrowed it into a generalised form of adaptationism . . . developmentalists have moved evolution toward constancy and unilinearity, whereas Darwin favoured polymorphism, change, and branching." Costall (1985, p. 30) observed that "according to the textbooks . . . Darwinian theory set developmental psychology in motion . . . [In fact] Darwinism undoubtedly set things moving but in quite the wrong direction." This approach is cogently argued by Costall and by his fellow-contributors to Charlesworth's 1986 symposium (Charlesworth, 1986a, 1986b; Costall, 1986; Ghiselin, 1986). Charlesworth concludes (1986a, p. 1) that "Darwin's impact upon developmental psychology has not been as positive and strong as one may think . . . At best the impact was weak and at worst somewhat misleading." Charlesworth continues "The concept of adaptation, so crucial in Darwin's formulation, never became part of his legacy to developmental psychology." Further (ibid., p. 2): "In short, Darwin simply did not bring about any paradigmatic change in child psychology, certainly not to any degree commensurate with the significance of his ideas." Costall (1986, p. 5) describes Darwinism's assimilation by psychology as "not only sporadic but partial." Finally, according to Ghiselin, the early developmentalists relied more on popularised versions of Darwin—including the writings of Spencer, Haeckel, and Huxley—than on detailed study of the original writings (Ghiselin, 1986, p. 14).

[6]Cairns (1983, p. 63). Again, for Danziger (1985, p. 319), "recapitulation theory soon collapsed under the weight of its many absurdities, leaving the field clear for other approaches which were more in tune with prevailing theoretical imperatives." The term "collapse" of course connotes inevitability—with hindsight.

[7]Where non-Darwinian influences are recognised they tend to be downplayed or even explained away. References in footnote 6 are general examples of this. More specifically, the Lamarckian influence on Freud is noted by Dixon and Lerner (1984, p. 19), with reference to Gould's *Ontogeny and phylogeny*. But an attempt is made to Darwinise this aspect of Freud: "Such a [psychoanalytic] characterisation of environment-organism interaction (minus the Lamarckian view of inheritance) is not antithetical to Darwin's evolutionary theory." Similarly, the "early" work of Piaget is described apologetically (ibid., p. 17) as containing "some endorsement of a modified recapitulation theory." Baldwin was (ibid., p. 16): "fundamentally a Darwinian evolutionist," a commitment manifested "less positively" by a (qualified) endorsement of recapitulation theory. Also see footnote 12.

[8]Dixon and Lerner (1985, p. 245). A similar exaggeration of the contemporary role of Darwinism is Borstelmann (1983, pp. 34–35). Danziger (1985, p. 319) is explicit that it was Darwin's natural selection theory as such which achieved domination, but this is certainly misleading.

[9]As described by Dixon and Lerner (1985, p. 245) contemporary developmentalists are embarked on a "mission of historical self-understanding . . . in keeping with the historical mission (which, on another level of analysis, is analogous to the developmental mission) the primal frontiers of developmental psychology are being ever more avidly explored." One hopes that it is only the style which derives from *Star trek*. A much earlier, and somewhat more sophisticated, analysis of the relations between development and the history of thought may be found in G.H. Mead (1936).

[10]It should be noted that Dixon and Lerner take care to disavow such a "Great Man" approach (1985, p. 247). But why then make such observations as (ibid., p. 251): "That Darwin was a young man was propitious indeed."

[11]Dixon and Lerner (1985, pp. 259–260).

[12]For example, Cairns (1983, p. 46) quotes Preyer as observing that "the brain comes into the world provided with a great number of impressions upon it. Some of these are quite obscure, some few are distinct." This Lamarckist statement should not, says Cairns, see

Preyer "written off as a naive nativist [since] it should be added that his position was closer to the bidirectional approach of modern psychobiology than to the innate ideas of Immanuel Kant . . . Preyer offers a *foresightful* statement of the bidirectional structure/function hypothesis, reaching the conclusion that 'The brain grows through its own activity' (emphasis added)." The "bidirectionality of structure/function relations" is a claim of modern research, which retrospectively legitimates Preyer's position. The actual reasons for Preyer making his claim—including associationist-hedonist assumptions on the deepening of sensory channels, and the Lamarckist process of growth through use—are ignored. "Foresight" is more satisfying.

[13]Some aspects of this process are discussed by Vonèche (in Broughton, 1987, p. 79):

> An appeal to the theory of evolution legitimised developmental psychology as something radically different from mere baby watching . . . By . . . conceptualising it, more or less, as a period for recapitulating the long process of hominisation . . . developmental psychologists managed to occupy a central position in the theory of knowledge of the time . . . Respectability was, at the time, the main concern of developmental psychologists. Hence the constant recourse to naturalisation [of social facts] and the theory of evolution, in order to present the norm of a developmental law conceived by a given observer in a given context of meanings in the guise of an observable fact immanent to the object under scrutiny.

[14]See, for example, the collection by Maynard Smith (1982); and, generally, the writings of S.J. Gould.

[15]For example, contemporary accounts of interactions between behaviour and evolution. Related issues are discussed in Butterworth et al. (1985); but also note the caveats by McGonigle (1987).

References

Note: Where appropriate, date of original publication is given first, followed by full details of a later edition or translation. In this case any page references in the text are to the latter.

Adlam, D., Henriques, J., Rose, N., Salfield, A., Venn, C., & Walkerdine, V. (1977). Psychology, ideology, and the human subject. *Ideology and Consciousness*, *1*, 5–56.

Ash, M. (1985a) Gestalt psychology: Origins in Germany and reception in the United States. In C. Buxton (Ed.), *Points of view in the modern history of psychology*. New York: Academic Press.

Ash, M. (1985b) The role of developmental concepts in the history of Gestalt theory: The work of Kurt Koffka. In G. Eckardt, W. Bringmann, & L. Sprung (Eds.), *Contributions to a history of developmental psychology*. Berlin: Mouton.

Atkinson, C. (1983). *Making sense of Piaget: The philosophical roots*. London: Routledge & Kegan Paul.

Baldwin, J. M. (1895). *Mental development in the child and the race. Methods and processes* (2nd Ed.). New York: MacMillan (1903).

Baldwin, J. M. (1897). *Social and ethical interpretations in mental development. A study in social psychology* (5th Ed.). New York: MacMillan (1913).

Baldwin, J. M. (1902). *Development and evolution*. New York: MacMillan.

Baldwin, J. M. (1904). The limits of pragmatism. *Psychological Review*, *11*, 30–60.

Baldwin, J. M. (1906–1911). *Thought and things. A study of the development and meaning of thought* (3 Vols.). London: Swan Sonnenschein.

Baldwin, J. M. (1913). *History of psychology. A sketch and an interpretation*. London: Watt's.

Baldwin, J. M. (1930). Autobiography. In C. Murchison (Ed.), *A history of psychology in autobiography*, *Vol. 1*. Worcester, Mass.: Clark University Press.

Baltes, P. (1983). Life-span developmental psychology: Observations on history and theory revisited. In R. Lerner (Ed.), *Developmental psychology: Historical and philosophical perspectives*. Hillsdale, N.J.: Lawrence Erlbaum Associates Inc.

Barlow, N. (1958). *The autobiography of Charles Darwin*. London: Collins.

Barthélemy-Madaule, M. (1979). *Lamarck the mythical precursor*. Cambridge, Mass.: The M.I.T. Press (1982).
Bateson, P. (1987). Biological approaches to the study of behavioural development. *International Journal of Behavioural Development, 10*, 1–22.
Beer, G. (1985). Darwin's reading and the fictions of development. In D. Kohn (Ed.), *The Darwinian heritage*. Princeton: Princeton University Press.
Berger, P. & Luckmann, T. (1967). *The social construction of reality*. Harmondsworth: Pelican.
Bergson, H. (1907). *Creative evolution*. London: MacMillan (1911).
Bettelheim, B. (1967). *The empty fortress: Infantile autism and the birth of the self*. New York: Free Press.
Bever, T. (Ed.) (1982). *Regressions in mental development*. Hillsdale, N.J.: Lawrence Erlbaum Associates Inc.
Bleuler, P. E. (1913). Autistic thinking. *American Journal of Insanity, 19*, 873–886.
Blumenthal, A. (1980). Wilhelm Wundt and early American psychology. In R. Rieber (Ed.), *Wilhelm Wundt and the making of a scientific psychology*. New York: Plenum Press.
Blumenthal, A. (1985). Wilhelm Wundt: Psychology as the propaedeutic science. In C. Buxton (Ed.), *Points of view in the modern history of psychology*. New York: Academic Press.
Boakes, R. (1984). *From Darwin to behaviourism*. Cambridge, U.K.: Cambridge University Press.
Boas, G. (1966). *The cult of childhood*. London: The Warburg Institute.
Bölsche, W. (1900). *Haeckel: His life and work*. London: T. Fisher Unwin (1906).
Bornstein, M. & Lamb, M. (Eds.) (1984). *Developmental psychology: An advanced textbook*. Hillsdale, N.J.: Lawrence Erlbaum Associates Inc.
Borstelmann, L. (1983). Children before psychology: Ideas about children from antiquity to late 1880s. In P. Mussen (Ed.), *Handbook of child psychology* (4th Ed.). *Vol. 1: History, theory and methods*. New York: Wiley.
Bower, T. G. R. (1979). *Human development*. San Francisco: Freeman.
Bower, T. G. R. (1982). *Development in infancy* (2nd ed.). San Francisco: Freeman.
Bowlby, J. (1953). *Child care and the growth of love* (2nd ed.). Harmondsworth: Penguin (1972).
Bowlby, J. (1969). *Attachment*. Harmondsworth: Penguin (1971).
Bowler, P. (1983). *The eclipse of Darwinism: Anti-Darwinian evolution theories in the decades around 1900*. Baltimore: Johns Hopkins University Press.
Bowler, P. (1984). *Evolution: the history of an idea*. Berkeley, California: University of California Press.
Bowler, P. (1987). *Theories of human evolution: A century of debate*. Baltimore: John Hopkins University Press.
Bowler, P. (1988). *The non-Darwinian revolution: Reinterpreting a historical myth*. Baltimore: Johns Hopkins University Press.
Bringmann, W., Bringmann, N., & Balance, W. (1985). Experimental approaches to developmental psychology before William Preyer. In G. Eckardt, W. Bringmann, & L. Sprung (Eds.), *Contributions to a history of developmental psychology*. Berlin: Mouton.
Bringuier, J.-C. (1980). *Conversations with Jean Piaget*. Chicago: University of Chicago Press.
Brome, V. (1978). *Jung: Man and myth*. London: Paladin.
Bronfenbrenner, U. (1979). *The ecology of human development: Experiments by nature and design*. Cambridge, Mass.: Harvard University Press.
Bronfenbrenner, U. & Crouter, A. (1983). The evolution of environmental models in developmental research. In P. Mussen (Ed.), *Handbook of child psychology* (4th Ed.). *Vol. 1: History, theory, and methods*. New York: Wiley.

Broughton, J. (1981). Piaget's structural developmental psychology III: Function and the problem of knowledge. *Human Development, 24,* 257–285.
Broughton, J. (1986). The psychology, history, and ideology of the self. In K. Larsen (Ed.), *Dialectics and ideology in psychology.* Norwood, N.J.: Ablex.
Broughton, J. (Ed.) (1987). *Critical theories of psychological development.* New York: Plenum Press.
Broughton, J. & Freeman-Moir. (Eds.) (1982). *The cognitive developmental psychology of James Mark Baldwin.* Norwood. N.J.: Ablex.
Browne, J. (1985). Darwin and the expression of the emotions. In D. Kohn (Ed.), *The Darwinian heritage.* Princeton: Princeton University Press.
Bruner, J. (1983). *Child's talk: Learning to use language.* Oxford: Oxford University Press.
Bruner, J. & Haste, H. (1987). *Making sense: The child's construction of the world.* London: Methuen.
Bryant, P. (1982). Piaget's questions. *British Journal of Psychology, 73,* 157–161.
Buck-Morss, S. (1975). Socioeconomic bias in Piaget's theory: Implications for cross-cultural studies. In A. Buss (Ed.), *Psychology in social context.* New York: Irvington (1979).
Bühler, C. (1927). *The first year of life.* New York: John Day (1930).
Bühler, C. & Hetzer, H. (1935). *Testing children's development from birth to school age.* New York: Farrar & Rinehart.
Bühler, K. (1919). *The mental development of the child* (5th Ed.). London: Kegan Paul, Trench, Trubner (1930).
Bullowa, M. (Ed.) (1979). *Before speech: The beginnings of interpersonal communication.* Cambridge, U.K.: Cambridge University Press.
Burkhardt, R. (1985). Darwin on animal behaviour and evolution. In D. Kohn (Ed.), *The Darwinian heritage.* Princeton: Princeton University Press.
Buss, A. (Ed.) (1979). *Psychology in social context.* New York: Irvington.
Butterworth, G. (Ed.) (1982). *Infancy and epistemology.* Brighton: Harvester.
Butterworth, G. (1987). *Main themes in European research on infant perception and cognition* (Annual Report (1986–1987) No. 10). Hokkaido, Japan: Research and Clinical Centre for Child Development, Hokkaido University.
Butterworth, G., Scaife, M., & Rutkowska, J. (Eds.) (1985). *Evolution and developmental psychology.* Brighton: Harvester Press.
Buxton, C. (1985). *Points of view in the modern history of psychology.* New York: Academic Press.
Cairns, R. (1980). Developmental psychology before Piaget: The remarkable contributions of James Mark Baldwin. *Contemporary Psychology, 25,* 438–440.
Cairns, R. (1983). The emergence of developmental psychology. In P. Mussen (Ed.), *Handbook of child psychology* (4th Ed.). *Vol. 1: History, theory, and methods.* New York: Wiley.
Cairns, R. & Ornstein, P. (1979). Developmental psychology. In E. Hearst (Ed.), *The first century of experimental psychology,* Hillsdale, N.J.: Lawrence Erlbaum Associates Inc.
Carey, S. (1985). *Conceptual change in childhood.* Cambridge, Mass.: The M.I.T. Press.
Carotenuto, A. (1982). *A secret symmetry: Sabina Spielrein between Jung and Freud.* New York: Pantheon.
Case, R. (1985). *Intellectual development: Birth to adulthood.* London: Academic Press.
Cavanaugh, J. (1985). Cognitive developmental psychology before Preyer: Biographical and educational records. In G. Eckardt, W. Bringmann, & L. Sprung (Eds.), *Contributions to a history of developmental psychology.* Berlin: Mouton.
Charles, D. (1970). Historical antecedents of lifespan developmental psychology. In L. Goulet & P. Baltes (Eds.), *Lifespan developmental psychology: Research and theory.* New York: Academic Press.

Charlesworth, W. (1986a). Darwin and developmental psychology: 100 years later. *Human Development, 29*, 1–4.
Charlesworth, W. (1986b). Darwin and developmental psychology: From the proximate to the ultimate. *Human Development, 29*, 22–35.
Chomsky, N. (1986). *Knowledge of language: Its nature, origin, and use*. New York: Praeger.
Claparède, E. (1905). *Experimental pedagogy and the psychology of the child* (4th Ed.). London: Edward Arnold (1911).
Claparède, E. (1930). Autobiography. In C. Murchison (Ed.), *A history of psychology in autobiography, Vol 1*. Worcester, Mass.: Clark University Press.
Codd, C. (1917). Reincarnation's answer to life's problems. In *Bibby's Annual* III/12, 13–14.
Cohen, D. (1979). *J. B. Watson, the founder of behaviourism: A biography*. London: Routledge & Kegan Paul.
Coleman, J. (1980). *The nature of adolescence*. London: Methuen.
Coles, R. (1970). *Erik H. Erikson: The growth of his work*. London: Souvenir Press (1973).
Compayré, G. (1887). *The history of pedagogy*. London: Swan Sonnenschein (1909).
Conan Doyle, A. (1981). *The Penguin complete Sherlock Holmes*. Harmondsworth: Penguin.
Costall, A. (1985). Specious origins? Darwinism and developmental theory. In G. Butterworth, M. Scaife, & J. Rutkowska (Eds.), *Evolution and developmental psychology*. Brighton: Harvester Press.
Costall, A. (1986). Evolutionary gradualism and the study of development. *Human Development, 29*, 4–11.
Coveney, P. (1957). *The image of childhood*. Harmondsworth: Penguin (revised ed. 1967).
Cox, M. (1986). *The child's point of view*. Brighton: Harvester.
Crain, W. (1980). *Theories of development: Concepts and applications*. Englewood Cliffs, N.J.: Prentice-Hall.
Crnic, L. & Penningtion, B. (1987). Developmental psychology and the neurosciences: An introduction. *Child Development, 58*, 533–538.
Crookshank, F. G. (1924). *The mongol in our midst; a study of man and his three faces*. London: Kegan Paul, Trench, Trubner.
Danziger, K. (1980). Wundt and the two traditions of psychology. In R. Rieber (Ed.), *Wilhelm Wundt and the making of a scientific psychology*. New York: Plenum Press.
Danziger, K. (1985). The problem of imitation and explanatory models in early developmental psychology. In G. Eckardt, W. Bringmann, & L. Sprung (Eds.), *Contributions to a history of developmental psychology*. Berlin: Mouton.
Darwin, C. (1859). *On the origin of species by means of natural selection*. London: John Murray.
Darwin, C. (1871). *The descent of man and selection in relation to sex*. Detroit: Gale Research Co. (1974).
Darwin, C. (1872). *The expression of the emotions in man and animals*. Chicago: University of Chicago Press (1965).
Darwin, C. (1877). A biographical sketch of an infant. In H. Gruber, *Darwin on man: A psychological study of scientific creativity*. London: Wildwood House (1974).
De Beer, G. (1958). *Embryos and ancestors* (3rd Ed.). Oxford: Clarendon Press.
Dixon, R. & Lerner, R. (1984). A history of systems in developmental psychology. In M. Bornstein & M. Lamb, *Developmental psychology: An advanced textbook*. Hillsdale, N.J.: Lawrence Erlbaum Associates Inc.
Dixon, R. & Lerner, R. (1985). Darwinism and the emergence of developmental psychology. In G. Eckardt, W. Bringmann, & L. Sprung (Eds.), *Contributions to a history of developmental psychology*. Berlin: Mouton.
Dixon, R. & Nesselroade, J. (1983). Pluralism and correlational analysis in developmental

psychology: Historical commonalities. In R. Lerner (Ed.), *Developmental psychology: Historical and philosophical perspectives*. Hillsdale, N.J.: Lawrence Erlbaum Associates Inc.

Donaldson, M. (1978). *Children's minds*. London: Fontana/Collins.

Drummond, W. (1908). *An introduction to child-study*. London: Edward Arnold.

Eckardt, G. (1985). Preyer's road to child psychology. In G. Eckardt, W. Bringmann, & L. Sprung (Eds.), *Contributions to a history of developmental psychology*. Berlin: Mouton.

Eckardt, G., Bringmann, W., & Sprung, L. (Eds.) (1985). *Contributions to a history of developmental psychology*. Berlin: Mouton.

Ellenberger, H. (1970). *The discovery of the unconscious: The history and evolution of dynamic psychiatry*. New York: Basic Books.

Erikson, E. (1946). Ego development and historical change. In *The psychoanalytic study of the child, Vol. II*. Imago Pub. Co. (1947).

Erikson, E. (1950). *Childhood and society*. Harmondsworth: Penguin (1965).

Evans, R. (1973). *Jean Piaget: The man and his ideas*. New York: Dutton.

Evans, R. (1975). *Konrad Lorenz: The man and his ideas*. New York: Dutton.

Farr, J. (1987). The way of hypotheses: Locke on method. *Journal of the History of Ideas*, *48*, 51–72.

Fodor, J. (1980). Methodological solipsism considered as a research strategy in cognitive psychology. *The Behavioural and Brain Sciences*, *3*, 63–109.

Freeman, D. (1984). *Margaret Mead and Samoa: The making and unmaking of an anthropological myth*. Harmondsworth: Pelican.

Freeman, N. (1972). Process and product in children's drawing. *Perception*, *1*, 123–140.

Freud, A. (1936). *The ego and the mechanisms of defence*. London: Hogarth Press (1968).

Freud, A. (1958). Adolescence. In *The writings of Anna Freud, Vol. V*. New York: International Universities Press (1969).

Freud, A. (1969). Discussion of John Bowlby's work on separation, grief and mourning. In *The writings of Anna Freud, Vol. V*. New York: International Universities Press.

Freud, S. (1900). *The interpretation of dreams, Vols. IV,V*, (Standard Ed.). London: Hogarth Press (1953–1974).

Freud, S. (1905). *Three essays on the theory of sexuality, Vol. VII* (Standard Ed.) (with 2nd Ed. 1910; 3rd Ed. 1915; 4th Ed. 1920). London: Hogarth Press (1953–1974).

Freud, S. (1911). Formulations on the two principles of mental functioning, *Vol. XII* (Standard Ed.). London: Hogarth Press (1953–1974).

Freud, S. (1912–1913). *Totem and taboo, Vol. XIII* (Standard Ed.). London: Hogarth Press (1953–1974).

Freud, S. (1915). Instincts and their vicissitudes, *Vol. XIV* (Standard Ed.). London: Hogarth Press (1953–1974).

Freud, S. (1923). *The ego and the id, Vol. XIX*. (Standard Edition) London: Hogarth Press (1953–1974).

Freud, S. (1925). Some psychical consequences of the anatomical distinction between the sexes, Vol. XIX (Standard Edition). London: Hogarth Press (1953–1974).

Gallop, J. (1985). *Reading Lacan*. Ithaca, N.Y.: Cornell University Press.

Gergen, K. (1982). *Toward transformation in social knowledge*. New York: Springer-Verlag.

Gergen, K. & Davis, K. (1985). *The social construction of the person*. New York: Springer-Verlag.

Gesell, A. (1946). The ontogenesis of infant behaviour. In L. Carmichael (Ed.), *Manual of child psychology*. New York: Wiley (1954).

Gesell, A. (1952). Autobiography. In E. Boring, H. Werner, R. Yerkes, & H. Langfeld (Eds.), *A history of psychology in autobiography, Vol. IV*. New York: Russell & Russell (1968).

Gesell, A., Halverson, H., Thompson, H., Ilg, F., Castner, B., Ames, L., & Amatruda, C. (1940). *The first five years of life, a guide to the study of the preschool child.* New York: Harper.

Ghiselin, M. (1986). The assimilation of Darwinism in developmental psychology. *Human Development, 29*, 12–22.

Gibson, E. J. (1985). Whosoever hath, to him shall be given. *New Ideas in Psychology, 3*, 73–75.

Gibson, J. J. (1979). *The ecological approach to visual perception.* Boston: Houghton Mifflin.

Giddens, A. (1984). *The constitution of society: Outline of the theory of structuration.* Cambridge, U.K.: Polity Press.

Glass, B., Temkin, O., & Strauss, W. (Eds.) (1968). *Forerunners of Darwin.* Baltimore: Johns Hopkins University Press.

Gollin, E. (1981). Development and plasticity. In E. Gollin, (Ed.), *Developmental plasticity: Behavioural and biological aspects of variations in development.* New York: Academic Press.

Gottlieb, G. (1979). Comparative psychology and ethology. In E. Hearst (Ed.), *The first century of experimental psychology.* Hillsdale, N.J.: Lawrence Erlbaum Associates Inc.

Gottlieb, G. (1983). The psychobiological approach to developmental issues. In M. Haith & J. Campos (Eds.), *Handbook of child psychology* (4th Ed.). *Vol II: Infancy and developmental psychobiology.* New York: Wiley.

Gould, S. J. (1977). *Ontogeny and phylogeny.* Cambridge, Mass.: Belknap Press/ Harvard University Press.

Gould, S. J. (1984). *The mismeasure of man.* Harmondsworth: Penguin.

Gould, S. J. (1985). The paradox of the first tier: An agenda for paleobiology. *Paleobiology, 11*, 2–12.

Gould, S. J. & Lewontin, R. (1979). The spandrels of San Marco and the Panglossian paradigm: A critique of the adaptationist programme. *Proceedings of the Royal Society of London, 205B*, 581–598.

Gould, S. J. & Vrba, E. (1982). Exaptation—A missing term in the science of form. *Paleobiology, 8*, 4–15.

Grinder, R. (1967). *A history of genetic psychology.* New York: Wiley.

Grinnell, G. (1985). The rise and fall of Darwin's second theory. *Journal of the History of Biology, 18*, 51–70.

Groffmann, K. (1970). Life-span developmental psychology in Europe: Past and present. In L. Goulet & P. Baltes (Eds.), *Life-span developmental psychology: Research and theory.* New York: Academic Press.

Groos, K. (1896). *The play of animals.* London: Chapman & Hall (1898).

Groos, K. (1898). *The play of man.* New York: Appleton (1901).

Gruber, H. (1974). *Darwin on man: A psychological study of scientific creativity.* London: Wildwood House.

Gruber, H. & Vonèche, J.-J. (1977). *The essential Piaget.* London: Routledge & Kegan Paul.

Haeckel, E. (1874). *The evolution of man.* London: Kegan Paul (1879).

Haeckel, E. (1899). *The riddle of the universe.* London: Watts (1906).

Haeckel, E. (1906). *Last words on evolution.* London: Owen.

Hall, G. S. (1904). *Adolescence: Its psychology and its relations to physiology, anthropology, sociology, sex, crime, religion, and education* (2 Vols.). New York: Appleton.

Hall, G. S. (1922). *Senescence, the last half of life.* New York: Appleton.

Hardesty, F. (1976a). Early European contributions to developmental psychology. In K. Riegel & J. Meacham (Eds.), *The developing individual in a changing world.* Chicago: Aldine.

Hardesty, F. (1976b). Louis William Stern: A new view of the Hamburg years. *Annals of the New York Academy of Sciences, 270*, 30–44.

Hardesty, F. (1977). William Stern and American psychology. *Annals of the New York Academy of Sciences, 273*, 33–46.
Harré, R. (1983). *Personal being*. Oxford: Blackwell.
Harré, R. (1986). The step to social constructionism. In M. Richards & P. Light (Eds.), *Children of social worlds*. Cambridge, U.K.: Polity Press.
Harré, R. (1987). Enlarging the paradigm. *New Ideas in Psychology, 5*, 3–12.
Hazlitt, V. (1933). *The psychology of infancy*. London: Methuen.
Hearnshaw, L. (1979). *Cyril Burt: Psychologist*. London: Hodder & Stoughton.
Hearst, E. (Ed.) (1979). *The first century of experimental psychology*. Hillsdale, N.J.: Lawrence Erlbaum Associates Inc.
Henriques, J., Hollway, W., Urwin, C., Venn, C., & Walkerdine, V. (1984). *Changing the subject: Psychology, social regulation, and subjectivity*. London: Methuen.
Hinde, R. (1983). Ethology and child development. In M. Haith & J. Campos (Eds.), *Handbook of child psychology* (4th Ed.). *Vol II: Infancy and developmental psychobiology*. New York: Wiley.
Hirst, P. (1975). *Durkheim, Bernard, and epistemology*. London: Routledge & Kegan Paul.
Hodos, W. & Campbell, C. (1969). Scala Naturae: Why there is no theory in comparative psychology. *Psychological Review, 76*, 337–350.
Hume, D. (1739). *A treatise of human nature*. Harmondsworth: Penguin (1969).
Ingleby, D. (1986). Development in social context. In M. Richards & P. Light (Eds.), *Children of social worlds*. Cambridge, U.K.: Polity Press.
Inhelder, B. & Piaget, J. (1955). *The growth of logical thinking from childhood to adolescence*. London: Routledge & Kegan Paul (1958).
Jaeger, S. (1982). Origins of child psychology: William Preyer. In W. Woodward & M. Ash (Eds.), *The problematic science: Psychology in nineteenth-century thought*. New York: Praeger.
Joas, H. (1985). *G. H. Mead: A contemporary re-examination of his thought*. Cambridge, U.K.: Polity Press.
Jones, G. (1980). *Social Darwinism and English thought*. Brighton: Harvester Press.
Jordanova, L. (1984). *Lamarck*. Oxford: Oxford University Press.
Jung, C. G. (1908). *The Freudian theory of hysteria. Collected Works, Vol. 4*. London: Routledge & Kegan Paul (1961).
Jung, C. G. (1912). *Symbols of transformation* (4th Ed.). *Collected Works, Vol. 5*. London: Routledge & Kegan Paul (1956).
Jung, C. G. (1963). *Memories, dreams, reflections*. London: Collins.
Jung, C. G. (1973). *Letters, Vol. 1*. London: Routledge & Kegan Paul.
Kagan, J. (1983). Classifications of the child. In P. Mussen (Ed.), *Handbook of child psychology* (4th Ed.). *Vol. 1: History, theory and methods*. New York: Wiley.
Kalikow, T. (1983). Konrad Lorenz's ethological theory: Explanation and ideology, 1938–1943. *Journal of the History of Biology, 16*, 39–73.
Kaplan, B. (1983). A trio of trials. In R. Lerner (Ed.), *Developmental psychology: Historical and philosophical perspectives*. Hillsdale, N.J.: Lawrence Erlbaum Associates Inc.
Keegan, R. & Gruber, H. (1985). Charles Darwin's unpublished "Diary of an infant": An early phase in his psychological work. In G. Eckardt, W. Bringmann, & L. Sprung (Eds.), *Contributions to a history of developmental psychology*. Berlin: Mouton.
Kessel, S. & Siegel, A. (Eds.) (1983). *The child and other cultural inventions*. New York: Praeger.
Kessen, W. (1965). *The child*. New York: Wiley.
King-Hele, D. (1977). *Doctor of revolution: The life and genius of Erasmus Darwin*. London: Faber & Faber.
Kirkpatrick, E. (1903). *Fundamentals of child study*. New York: MacMillan (1922).
Kitchener, R. (1983). Changing conceptions of the philosophy of science and the foundations

of developmental psychology. In D. Kuhn & J. Meacham (Eds.), *On the development of developmental psychology. Contributions to human development 8*. Basel: Karger.

Koffka, K. (1921). *The growth of the mind*. London: Kegan Paul, Trench, Trubner (1928).

Kohlberg, L., Levine, C., & Hewer, A. (1983). *Moral stages: A current formulation and a response to critics*. Basel: Karger.

Kohn, D. (Ed.) (1985). *The Darwinian heritage*. Princeton: Princeton University Press.

Kramer, R. (1976). *Maria Montessori*. Oxford: Basil Blackwell.

Kuhn, D. (1983). On the dual executive and its significance in the development of developmental psychology. In D. Kuhn & J. Meacham (Eds.), *On the development of developmental psychology. Contributions to human development 8*. Basel: Karger.

Kuhn, D. & Meacham, J. (Eds.) (1983). *On the development of developmental psychology. Contributions to human development 8*. Basel: Karger.

Kurtzman, H. (1987). Deconstruction and psychology: An introduction. *New Ideas in Psychology*, *5*, 33–71.

Labouvie-Vief, G. & Chandler, M. (1978). Cognitive development and life-span developmental theories: Idealistic versus contextual perspectives. In P. Baltes, (Ed.), *Life-span development and behaviour. Vol. 1*. New York: Academic Press.

Lacan, J. (1977). *Ecrits*. London: Tavistock.

Lamarck, J.-B. de (1809). *Zoological philosophy*. London: MacMillan (1914).

Leahey, T. (1986). History without a past: Review of Kimble and Schlesinger (Eds.), "Topics in the history of psychology." *Contemporary Psychology*, *31*, 648–649.

Le Dantec, F. (1907). *The nature and origin of life*. London: Hodder & Stoughton.

Lee, D., Young, D., & McLaughlin, C. (1984). A roadside simulation of road crossing for children. *Ergonomics*, *27*, 1271–1281.

Leichtman, M. (1979). Gestalt theory and the revolt against positivism. In A. Buss (Ed.), *Psychology in social context*. New York: Irvington.

Leonard, P. (1984). *Personality and ideology: Towards a materialist understanding of the individual*. London: MacMillan.

Lerner, R. (Ed.) (1983). *Developmental psychology: Historical and philosophical perspectives*. Hillsdale, N.J.: Lawrence Erlbaum Associates Inc.

Lerner, R. (1986). *Concepts and theories of human development* (2nd Ed.). Reading, Mass.: Addison-Wesley.

Lewin, K. (1946). Behaviour and development as a function of the total situation. In L. Carmichael (Ed.), *Manual of child psychology*. New York: Wiley (1954).

Lewis, J. & Smith, R. (1980). *American sociology and pragmatism*. Chicago: University of Chicago Press.

Light, P. & McEwen, F. (1987). Drawings as messages: The effect of a communication game upon production of view-specific drawings. *British Journal of Developmental Psychology*, *5*, 53–60.

Locke, J. (1689). *An essay concerning human understanding*. London: Fontana/Collins (1964).

Loeb, L. (1981). *From Descartes to Hume: Continental metaphysics and the development of modern philosophy*. Ithaca, N.Y.: Cornell University Press.

Logue, A. (1985). The origins of behaviourism: Origins and proclamation. In C. Buxton (Ed.), *Points of view in the modern history of psychology*. New York: Academic Press.

Lorenz, K. (1965). *Evolution and modification of behaviour*. London: Methuen (1966).

Lorenz, K. (1973). *Behind the mirror: A search for the natural history of human knowledge*. London: Methuen (1977).

Lorenz, K. (1978). *The foundations of ethology*. New York: Springer-Verlag (1981).

Luquet, G. (1913). *Les dessins d'un enfant*. Paris: Alcan.

Luria, A. (1979). *The making of mind*. Cambridge, Mass.: Harvard University Press.

Lynn, R. (1987). The intelligence of the mongoloids: A psychometric, evolutionary, and neurological theory. *Personality and Individual Differences, 8*, 813–844.
McCullers, J. (1969). G. Stanley Hall's conception of mental development and some indications of its influence on developmental psychology. *American Psychologist, 24*, 1109–1114.
McGonigle, B. (1987). Review of Butterworth et al., "Evolution and developmental psychology." *British Journal of Developmental Psychology, 5*, 202–203.
McGuire, W. (Ed.) (1974). *The Freud/Jung letters*. London: Hogarth Press.
McKim, R. (1987). Luce's account of the development of Berkeley's immaterialism. *Journal of the History of Ideas, 48*, 649–669.
McLeish, J. (1975). *Soviet psychology: History, theory, content*. London: Methuen.
Mahler, M., Pine, F., & Bergman, A. (1975). *The psychological birth of the human infant*. New York: Basic Books.
Manicas, P. (1987). *A history and philosophy of the social sciences*. Oxford: Blackwell.
Marcuse, H. (1955). *Eros and civilisation: A philosophical enquiry into Freud*. New York: Vintage Books.
Margolis, J., Manicas, P., Harré, R., & Secord, P. (1986). *Psychology: Designing the discipline*. Oxford: Blackwell.
Marx, K. (1845). Theses on Feuerbach. In J. Elster (Ed.), *Karl Marx: A reader*. Cambridge, U.K.: Cambridge University Press.
Marx, K. (1859). Preface to "A contribution to the critique of political economy". In J. Elster (Ed.), *Karl Marx: A reader*. Cambridge, U.K.: Cambridge University Press.
Maynard Smith, J. (Ed.) (1982). *Evolution now: A century after Darwin*. London: MacMillan/Nature.
Mayr, E. (1982). *The growth of biological thought*. Cambridge, Mass.: Belknap Press of Harvard University Press.
Mayr, E. (1985). Weismann and evolution. *Journal of the History of Biology, 18*, 295–329.
Mays, W. (1982). *Piaget and Freud*. Manchester: Institute of Advanced Studies, Manchester Polytechnic.
Mead, G. H. (1934). *Mind, self, and society*. Chicago: University of Chicago Press.
Mead, G. H. (1936). *Movements of thought in the nineteenth century*. Chicago: University of Chicago Press.
Mead, G. H. (1938). *The philosophy of the act*. Chicago: University of Chicago Press.
Mead, M. (1928). *Coming of age in Samoa: A psychological study in primitive youth for Western civilisation*. Harmondsworth: Penguin (1943).
Mead, M. (1950). *Male and female*. Harmondsworth: Pelican (1962).
Meyer, E. (1935). La représentation des relations spatiales chez l'enfant. *Cahiers de pédagogie expérimentale et de psychologie de l'enfant, No. 8*. Université de Genève.
Miller, J. (1983). *States of mind: Conversations with psychological investigators*. London: B.B.C.
Miller, P. (1983). *Theories of developmental psychology*. San Francisco: Freeman.
Mobasser, N. (1987). Marx and self-realisation. *New Left Review*, No. 161, 119–128.
Moore, J. (1977). Could Darwinism be introduced in France? *British Journal for the History of Science, 10*, 246–251.
Moore, J. (1986). Socialising Darwinism: Historiography and the fortunes of a phrase. In L. Levidow (Ed.), *Science as politics*. London: Free Association Books.
Morgan, M. (1977). *Molyneaux's question*. Cambridge, U.K.: Cambridge University Press.
Morgan, T. (1903). *Evolution and adaptation*. New York: MacMillan.
Morss, J. R. (1983). The closed minds of Piaget and Freud: A comment on Furth. *New Ideas in Psychology, 1*, 281–282.
Morss, J. R. (1984). "The primacy of the abstract": Differentiation without loss as a theory

of development. An interview with T. G. R. Bower. *New Ideas in Psychology*, *2*, 257–267.
Morss, J. R. (1985a). Early cognitive development: Difference or delay? In D. Lane & B. Stratford (Eds.), *Current approaches to Down's Syndrome*. London: Holt, Rinehart, Winston.
Morss, J. R. (1985b). Old Mead in new bottles: The impersonal and the interpersonal in infant knowledge. *New Ideas in Psychology*, *3*, 165–176.
Morss, J. R. (1986). The practices of subjection: Review of Henriques et al., "Changing the subject." *New Ideas in Psychology*, *4*, 401–406.
Morss, J. R. (1987a). The construction of perspectives: Piaget's alternative to spatial egocentrism. *International Journal of Behavioural Development*, *10*, 263–279.
Morss, J. R. (1987b). "The dialectic of personal growth": Theory, practice and human being. An interview with Rom Harré. *New Ideas in Psychology*, *5*, 127–135.
Morss, J. R. (1988). The public world of childhood. *Journal for the Theory of Social Behaviour*, *18*, 323–343.
Morss. J. R. (1989). Misconceiving Gibson: Review of Russell, "Explaining mental life." *New Ideas in Psychology*, *7*.
Mouzelis, N. (1988). Marxism or post-Marxism? *New Left Review*, No. 167, 107–123.
Mueller, R. (1976). A chapter in the history of the relationship between psychology and sociology in America: James Mark Baldwin. *Journal for the History of the Behavioural Sciences*, *12*, 240–253.
Mussen, P. (Ed.) (1983). *Handbook of child psychology* (4th Ed.). New York: Wiley.
Muuss, R. (1968). *Theories of adolescence* (2nd Ed.). New York: Random House.
Novack, G. (1972). *Understanding history: Marxist essays*. New York: Pathfinder Press.
Olssen, M. (1988). *Mental testing in New Zealand: Critical and oppositional perspectives*. Dunedin: University of Otago Press.
Perez, B. (1878). *The first three years of childhood*. London: Swan, Sonnenschein (1885).
Piaget, J. (1918a). Biology and war. In H. Gruber & J.-H. Vonèche (Eds.), *The essential Piaget*. London: Routledge & Kegan Paul (1977).
Piaget, J. (1918b). *Recherche*. Extracted in H. Gruber, & J.-J. Vonèche (Eds.), *The essential Piaget*. London: Routledge & Kegan Paul (1977).
Piaget, J. (1920). Psychoanalysis in its relations with child psychology. In H. Gruber & J.-J. Vonèche (Eds.), *The essential Piaget*. London: Routledge & Kegan Paul (1977).
Piaget, J. (1923a). La pensée symbolique et la pensée de l'enfant. *Archives de Psychologie*, *18*, 273–304.
Piaget, J. (1923b). *The language and thought of the child*. London: Routledge & Kegan Paul (1959).
Piaget, J. (1924). *Judgment and reasoning in the child*. London: Kegan Paul, Trench, Trubner (1928).
Piaget, J. (1926). *The child's conception of the world*. London: Paladin (1973).
Piaget, J. (1927a). *The child's conception of physical causality*. London: Kegan Paul, Trench, Trubner (1930).
Piaget, J. (1927b). The first year of life of the child. In H. Gruber & J.-J. Vonèche (Eds.), *The essential Piaget*. London: Routledge & Kegan Paul (1977).
Piaget, J. (1932). *The moral judgment of the child*. Harmondsworth: Penguin (1977).
Piaget, J. (1936). *The origin of intelligence in the child*. Harmondsworth: Penguin (1977).
Piaget, J. (1937). *The construction of reality in the child*. New York: Ballantine Books (1971).
Piaget, J. (1940). The mental development of the child. In J. Piaget, *Six psychological studies*. New York: Vintage Books (1967).
Piaget, J. (1941). *The child's conception of number*. London: Routledge & Kegan Paul (1952).
Piaget, J. (1945). *Play, dreams, and imitation in childhood*. London: Routledge & Kegan Paul (1962).

Piaget, J. (1947). *The psychology of intelligence*. London: Routledge & Kegan Paul (1964).
Piaget, J. (1952). Autobiography. In E. Boring, H. Werner, R. Yerkes, & H. Langfeld (Eds.), *A history of psychology in autobiography, Vol. IV*. New York: Russell & Russell (1968).
Piaget, J. (1967). *Biology and knowledge*. Edinburgh: Edinburgh University Press (1971).
Piaget, J. (1970a). *Psychology and epistemology*. Harmondsworth: Penguin (1972a).
Piaget, J. (1970b). *Principles of genetic epistemology*. London: Routledge & Kegan Paul (1972b).
Piaget, J. (1974). *Adaptation and intelligence: Organic selection and phenocopy*. Chicago: University of Chicago Press (1980).
Piaget, J. (1975). *The development of thought*. Oxford: Blackwell (1978).
Piaget, J. (1976). *Behaviour and evolution*. London: Routledge & Kegan Paul (1979).
Piaget, J. & Inhelder, B. (1948). *The child's conception of space*. London: Routledge & Kegan Paul (1956).
Preyer, W. (1882). *The mind of the child. Vol. 1: The senses and the will*. New York: Appleton (1914). *Vol 2: The development of the intellect*. New York: Appleton (1892).
Pueschel, S., Tingey, C., Rynders, J., Crocker, A., & Crutcher, D. (Eds.) (1987). *New perspectives on Downs Syndrome*. Baltimore: P. H. Brookes.
Radford, J. (1988). Sherlock Holmes and the history of psychology. *The Psychologist: Bulletin of the British Psychological Society*, *1*, 143–146.
Reese, H. & Overton, W. (1970). Models of development and theories of development. In L. Goulet & P. Baltes (Eds.), *Life-span developmental psychology: Research and theory*. New York: Academic Press.
Reinert, G. (1979). Prolegomena to a history of lifespan developmental psychology. In P. Baltes & O. Brim (Eds.), *Lifespan development and behaviour, Vol. 2*. New York: Academic Press.
Reiss, T. (1982). *The discourse of modernism*. Ithaca, N.Y.: Cornell University Press.
Richards, M. (Ed.) (1974). *The integration of a child into a social world*. Cambridge, U.K.: Cambridge University Press.
Richards, M. & Light, P. (Eds.) (1986). *Children of social worlds*. Cambridge, U.K.: Polity Press.
Richards, R. (1977). Lloyd Morgan's theory of instinct: From Darwinism to neo-Darwinism. *Journal for the History of the Behavioural Sciences*, *13*, 12–32.
Richards, R. (1979). Influence of sensationalist tradition on early theories of the evolution of behaviour. *Journal of the History of Ideas*, *40*, 85–105.
Richards, R. (1981). Instinct and intelligence in British natural theology: Some contributions to Darwin's theory of the evolution of behaviour. *Journal of the History of Biology*, *14*, 193–230.
Richards, R. (1982). The emergence of evolutionary biology of behaviour in the early nineteenth century. *British Journal for the History of Science*, *15*, 241–280.
Richards, R. (1987). *Darwin and the emergence of evolutionary theories of mind and behaviour*. Chicago: University of Chicago Press.
Richter, I. (1952). *The Leonardo notebooks: Selections*. Oxford: Oxford University Press.
Ridley, M. (1982). Coadaptation and the inadequacy of natural selection. *British Journal for the History of Science*, *15*, 45–68.
Rieber, R. (1980). *Wilhelm Wundt and the making of a scientific psychology*. New York: Plenum Press.
Riegel, K. (1976). *Psychology of development and history*. New York: Plenum.
Riegel, K. (1977). History of psychological gerontology. In J. Birren & K. Schaie (Eds.), *Handbook of the psychology of ageing*. New York: Van Nostrand-Reinhold.
Reigel, K. & Meacham, J. (Eds.) (1976). *The developing individual in a changing world*. Chicago: Aldine.

Riley, D. (1978). Developmental psychology, biology, and Marxism. *Ideology and Consciousness*, *4*, 73–92.
Riley, D. (1983). *War in the nursery*. London: Virago Press.
Roazen, P. (1974). *Freud and his followers*. Harmondsworth: Penguin.
Romanes, G. (1888). *Mental evolution in man: Origin of human faculty*. London: Kegan Paul, Trench.
Romanes, G. (1892). *Darwin, and after Darwin*. London: Longmans, Green (1897).
Ross, D. (1972). *G. Stanley Hall: The psychologist as prophet*. Chicago: University of Chicago Press.
Rotman, B. (1977). *Jean Piaget: Psychologist of the real*. Hassocks: Harvester Press.
Rousseau, J.-J. (1762). *Emile, or, on education*. New York: Basic Books (1979).
Rubinstein, D. (1981). *Marx and Wittgenstein: Social praxis and social explanation*. London: Routledge & Kegan Paul.
Russell, E. (1916). *Form and function: A contribution to the history of animal morphology*. London: John Murray.
Russell, J. (1978). *The acquisition of knowledge*. London: MacMillan.
Russell, J. (1984). *Explaining mental life: Some philosophical issues in psychology*. New York: St. Martin's Press.
Russell, J. (Ed.) (1987). *Philosophical perspectives on developmental psychology*. Oxford: Blackwell.
Sanford, E. (1902). Mental growth and decay. *American Journal of Psychology*, *13*, 426–449.
Scarr, S. (1986). How plastic are we? Review of Lerner, "On the nature of human plasticity." *Contemporary Psychology*, *31*, 565–567.
Schaie, K. W. (1983). What can we learn from the longitudinal study of adult psychological development? In K. W. Schaie (Ed.), *Longitudinal studies of adult psychological development*. New York: The Guilford Press.
Scribner, S. (1985). Vygotsky's use of history. In J. Wertsch (Ed.), *Culture, communication, and cognition: Vygotskian perspectives*. Cambridge, U.K.: Cambridge University Press.
Scudo, F. & Acanfora, M. (1985). Darwin and Russian evolutionary biology. In D. Kohn (Ed.), *The Darwinian heritage*. Princeton: Princeton University Press.
Sears, R. (1975). Your ancients revisited: A history of child development. In M. Hetherington (Ed.), *Review of research in child development, Vol. 5*. Chicago: University of Chicago Press.
Senn, M. (1975). Insights on the child development movement in the United States. *Monographs of the Society for Research in Child Development*, *40*, No. 161, 3–4.
Sève, L. (1974). *Man in Marxist theory and the psychology of personality* (3rd ed.). Brighton: Harvester (1978).
Shinn, M. (1900). *The biography of a baby*. Boston: Houghton Mifflin.
Shotter, J. (1984). *Social accountability and selfhood*. Oxford: Blackwell.
Shotter, J. (1986). A sense of place: Vico and the social production of social identities. *British Journal of Social Psychology*, *25*, 199–211.
Siegler, R. (1983a). Five generalisations about cognitive development. *American Psychologist*, *38*, 263–277.
Siegler, R. (1983b). Information processing approaches to development. In P. Mussen (Ed.), *Handbook of child psychology, Vol. 1: History, theory, and methods*. New York: Wiley.
Sinha, C. (1988). *Language and representation: A socio-naturalistic approach to human development*. New York: Harvester.
Smith, C. (1982a). Evolution and the problem of mind: Part I. Herbert Spencer. *Journal of the History of Biology*, *15*, 55–88.
Smith, C. (1982b). Evolution and the problem of mind: Part II. John Hughlings Jackson. *Journal of the History of Biology*, *15*, 241–262.

Spencer, H. (1860). *Education: Intellectual, moral, and physical.* New York: Appleton (1896).
Spencer, H. (1864). *First principles.* New York: Appleton.
Spencer, R. (1957). Evolution and development: A veiw of anthropology. In D. Harris (Ed.), *The concept of development.* Minneapolis: University of Minnesota Press.
Spielrein, S. (1912). Die Destruktion als Ursache des Werdens. *Jahrbuch für psychoanalytische und psychopathologische Forschungen, 4,* 465–503.
Spielrein, S. (1923a). Die Zeit im unterschwelligen Seelenleben. *Imago, 9,* 300–317.
Spielrein, S. (1923b). Quelques analogies entre la pensée de l'enfant, celle de l'aphisique et la pensée subconsciente. *Archives de Psychologie, 18,* 305–322.
Spranger, E. (1924). *Psychologie des Jugendalters* (24th Ed.). Heidelberg: Quelle & Meyer (1955).
Spranger, E. (1928). *Types of men* (5th Ed.). Halle: Niemeyer Verlag.
Steedman, C., Urwin, C., & Walkerdine, V. (Eds.) (1985). *Language, gender, and childhood.* London: Routledge & Kegan Paul.
Stern, W. (1914). *The psychology of early childhood* (3rd Ed.). New York: Holt (1923).
Stern, W. (1930). Autobiography. In C. Murchison (Ed.), *A history of psychology in autobiography, Vol. 1.* Worcester, Mass.: Clark University Press.
Stocking, G. (1968). *Race, culture, and evolution.* New York: Free Press.
Strauss, S. (Ed.) (1982). *U-shaped behavioural growth.* New York: Academic Press.
Sugarman, S. (1987). *Piaget's construction of the child's reality.* Cambridge, U.K.: Cambridge University Press.
Sulloway, F. (1979). *Freud: Biologist of the mind: Beyond the psychoanalytic legend.* New York: Basic Books.
Sully, J. (1886). *The teacher's handbook of psychology, on the basis of 'Outlines of psychology'* (Rev. Ed.). New York: Appleton (1894).
Sully, J. (1895). *Studies of childhood.* London: Longmans, Green & Co.
Sully, J. (1918). *My life and friends: A psychologist's memories.* London: T. Fisher Unwin.
Sutton, A. (1983). An introduction to Soviet developmental psychology. In S. Meadows (Ed.), *Developing thinking: Approaches to children's cognitive development.* London: Methuen.
Thorndike, E. (1914). *Educational psychology: Briefer course.* New York: Teachers College, Columbia University (1923).
Tiedemann, D. (1787). Tiedemann's observations on the development of the mental faculties of children (Trans. C. Murchison & S. Langer). *Pedagogical Seminary,* 1927, 205–230.
Tobach, E. (1985). The relationship between Preyer's concept of psychogenesis and his views of Darwin's theory of evolution. In G. Eckardt, W. Bringmann, & L. Sprung (Eds.), *Contributions to a history of developmental psychology.* Berlin: Mouton.
Toulmin, S. (1981). Epistemology and development. In E. Gollin (Ed.), *Development and plasticity.* New York: Academic Press.
Toulmin, S. (1982). *The return to cosmology.* Berkeley, California: University of California Press.
Toulmin, S. (1985). *The inner life: The outer mind.* (Heinz Werner memorial lecture). Worcester, Mass.: Clark University Press.
Tylor, E. B. (1871). *Primitive culture: Researches into the development of mythology, philosophy, religion, language, art, and custom.* London: J. Murray.
Urwin, C. (1985). Constructing motherhood: The persuasion of normal development. In C. Steedman, C. Urwin, & V. Walkerdine (Eds.), *Language, gender, and childhood.* London: Routledge & Kegan Paul.
Urwin, C. (1986a). Developmental psychology and psychoanalysis: Splitting the difference.

In M. Richards & P. Light (Eds.), *Children of social worlds*. Cambridge, U.K.: Polity Press.
Urwin, C. (1986b). Review of Schaffer, "The child's entry into a social world." *British Journal of Developmental Psychology*, *4*, 394–397.
Valsiner, J. (1988). *Developmental psychology in the Soviet Union*. Brighton: Harvester.
Vidal, F., Buscaglia, M., & Vonèche, J. (1983). Darwinism and developmental psychology. *Journal for the History of the Behavioural Sciences*, *19*, 81–94.
Voyat, G. & Birns, B. (Eds.) (1973). Henri Wallon: His world, his work. *International Journal of Mental Health*, *1/4*.
Vygotsky, L. (1962). *Thought and language*. Cambridge, Mass.: M.I.T. Press.
Vygotsky, L. (1978). *Mind in society*. Cambridge, Mass.: Harvard University Press.
Vygotsky, L. (1986). *Thought and language*. Newly translated by A. Kozulin. Cambridge, Mass.: M.I.T. Press.
Wade, I. (1971). *The intellectual origins of the French enlightenment*. Princeton, N.J.: Princeton University Press.
Walkerdine, V. (1985). Psychological knowledge and educational practice: Producing the truth about schools. In G. Claxton, W. Swann, P. Salmon, V. Walkerdine, B. Jacobsen, & J. White, *Psychology and schooling: What's the matter*? Bedford Way Papers 25. London: Institute of Education, University of London.
Walkerdine, V. (1987). *The mastery of reason: Cognitive development and the production of rationality*. London: Routledge & Kegan Paul.
Wapner, S. & Kaplan, B. (Eds.) (1983). *Toward a holistic developmental psychology*. Hillsdale, N.J.: Lawrence Erlbaum Associates Inc.
Wartofsky, M. (1983). From genetic epistemology to historical epistemology: Kant, Marx, and Piaget. In L. Liben (Ed.), *Piaget and the foundations of knowledge*. Hillsdale, N.J.: Lawrence Erlbaum Associates Inc.
Werner, H. (1926). *The comparative psychology of mental development* (Rev. Ed.). New York: International Universities Press (1948).
Werner, H. (1957). The concept of development from a comparative and organismic point of view. In D. Harris (Ed.), *The concept of development*. Minneapolis: University of Minnesota Press.
Wertheimer, M. (1985). The evolution of the concept of development in the history of psychology. In G. Eckardt, W. Bringmann, & L. Sprung (Eds.), *Contributions to a history of developmental psychology*. Berlin: Mouton.
Wertsch, J. (Ed.) (1985). *Culture, communication, and cognition: Vygotskian perspectives*. Cambridge, U.K.: Cambridge University Press.
White, S. (1968). The learning-maturation controversy: Hall to Hull. *Merrill-Palmer Quarterly*, *14*, 187–196.
White, S. (1983). The idea of development in developmental psychology. In R. Lerner (Ed.), *Developmental psychology: Historical and philosophical perspectives*. Hillsdale, N.J.: Lawrence Erlbaum Associates Inc.
Wolf, T. (1973). *Alfred Binet*. Chicago: University of Chicago Press.
Woodward, W. (1979). Young Piaget revisited: From the grasp of consciousness to *décalage*. *Genetic Psychology Monographs*, *99*, 131–161.
Woodward, W. & Ash, M. (Eds.) (1982). *The problematic science: Psychology in nineteenth-century thought*. New York: Praeger.
Wordsworth, J. (1982). *William Wordsworth: The borders of vision*. Oxford: Clarendon Press.
Yolton, J. (1977). *The Locke reader*. Cambridge, U.K.: Cambridge University Press.
Young, R. (1985a). Darwinism *is* social. In D. Kohn (Ed.), *The Darwinian heritage*. Princeton: Princeton University Press.

Young, R. (1985b). Is nature a labour process? In L. Levidow & R. Young (Eds.), *Science, technology, and the labour process: Marxist studies, Vol. 2*. London: Free Association Books.
Youniss, J. (1983a). Social construction of adolescence by adolescents and parents. In H. Grotevant & C. Cooper (Eds.), *Adolescent development in the family. New directions for child development, No. 22*. San Francisco: Jossey-Bass.
Youniss, J. (1983b). Beyond ideology to the universals of development. In D. Kuhn & J. Meacham (Eds.), *On the developmental psychology. Contributions to Human Development, 8*. Basel: Karger.

Reference Notes

1. Bowler, P. (1985). *The non-Darwinian revolution*. Symposium paper, Why developmental psychology is not Darwinian': Annual Conference, British Psychological Society (Developmental Section), Queen's University, Belfast.
2. Kern, S. (1970). *Freud and the emergence of child psychology: 1880–1910*. Unpublished Ph.D. thesis, Columbia University, U.S.A.
3. Strickland, C. (1963). *The child and the race: The doctrines of recapitulation and culture epochs in the rise of the child-centred ideal in American educational thought, 1875–1900*. Unpublished Ph.D. thesis, University of Wisconsin, U.S.A.
4. Young, R. (1983). *How societies constitute their knowledge: Prolegomena to a labour process perspective*. Unpublished Manuscript.

Author Index

Acanfora, M., 27n11
Adlam, D., 225n69
Ainsworth, M., 114n50
Ash, M., 26n1, 70nn5–6, 195n15
Atkinson, C., 70n14, 82n20

Bain, A., 42, 53
Baldwin, J. M., 8, 25, 27n11, 37–43, 52–53, 60–62, 64–66, 89, 92–93, 96, 98, 103–107, 110–111, 123, 128, 132, 144, 149n41, 176–178, 181–182, 184–185, 187, 200, 230–231, 235n7
Baltes, P., 205, 220n16, 221nn24,26
Barlow, N., 27n12
Barthélemy-Madaule, M., 9n5, 26n7, 27nn16–17, 71n16
Bateson, G., 165
Bateson, P., 220n15, 221n25
Beer, G., 26n3
Berger, P., 223n46
Bergson, H., 7, 60, 176
Berkeley, G., 76, 78
Bernard, C., 182
Bettelheim, B., 114n45
Bevan, W., 49n11, 70n7
Bever, T., 194n3
Binet, A., 54, 153–155
Birns, B., 114n40
Bleuler, P. E., 116–119, 184
Blumenthal, A., 9n12, 70n6
Boakes, R., 26n1, 27n23
Boas, F., 37, 164
Boas, G., 48n2, 49n14
Bölsche, W., 27n18, 200, 219n3
Bornstein, M., 219n1
Borstelmann, L., 235n8
Bower, T. G. R., 112, 112n2, 113n28, 210
Bowlby, J., 111, 114n45, 200–201, 220n10
Bowler, P., 9nn3,4,7, 27nn2,7, 27n13, 71n18
Bradley, B., 112n1
Breuer, J., 43
Bringmann, W., 113n3
Bringuier, J.-C., 71n21
Brome, V., 147n5
Bronfenbrenner, U., 212–214
Broughton, J., 49n11, 195n14, 221n27, 226n74
Browne, J., 26n6
Bruner, J., 148n7, 223n51
Bryant, P., 222n36
Buck-Morss, S., 223nn47,49
Bühler, C., 56, 58, 89, 95–96, 121

Bühler, K., 56, 58, 89, 95–96, 121, 133–134
Bullowa, M., 112n2
Burkhardt, R., 26n8
Burt, C., 154–155
Buss, A., 223n47
Butterworth, G., 112n2, 222n34, 234n2, 236n15
Buxton, C., 9n12, 49n11, 70n7, 82n17

Cabanis, P.-J., 5–6, 81n9
Cairns, R., 9nl, 28n25, 49n11, 230, 235n12
Campbell, C., 27n14
Campbell, D. T., 220n6
Carey, S., 148n14
Carotenuto, A., 49n19, 147n5
Case, R., 222n31
Cavanaugh, J., 28n28
Chamberlain, A., 24
Chandler, M., 194n2, 220n16, 221n28, 225n68
Charlesworth, W., 9n1, 235n5
Chomsky, N., 209–210, 222n33
Claparède, E., 55, 98, 183–185, 209
Codd, C., 49n18
Coleman, J., 170n1
Coles, R., 171n19
Compayré, G., 48n6, 82n16
Comte, A., 6, 80, 149n46, 224n57
Conan Doyle, A., 29n38
Condillac, Abbé de, 48n6, 77–79
Condorcet, M., 5–6, 80
Corsi, P., 71n18
Costall, A., 9n1, 222n34, 235n5
Coveney, P., 81n11, 82n15, 112n1
Cox, M., 148nn23,27
Crain, W., 9n1
Crnic, L., 220n15
Crookshank, F. G., 29n34
Crouter, A., 222n41
Cuvier, G., 17, 27n16

Danziger, K., 9n12, 48n10, 114n37, 225n6
Darwin, C., 1–3, 5–7, 11–21, 23–29, 32, 38–39, 42, 52, 55, 70nn8,16, 71n18, 77, 81nn1,9, 84, 119, 175–177, 194n11, 199–201, 219n3, 228, 230–232, 234n5
Darwin, E., 77, 82n11
Davis, K., 223n50
Davydov, V., 70n9, 225n61
De Beer, G., 9n8, 27n18
Descartes, R., 74–75, 77, 85, 188
Dixon, R., 9n1, 27n11, 221n23, 235nn7–11
Donaldson, M., 211
Drummond, W., 48nn6–7, 113n11
Ducret, J., 70n14
Durkheim, E., 145–146

Eckardt, G., 28n25, 70n1
Ellenberger, H., 49n14, 147n1, 195n12
Engels, F., 58, 224n56
Erikson, E., 152, 163, 165–170, 180, 183
Evans, R., 70n14, 219n3
Eyferth, K., 70n8

Farr, J., 81n2
Fechner, G., 7, 38
Fichte, J. G., 6
Fliess, W., 44–45
Flynn, J., 170n3
Fodor, J., 209–210
Foucault, M., 217
Freeman, D., 171n17
Freeman, N., 148n27
Freeman-Moir, J., 49n11
Freud, A., 109, 114n48, 161–163, 167–168
Freud, S., 24–25, 36, 39, 43–48, 52, 54, 107–111, 114n48, 116–118, 123, 125, 140–145, 147n5, 152, 160–163, 165, 167, 169–170, 179–180, 182–183, 187, 203, 217, 230, 234n1, 235n7
Froebel, F., 79, 82n16
Fromm, E., 110, 114n48

Gallop, J., 114n46
Galton, F., 154

Gassendi, P., 5, 74–75
Gergen, K., 194n3, 220n16, 223nn47,50
Gesell, A., 51, 53, 55, 160, 175, 180, 193, 193n1
Ghiselin, M., 9n1, 70n16, 219n3, 235n5
Gibson, E. J., 210, 222n35
Gibson, J. J., 210, 222n33, 223n51
Giddens, A., 8, 10n14
Glass, B., 27n14
Goddard, H., 154
Goethe, J. W. von, 48n6, 63, 69, 190
Gollin, E., 194n3
Gottlieb, G., 26n1, 82n14, 202–204
Gould, S. J., 9nn6,8, 10n14, 27nn11,18, 28n32, 29n34, 48nn2,6, 70n10, 113n10, 170nn3,5, 195n15, 199, 201–202, 219n2, 235n7, 236n14
Grinnell, G., 26n8, 27n16, 194n7
Groos, K., 36, 49n13, 148n24
Gruber, H., 26n4, 70n14

Haeckel, E., 4, 7, 18, 20–21, 25, 32, 42–43, 49n21, 54, 58, 65, 68, 200, 202, 219n3, 224n58
Hall, G. S., 24–25, 32–38, 42, 45, 52–53, 57, 68, 160, 164, 170n8, 178, 230–231
Hardesty, F., 70n8
Harré, R., 212, 215, 225n66, 234n1
Harris, A., 114n51
Harris, B., 70n1
Hartley, D., 76
Haste, H., 223n51
Havelock Ellis, H., 23, 25
Hearst, E., 26n1
Hegel, G. W. F., 6, 38, 105
Henriques, J., 225n70
Herbart, J. F., 6
Hinde, R., 200–201
Hirst, P., 81n2, 149n46, 194n11
Hobbes, T., 39, 74
Hodos, W., 27n14
Horney, K., 110, 114n48
Hughlings Jackson, J., 23–24, 44, 203
Hume, D., 76–77, 223n54

Ingleby, D., 222nn37,45
Inhelder, B., 138

Jaeger, S., 27n19, 112n3
James, W., 33, 144, 188
Janet, P., 43, 66, 123, 128, 183
Joas, H., 149n41
Jones, E., 160
Jones, G., 27n20
Jordanova, L., 27n16
Jung, C. G., 36, 44, 47, 116–119, 147n5, 184

Kagan, J., 194nn3–4
Kalikow, T., 219n3, 220n6
Kant, I., 24, 94, 101, 200, 219n5
Kaplan, B., 71n28, 221nn23–24, 222n41, 234n1
Keegan, R., 26n4
Kern, S., 48n6, 49n14
Kessel, S., 49n11, 70n7, 223n48
Kessen, W., 28n32
Kirkpatrick, E., 113n11
Kitchener, R., 221nn24–25, 234n4
Klahr, D., 222n30
Klein, M., 110
Koffka, K., 188–189, 191, 210
Kohlberg, L., 149n47, 194n3, 212
Köhler, W., 56, 58, 94–95, 111, 121, 190
Kohn, D., 9n3, 26n2
Kramer, R., 82n16, 171n19
Kuhn, D., 222n31, 223n51
Kurtzman, H., 222n45, 234n1

Labouvie-Vief, G., 194n2, 220n16, 221n28, 225n68
Lacan, J., 110
Lamarck, J.-B. de, 2–3, 6, 13, 16–17, 26–27, 32, 64, 81n9, 82n11, 112n3, 176, 195n13, 220n5, 228, 235n7
Lamb, M., 219n1
Langdon Down, J., 24
Leahey, T., 9nn2,12, 81n2

Le Dantec, F., 61–62, 71n18, 184, 195n13
Lee, D., 222n34
Leichtman, M., 70n6, 195n15
Lenin, V. I., 224n57
Leonard, P., 225n64
Leont'ev, A. N., 149n42, 216
Lerner, R., 9n1, 27n11, 194n2, 221n25, 235nn7–11
Lévy-Bruhl, L., 125
Lewin, K., 188–190, 212, 225n66
Lewis, J., 149n41
Lewontin, R., 10n14, 219n2
Light, P., 222nn37,39, 225n74
Lloyd Morgan, C., 100, 176
Locke, J., 5, 74–77
Logue, A., 70n1
Lombroso, C., 24
Lorenz, K., 68, 71n30, 111, 169, 200, 223n46
Lovejoy, A., 27n14
Luckmann, T., 233n46
Luquet, G., 134–135
Luria, A., 224n59
Lynn, R., 29n34

McCullers, J., 48n3
McEwen, F., 222n39
McGonigle, B., 236n15
McGuire, W., 147n5
McKim, R., 81n10
McLeish, J., 148n45
Mahler, M., 114n45
Manicas, P., 9nn10,12, 27n20, 82n17, 149n46, 224n57, 234n4
Marcuse, H., 114n48, 147n1
Margolis, J., 234n4
Marx, K., 58, 215–217
Maynard Smith, J., 236n14
Mayr, E., 9n8, 16, 26nn2,7, 27n17
Mays, W., 222n38
Mead, G. H., 8, 110, 143–144, 212, 215, 222n44, 223n51, 235n9
Mead, M., 37, 152, 164–166
Mehler, J., 222n32
Meyer, E., 136–139
Meynert, T., 25
Mill, J., 6, 79
Mill, J. S., 79
Miller, P., 9n1
Mobasser, N., 223n54
Montessori, M., 79, 82n16, 167, 171n19
Moore, J., 9n13, 71n18
Morgan, M., 81n10, 82n14
Morss, J. R., 29n34, 148nn23,30, 149n42, 222nn34–35, 223nn46,50–51
Mounoud, P., 222n32
Mouzelis, N., 224n57
Mueller, R., 49n11
Mussen, P., 219n1
Muuss, R., 170nn1,8

Nesselroade, J., 221n23
Novack, G., 224n58

Olssen, M., 170n3
Osborn, H. F., 176
Overton, W., 193n2

Pavlov, I., 216
Pennington, B., 220n15
Perez, B., 28n38, 34
Pestalozzi, J. H., 48n6, 79, 82n16
Piaget, J., 27n11, 43, 49n19, 57, 59–67, 88–91, 96–101, 105–106, 109, 115–116, 118–119, 122–132, 134–140, 144–147, 154–159, 163, 174, 176, 178–179, 181–186, 191–193, 194n11, 200, 203, 207–211, 222n31
Plekhanov, G. V., 224nn57–58
Preyer, W., 19–20, 34, 57, 79, 84–93, 95, 97, 102, 121, 181, 195n11, 202, 230–231, 235n12
Pueschel, S., 29n34

Radford, J., 29n38
Radzikhovskii, L., 70n9, 225n61
Rahmani, L., 70n9, 149n42, 224n59, 225n61
Reese, H., 193n2, 220n16
Reinert, G., 9n1, 221n26, 234n5
Reiss, T., 234n4

Richards, D., 222n30
Richards, M., 225n74
Richards, R., 9n9, 26nn6,8, 27nn16,20,23, 81nn1,9
Richter, I., 26n7
Ridley, M., 27nn17,20,23, 49n10
Riegel, K., 70n10, 206, 214, 216–217, 225n61
Riley, D., 114n47, 225n69
Roazen, P., 49n14
Romanes, G., 19–21, 27n24, 34, 42, 52, 119
Ross, D., 48n3
Rotman, B., 70n14
Rousseau, J.-J., 6, 33, 35, 48n6, 63, 77–79, 85, 125, 153, 159, 183
Royce, J., 105, 132
Rubinstein, D., 222n42, 223n46
Rubinstein, S.L., 216, 149n42
Russell, E., 71n23
Russell, J., 49n11, 82n20, 194n9, 221n29, 222nn33–34
Rynders, J., 29n34

Sanford, E., 160
Scarr, S., 221n25
Schaie, K. W., 221nn17,22
Schopenhauer, A., 6, 24
Schutz, A., 212
Scribner, S., 70n13
Scudo, F., 27n11
Sears, R., 70n4
Segal, H., 114n45
Senn, M., 70n4
Serres, E., 6, 65
Sève, L., 70n10, 170n5, 195n12, 217, 223n54
Shinn, M., 88, 93–94, 103
Shotter, J., 215
Siegel, A., 223n48
Siegler, R., 209, 222n30
Simon, T., 153
Sinha, C., 225n69
Smith, C., 27n20, 28n31
Smith, R., 149n41
Spalding, D., 87
Spencer, H., 19–20, 22–23, 38, 42, 48n6, 53, 80, 183, 187, 203, 224n57
Spencer, R., 28n30, 49n18
Spielrein, S., 49n19, 118, 123
Spranger, E., 159
Stern, W., 57, 67–68, 88, 94–95, 98, 105, 120–121, 133, 139, 188–191
Stocking, G., 28n32
Stone, C. A., 195n12, 225n60
Strauss, S., 194n3, 222n35
Strickland, C., 28n32, 48n6
Sugarman, S., 148n14
Sullivan, H. S., 110, 114n48
Sulloway, F., 9nn5,8, 27n23, 28nn31–32, 37, 48n1, 49nn14,19
Sully, J., 19, 21–23, 25, 102, 119, 125, 132–133, 173
Suttie, I., 110
Sutton, A., 224n59, 225n62

Terman, L., 54, 154, 160
Thomae, H., 170n8
Thorndike, E., 52, 189
Tiedemann, D., 84
Tobach, E., 28n25
Toulmin, S., 17, 27n11, 194nn3,11, 223n46, 234n4
Tylor, E., 22, 28n30, 47

Urwin, C., 114n46, 218, 222n37

Valsiner, J., 70n9, 224n59
Van der Veer, R., 70n9
Vidal, F., 70n16, 81n1, 234n5
Von Baer, K., 15, 19, 27n11, 65, 69, 186
Vonèche, J.-J., 70n14, 193n1, 236n13
Von Uexküll, J., 68, 175, 200–201, 220nn5,9, 223n46
Voyat, G., 114n40, 170n3
Vrba, E., 9n6, 10n14, 219n2
Vygotsky, L. S., 8, 57–59, 106, 121–122, 124–127, 144, 178, 213, 215–216, 223n51, 224n59

Waddington, C., 178–179
Wade, I., 81n2

Walkerdine, V., 171n19, 218, 222n37, 225n73
Wallon, H., 106, 110
Wapner, S., 71n28
Wartofsky, M., 82n20
Watson, J. B., 52, 55, 181
Weindling, P., 71n18
Weismann, A., 17, 25, 41, 61, 177
Werner, H., 57–58, 67–69, 126–127, 175, 178, 187–193, 193n2, 203
Wertheimer, M., 27n14, 28n32
Wertsch, J., 70n9, 195n12, 224n59, 225n60
White, S., 27n22
Wolf, T., 170n3
Woodward, W., 26n1
Wordsworth, J., 81n11
Wordsworth, W., 81n11, 112n1
Wundt, W., 7, 9n12, 24, 33, 56, 94

Young, R., 9n13, 223n55, 224nn56–58
Youniss, J., 170n1, 234n4

Zinchenko, V., 70n9, 225n61

Subject Index

Accommodation
  and Baldwin, 41–42, 176–177, 182
  and Piaget, 61–62, 90, 96, 184–185; *See also* Adaptation; Learning
Adaptation, 41–42, 55–56, 60, 176, 199–201, 209–210; *See also* Learning
Adolescence, 34–36, 131, 151–170
Animism, 22, 47, 125
Anthropology, 37, 164
Assimilation, 61–62, 90, 96, 128, 181, 184–185, 192
Associationism, 6, 22, 79–80, 94, 153, 208
  and child, 120, 133–134
  and infant, 74–76, 78, 93–94, 96, 100–102, 188
  and newborn, 86–88
Attachment, 111, 200
Autistic thinking, 96, 116–119, 122

'Berkeleyan' state (of perception), 23, 76–78, 85, 92, 137
Biogenetic law (Haeckel), 4, 18, 25; *See also* Recapitulation, ancestral

Circular reaction
  and Baldwin, 42, 93, 185
  and Piaget, 89, 96, 99, 185
Civilisation, 5, 43, 46, 63, 179; *See also* Recapitulation, cultural
Communication
  and cognitive development, 211–212
  early, 20, 119, 121
Continuity between animals and mankind, 5, 20, 58, 69, 75, 77, 119
  and Darwin, 12, 24, 36, 119
Criminal, 24, 36

Darwinian theory, influence of, 1–2, 7, 16, 23, 32, 175–177, 230–232
  contemporary, 199, 201
  specific applications, 52, 55, 60–61, 189; *See also* Natural selection
Developmental psychology, history of, 1, 7, 230–231
Direction in development, 54, 69, 168, 175–180
Drawings, children's, 22, 132–135, 138, 212
Dreams, dreaming, 22, 24–25, 44

Economic (energy) model, 43, 183–184; *See also* Equilibrium
Education, 33–34, 63, 79
Egocentrism, 118, 122–124, 126, 135, 193

infancy, 96
spatial, 137–140
Embryo, embryogenesis, 14–15, 18, 19, 187
and Piaget, 65, 178–179
Emotion, expression of, 12–13, 23–24, 104–106, 121, 191
smiling, 87, 102–103, 111
Empiricism, 74, 80, 94, 188–189, 206, *See also* Positivism
Equilibrium, 182–184
and Piaget, 62, 156–159, 178–179, 184–186
Evolutionism, 8, 23–26, 38, 165; *See also* Lamarckism; non-Darwinian biology; Recapitulation

Fears, children's, 14, 21, 36
Formal reasoning, 127, 131, 153, 155–159
Functional approach, 55–56, 58

Genetic epistemology, 38, 60, 63, 78, 178
Genetic psychology, 34, 53
Gestalt psychology, 56, 94–95, 100, 174–175, 210
and differentiation, 187–192
Great Chain of Being, the, 17, 23
Group, grouping (Piaget), 99–100, 130, 132, 157

Idealism, 6–7, 37–38, 68–69, 80, 105, 121, 156
Imitation, 61–62, 102, 104–106
Infancy, 25, 52–53, 78, 83–112, 200, 210
and Baldwin, 39, 93, 103–106, 182
and Bowlby, 111, 200
and Darwin, 11–12
and S. Freud, 45–46, 107–109
and Piaget, 63, 89–91, 96–101, 105–106, 184–185
and Preyer, 84–88, 92, 102
and Vygotsky, 58–59, 106; *See also* Newborn
Inheritance of acquired character, *see* Lamarckism
Instinct, 37, 40, 45, 52, 77, 108, 111, 162–163, 200–201
and newborn, 87, 89
Intelligence, *see* Mental testing

Lamarckism, 3, 13, 16–19, 25, 31–32, 35, 73, 79–80, 228
and Baldwin, 41
and Darwin, 13–14
and Erikson, 167
and A. Freud, 163
and S. Freud, 47, 141–142
and Jung, 47, 117
and Piaget, 60–61, 64–65, 90
and Preyer, 21, 87
and Shinn, 88
and Sully, 22
Language, 20, 58–59, 79, 119–124, 134
Latency (Freud), 46, 141, 160, 166
Learning, 52–53, 181, 201
in newborn, 84, 86–87, 90–91
Lifespan development, 151, 204–207

Marxism, 58, 106, 122, 215–217
Mental retardation, 24, 153
Mental testing, 54, 96, 153–155, 189, 205
Morality, moral development, 142–146, 167, 212

Natural selection, 17, 41, 61, 177, 200
and Darwin, 13, 16, 23, 177
Nature-philosophy, 6, 8, 33, 38, 63
Neurology and physiology,
as developmental explanation, 23–25, 43–44, 52–53, 162, 202–204
and infant, 92–93, 181–182
and newborn, 85, 88, 90
Newborn, 53, 75, 84–91, 189–191, 193, 203
Non-Darwinian biology, 2–3, 16–17, 21–22, 60, 175–176, 200; *See also* Lamarckism, Recapitulation

Organic selection (Baldwin), 41, 61, 64–65, 176–177

Pathology (madness), 24, 46, 116, 168, 200
Perception, 22, 76, 79, 191, 210
  in child, 125, 135, 137
  in infant, 85, 91–92, 94–95, 98, 210; *See also* 'Berkeleyan' state
Periodicity, 32, 36, 44
Play, 36, 146, 167
Positivism, 6–7, 80, 213, 216, 230
Prehistoric man, 23, 35, 44–45, 47, 66
Primitive thought, 115, 125, 127, 191; *See also* 'Savage'
Progress, 5–6, 80, 175–180, 228–229
Psychology
  behaviourism, 52–53
  cognitive, 208
  comparative, 52, 56, 58, 95
  experimental, 33, 38, 56, 117, 119
  history of, 7, 40, 80
  social, 56; *See also* Gestalt psychology; Soviet psychology
Psychophysics, 7, 38, 56

Racism, racial comparison, 24, 32, 87, 154
Reaching, grasping, 78, 87, 92–93, 95, 97, 99
Recapitulation, ancestral, 4, 7, 18, 25, 32; *See also* Recapitulation, developmentalists and
Recapitulation, claims and general impact of, 3–4, 7, 16–19, 23–25, 79, 120, 201–202, 229
Recapitulation, cultural, 39, 63, 79–80, 145–146
  and educational theory, 33–34, 63, 79
  and history of science, 158, 176, 179
Recapitulation, developmentalists and:
  Baldwin, 39–40, 42
  K. Bühler, 56, 134
  Darwin, 14–16
  S. Freud, 44–47, 107–109, 141
  Gesell, 53
  Haeckel, 18
  Hall, 33–37, 52, 160
  Jung, 47, 117
  Koffka, 189
  Lacan, 111
  Le Dantec, 61
  M. Mead, 166
  Piaget, 63, 65–66, 146
  Preyer, 21, 86–87, 102
  Romanes, 20
  Shinn, 88
  Stern, 57, 120
  Sully, 21
  Vygotsky, 59
  Werner, 68–69
Recapitulation, hierarchical, 4, 6; *See also* Recapitulation, cultural; Recapitulation, developmentalists and; Recapitulation, repetition within development as
Recapitulation, repetition within development as, 63, 135–137, 141, 161
Reflex, 84, 86, 88–91
Regression, 25, 137, 179, 190
Repetition, 32, 47, 63, 135–137, 141, 161, 203
Romanticism, 6, 63

'Savage', 22–23, 32, 46, 68, 117, 132, 191; *See also* Primitive thought
Sensationism, sensationalism, 5–6, 73–81, 84–85, 101, 191, 228
Sensory modalities, 76, 92, 210, 229
Sex, sexuality, 25, 35, 165–166
  and A. Freud, 162–163
  and S. Freud, 43–46, 107–108, 140–143, 160
Single track, as model of development, 16, 23, 32, 35, 66, 202
Social nature of human development, 59, 106, 124, 144, 214–219
  and Baldwin 39, 104–105
  and Piaget, 128, 132, 146

Soviet psychology, 58, 215–217
Space, 95, 98–101, 135–140
Stage, developmental, 32, 40, 80, 174, 207, 212
  and Erikson, 169, 180
  and S. Freud, 46, 107–108
  and Piaget, 64–66, 98, 127, 185
  and Werner, 67
Storm and stress, 36, 159, 164–165
Suggestibility, 93, 103–104, 145, 185
Syncretic thinking, 126, 191

Utilitarianism, psychological (Spencer-Bain), 42, 53, 88

Weismannism, 17, 25, 41, 61
Women, biological/recapitulationary framework and, 23, 36, 142–143, 165–166

For Product Safety Concerns and Information please contact our EU
representative GPSR@taylorandfrancis.com
Taylor & Francis Verlag GmbH, Kaufingerstraße 24, 80331 München, Germany

www.ingramcontent.com/pod-product-compliance
Ingram Content Group UK Ltd.
Pitfield, Milton Keynes, MK11 3LW, UK
UKHW020013200926
475702UK00014B/1869

* 9 7 8 1 1 3 8 0 3 7 8 3 0 *